Triumph and Disas

150 years of Rochdale Hor

Jim Stringer & Mark Wynn

London League Publications Ltd

Triumph and Disaster
150 years of Rochdale Hornets

© Jim Stringer & Mark Wynn
Foreword © Paul Ormerod
The moral right of Jim Stringer and Mark Wynn to be identified as the authors has been asserted.

Front & back cover design @ Stephen McCarthy.

All photographs are from private collections unless otherwise credited to the photographer or provider of the photo. No copyright has been intentionally breached; please contact London League Publications Ltd if you believe there has been a breach of copyright.

Front cover photos: 2013 Rochdale Hornets team that beat Oldham to win the Championship One Grand Final; early Rochdale Hornets logo. Back cover: 1922 Challenge Cup winning team and Chris Riley playing against Toulouse in 2016 League 1 Promotion Final.

A CIP catalogue record for this book is available from the British Library.

Published in November 2021 by London League Publications Ltd, PO Box 65784, London NW2 9NS

ISBN: 978-1-909885-28-8

Cover design by Stephen McCarthy Graphic Design
46, Clarence Road, London N15 5BB.

Editing and layout by Peter Lush

Printed and bound in Great Britain by Ashford Colour Press Ltd, Gosport, Hants PO13 0FW

Foreword

Jim Stringer and Mark Wynn, the authors of this book, have each done a great deal for Rochdale Hornets Rugby Football League club in recent decades. But even by their own demanding standards, this book is a major undertaking. It is an honour to be asked to write the Foreword.

At one level, the book does exactly what it says in the sub-title. It is a history of 150 years of Hornets. An immense amount of work has gone into reading the original sources, often the *Rochdale Observer*, to describe events and results on the field of play.

In terms of the playing record over the years, every Hornets fan will readily empathise with the main title *Triumph and Disaster*. Indeed, we often see these two qualities displayed during the course of a single game.

But the book is much more than simply a record of how the team has performed. Its messages extend far beyond the sport of rugby league itself or the borough of Rochdale.

It gives us a fascinating and detailed history of a business, of its ups and downs, of how key decisions were made and of the conflicts which often surrounded them. On the latter point, as a Rochdalian myself, I sometimes think, only to some extent frivolously, that the town's main sport is neither soccer nor rugby, but feuding.

On a more serious note, Jim and Mark have produced a rare and valuable document. It is a history of what we now call an SME, a small and medium sized enterprise. There are histories of great institutions such as the Bank of England and of large companies. But there are virtually none which describe the decision-making processes and commercial successes and failures of a small company, which in corporate terms is what Hornets has always been.

These descriptions of corporate decision-making show how hard it is to make good ones. With hindsight, everything is easy. In advance, there is always massive uncertainty.

This problem exists regardless of the scale of the company. In the 1980s, for example, Microsoft was about to abandon Windows as its main operating system. It was only through a purely fortuitous set of events that they stuck with it, and the rest is history.

Just one example from the book will suffice in the case of Hornets. Following the sale of the Athletic Grounds in the late 1980s, the club found itself not only owning 47.5 per cent of Spotland Stadium. It had over £1 million in the bank.

What to do with the cash? If it had been invested in shares, the club would now be sitting on several millions, and would have enjoyed a substantial income from dividends every year. Looking back, that seems the obvious decision to have made.

But the directors took the decision to invest in the team. If the gamble had paid off and the initial success had continued, the club would have been a candidate for the inaugural Super League in 1996, only a few years later.

The decision to invest in the team was not surprising given the nature of professional sports teams. Most of them are companies just like any other company. But they are unusual.

The vast majority of economic activity is carried out by companies owned by shareholders. The principal motivation and purpose of such companies is to make as much profit as possible for the shareholders. There are all sorts of nuances and qualifications which can be made to this. But, stripped down to its essentials, most companies exist to make a profit.

Professional sports clubs are different. They are more interested in maximising costs than they are to boost profits. The reason is simple. Clubs are judged not on how much profit they make, but how they perform on the field.

The more a club spends on its players, the more successful it is likely to be. The correlation between spending and playing success is not perfect. But it is strong across all professional team sports. Against this background, the longevity of most professional clubs is remarkable.

Most companies disappear within a handful of years of their formation. There are examples within rugby league itself, from the abortive attempts to establish the game in South Wales just before the First World War, to the failures in London in the 1930s, right through to the exotically named clubs of recent years such as Southend Invicta and Mansfield Marksman.

But of the 22 clubs which, following the historic meeting in Huddersfield in 1895 to form the Northern Union, took part in rugby league's first ever season, 15 still exist.

To put this in context, Les Hannah, a Manchester lad and top economic historian, looked at the world's 100 *largest* industrial companies in 1912 and tracked what had happened to them by 1995. No fewer than 48 of these gigantic mammoths no longer existed and only 19 remained in the top 100.

As Jim and Mark make clear, Hornets was on the brink on several occasions, and indeed in 2009 the club found itself in administration. But it has survived 150 years, much longer than almost any other company.

The book gives us detailed descriptions of how exactly the company managed to survive these various mortal threats. This in itself makes it worthy of a much wider audience than the loyal band of Hornets supporters.

There is a common theme in the survival process. Namely that Rochdale Hornets *does* inspire intense loyalty. The club is deeply rooted in the community, rooted in Rochdale.

Uncertain times lie ahead not just for Hornets but for rugby league in general. But *Triumph and Disaster* serves as an inspiration. We have overcome difficult, adverse conditions in the past and we will do so again. Onward, Hornets. Onward!

Paul Ormerod
President, Rochdale Hornets Rugby League Football Club

About the authors

Jim Stringer first watched Rochdale Hornets in 1971 – their centenary year. Since then, he has been a ball-boy, a player in the club's junior ranks, programme designer/editor, fanzine editor, supporter's association founder, chair of the co-operative, blog writer, vlogger and fundraiser. He is currently Hornets' stadium announcer and contributes a heritage column to the match day programme.

He has seen Rochdale Hornets play home and away from Llanelli to London and Toulouse to Toronto. He also owns over 300 rugby league jerseys. For over 30 years he has worked in advertising as a writer and strategist.

Mark Wynn was born and raised in Rochdale and still lives in the town. Introduced to Rugby League by his father Derek, Mark has been a lifelong Rochdale Hornets fan as well playing for local amateur Rugby League side Milnrow and Newhey.

Mark first became involved with Rochdale Hornets other than as a supporter by helping with fundraising and being a member of the 'Nest-Egg', a Hornets supporters group.

Mark formed the successful Rochdale Swarm, the Rochdale Hornets supporters' team which played the various derivatives of rugby league, Tag, Touch and Masters, as well as hosting large scale rugby league festivals.

Mark was the chairman of Rochdale Hornets for 10 seasons. He is currently the chair of the Rochdale Hornets Sporting Foundation, and a non-executive director of the Bristol based All Golds Rugby League Club.

Away from rugby league Mark is a social entrepreneur and runs an awarding social enterprise, Heywood, Middleton & Rochdale Circle as well as having a consultancy business aimed at supporting other social enterprises and sporting organisations. Mark has been married for over 30 years to Deborah and has two grown up children, Emily and Olivia.

The origins of this book

As Mark Wynn reminded me recently, the origins of this book date back to 2015 (or even 1871!). I was invited by Gary Slater, a Warrington supporter and one of London League Publications Ltd.'s regular authors, to attend a reception at the Houses of Parliament organised by the All-Party Rugby League Parliamentary Group. It was in support of the forthcoming test series against New Zealand. Mark was there as club chairman of Rochdale Hornets. We started talking and he told me about the idea of producing a book to mark the club's 150th anniversary. We later signed an agreement, with a 'get-out' clause for both sides. I must admit that I didn't hear anything for some time, and reading the book I understand why. Mark and his colleagues had other things to worry about!

Anyway, Mark contacted me before the pandemic, saying that the book was going to happen. We had a Zoom meeting, so at least I have met most people involved over the internet, and look forward to meeting them in person in the future. The book was delayed because local history centres were closed due to the pandemic, but I'm pleased to say we got there in the end.

I have watched Hornets on occasions over the years, usually when they were playing Fulham or the London Crusaders. They were the first team I saw beat Fulham. The story at the time was that they were the first team to travel down to London the day before the game. It paid dividends for them. And of course, Fulham signed Shaun Hoare from Rochdale, a young hard-working tall forward. While I accept that Fulham had good wingers, if Fulham had signed Henderson Gill from Rochdale with their £30,000, he would have been a sensation in London. Sadly, he ended up at Wigan.

As has been said elsewhere, times are tough for the smaller clubs in professional sport. However, in future I will look out for Hornets results, and will try to get to a game to watch them. Forward to another 150 years!

Peter Lush
London League Publications Ltd

Thank you
This book was very much a team effort – even a co-operative one. Jim and Mark would like to thank the following people for their help and support in contributing to this book: Chris Churm, Emon Ratu, Neil Bruckshaw, Ryan Bradley, Carl Parr, Paul Ormerod, Julie Clarke, Malcolm Journeaux (photographer), Jackie Meredith (photographer) and Jenny Driver & Sarah Hodkinson of Touchstone Rochdale.

London League Publications Ltd would like to thank everyone who contributed photos to the book, Steve McCarthy for designing the cover and the staff of Ashford Colour Press for printing the book.

Contents

1. In the beginning   1

2. 1871: Wasps, Butterflies and Grasshoppers   3

3. 1895: The great split   11

4. 1911: In the shadow of war   19

5. 1922: Challenge Cup glory   33

6. 1928 to 1939: The brink   39

7. 1948 to 1958: The weight of expectations   53

8. 1961: Vinaka Fiji   71

9. 1971: Myler   87

10. 1975 to 1979: The yo-yo years   95

11. 1980: Decline and fall   113

12. 1990: Never a dull moment   131

13. 2000: Turmoil   147

14. 2008: Downfall   159

15. A new hope: The birth of a Co-operative Club   165

16. A new start – with a less than clean slate   173

17. Writing new history   179

18. Miracles happen   185

19. Optimism and change   195

20. 2019 to 2021: The end of the beginning   199

Appendix 1: Statistics and records   212

Appendix 2: Player Heritage Numbers   221

A BDV cigarettes 'silk' from the 1920s (Courtesy Jim Stringer)

1. In the beginning

It is important to remember that the game that evolved into rugby league was – in the beginning – very different to that played today. From its earliest days, any game in which a ball was handled, kicked or passed between players was called 'football' or 'foot-ball'.

The earliest record of 'foot-ball' in Rochdale reports that games between the various hamlets around the town were played as far back as 1775. These were effectively 'mob football' games: chaotic affairs with few rules and an unlimited number of players who used any means necessary to convey a pig's bladder from one side of town to the other.

According to local historian Henry Fishwick, games were "... played in the streets of Rochdale, with an occasional divergence into the bed of the river." Such games faded from the sporting scene after the Highway Act of 1835 banned the playing of football in the street, stating: "If any person shall play at Foot-ball or any other Game on any Part of the said Highways, to the Annoyance of any Passenger or Passengers they shall pay any Sum not exceeding Forty Shillings." By the early 19th Century, organised football was mostly played to local rules, with anything up to 20 or 30 players a side.

The first contest between two Rochdale clubs took place in December 1841, when The Body-Guard Club based at the Grapes Inn on Baillie Street accepted the challenge of the Fear-Nought Club to "... play them at foot-ball for their proposed sum, two games out of three, 12 on each side. After that they will play them for half a barrel of Old Tom, one single game; the Fear-Nought Club to fix the time as early as possible."

The match was played on Christmas Day 1841 under 'rules agreed by both parties' and overseen by an umpire from each team. The aim was to kick the ball over the fence at the opponent's end of the ground. But neither side could score.

The match was eventually settled when a tired Body-Guards player called a spectator onto the field to take a kick for him. This infringement of the rules was deemed 'foul play' by his own umpire, who awarded the game to The Fear-Noughts.

As 'football' gained popularity across the country and teams began to play opponents from other areas, there was a need to codify a common set of rules. The rules adopted by the majority of clubs – and eventually the governing body – were based on those laid down at Rugby School; The Rugby Rules. This was the point at which the game became known as 'Rugby Football' and it was, by far, the dominant football code in the Rochdale area.

With this evolution in mind that, in this book we call the game that Hornets and their precedents played by whatever name was used to describe it at the time, be that 'football', 'rugby football' or 'rugby league'.

It is interesting to note that another set of football rules that also allowed the handling of the ball in open play, but did not permit players to run with it, was established in 1863 by the newly formed Football Association.

Their game became 'Association Football': soccer. However, as Rochdale AFC wasn't founded until 1907, there really was only one 'football' in town for close on half a century.

Football arrives: From *The Rochdale Observer,* Saturday 18 January 1868

"Within the past few weeks a club called the Rochdale Football Club has been established by a number of local gentlemen desirous of providing, in the absence of skating, a means of healthy outdoor exercise.

The football has long been an English 'institution' and at Rugby, Eton and other scholastic establishments of high order has formed a chief winter's game.

Any fine winter's day will do for a game of football, a game which we had almost said has no dangers about it whatsoever - at all events they are reduced to the minimum, even if the play is not shorn of the 'hacking', which is a characteristic of the Rugby rules - the rules being arbitrary in different districts.

This game brings all the muscles of the body into exercise, and results in a warm glow and a bracing energy which hundreds of our pale-faced factory lads and other confined operatives would be all the better for.

They would relish a night's reading or in-door entertainment with greater enjoyment and profit, if it was varied now and then by an hour or two of football kicking; and this would be much more ennobling than many ways of spending Saturday afternoon and other occasional spare hours.

The observance of a good set of rules is calculated to improve men morally as well as physically, because unlike cricket for instance, all the men play at once and are strictly forbidden from taking undue advantages which the exigences of play frequently afford and which are sometimes very tempting, in order to prevent an adversary goaling the ball."

And so it began...

References
Bell's Life in London and Sporting Chronicle - 12 December 1841 & 2 January 1842
The History of the Parish of Rochdale in the County of Lancaster - Henry Fishwick, 1889
legislation.gov.uk: Highway Act 1835 – LXXII Penalty on Persons committing Nuisances by riding on Footpaths, &c.

2. 1871: Wasps, Butterflies and Grasshoppers

Rugby football in Rochdale began in 1867. The Rochdale Football Club was formed by a magistrate, the lord of the manor, a clerk, a watchmaker, a managing director, a tobacconist, a draper, a 'smallware dealer', a solicitor, a publican, a builder, a shop-keeper and a cotton merchant.

The first reference we can find for a game is on Saturday 21 December 1867, an advertisement in *The Rochdale Observer* that says: "A MATCH will be PLAYED (weather permitting) on the new ground at Sparth Bottoms THIS DAY, the 21st inst. at 3.0pm - R.S.D Colley, Hon. Sec."

The club elected to play to the Rugby rules – without 'hacking'. Hacking permitted players to trip their opponents by kicking them in the shins.

The Rochdale Observer described the club as: "... composed of the sons of our wealthier inhabitants and includes players from different first class schools".

This led to a football boom in the town and other clubs quickly followed, among them Rochdale Wasps, St Clement's, Rochdale Juniors, Rochdale Athletic Club and Rakebank. Juniors and Rakebank merged in 1871 to form Rochdale United.

In the South of England, football was recognised as one of the most popular winter pastimes for gentlemen. In April 1871 a meeting was called inviting the growing number of London clubs to form a Rugby Football Union, with 'upwards of 30 clubs' appointing a committee to revise, codify and approve a set of official rules that would enable the spread of the code across the country.

The new Rugby Football Union had its eyes on the regional footballing hotbeds. It said: "The London Clubs have done well in taking the initiative. We trust that such nurseries of the game in Manchester, Liverpool, Rochdale and Sheffield will enrol themselves under the standard of the Union."

Having seen the Rugby Football code take hold across the North, the directors of Rochdale Wasps, Rochdale United and Rochdale Football Club saw the potential in joining forces to form a senior team to represent the whole town.

Their first meeting was held on Thursday 20 April 1871 at the Roebuck Hotel in Rochdale, with a key discussion focusing on a name for the new club. Rochdale Wasps, Rochdale Butterflies and Rochdale Grasshoppers were all suggested. The report from the inaugural meeting records the decision: "Resolved: That the present name of the club be changed to the Rochdale Hornets Football Club."

The first elected officers of the new club were: president, James Schofield; vice-president RM Jones; secretary, JW Sellars and treasurer Edward Healey. The committee comprised R Butterworth, JW Baron, A Taylor, J Buckley, J Davies, W Peters, T Irving and RR Osborne – who was named as Rochdale Hornets' first ever captain. The new club boasted 66 members – and playing members had to provide themselves with two jerseys: one black and amber, the other white.

When Hornets' inaugural season came around, the club was announced onto the local sporting scene in unassuming fashion. A three line notice on the front page of the *Rochdale*

Observer read: "THE ROCHDALE HORNETS FOOTBALL CLUB. The opening match will be played THIS DAY (Saturday 7 October) on the club ground, Milnrow Road. Fifteen against the rest. Kick off at three o'clock. Admission 6d and 2d."

It is interesting to note that, at its foundation, Hornets was still 'wholly composed of men of the public school or college type'. But within a year, 'working men' were permitted to play alongside the businessmen, tradesmen and the gentry. The first 'working man' to break the mould was Jesse Wilson, who had cut his footballing teeth with Castleton Moor. His reputation for playing 'a dour, determined game' saw him invited to join the town's senior team and he became 'the forerunner of a grand set of working class players who made the club famous throughout Lancashire and Yorkshire.'

Hornets' first home was the old Athletic Grounds at Newbold. From there they moved to the Rochdale Cricket Club on Vavasour Street, off Milnrow Road in Newbold, for which the club paid £4 per year rent. Where Hornets differed from other emerging clubs of the era was that they had an enclosed ground. This meant they could charge admission at the gate, unlike other clubs where supporters were invited to pay only when a collection box was taken round. The cost of admission was adults 6d, boys 3d – ladies free.

The balance sheet for the first season showed receipts as £16 6s 10d and expenses as £15 11s 0d: a profit of 15s 10d.

Such was the popularity of football in the borough in the early years, that the 1873 season was ended with a 'district football match' – the town's own 'area of origin' - where the best players from North and South of the River Roch took part in a 20-a-side game at Rochdale Athletic Club in front of a substantial crowd. The North emerged victorious by 'two touchdowns, a rouge and four touches in-goal to nothing'.

When the cricket ground was sold for building in 1877 – Newbold School was built on the site – Hornets moved with the cricket club to their new home in Dane Street, where admission charges became: pavilion 6d, rest of ground 3d, horses 1 shilling, ladies free.

The harsh winter of 1878–79 saw football fixtures suspended. *The Rochdale Observer* saw it as an opportunity to review the footballing landscape in the town – and the article gives us a snapshot of the makeshift way the game was played.

"Weather permitting, we hope to see you kick-off again - Rangers, Wanderers, Rovers, Hornets, Wasps and the rest of you: but this long spell of being 'frozen out' should have given you time to think over your pet game and how you play it."

"We have missed you, but we have had our leisure to realise several ways in which you mar our enjoyment of the game - comparatively small matters entirely in your power to alter, the removal of which would popularise football wonderfully."

They went on to list their gripes: "First, you lack punctuality: you say 3 o'clock when sometimes your opponents' train will not bring them before 3.30; or, more annoying still, two or three of your own team stroll on the field having still to undress and prepare for play, after your opponents are stripped, ready and waiting in the cold."

"Then you lack discipline; there is a parade of choosing a captain, a labour lost for you too often have 15 of them in a team, and the nominal captain's chief duty is to try and keep peace among his men."

A Rochdale Hornets team in 1875. (Courtesy Jim Stringer)

Respect for the umpire was seen as somewhat lacking: "You make us think he ought always to be guided only by the shouts of the players, for if his decision does not happen to suit the team he is set aside in a very summary fashion. This is a sorry compliment to your own umpire." It seems that respect for the decisions umpires did make was also a little thin on the ground: "You lack temper and generosity too, or we should not so often see the tedious wrangles, the interruptions of the game, the walking off in a huff, the disputed tries, protested goals and the rest of it that are an unfair infliction on those who like the game and pay their money expecting to see a friendly, gentlemanly contest."

It's little wonder that decisions were questioned so frequently. Each team provided their own umpire and there were often lengthy disputes on the legality of scores. Match reports of the time even refer to such scores as 'disputed tries'.

In an attempt to mitigate such disputes, neutral referees were appointed – but they were only called into play when the umpires could not agree. Over time, the referees were given sole charge of play – and the umpires became touch judges.

In those initial years, the sport bore only a passing resemblance to the modern game of rugby league. Under early Rugby rules, the game would restart after every tackle with a scrum; passing hand-to-hand was rare and progress was made by pushing the opposing pack back at a scrum or by kicking the ball downfield, where another scrum could be formed.

Winning the game meant navigating a complex scoring system. In the earliest days, the only scores that counted came from goals. In order to secure an attempt at a scoring kick, a side had to earn a 'Try at Goal'.

Hornets Football Club first team 1883–84 at the Pavilion at Rochdale Cricket Club, Dane Street.
WA Scholes, J Groves, G Dovey; J Nolan, JW Calvert; J Holt (captain), TB Lord, J Buckley, A Bamford,
R Wrigley, JW Griffiths; W Brierley, S Jackson, H Lord, J Wilson, B Binns, E Wild.
(Rochdale Hornets Heritage collection)

W Smith Trading Card
One of the earliest pieces of Hornets merchandise, this 1886 Holts The Hatter trading card shows Hornets half-back W Smith. Holts – of Lord Street in Rochdale – used to manufacture the presentation club caps awarded to players for playing regular first-team football. (Courtesy Jim Stringer)

A 'Try' was achieved by the attacking team touching down the ball behind the opponents' goal line. The 'Try' itself yielded no points – only the chance to score a goal from the resulting kick.

In 1875, the number of tries achieved by each team came into the reckoning – but only then as a deciding factor in a result if the number of goals were equal, or if no goals had been scored. To complicate matters further, there was also an opportunity to score a 'minor point' or a 'rouge', where the defending team could touch down a loose ball in their own in-goal or kick it over the dead-ball line.

It took 15 years after Hornets' foundation for the RFU to adopt a scoring system that allocated points for goals and tries – three points for a goal, one point for a try – but, even then, if a try were converted, only the goal would count.

June 1879 saw Hornets strengthen their base in the town when the Rochdale Rovers club members moved en-masse across to Hornets. Effectively a merger, the conditions of the move were that all Rovers members would pay Hornets' five shillings annual subscription - and that the club should hand over all of its assets.

That wasn't the only major change at the club. Despite a long-standing relationship with the cricket club, Hornets leased a ground behind Oakenrod Hall off Bury Road. Little is known about the set-up at Oakenrod because the move there only lasted one season.

What we can assume, having looked at the Ordnance Survey maps of the time, is that it would have been a pretty small playing field: the area hemmed in between the Hall, the River Roch and Oakenrod Mill barely big enough to accommodate a football pitch.

Access wasn't great either; advertisements for games in the local press carried the instruction: "Entrance through Oakenrod Mill only." Very salubrious.

The Rochdale Observer of 16 August 1879 was at a loss as to why Hornets would turn their backs on a new ground in the centre of town. They said: "Now we hear of 'Hornets at Oakenrod Hall' for the coming season. This sounds strange." The article continued: "We are not in the secrets of either club, but entertained the idea that the RCC and the Hornets FC had formed an alliance which has been mutually advantageous. It would seem at first sight that the Hornets might go farther than Manchester Road and fare worse, both in the matter of proximity to the town, accommodation, attendance and gate money."

The Rochdale Observer did, though, ponder the reasons for the move: "Perhaps they fancy the benefit has been too much on one side, because the cricketers have been landlords all the year round, and thus had entrée to the ground. There are, however, advantages on the other hand not too far to seek. It seems a pity that some equitable arrangement has not been found and agreed on."

At the season's end, the move to Oakenrod Hall was deemed an abject failure and, owing to poor gates, they returned to Dane Street – where they reconfigured the pitch to run at 90° to its previous position.

The period following Hornets' formation saw a multitude of clubs spring up 'almost like mushrooms' according to *The Green Final.* It said: "The working class lads, having watched and learnt the game, fell to it like ducks to water." And you can see the fervour with which Rugby football was being played in the town.

7

A glimpse down the weekly fixtures reveals teams across the borough and beyond: St Mary's Balderstone, Albion, Grammar School, Wasps, Wanderers, Crossfield Rovers, St Chad's, St James's, Balderstone Grasshoppers, Sparrow Hill, Castleton Hornets, Falinge, Wardle, Sudden Rangers, St Clement's, Castleton Moor, Belfield Boxers, Syke, Little Bent (Facit), Bacup Grasshoppers, Healey Rangers, Royton Rangers, Britannia, Unitarians and Oakenrod.

Within a decade of Hornets' formation, there were 60 clubs fielding 80 teams – 1,200 players – within a three mile radius. Sixteen local junior sides contested the first Rochdale Charity Cup in 1887 and a year later an estimated crowd of 10,000 people watched the final at Dane Street.

From the outset, though, Hornets looked beyond the town for fixtures, with reports naming Harrogate, Stalybridge, Manchester, Crewe, Leeds St John's, Huddersfield, Sale, Monsall, Warrington, Didsbury Free Wanderers and Bury amongst their opponents.

This 'Northern nursery' had grown up – and it was ready to play with the big boys.

References
Rochdale Observer - Saturday 18 January 1868
Rochdale Observer - Saturday 18 June 1870
Rochdale Observer - Saturday 23 March 1872
Rochdale Times - Saturday 4 May 1878
The Rochdale Observer - Saturday 16 August 1878
Rochdale Observer - Saturday 8 February 1879
The Rochdale Observer - Saturday 22 November 1879
Rochdale Times - Saturday 4 May 1878
Bell's Life in London and Sporting Chronicle - Saturday 22 April 1871
The Green Final: 'Old Stalwarts of the Hornets: J.R. Hartley' - Saturday 22 September 1923
The Green Final: 'Old Stalwarts of the Hornets: The Late Jesse Wilson' - Saturday 13 October 1923
The Rochdale Hornets Centenary - Bob Fletcher, 1971
'*The Oval World*': Tony Collins, 2015
bathrugbyheritage.org: 'The early days of Rugby Union scoring': Brian Jenkins
The New Annals of Rochdale - T.T. Heywood, 1931

✤ RULES. ✤

1.—That this Club be called "THE ROCHDALE HORNETS' FOOTBALL CLUB."

2.—That the Club be managed by a President, two Vice-Presidents, and a Committee of ten members, with power to add; five to form a quorum.

3.—That a Captain for the season be appointed. Also that a Captain be appointed for the second team.

4.—That the Subscription be Five Shillings per annum (with an Entrance Fee of Five Shillings), payable before October 1st, and that the Committee have power to remit the Entrance Fee to playing members in cases they deem advisable.

5.—That the Club be governed by the Rules of the Rugby Union.

6.—That the President and Secretaries, or Vice-Presidents and Secretaries, have power to call a Special General Meeting at any time they may deem it necessary, or on a receipt of a requisition to that effect, signed by ten or more members. All Special Meetings to be convened by circular.

7.—That the Committee shall have the power of expelling any member for ungentlemanly conduct, such member having the right to appeal to a General Meeting of members within a period of fourteen days after receiving the notice thereof.

8.—That the Club Colours be WHITE, and that no member be allowed to play unless in club colours.

9.—That any gentleman desirous of joining the Club be proposed and seconded by two members. The election to be by ballot—two black balls in eight, or one in five to exclude.

10.—That any member wishing to resign must give notice in writing to one of the Secretaries previous to the Annual Meeting, and when he has paid all Subscriptions and Fines due, his name shall be erased from the books.

11.—That any member receiving due notice to play in a match and NOT REPLYING DEFINITELY to one of the Secretaries THREE DAYS before, or not playing after promising to play, shall be fined, at the discretion of the Committee, such fine not to exceed 2s. 6d.

12.—That the Committee shall have power to make bye-laws at any time.

13.—That full third class railway fare be paid to each member playing in a match away from home.

J. R. HARTLEY, CHAIRMAN.

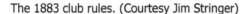

N.B.—Rule Eleven will be Strictly Enforced.

The 1883 club rules. (Courtesy Jim Stringer)

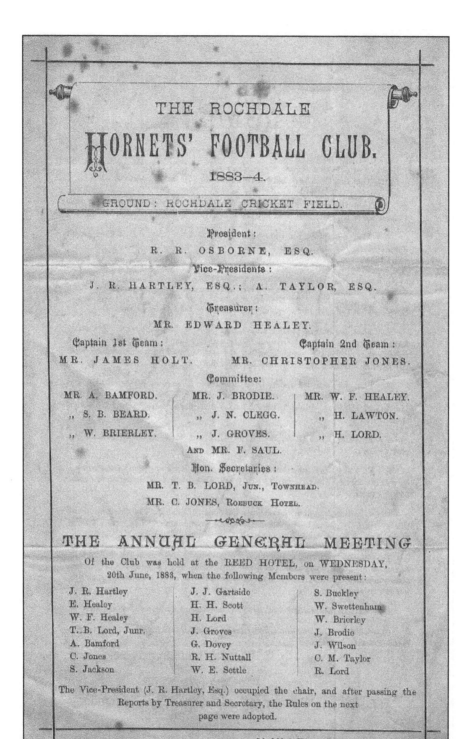

THE ROCHDALE
HORNETS' FOOTBALL CLUB.
1883—4.

GROUND: ROCHDALE CRICKET FIELD.

President:
R. R. OSBORNE, ESQ.

Vice-Presidents:
J. R. HARTLEY, ESQ.; A. TAYLOR, ESQ.

Treasurer:
MR. EDWARD HEALEY.

Captain 1st Team: Captain 2nd Team:
MR. JAMES HOLT.   MR. CHRISTOPHER JONES.

Committee:

MR. A. BAMFORD.	MR. J. BRODIE.	MR. W. F. HEALEY.
„ S. B. BEARD.	„ J. N. CLEGG.	„ H. LAWTON.
„ W. BRIERLEY.	„ J. GROVES.	„ H. LORD.

AND MR. F. SAUL.

Hon. Secretaries:

MR. T. B. LORD, JUN., TOWNHEAD.

MR. C. JONES, ROEBUCK HOTEL.

THE ANNUAL GENERAL MEETING

Of the Club was held at the REED HOTEL, on WEDNESDAY, 20th June, 1883, when the following Members were present:

J. R. Hartley	J. J. Gartside	S. Buckley
E. Healey	H. H. Scott	W. Swettenham
W. F. Healey	H. Lord	W. Brierley
T. B. Lord, Junr.	J. Groves	J. Brodie
A. Bamford	G. Dovey	J. Wilson
C. Jones	R. H. Nuttall	C. M. Taylor
S. Jackson	W. E. Settle	R. Lord

The Vice-President (J. R. Hartley, Esq.) occupied the chair, and after passing the Reports by Treasurer and Secretary, the Rules on the next page were adopted.

Schofield & Hoblyn, Printers, Rochdale.

The cover of the 1883–84 Annual Report. (Courtesy Jim Stringer)

10

3. 1895: The great split

By the early 1890s the clubs in the North had a huge player pool, growing crowds, increasing revenues and the biggest potential. And the London-based Rugby Football Union didn't like it one bit.

251 of the 481 clubs affiliated to the RFU were located in Northern England and the Union felt threatened. Particularly by the popularity and power of the clubs in Yorkshire and Lancashire.

The strength of the game on both sides of the Pennines brought a craving for greater competition – and the rewards that came with it. The creation of independent Yorkshire and West Lancashire & Border Towns challenge cups had drawn big crowds, bolstering the North as a rugby stronghold.

The next step was for the Yorkshire and Lancashire competitions to form leagues that would provide big games against local rivals on a regular basis – with shared gate money. In 1889 Lancashire abandoned its cup in favour of a fledgling league competition. Yorkshire clubs were strictly forbidden to follow suit by their county Union. But in March 1892 – in open defiance of the RFU in London – the 10 biggest clubs in Yorkshire formed their own self-governing senior competition, followed later in the year by creation of the Lancashire Club Championship. Such actions were clear steps towards greater autonomy.

In the South, rugby football was considered a leisure activity for privately educated sons of wealthy industrialists and the gentry. Games being played on a Saturday didn't worry them at all – but for the working players in the North, playing rugby on a Saturday could mean losing half a day's pay.

So, the Northern Clubs lobbied the RFU to allow them to make 'broken time' payments to their players – in lieu of the pay they lost. This was anathema to the strictly amateur ethos of the RFU. They saw it as being paid to play: a stain of professionalism on their Corinthian conscience.

One Rugby Football Union representative said: "If the working man cannot afford to play the game, he should do without it." Another said that, as the public schools had invented the game, "why should we hand it over to the working classes?"

Hornets' president, Mr James Hartley, was adamant. "If a man loses a portion or all of his day's wages through playing a match, he was to be paid a certain amount of money. It was not intended that a man should be paid as a professional for services rendered as a player". But anything considered a 'payment' raised the anger of the RFU: even post-match meals for players were investigated.

One report suggests that Hornets were already paying broken time payments to their players. Hornets player Ned Wild said: "I cannot for the life of me see why a working man should lose his amateur status because he is paid wages lost through having to leave work. I fought for that myself and got it for the players in my time."

Wild later admitted that payments were made to the working players "… long before the Northern Union was thought of…". These took the form of half a crown for each man who had to get off work and travel with the team. He also spoke of players being handed a sovereign per man as 'pocket money' when Hornets played fixtures in the South of England against Oxford University and Kensington.

James Hartley said that Hornets had covered all of their own expenses for the two matches in the South. However, in an act of supreme hypocrisy, Oxford would not fulfil the return fixture until Hornets agreed to "… guarantee all their expenses, including very generous hotel bills and railway fares."

At a meeting of the RFU in London in September 1893, representatives from Northern clubs proposed that players be compensated for a bona-fide loss of time. In response the Secretary of the RFU suggested an amendment to the proposal. They wanted to add… 'contrary to the true interest of the game and its spirit'.

The proposal was defeated by 282 votes to 136, and the RFU passed a motion decreeing that "only clubs composed entirely of amateurs shall be eligible for membership, and its headquarters shall be in London where all general meetings shall be held".

Over the next 23 months, bans, suspensions and trials became the order of the day as the RFU sought to quell this Northern affront to their amateur ethos and, in 1894, Hornets became embroiled in a major dispute in which all but three clubs in the Lancashire Championship were accused of paying their players.

Compounded by squabbling over control of county competitions – by May 1895, Lancashire's senior clubs had already resigned from their county union, Yorkshire senior clubs followed suit in June – relationships between clubs and the RFU were at breaking point.

On 13 August, the press reported even tougher RFU regulations against professionalism - including forbidding clubs to take money at the gate. It was the final straw. The Northern clubs had little choice but to take control of their own destiny.

A special meeting of clubs was called for Wednesday 29 August 1895. The proposal on the table: mass resignation from the Rugby Football Union and the formation of a Northern Rugby Union that allowed clubs to pay players legitimate broken time payments of six shillings per day.

Representatives of 21 'rebel' clubs gathered at the George Hotel in Huddersfield. Around the table were Batley, Bradford, Brighouse Rangers, Broughton Rangers, Dewsbury, Halifax, Huddersfield, Hull, Hunslet, Leeds, Leigh, Liversedge, Manningham, Oldham, Rochdale Hornets, Runcorn, St Helens, Tyldesley, Wakefield Trinity, Warrington, Widnes and Wigan. Stockport was not present at the meeting but were asked to join and immediately dispatched a representative to take part in the meeting. Rochdale Hornets sent club secretary Mr William Brierley.

Twenty of the delegates present backed the resolution "that the clubs here represented decide to form a Northern Rugby Football Union, and pledge themselves to push forward, without delay, its establishment on the principle of payment for bona-fide broken-time only". Only Dewsbury declined.

The deed was done and, having lit the fuse, things moved quickly. The following evening there was a meeting of the Hornets committee at the Albion Hotel, Yorkshire Street – to discuss the club's attitude towards the new Northern Football Union, formed by 12 Yorkshire clubs and the nine which had resigned from the Lancashire Club Championship Competition.

On Saturday 31 August, *The Rochdale Observer* reported the secession from the Union in a footnote at the bottom of page five: "At a meeting held at the George Hotel, Huddersfield on Thursday evening, the Hornets being among the clubs represented, it was decided to form a Northern Union and to work on the principle of payment for lost time."

Its front page carried a modest five line announcement: "Hornets FC – a special general meeting of the members will be held on Monday next (2nd September) at the Lecture Rooms Public Hall at 8.0pm. Business: To confirm the action of the Committee in joining the Northern Rugby Union."

In reference to the members' meeting, *The Rochdale Observer* commented: "This is undoubtedly the proper thing to do, though it might with advantage have been done earlier." Though how that would have been possible is hard to tell, given that William Brierley was required to give an answer on Rochdale Hornets' support of the Northern Union on the Thursday evening – and the Saturday *Rochdale Observer* would have been the first available opportunity to announce the meeting.

Chairman James Hartley addressed the members, making clear the position of the 22 clubs that any payments were solely a compensation for broken time. Secretary William Brierley reiterated the chairman's statement, saying that every club in the Northern Union was "... dead against professionalism."

He went on to reassure members that "... if the Hornets joined the new union they would have 42 matches with the best clubs in Lancashire and Yorkshire; if they did not, they would only get about 14 matches."

With this in mind, the members ratified the decision taken by the club's committee, only three voting against. Hornets would join the Northern Union.

A short article in *The Rochdale Observer* that week headlined 'The Hornets and the New League' offered more detail of the proposed split and how it would affect Hornets' immediate future: including the creation of a rift in the game in Rochdale that would reshape the town's footballing landscape.

It said: "The League proposes to allow payment for players' 'broken time'. If the Hornets join it - and there was a general feeling at the committee meeting in favour of it - they would have to cancel their fixtures with St Clement's and the other clubs outside the new union, but, on the other hand, they would be assured of meeting some of the best teams in Lancashire and Yorkshire."

Clubs loyal to the RFU, asked their governing body if they would still be permitted to play the matches already arranged with clubs which have joined the new Northern Union. Mr Rowland Hill (an RFU official) replied "I am directed by my committee to inform you that no club belonging to our union will be permitted to play matches with any other club which is in membership with the Northern Union."

Harvey Rigg, secretary of St Clement's understood the potential impact on his and other local clubs. He had been seen at the George Hotel on the evening of the meeting, but denied that he'd been there to consider joining the Northern Union. In a letter to *The Rochdale Observer* he wrote, "It is necessary for me to say that although present at the hotel in the interests of my club I was not at the meeting. I had arranged matches with the Hornets,

Widnes, Broughton Rangers, Leigh and Tyldesley and it was to know their fate that I travelled to Huddersfield. The new union has been formed and these are cancelled."

Despite their initial reticence to split from the RFU, St Clement's flirted briefly with the Northern Union for a season, but disbanded in September 1897. Harvey Rigg would go on to become a founding director of the Rochdale Association Football Club, which would play its games on the former St Clement's ground at Wilbutts Lane, Spotland.

With the rugby football game in such flux, plans for the 1895–96 Northern Union season were uncertain. *The Yorkshire Evening Post* said: "Probably there will be instituted in the vague future some county championship scheme to provide the attraction, which will have been cut away by the secession from the Union. Possibly also, in the nebulous yet to be, there will be an Inter-County Challenge Cup contest. These things are in the clouds as yet, but are being mooted."

The first acts of the Northern Union were to elect Mr Henry Hirst Waller, chairman of the Brighouse club, as the first chairman of the Northern Rugby Football Union and to appoint a sub-committee to 'consider rules and by-laws'. It was also agreed that meetings of the new union would be held alternately in Manchester and Huddersfield. A resolution to run senior competitions in Lancashire and Yorkshire was agreed and a meeting of the club secretaries was called for the following Tuesday, 3 September at the Spread Eagle Hotel in Manchester.

Twenty-two clubs attended the Manchester meeting. For four and a half hours, they worked not only to develop the terms of the new union, but also arrange its first fixtures, which were ambitiously scheduled for the coming Saturday – giving clubs four days to arrange transport and match officials.

Hornets were to travel to St Helens. What is interesting is that there was no real pre-season preparation for such a historic game. *The Rochdale Observer* noted: "It is very unfortunate for the Hornets that they have to enter the field today against St Helens after only one trial match. The players should have commenced practicing on Tuesday, but the showery weather prevented this, and on Thursday the conditions were hardly more favourable. Some rain fell during the day and in the evening darkness set in very early. The consequence was that only 20 players put on their jerseys and barely an hour's play was possible."

They continued: "The players contented themselves with knocking the ball about until there were a sufficient number of men on the field to form scratch sides. The game was played under difficulties as the goal posts have not yet been fixed up, and there were no goal or touch lines. The play was chiefly of a rough and tumble character and little science was exhibited. Of course, this was all that was expected by anybody, and if it has "loosened the limbs" of the players it will have achieved its object. Teddy Buckley seemed as lively and tricky as ever, and before the game commenced, he endeavoured to coach some of his colleagues in the art of passing."

On Saturday 7 September – just 10 days after the meeting at the George Hotel – the first Northern Union matches were played. Notably, it was the weekend before the official opening of the Rugby Football Union season.

The Hornets team selected for the game at St Helens was: Joe Wood, J Hill, Teddy Buckley, C Midgley, F Uttley, A Mason, S Sucksmith, GT Dex, A Hill, F Kershaw, A Dearden, C Trevor, Peter Leach, Jack Leach and Alf Leach.

The referee for Hornets' inaugural Northern Union game was Mr H Court of Oldham, with Mr H Taylor of Tyldesley and Mr J Potts of Stockport named as touch judges.

The game kicked off at 4.50pm. Hornets arrived an hour late after missing a connecting train in Manchester. Not a good start.

With Teddy Buckley pulling the strings, Hornets gave a good account of themselves in the first half, but errors and penalties gave Saints the opportunity to open the scoring. Saints were in again when they charged down a Hornets 25-yard drop-out to score.

It is reported that 'in the second half Hornets held the advantage all through', with play concentrated in the forwards and little open football. Joe Wood attempted a drop-goal, worth four points, but missed the mark. Hornets continued to press and the pressure told when Saints were caught offside in front of their own posts. Midgley landed the penalty to put Hornets on the board.

Sucksmith came close to scoring Hornets' inaugural Northern Union try, but as he dived to touch down, the ball was 'kicked from under him as he was dropping on it'. With time running out, Midgley took a penalty kick at goal from near halfway, but the attempt fell short. Final score St Helens 8 Hornets 3.

The Yorkshire Post reported: "The encounter between St Helens and Rochdale Hornets caused great excitement in the former town, and it says much for the energy and determination which Hornets put into their work that, with eight points against them at half time, they were not only able to prevent their opponents from scoring further, but succeeded in placing them on the defensive, and placing a penalty goal to their own credit."

As the season progressed, things didn't improve a great deal. The first five games were all lost before a 3–3 draw with Stockport halted the run. The following game against Broughton Rangers, on 12 October, saw Hornets secure their first win in the Northern Union in front of a Dane Street crowd of 5,000.

A further five games passed without a win, but hopes were raised briefly in November by back-to-back victories against Widnes, (6–0) and Wakefield (5–0). The following week Hornets travelled to Oldham for their first ever Northern Union clash. A 13–8 defeat became the first of 18 games without a win; a horrendous run punctuated only by four draws - three of them 0–0.

A 7–3 Good Friday win over Stockport briefly raised spirits, but that heralded a run-in of 10 straight defeats, during which Hornets were nilled six times.

In a season that yielded only 19 tries, 10 goals and a drop-goal, Hornets leading try, goal and point scorer was centre C Midgley with three tries, four goals and two drop-goals for 20 points. The season that had begun with such rebellion and potential ended with a 21–0 defeat at Leeds. The final tally: Played 42: Won 4: Drew 8: Lost 30.

The Rochdale Times commented that it must have been with a sigh of relief that the inaugural season of the Northern Union was brought to a close: "From the commencement of the season the club have battled against great odds. They won less matches than ever they have done before in a single season, and have suffered the indignity of having their ground closed for nearly two months, and robbing them of some of their best drawing fixtures through the attitude of a few reckless supporters."

"There is little doubt that all connected with the club are glad the curtain has fallen and look forward to next season as giving promise of much better things."

Indeed, in a way that has become familiar to all of us over the years, the long-suffering Hornets fans drew praise in *The Rochdale Times'* review of the season: "Through all the bad luck which they have had throughout the season, this can be said of the of the Hornets supporters: that they have stuck to their club loyally."

"To turn up Saturday after Saturday to watch their team suffer defeat after defeat is enough to make anyone downhearted, but they have clung to the hope that their favourites would improve, and now the end of the season has arrived and they haven't, they are positive that the team will be a 'rattler' next season. Such faith as they have shown is highly commendable, and deserves a better return than it has had so far."

But even though Hornets finished stone-cold last with just four wins from 42 games, the NU's first season was a commercial success: the club made a profit of £96.

Off the field, though, the partisan excitement of the new Northern Union stirred-up trouble. Indeed, after a home game against Brighouse Rangers – in which "several obviously wrong decisions were given" – referee Mr Slevin fell foul of angry Hornets supporters. At the end of the game spectators invaded the pitch and mobbed the referee. Despite the best efforts of police, the players and private detectives he was 'struck several times with sticks and umbrellas'.

Eventually jostled from the field, there was an attempt to smuggle him out of the ground via a back entrance only for him to be intercepted by the crowd. He was eventually put in a Hansom Cab with a detective and one of the Hornets' players for protection. But the cab was followed and forced to stop, so the driver had to look for another escape route. During the melee, the referee fell out of the cab, but was not seriously hurt. Bundled back aboard, he was then driven three miles to Heywood in order to shake off the mob.

Anticipating that poor Mr Slevin would return to Rochdale by train, a large crowd gathered to wait for him at Rochdale station, but after waiting some time they gave up and went home.

Following a complaint by Mr Slevin, a meeting of the Northern Union Lancashire Committee considered appropriate action. Their decision was to suspend Hornets' use of their home ground for six weeks, depriving them of home advantage and vital revenue for some of their most attractive fixtures.

Having lost somewhere in the region of £200 in the first three weeks of the ban, Hornets President James Hartley appealed to the Northern Union, saying that the affair had been greatly exaggerated, that the sentence of the Lancashire Committee was too severe and that it could lead to the downfall of the club.

The Northern Union dismissed the appeal unanimously and Hornets had to appeal to supporters for donations to get through the next three weeks. But help came from an unlikely source. Hornets were due to play Oldham at home during the suspension. Not only did Oldham offer Hornets use of their ground for the game, having attracted a crowd of 13,000 they also handed over the gate receipts of £156 – less £10 to cover their own costs.

The ban was the first of three times between February 1896 and December 1897 that Hornets were punished for poor supporter behaviour. On the second incident – an attack on opponents – the Northern Union ordered Hornets' ground to be closed for five weeks. In the third case, following 'rowdy behaviour by young spectators at the ground', Hornets were ordered to display 200 behaviour notices in the town and double the admission for boys to the full adult price of sixpence.

Keen to make the game as attractive as possible to paying spectators, the Northern Union began making changes to the game that would separate it forever from its Rugby Union roots. In 1897, line-outs were abolished and all goals were reduced to two points to place greater emphasis on scoring tries.

In 1898, the great rugby union taboo of professionalism was embraced. Payments for playing were legalised on the proviso that players had to be in 'bone-fide employment'. Working for their club or in spurious roles such as 'waiter' or 'billiard scorer' were still frowned upon.

The Northern Union's final split from its rugby union roots came in 1906 when teams were reduced from 15-a-side to 13. The chaos of a ruck after every tackle was also done away with. It was replaced by 'an orderly play the ball' in which the tackled player was required to regain his feet and roll the ball backwards with his foot.

In doing this, the Northern Union created a sport that was distinctively different to its ancestor. And, while rugby union remained resolutely anchored in the 19th century, this new, exciting footballing code had its eyes fixed firmly on the future.

References

'The History of Rugby League Football' - K Macklin, 1962

https://www.irishexaminer.com/opinion/columnists/arid–20428917.html: 'How class warfare split rugby in England' - P Mills November 2016

Rochdale Observer Saturday 31 August 1895

'A People's Game' - Geoffrey Moorhouse, 1995

'Rugby League in Twentieth Century Britain: A Social and Cultural History' - Tony Collins, 2006

http://www.rlhalloffame.org.uk/season1.htm

Yorkshire Post 9th September 1895

Rochdale Observer 7th September 1895

Rochdale Times - Saturday 2 May 1896

Green Final: 'Old Stalwarts of the Hornets - Mr JR Hartley' - 22 September 1923

Green Final: 'Old Stalwarts of the Hornets - Ned Wild' - 20 October 1923

'First Season In The Northern Union 1895–1896 - A Factual Record' - C Atkin 1995

A pre-World War One Hornets team including Walter Roman and several other west-country players.
(Courtesy *Rugby League Journal*)

Rochdale Observer sketches of Hornets signings from Bridgewater in Somerset, Walter Roman
and Tommy Woods (Courtesy Jim Stringer)

4. 1911: In the shadow of war

Hornets started the 20th century looking further afield for quality players. Around the same time, in the rugby union heartlands of Wales and the South West, some of the country's best rugby players were looking to the Northern Union for an opportunity to shine in the professional game.

Joe Corsi and Ernest Jenkins (Wales), Ernest Jones, Tommy Woods, Walter Roman, Tom West, Jack Robinson and Vic Slade (Somerset), George Prudence and Dickie Paddon (Devon) and Sammy Carter (Cornwall) all came North to pull on a Rochdale Hornets jersey.

In the years leading up to the First World War, Hornets were becoming a force to be reckoned with in Lancashire. With a feared pack, named The Terrible Six for their uncompromising approach, and a back line featuring some of the country's most exciting rugby potential, they overcame poor league form to dominate the county cup competition.

In the 1911–12 season, Hornets won the Lancashire Senior Cup for the first time in their history. Rounds one and two were straightforward victories, Hornets beating Swinton 13–0 at the Athletic Grounds and Broughton Rangers 18–3 at Wheater's Field. The semi-final proved more of a challenge. An 8–8 draw with Widnes at the Athletic Grounds meant a replay on the following Wednesday evening at Lowerhouse Lane. Hornets were ruthless and came away from Widnes with an impressive 11–0 win.

Already waiting for them in the Final was a formidable Oldham side that had only conceded a solitary goal in their three games against Barrow, Leigh and Wigan.

The Final was played at Wheater's Field, Broughton on Saturday 2 December 1911. The Hornets team was: Baxter, West, Robinson, English, Paddon, Schofield, Jones, Woods, Fitzsimmons, Dearden, Roman, Jenkins and Turner.

One report says that, in a crowd of 16,399, "The supporters of both clubs were there in strong force and the club colours – the green and black of Hornets and the red and white of Oldham – were conspicuously worn, and it was significant that the green and black largely predominated. Throughout the game, indeed, the Hornets were obviously the favourites, and their sallies received far greater encouragement than those of Oldham."

The early exchanges were cagey. Hornets took the lead on the quarter-mark with a Paddon penalty, and he added another on the half hour to give Hornets a 4–0 half-time lead. Oldham started the second half with a drop-goal to edge within two points, but Hornets struck back in style: Schofield broke from a scrum, drawing defenders to find Turner in support who dived in to score. Hornets were on the board again when English dropped a goal to stretch their lead. With 11 minutes to play, Oldham scored a try out wide to close the gap to 9–5, but with just two minutes remaining, Hornets mounted a last attack. From a scrum close to the Oldham line Schofield found Jones up the blind-side who had enough pace to round the defender and score. The referee blew for time as Paddon's conversion attempt pulled wide. Hornets 12 Oldham 5.

This stirring victory gave John Baxter the honour of being the first Rochdale Hornets captain to lift a trophy. Doubly special for him, as it was also his birthday. In receiving the cup, he said: "This is the preliminary run for the Northern Union Cup."

The Hornets Fallen: Hornets won the 1911-12 Lancashire Cup beating Oldham 12–5 at Broughton in front of a capacity 20,000 crowd. The team featured Walter Roman (back row, extreme right) and Tom West (middle row, left of the cup) who were both killed in The First World War.
(Rochdale Hornets Heritage Archive)

After a 40 year wait John Baxter became the first Rochdale Hornets captain to lift a trophy, the 1911 Lancashire Senior Cup. (Rochdale Hornets Heritage Archive)

The supporter celebrations began long before people got back to Rochdale. One report speaks of 'lively scenes' of celebrating fans on packed trains departing Victoria Station – and when the Hornets team arrived at Victoria to catch their train back, there were "terrific cheers and a furious waving of caps and hats" from crowds of supporters. The team's return was met with another sizeable crowd at Rochdale Station, where a mounted policeman and a number of officers were required to hold back supporters to enable the players to board their wagonette.

The Rochdale Times said of the scenes: "Thousands of people, most of whom sported the popular green and black colours in the form or rosettes or miniature cups with pieces of ribbon attached, cheered and cheered again the men who had brought honour to the town. Hats and sticks waved in the air, every time the Hornets captain held the cup aloft the cheers rang out afresh and the trumpets and rattles in the possession of scores of the crowd were brought into action."

The throng followed the team on their way to the Albion Hotel, Yorkshire Street for post-match celebrations. And what a parade it was. Led by mounted police, the Rochdale Old Band played lively music ahead of the wagonette. The streets so full it became impossible to walk on the pavements and shopkeepers feared for their windows. Turning from Drake Street into the town centre, the players were faced with an even bigger crowd and, when the Albion was finally reached, they refused to disperse until Johnny Baxter appeared at a window with the trophy.

Inside, the cup was filed with champagne and passed round to toast the skipper's birthday. Chairman JR Hartley made the toast: "Very good health to the captain, to our supporters and last but not least to all our players."

The Rochdale Times summed up the day: "Altogether a rare sprit of buoyancy pervaded the atmosphere and Saturday evening will live long in the memory not only of the patrons of the Hornets, but of the townspeople generally."

The following year, Hornets again got to the final. Having got a bye in round one, they drew 0–0 away to Broughton Rangers in round two, and beat them 18–4 in the replay at home three days later.

On the day of the semi-final, Rochdale woke to a blanket of thick fog and there were 'grave doubts' as late as 2pm as to whether the game would go ahead. By 2.30 both sets of posts were visible from the grandstand, referee Mr Renton of Hunslet declared the game on and fans were allowed into the ground.

Two first half Walter Roman tries and two Dickie Paddon goals gave Hornets a 10–3 lead. In the second half, St Helens clawed their way back into contention with a converted try to make it 10–8. Both sides exchanged missed penalties as they strove to gain an advantage, and what looked like a late Saints try was struck off for a forward pass. Hornets clung on to win by a two point margin.

The final took place on Wednesday 11 December 1912 at The Willows – the crowd of 'well over 10,000' was considered a 'fine attendance for a mid-week rugby match

Despite an early Paddon try and a 5–0 lead, Hornets went down to Wigan by 21–5. Hornets were unlucky to lose Tom West in the first half with an ankle injury – there were no substitutes – but Wigan struggled to make the numerical advantage count.

Two late tries extended the scoreline. *The Rochdale Times* report said: "The Hornets did not infuse into their play the energy and resources which characterised their efforts against Broughton in the second round replay; had they been able to do so the story to be told might have been a very different one."

Having been to two consecutive finals, expectations were high for the following season's Lancashire Cup, but Hornets were again undone by Wigan – this time in a 9–2 first round defeat at Central Park. In typical bogey-team fashion, Wigan also knocked Hornets out of that year's Challenge Cup – 16–0 at the Athletic Grounds.

Despite a lack of cup success Hornets fared better in the league, finishing 4th in the Lancashire League and 12th in the Northern League.

The Annual Report also declared: "During the past season the directors have been able to complete the purchase of the Athletic Grounds and it must be pleasing to both the shareholders and the supporters of the club to know that the company now possess what is generally considered to be the finest Football and Athletic Grounds in the North of England."

The 1913–14 season was one of steady consolidation. Despite a quarter final exit from the Challenge Cup and a first round exit at the hands of Wigan in the Lancashire cup, Hornets showed up well in the league, culminating in their highest ever finish in 7th.

The Annual Report also congratulated Walter Roman and Jack Robinson for their selection for the Northern Union team to play in Australia. It says: "We trust that they will have a very pleasant and successful tour."

However, on 12 August 1914, while the pair were still on tour, war was declared. As reservists, Walter and Jack presented themselves at Victoria Barracks in Sydney requesting the earliest passage back to the UK. The earliest ship was the one on which the England team was to return.

On returning from the tour, Walter Roman said: "I think our team one of the greatest combinations that ever left England. Our last match was a revelation of Bulldog Courage and British pluck. I now have sterner work to face for King and Country. I shall do my best in this great game just as I always do in football."

Despite the outbreak of war before the 1914–15 season began, the decision was made to play both the regular season and the cup competitions to a conclusion. But the impact of the war was evident in the lower attendances at matches and with many teams missing players who had already signed up for the Armed Forces.

In the first round of the Lancashire Senior Cup, Hornets beat Broughton Rangers 8–5 at the Cliff. In round two Hornets drew 0–0 with Widnes at the Athletic Grounds, winning the replay 12–0.

In the semi-final Hornets took on Warrington at Wilderspool. 12-man Hornets won 13–5. Forward Bowers was dismissed in the first half for a much disputed late challenge on the Wire full-back after he'd kicked clear. The report in *The Rochdale Times* described the dismissal as 'ridiculously severe punishment for what was more a technical offence more than anything else.'

But it didn't faze Hornets at all, one match report said: 'There could not be the slightest doubt as to which was the better side at Warrington on Saturday. The Visitors were never behind, and though Warrington drew level in the earlier stages of the second half, they never really seemed likely to pull the game off. The confidence with which the Hornets buckled down to their work and regained the lead fairly delighted the good number of supporters who had patronised the excursion."

Their reward was a final against bogey-team Wigan at the Willows. On the day of the final, the weather was awful - sleet and rain whipped by cold winds. This and the increasing number of men enlisted kept the crowd down to only 4,000 hardy souls – 1,000 of them from Rochdale.

Despite Hornets playing with the wind in the first half, Wigan opened the scoring with a penalty after Schofield was caught offside at a scrum. For 10 minutes Hornets lay siege to the Wigan line, doing everything but score. First Jones tripped chasing his charge-down over the goal line; then a try by Hopwood was declined to the surprise of the Hornets players; then Hopwood again knocking-on over the line as he reached to score.

With the game locked in a struggle, it took a moment of individual ingenuity to snatch victory. Having won a scrum close to their own line, Wigan's Thomas passed the ball to Seddon; Hornets' Ernest Jones "pounced and, taking the ball from him, scored what proved to be the winning try."

Try as they might, Wigan could not break Hornets' stern defence and when in possession, "Jones' touch kicking repeatedly drove back the Wiganers and upset their plans."

Late in the game Wigan were awarded a penalty in front of the posts for a dubious high tackle. *The Rochdale Observer* said: "To the delight of the Rochdalians, Thomas' shot went wide." `The bogey was laid: Hornets sneaked home 3–2.

After receiving the Cup, captain George Prudence was carried shoulder high from the field by his team-mates. The victorious Hornets team was: Mick English, Jack Hopwood, Joe Corsi, George Prudence, J Fairhurst, Bobby Schofield, Ernest Jones, Jack Fitzsimmons, Sammy Carter, Billy Ashworth, Victor Slade, GD Webb and Joe Bowers.

During the post-match speeches at the Albion Hotel, Yorkshire Street, George Prudence said he felt proud to be the captain of such a fine team and he hoped that they would all work together in the future.

Councillor Watson said that the directors were exceedingly pleased with the way the players had risen to the occasion. He spoke of how Hornets: "... had lost a lot of good men owing to the calls of the Army, but the others had put in all that they knew how to make up for that, and they had done splendidly."

The fact that the match report appeared on the same page of *The Rochdale Observer* as a report on Rochdalians wounded at Ypres was an indication that things were about to change dramatically.

By the time the Club's Annual Report & Accounts were released on 31 May 1915, 24 Hornets players had already departed to join the fighting.

In an article headlined 'Football Prospects', *The Rochdale Observer* reported: "On account of the war and the large number of players who have enlisted, football will hardly be the attraction during the forthcoming season as is usually the case. The Hornets have a particularly pleasing list of players who have responded to their country's call."

Hornets captain George Prudence with the 1914–15 Lancashire Cup.
Hornets beat Wigan 3–2 to win the final.
(Rochdale Hornets Heritage Archive)

With 1,500 players serving their country, attendances in severe decline and conscription imminent, the Northern Union decided at its AGM in June 2015 to suspend professional football for the remainder of the war.

This move saw the emergence of the Wartime Emergency League where games were to be played on a friendly basis only, arranged between the clubs themselves, with players receiving a standard expenses payment of 2s 6d.

There was also a relaxation of player registration rules, which enabled players to turn out for the club nearest their workplace or military posting. This meant that team line-ups changed week by week – with many clubs fielding scratch teams made-up of other clubs' players, local amateurs and whoever else was available to play.

Given the uncertainties of the time, each club played a different number of fixtures. These were kept local to reduce travelling time, minimise cost and conserve precious war resources.

24 clubs played friendly matches in the 1915–16 season, and Hornets was one of them. What was clear from the outset was that the term 'friendly' was used loosely, with Hornets' game at Brighouse in September 1915 abandoned due to crowd trouble.

In a generous effort to support the growing number of enlisted players, Hornets supporters organised a collection at the Athletic Grounds on 16 October 1915. £8 3s 6 ½ d was raised to purchase footballs for soldiers in France and those still training at home. The Annual Report & Accounts from that financial year notes "The letters to hand acknowledging the receipt of the footballs show how very much the club's supporters' generosity has been appreciated".

While there was no 'official' league table for the 1915–16 season, the press did compile an unofficial one based on win percentages. The records show that Hornets played 33 games, winning nine and drawing three to finish 19th with a 32 percent win record.

The 1916–17 season was played on the same emergency basis and Hornets were beginning to struggle, finishing third bottom of the unofficial table.

Going into a third season of wartime football proved too much and it soon became clear that Hornets' game was up. At a meeting of the directors on Monday 3 December 1917, the board was compelled to abandon all remaining fixtures for the season as it was proving impossible to raise a competitive team and attendances had dwindled.

The Rochdale Observer of Wednesday 5 December 1917 reported: "The question of continuing to play football under the present abnormal conditions was considered. The directors decided not to play football at present and this practically means the abandoning of the fixtures arranged for this season."

The Observer continued: "Just before the war broke out interest in rugby football had been strongly revived. A good team had been got together and they were playing very attractive football. Since the outbreak of hostilities and the players began to enlist the difficulties with which the directors had to contend have been increased. In the 1914–15 season the team won 18 of the 34 games played: in 1915–16 nine out of 32, and on 1916–17 nine out of 32 played. During the present season they have not won a game of the seven played."

In the Saturday edition of *The Observer*, the scale of the challenge was made clear: "The Rochdale Hornets football club directors decided on Monday that no more matches be played at present. The reason for this decision is that practically all of the usual players have enlisted, with the result that the quality of play has been poor and that attendance of the public at the matches small."

"So far this season seven games have been played and the club has not won a single one of them. Shortly after the declaration of war practically the whole of the first and 'A' teams volunteered and, in all, 41 active players have joined the forces."

"Four have been killed and two permanently injured. All this has militated against the club's success. The losses on the last three seasons total over £1,100. As an indication on the fall in the numbers of spectators it may be mentioned that, while in 1913–14 spectators at home matches numbered 159,249, they dropped last season to 8,625."

Hornets' Annual Report for this truncated season makes miserable reading: "The team has only played seven matches, all of which were lost, scoring 7 points against 156 by our opponents. At the beginning of December, it was found impossible to raise a team to continue playing football, there being only three local players available and the Directors were reluctantly compelled to abandon all fixtures for the season."

"Financially, the year's working has resulted in a loss of £229 8s 8d. In November a subscription list was opened and an appeal made for funds to assist the club to carry on until peace is declared. The amount received to date being £32 8s 0d: any further subscription forwarded would be gratefully acknowledged."

The Hornets Fallen

These days the word 'hero' gets used lightly in a sporting context. Let us not forget that four Rochdale Hornets players were killed in the Great War. They served our club, our town and our country with distinction.

John Twigg

Born in Ibstock, Leicestershire, John Twigg had previously been an Army regular - which explains his early mobilisation in the war.

He had served with the 2nd Leicester Regiment in India for six years – and represented his regiment at rugby football on a tour of Ceylon where he played against Kundy, Colombo and a Ceylon national select side.

He returned to play for his local club Coalville before being picked up by Leicester Tigers. In his two years there he won six county caps – and it was at a Midland Counties versus Cornwall game where he was spotted by Hornets directors on a scouting mission. It is reported that they were 'favourably impressed'.

He was reported as having signed for Hornets on Monday 16 March 1914, having played his last game for Leicester versus Gloucester on the Saturday.

Described as a 'strong, sturdy forward, six feet in height and weighing 13st 8lb' it was expected that 'He should make a name for himself in Northern Union Football'.

John Twigg was killed in action on 13 March 1915 at Neuve Chappelle during the France and Flanders campaign. In an interview with the Rochdale Observer his Comrade Private Clacey said: "Before our infantry were given the order to charge, the artillery opened fire, maintaining a fierce bombardment. The Germans replied, one of their shells dropping into the trench where Twigg was. He was struck on the head with a big splinter and so severely injured that death was instantaneous."

He went on: "He was a very popular soldier and his death was much regretted. When out there Sergeant Twigg used to often talk about Rochdale Hornets and his friends at Rochdale – and he regularly received some fine hampers from the town."

John is remembered on the Leicester Tigers Roll of honour, and on Le Touret Memorial, Pas de Calais, France.

Rochdale Hornets Annual Report commented: "We have unfortunately to announce the severe loss we have sustained in the death of a player with great ability, much esteemed by the club, Sergeant Twigg, who fell gallantly fighting for king and country in France."

Ernest Thomas 'Tom' West

The third son of Mr. and Mrs. Walter West, of Twerton near Bath, 'Tom' began playing rugby at half-back for Oldfield Park Wesleyans – a Sunday School team. He switched to playing soccer for three seasons, but was drawn back to rugby by his local Twerton club. From there he progressed into Bath's second team, and his prowess as a sprinter saw him make the transition into the three-quarters. After four seasons with Bath, his job took him to Gloucester where he played for half a season, but struggled to get into a first team packed with England internationals.

His return to Bath saw him made first-team captain and he played alongside Jack Robinson – who also joined Hornets, and who was selected for the 1914 Australia and New Zealand tour with Walter Roman. While captaining Bath, Tom won six county caps, playing in a Somerset side captained by another future Hornet, Tommy Woods.

Tom West signed for Hornets in 1909 and, in 1911, won the Lancashire Senior Cup playing in the same side as fellow Somerset-men Walter Roman and Tommy Woods.

Tom West was an early volunteer, joining the Rifle Corps on 5 September of 1914. He was killed in action on the morning of 29 September 1915. He was on sentry duty alongside his fellow Bath centre Bert Lewis when he was hit by a bullet that killed him instantly.

Notice of his death was delivered to his mother along with a letter that he hadn't lived to dispatch. It read: "I may not have the opportunity of writing to you for a little while, so you must not worry if you don't hear from me. I shall be quite all right..."

Tom's Rochdalian comrade, Rifleman Pomfret, wrote home: "I regret to inform that my greatest chum Tommy West - the well-known Hornets player... met his death this Wednesday morning whilst doing his duty. The bullet passed through the side of his face and there was no hope for him. He died immediately without saying a word." In six seasons with Hornets Tom West made 146 appearances, scored 50 tries and five goals.

Charles Burton

Charles John Inglis Burton was born in the Dragoon Guards barracks in Athlone in 1881 - suggesting that his father was a regular. A centre, Charles played for several years as a stalwart of Hornets 'A' Team. Other than listings in 'A' team line-ups and mentions in occasional match reports of the time, he seems to have had a low-key Hornets career.

in a four line obituary, *The Rochdale Observer* reports that he joined-up shortly after the war commenced. We pieced his story together via his listing on the Wigan War memorial, which led us to the casualty records of the 3rd Battalion of the Worcestershire Regiment.

The Hornets Report & Accounts of 1916 – and *The Rochdale Observer* of 13 May that year – reported him as 'killed in action'. His regimental record shows he died in the France & Flanders campaign on 29 April 1916. He was 35 years old.

Walter Roman

Nicknamed 'Rattler', Walter Roman was no stranger to conflict: he had previously been a 'regular' in the 2nd Battalion of the Somerset Light Infantry in 1899. He saw service in the Boer War, and was awarded the Queen's South Africa Medal & Bars, Cape Colony, Orange Free State, Transvaal, and the King's South Africa Medal. In 1901 he transferred to the 1st Battalion of the SLI and served in India for five years.

He left the Army in 1907 and resumed his rugby career, going on to play rugby union for Somerset and England. He signed for Rochdale Hornets in January 1910, for what was rumoured to be a substantial signing on fee of £200. He was one the hottest rugby properties in the country at that time – and became Hornets' captain, leading the side to the 1911 Lancashire Senior Cup victory.

He was selected for the 1914 Northern Union tour of Australia and New Zealand, which went on to become famous for the 'Rorke's Drift' test. Although he never won a test cap, he played in seven games and scored one try.

Walter was in Australia when war was declared and returned to England at the earliest opportunity. He arrived back in England on a Saturday and reported to his regiment in Taunton 48 hours later, via a brief return to Rochdale.

Familiar with the horrors of war, he said: "I shall do my best in this great game just as I always do in football."

Walter Roman played one more game for Hornets a year later, against Broughton Rangers while on leave. The *Rochdale Observer* reported the crowd's roar of appreciation as he led his team into battle on the football field for what would be the last time.

On the first day of the Battle of the Somme on Saturday 1 July 1916, his 36th birthday, Walter's unit went over the top of their trench into no-man's land and advanced towards the German positions. While charging forward he was savagely wounded down one side. He was dragged from the battlefield and shipped back to a military hospital in Cheltenham. Despite rallying, he died of his wounds.

His body was taken back to Bridgwater where his funeral was held in a packed Holy Trinity church. The *Bridgewater Mercury* reported "Throngs of people lined the streets and the procession took a long time to reach his grave, such was the outpouring of grief at the loss of this famous individual."

Hornets directors Messrs Aspinall and Hudson attended. The players were represented by Hornets captain George Prudence, fellow England tourist Jack Robinson, Alf Turner and Johnny Baxter. In a five year Hornets career Walter Roman scored 44 tries and 15 goals.

The Hornets Annual Report for the 1916–17 season pays tribute: "It is with very deep feelings of regret that we have to record the loss of Mr WJ Roman who died through injuries received whilst fighting in France. He had been Captain of the club for two seasons and had at all times been a credit to the Club, County and Country which he represented on the field of play."

The end of the War brought uncertainty. While there was an appetite to return to competition, soldiers were released from their service according to the importance of their civilian occupations, and caught up in this process were hundreds of players awaiting demobilisation.

This meant that assembling teams to kick off any sort of new season was a difficult process. The Hornets' team had been pulled apart by the war. Roman, Twigg, Burton and West were lost; Fairhurst, Heaton and Bennett spent the war playing at Wigan, Brannan at Broughton Rangers. Jones and Slade still awaited demobilisation.

But slowly players returned, and with Jones and Slade prepared to play while on leave, Hornets announced that they would resume playing on Christmas Day, with a friendly at Watersheddings against Oldham.

It was the first step to a bigger return, a report on 21 December 1918 saying: "It is intended to run a team for the rest of the season, and to commence playing league matches in the middle of January. A meeting of secretaries to arrange fixtures will be held on Monday."

On 25 December 1918, 4,000 people turned out to watch Hornets and Oldham resume one of the game's great rivalries. The Hornets team was: Kay, Ellis, Low, Prudence, AN Other, Jones, Spencer, Bowers, Slade, Carter, Bowmer, Groves and Fitzsimmons.

The Rochdale Times reported on a close game and a lucky Oldham win. "The Hornets did by far most of the attacking throughout the game, but they could not score, and it was only in the last five minutes that the Oldham men secured the only try of the match and won by it. It was a fluky sort of point. Kay knocked on in taking a high ball and from the breakaway which followed the ball was kicked over the line and the referee awarded the try to Tetlow, although the Hornets wing claimed to have been first to touch down."

"On the general play the Hornets were much the better side. Their forwards were far too good for those of Oldham, and got possession four out of five scrummages. Behind them Jones was one of the two outstanding figures in the game, but he received somewhat poor support from the threequarters, of whom Prudence was the best."

And the verdict after such a long break? "Play was contested throughout in a good spirit and the match was attractive and open, many of the movements being surprisingly good, considering that the men were practically without training. Result: Oldham 3 Hornets 0."

Hornets were due to play Oldham in a return game at the Athletic Grounds on New Year's Day, but Hornets' secretary Mr Hudson received a telegram from his Oldham counterpart saying that he "... regretted he was compelled to cancel the match." No reason was given.

On 11 January 1919 Hornets played at home for the first time in almost 15 months, an 8–3 defeat to Halifax: a friendly with a shared gate.

Played in front of a crowd of 3,000, *The Rochdale Times* said it "... proved that the love of rugby football is as strong as ever in the town..." and described it as "... a really good re-start for the rugby game in Rochdale and everybody seemed delighted with the play."

On the same day, *The Rochdale Times* published fixtures for the remainder of the 1919 season: home and away games against Oldham, Broughton Rangers, Salford, Warrington and Swinton. Among those games, scheduled for 5 April 1919, was the first round of the Lancashire Cup. Hornets were effectively still the holders having won the trophy in 1914 before the competition's suspension.

Despite the tribulations of the war, Hornets continued their domination of the competition as top class players made their way back from active service. Having beaten Salford 7–5 in Round 1 and St Helens Recs by 16–2 in Round 2, Hornets thumped Wigan 40–0 in front of 10,958 people at the Athletic Grounds in the semi-final.

Having led 14–0 at the break, The Hornets forward pack over-ran Wigan in the second half. One report says: "They played a brilliant game ... the most decisive victory the Hornets have ever scored against a side with pretentions of class." It was also the club's record score as a senior team. Hornets' reward: another final against Oldham.

In the build up to the final, *The Rochdale Times* (10 May 1919) was fulsome in its praise for Hornets' post-war resurgence: "The Rochdale Hornets Football Club has recovered from the effects of the war in a manner which has been perfectly astonishing even to those who are keenly interested in the doings of the club. In the autumn of 1917, the organisation was compelled to suspend its active operations owing to the dearth of players, most of whom were in the Army, whilst others were so closely engaged on war work that they had not the opportunity of helping to keep the game going."

"Although one or two are yet to return and several others will be seen no more, the team are now probably as powerful as at any time in their history."

"Today they meet Oldham in the final tie of the Lancashire Cup competition and are strong favourites: and only a victory in the remaining league match with Swinton next week is necessary to secure also the championship of the Lancashire section of the Northern Union League."

"It has been a remarkable revival and the club as a result should again be in a sound financial position."

A large crowd was anticipated at the Willows to see the two local rivals battle it out in a cup final, Salford club officials made 'special arrangements for a great assembly'. And Hornets went into the game as favourites – tipped to win by one newspaper pundit by 'anything up to a dozen points'.

The Hornets' players made the trip to the Willows on the supporters' special train that left Rochdale at 1.50pm. In support, it was estimated that at least five thousand Hornets fans made the trip to Salford. One newspaper report remarked on the determination of the supporters to see their team play: "They made the journey in all manner of ways. Two 'specials' which were run from the town direct to Weaste were packed to their utmost capacity, and the ordinary trains during the morning and shortly after noon were all crowded. So were the (tram)cars Manchester way. And cycles, motor-cycles, traps, motor cars, and motor chars-a-banc were all pressed into service."

Amazingly, several groups of enthusiastic fans walked the 12 miles to Weaste during the morning and there were hundreds more who opted to walk from Manchester due to over-crowding on the trams.

The attendance was a bumper 18,617, and the determination of the Hornets supporters was rewarded with a 22–0 pasting of the Roughyeds.

At full-time, a large crowd of Hornets supporters gathered in front of the stand to see captain George Prudence receive the Lancashire Cup from the Mayor of Salford.

It was almost 8pm when the Hornets team arrived back at Rochdale Station, where a large and enthusiastic crowd had waited over an hour to welcome them. As the players climbed aboard a wagonette for their short journey into town, the crowd cheered George Prudence as he took his place at the front of the vehicle with the trophy. The route along Maclure Road and down Drake Street was lined with spectators and the crowd followed on behind to the Wellington Hotel where the team would eat dinner and receive their medals.

In his presentation speech, Hornets Chairman Mr JR Hartley congratulated the team, not only on behalf of the club, but on behalf of the inhabitants of the town who, he said, had shown through their welcome how much they appreciated the victory.

It was an emotional speech too. Mr Hartley spoke of how it had been some years since they had been able to meet on such an occasion and how, since that time, they had gone through so many difficult experiences. He congratulated the players who had been fighting on their safe return and remarked that they could not allow the occasion to pass without an expression of feeling for their team mates who had lost their lives.

But this extraordinary season's business was not yet over. There was the small matter of a game at Swinton to clinch the Lancashire League title and secure the double. Rearranged after a postponement, the game took place on the Wednesday evening - just four days after the Lancashire Cup Final. Again, a large number of Rochdalians followed their team and gave them a 'rousing cheer' as they entered the field.

After soaking up some early Swinton pressure and 'wild-cat' spoiling tactics Dewhurst gave Hornets the lead with a try in the corner. Swinton's only real chances a couple of missed penalties.

Then Hornets produced some magic. Jones received the ball in his own half, racing away he found Corsi who slipped the ball to winger Dewhurst. He stepped inside two covering defenders to race half the length of the field to score under the posts. Jones landed the conversion. Hornets ahead at the break 8–0.

The second half saw Hornets take command. Bennett broke into space, he found Hopwood who was tackled just short. Thinking quickly, he jumped to his feet, tapped the ball across the goal-line and dived in to score.

Hornets continued to play the better football, but an injury to Corsi gave Swinton an opportunity to score an unconverted try. Hornets hit back when Hesketh kicked through from a scrum on half-way, then dribbled the ball to the line to score a brilliant try. Final score Swinton 3 Hornets 16. Hornets were crowned Champions of Lancashire.

In an article headlined: 'The Hornets Double Honour' *The Rochdale Times* acknowledged the club's incredible season: "It is a record they have never before reached; although they have won the knock-out competition twice previously it is the first time in their career as a club that they have gained the honour in the league tournament, and the accomplishment of the double feat in one season is a performance to be proud of."

"It is all the more notable on account of the fact that the club had not taken part in football for some fifteen months owing to the lack of players, and that the side had to be built up gradually after play recommenced in the new year."

The Hornets Annual Report for the season said: "From a playing standpoint the features of the season have been the winning of the Lancashire Senior Cup for the third time during the last five seasons it has been competed for, scoring 85 points against 7; also winning the Lancashire League Competition for the first time since its formation."

"The football played has been of a very high standard, it being remarkable how the players have returned to their best form after so long a lapse in the activities of the Northern Union game, owing to the call on the players for their assistance in aid of their country during the War."

"With players again available, we have every confidence in looking forward to another successful season..."

Indeed, against the odds, Hornets emerged from the shadow of war as Kings of Lancashire. But with the roaring twenties on the horizon, it felt like there were bigger prizes to be had.

References
'The History of Rugby League Football' - K. Macklin, 1962
Rochdale Times - Wednesday 6 December 1911
Rochdale Times - Wednesday 9 December 1914
Rochdale Observer - Wednesday 9 December 1914
Rochdale Times 21 December 1918
Rochdale Times - Wednesday 14 May 1919
Rochdale Times - Wednesday 15 January 1919
Rochdale Hornets Report and Accounts 1918–19
Rochdale Times - Saturday 28 December 1918
'Cost Comparison 1910 to Today' - S. Rimmer

5. 1922: Challenge Cup glory

At the start of 1922, Hornets were the team in form. From January through to April, they won 14 and drew one of the 18 games they played. And when the Challenge Cup came round in February, Hornets already had momentum.

In the first round, on 25 February, Hornets hammered Cumberland League side Broughton Moor 54–2. This earned them a plum tie at home a fortnight later, Hornets beating the mighty Leeds 15–7. The quarter final, on 25 March, saw Hornets drawn at home again – this time dispatching arch-rivals and eventual champions Oldham 5–2 in a gruelling battle.

The Rochdale Times said of the cup run: "The first round was a gift, but they had the luck of the draw at home in the second and third rounds against Leeds and Oldham. The brilliance of the victory over the Headingley men and the stubborn manner in which they contested the issue against Oldham under adverse circumstances stamped them as a side with distinct Cup possibilities."

The semi-finals saw reigning champions Hull drawn against Wigan and Hornets paired with Widnes. On 8 April, Hull beat Wigan 18–5 at Headingley. On the same day, in front of a 10,000 crowd at the Willows, Hornets overcame Widnes 23–3 to secure a place in their first ever Challenge Cup Final. *The Rochdale Times* was impressed: "For 20 minutes at the opening of the game the followers of the club had a delirious joy while the players piled up a score of eighteen points against their opponents Widnes and although the game had to proceed for the usual 80 minutes, it was as good as over in a quarter of the time."

In an article headlined "The Hornets Honour", *The Rochdale Times* also wrote: "For the first time since the inauguration of the competition 25 years ago, The Hornets Club have reached the final tie for the Northern Union Challenge Cup, the blue riband of Rugby Football in the North."

"Three times previously they have fallen at the last obstacle but one, but that fact by no means robbed their supporters of confidence last Saturday and the team thoroughly justified the trust placed in it."

Looking ahead, the report said: "Whether the side will meet with similar success in the final tie against Hull, which is to be played at Leeds on the 29th of the month, remains to be seen, but whether they succeed or fail, the side have given their supporters something to think and talk about."

"There is an irresistible fascination with cup ties which somehow ordinary games do not provide and it is certain there will be a big exodus from Rochdale to Leeds on the 29th, in spite of trade depression and shortage of money."

"The easy fashion in which they disposed of the pretentions of Widnes in the semi-final at Salford emphasised their ability, and if they do not start favourites on Saturday against Hull, there are few I fancy who do not consider they have an equal chance."

On the Wednesday before the game, *The Rochdale Times* printed vital details for fans planning to make the trip to Leeds "... in spite of the distance..."

"The Railway Company are running three long special trains leaving at a few minutes to 11, a few minutes to 12 and one o'clock. The Hornets players will travel on the 12.46 ordinary train, reaching Leeds at 1.48 and they will proceed direct to the ground. After the match, win or lose, the Hornets players and officials will have tea at the Griffin Hotel, Leeds and will leave for Rochdale on the 7.15 train, driving here at 8.30."

Ahead of the game, the mood in the Hornets camp was positive. *The Rochdale Times* reported: "The players have been doing their training quietly at the Athletic Grounds and are following their ordinary employment. On Saturday, they went to Wigan to see Hull play that club in the league semi-final and the general opinion was that, on the form then shown by the Hull men, there was no doubt as to the result."

The 1921–22 Challenge Cup Final was played at Headingley on Saturday 29 April. Hornets played a Hull FC team packed with internationals, including the world famous Great Britain centre Billy Batten.

There was a general assumption that Hornets were the inferior side and all Hull had to do to win was turn up. In his match preview, *Hull Daily Mail* journalist 'Vedette' wrote: "I have no doubt that Hull's superiority in the matter of polish and the finer arts of the game will gain them the day."

And even the official programme notes said: "The Hull side are reported to be in splendid condition and are popular favourites. Hornets' backs are generally supposed to be much weaker than the men from Hull."

The Hornets team on the day was: Frank Prescott, Joe Corsi, Teddy McLaughlin, Fred Wild, Tommy Fitton, J Kynan, J Heaton, Tommy Woods, Jack Bennett, Thomas Harris, Dai Edwards, Dicky Paddon and Louis Corsi. They had other ideas.

There was much talk of an 'exodus' from Rochdale to see Hornets play in the final, with Hornets selling out their entire allocation of stand tickets. With kick-off approaching - for the first time in the history of the Leeds Club - the gates were closed with thousands of fans still gathering outside, many from Rochdale who had suffered train delays. Officials ordered the gates to be opened. Inside, the crash barriers gave way and the hundreds of fans spilling onto the pitch had to be pushed back by mounted police before play could commence. Fortunately, no-one was injured.

In the opening exchanges, Hornets' pack dominated; Hull relying on the defensive efforts of Batten to keep his side in the game. Against the run of play, Hull were first to score. Just eight minutes in, winger Kennedy charged down a clearing kick from Heaton. The centre gathered the ball to run clear and score. He failed to convert his own try, hitting the crossbar.

Hornets piled on the pressure: two Dicky Paddon penalties edged them ahead before Tommy Fitton bored his way through for a try in the corner. Just before Half time, Casewell broke clear for Hull. He found Stone, who released Batten into space. As Hornets fullback Prescott went to make the tackle, Batten leaped over the full-back to score. The conversion missed. Hornets held a slim half-time lead of 7–6.

Hull began the second half with a bang. Kennedy intercepted a Hornets pass, and he sent Morgan skirting round Prescott for what looked a certain try - only for the move to be called back for a foot in touch. The game became a tense affair as play went from end to end in an exciting second half.

Eventually, Heaton and Wild combined to send in Tommy Fitton for a second Hornets try. The spectators who were stood right up to the touchline had to be moved back so that Dicky Paddon could take the conversion attempt. He missed: 10–6.

Hull battled back. In the dying minutes, their second rower Taylor crashed in for a try to make it 10–9. One report of the game says: "As Stone took the kick, the crowd breathed in. The international winger was wide and Rochdale had won the cup."

Mrs Fillan, wife of the Northern Union Chairman, presented the trophy to Hornets captain Jack Bennett: the first – and as yet only – Hornets captain to lift the game's most prestigious piece of silverware. In accepting the trophy, he declared that Hull had played well, but they'd won the cup before and now it was Hornets' turn.

The game was the last Challenge Cup Final to be played under the Northern Union banner before the governing body changed its name to the Rugby Football League, thus creating 'Rugby League'. It drew the largest crowd that had ever gathered to witness a Northern Union game in this country. The official attendance, depending on whose report you read, was close to 35,000, with some estimating at least a couple of thousand more. Receipts were £2,964.

The Rochdale Times match report described the game. "The last 10 or 12 minutes of the game will long be remembered by those who watched it. The tension was painful and I have heard of men who were made really ill by the excitement. Even the Leeds people who were not so directly interested in the result as those from Rochdale and Hull were held spellbound by the magnitude of the struggle, and the match will go down to history as the finest final tie since the competition was inaugurated."

Despite claiming throughout its match report how Hornets had only won through fortuitous luck, even the *Hull Daily Mail* had to grudgingly concede that the Boulevarders' star-studded team was handed a lesson in teamwork, hard work and strong forward play: "The keynote of the Hornets' success was undoubtedly forward. The Lancastrians won by reason of hard-fought scrimmaging of the old-fashioned type, in which every man pushed in the scrums for all he was worth. Compared to the Hornets methods, the Hull pack appeared too loose, and even when the Yorkshire forwards obtained possession, they allowed the Hornets six to wheel the scrum and take the ball with them."

"On the day's showing, the Rochdale pack was the best seen this season ... Paddon, Bennett and Louis Corsi stood out conspicuously. Putting aside the element of luck, the Lancastrians just about deserved that odd-point victory by virtue of their forwards' supreme efforts. Prescott, the winners' full-back, was also a huge factor in his team's success. When severely tested, he never made a mistake and was the essence of coolness "under fire"."

In the wake of the victory, congratulatory messages poured in to Hornets club secretary Mr Hudson. Among them, one from his Rochdale AFC counterpart Mr Lomax who wrote: "Accept hearty congratulations from the Rochdale Association Club and from myself on your club winning the Northern Union Cup"

Congratulations also came from official sources. Mr Jones of Widnes, the referee in charge of the final, sent a letter that read: "I had not the opportunity of congratulating your team on their great victory yesterday and I wish you to convey to them my heartiest congratulations on a victory so well won and well deserved after a hard and clean game."

Hornets captain Jack Bennett with the 1921–22 Northern Union Challenge Cup, the last
year it was contested under that name, before the sport became Rugby League.
(Rochdale Hornets Heritage Archive)

Jack Wilson, secretary of the Northern Union and former Hull FC official, wrote: "Allow me to congratulate you and your club on winning the cup. Although the margin was small it sufficed and it is generally conceded that the honour went to the better side. What fleeting glimpses I got of play impressed me that way."

On their return to Rochdale on Saturday evening, presumably after tea at the Griffin Hotel, the players were met at Rochdale Station by a crowd reported as numbering 'several thousand'. One report said: "When Bennett, the captain, emerged carrying the trophy, followed by the other players and club officials, a great roar of welcome went up. Cheer after cheer was raised as the players and officials entered a couple of charabancs and drove through the crowded streets to the Town Hall where the Mayor Alderman S. Diggle accorded them a civic reception."

With the Town Hall Square 'literally packed' with a crowd estimated at 40,000: "... it was only with difficulty that the players could make their way into the building, owing to the enthusiasm of their supporters."

The club's Annual Report was somewhat more measured in its celebrations: "The first team have, this season, realised the height of their ambition by winning the Northern Union Challenge Cup for the first time in the history of the Club. Every credit is due to the players for the splendid games they played throughout the cup ties, and in the Final Tie which took place before a record crowd of 35,000 people. It was generally agreed that it was one of the best games ever played under Northern Union Rules."

The following season, round one of the now Rugby League Challenge Cup was played on 17 February. Hornets were drawn at home to Huddersfield. Hornets lost 5–3. A repeat of cup glory would have to wait.

Photo: Hornets forward Sam Carter outside his pub, the Golden Fleece on Oldham Road, with Joe Corsi (left) and Louis Corsi (right). The Corsi brothers played in the 1922 Challenge Cup Final. Sam Carter was so proud of his association with Hornets that he put the club's name over the door with his own. (Rochdale Hornets Heritage Archive)

References:
'The History of Rugby League Football' - K Macklin, 1962
www.rugbyleagueproject.org/matches/32595
'Rugby League Challenge Cup: An Illustrated History 1897–1998' - L Hoole, 1998
Rochdale Times - 15 April 1922
Rochdale Times - Wednesday 26 April 1922
Rochdale Times - Saturday 6 May 1922
Hull Daily Mail Monday1 May 1922

Yorkshire Post and Leeds Intelligencer Saturday 29 April 1922
Sunday Mirror - Sunday 30 April 1922
Athletic News Monday 1 May 1922
Yorkshire Post and Leeds Intelligencer - Monday 1 May 1922
Westminster Gazette - Monday 1 May 1922

The Rochdale Hornets Football Club
Company Limited.

DIRECTORS:

Mr. J. R. HARTLEY, Chairman.

Mr. F. GREEN, Mr. J. R. DEX, Mr. A. E. ASHWORTH, Mr. R. HERBERT, Mr. R. BRIERLEY,
Mr. F. BUTTERWORTH, Mr. A. TURNER, Mr. J. HIGGIN, Mr. J. E. TWEEDALE,
Mr. W. SPENCER.

ATTENDANCES:
MEETINGS 55.

Mr. F. BUTTERWORTH 43	Mr. A. E. ASHWORTH 38
Mr. R. BRIERLEY 42	Mr. A. TURNER 38
Mr. W. SPENCER 42	Mr. J. HIGGIN... 37
Mr. R. HERBERT 42	Mr. J. R. HARTLEY... 16
Mr. J. E. TWEEDALE 42	*Mr. J. R. DEX... 15

Mr. F. GREEN 7

*Died October 15th, 1921.

REPORT:

To the Shareholders of the Rochdale Hornets Football Club Company Limited.

The Directors beg to submit their Sixteenth Annual Report and Balance Sheet of the Company.

The First Team have played 41 Matches, of which 25 were won, 14 lost and 2 drawn, scoring 461 points against 266 by our opponents.

The "A" Team have played 31 Matches, of which 16 were won, 12 lost and 3 drawn, scoring 332 points against 209 by our opponents.

From a playing standpoint the First Team have this Season realized the height of their ambition by winning the Northern Union Challenge Cup for the first time in the history of the Club. Every credit is due to the players for the splendid games they played throughout the Cup Ties, and in the Final Tie, which took place at Leeds before a record crowd of over 35,000 people, it was generally agreed that it was one of the best games ever played under Northern Union Rules. The Team's performances in League Matches up to Xmas were not very convincing, but from that period to the end of the Season showed a wonderful improvement, as they only lost four matches out of the last eighteen played, their position in the League being 7th against 10th in Season 1920-21, they also finished 3rd in the Lancashire League. The "A" Team commenced very well, but unaccountedly their play was very disappointing during the latter part of the Season.

During the Season an "A" Team Match was set aside for the benefit of W. Ashworth and J. W. Fairhurst, both of whom have rendered long and faithful service to the Club.

Financially the year's working has resulted in a heavy loss which is accounted for principally by the depression in trade as shown by the decrease in gate receipts, which were over £2,250 less than in the previous Season, also the sale of Season Tickets was £340 less. Drainage and other work on the grounds caused heavy expenditure last Season.

It is with very great regret that we have to record the death of Mr. J. R. Dex, one of the oldest Directors of the Company, and one whose experience and valuable assistance, given so generously for the welfare of the Company, has been sadly missed by all who worked with him in the interests of the Club. We also have to record the death of one of our young players, R. Winstanley, whose sudden death at the early age of 21 years, came as a great blow both to the officials and his fellow players.

Messrs. A. E. Ashworth, R. Brierley, F. Green and J. Higgin are the retiring Directors.

Mr. J. Brown is the retiring Auditor.

Nominations for Directors and Auditor to be appointed at the Annual General Meeting to be held on June 27th, must be forwarded to the Secretary of the Company, 14, Nelson Street, Rochdale, signed by two Shareholders as Proposer and Seconder of the Nominations on or before Friday, June 23rd, 1922.

W. SPENCER,
J. E. TWEEDALE, } DIRECTORS.

June 7th, 1922.

FRED. T. HUDSON, SECRETARY.

The cover of the 1922 Annual Report. (Courtesy Jim Stringer)

6. 1928 to 1939: The brink

By 1928, the optimism of the Challenge Cup win six years previously had evaporated. Hit by the death of long-standing chairman JR Hartley, dreadful league form, an exit from the Challenge Cup at home in the first round, plummeting gates and a collapse in match-day revenues, Hornets faced an existential crisis.

The board was brutally honest in its appraisal of the situation. "Gate receipts for the whole season only amount to £2,362 17s 6d ... £2,806 1s less than the previous season, and it is evident to us that unless increased support is given to the club, there will be no alternative but to close down, which will be a most serious matter to all who have the game at heart."

There were, however, greater tests to come. At the start of the 20th century, 80 percent of the cotton industry's workforce in the UK was located in Lancashire – and Rochdale had staked its economic standing on King Cotton. Unlike the towns around it, not only was Rochdale a producer of spun yarn, it was also one of Lancashire's leading manufacturers of woven cotton cloth. But between the wars, the demand for British cotton slumped.

Working 24 hours a day, Japan had become the world's largest cotton manufacturer. Not only had it taken many of Lancashire's Eastern markets, it flooded the UK with cheap cloth. Meanwhile, in India, one of the county's biggest export markets, Gandhi stoked a boycott of Lancashire textiles as his country strove for independence.

Rochdale's fortunes reflected the decline of the industry. From a population of 95,000, half of Rochdale's workforce was employed in the textile industry. Unsurprising, then, that cotton's decline hit the town hard: 4,500 Rochdalians unemployed, with a further 24,000 on short time. By 1930, Rochdale had already lost 10 of its 65 mills.

Times were hard and, it seems, Hornets were caught in the slipstream. The club's 1929 Report and Accounts said: "In addition to the lack of support of the public we do not seem to get the support from the Employers of Labour that we formerly got, which not only causes us much more expense in finding players work on the ground, but also prevents us from securing any player of note, as work is always one of their conditions of signing on."

Bemoaning 'the bad state of trade' in the town, the directors blamed "... admitting the unemployed at a reduced rate" as a factor in falling gate receipts.

The board had reiterated its plea for help with finding jobs for players: "(we) appeal to the Employers of Labour to give us the support they have done in the past, by finding employment for new players..." But with over 30,000 Rochdalians either out of work or on short time, jobs in the town were hard to come by.

An attempt to plug the holes in the squad by signing local players was considered a failure: "We have given extended trials to several players, including local juniors, who unfortunately have not come up to expectations. We have expended in this connection, just this season, a matter of nearly £450."

Certainly, one of the reasons for Hornets' struggle was the 'win-percentage' system that the Northern Rugby League operated under at the time. The Championship comprised 28 teams, in which some teams played 40 games and others, including Hornets, played only 34.

Within that, there were restrictions on which clubs were played, so there was no assurance that a club would play money-spinning games against the bigger names in the league.

It was a system seen as disadvantageous for some clubs, and difficult for most supporters to follow. In a report on how Hull KR had made a profit from the system, the *Hull Daily Mail* reported that: "... clubs such as Bramley, Barrow, Batley, Rochdale Hornets and Keighley are in a poor way and one or two of them will need the practical help of the League if they are to continue. Yet because the authorities are afraid of losing some of the weaklings, they will not throw overboard the decimal system which confuses so many people as to the whereabouts of their own particular club in the league table."

Hornets ended the 1928–29 season third bottom with a win percentage of 29.4. As a cost-cutting exercise, the directors pared expenses to the 'very minimum' and had paid all their own travelling expenses. Having made sacrifices themselves, they believed that at least some of the responsibility for the club's parlous state lay at the door of the Rugby League.

There was a belief among directors that Rochdale was being overlooked as a potential venue for the RFL's big games. They said: "We have not received at the hands of the Rugby League the support we expect to receive in connection with the playing of representative matches on our ground."

"As the members know, very large sums of money have been expended for many years on the making of our ground suitable for any important matches; but unfortunately, we seem to be forgotten when these are fixed up. One of these matches would not only have helped us considerably financially, but would also have revived interest in our game locally."

Miraculously, within a month of bemoaning the lack of representative games Hornets were named as the first opponents for the Kangaroos on the upcoming Australian tour. The game had originally been scheduled against Broughton Rangers, but was switched after it clashed with a horse race at nearby Castle Irwell.

The hope then was that the club would actually make it through the close season. A report in *The Athletic News* viewed Hornets' pre-season preparations with cautious optimism: "As far as their finances have permitted, the Rochdale Hornets directorate have been indulging in team building during the close season. It is generally recognised that another season as disastrous as the last would mean the end of the Hornets..."

The season opened with a 19–15 home defeat to St Helens Recs. Hornets staged a 'remarkable rally' after trailing 19–0. Hornets' next opponents: Australia.

The Lancashire Post previewed the game in a somewhat understated way: "The Australians open their tour against Rochdale Hornets at Rochdale tomorrow. They have been training well at Ilkley and are quite hopeful of doing well. The Hornets cannot be regarded as exceptionally strong opposition, but they are pretty dour, and the fixture should attract a large crowd of spectators."

The Yorkshire Post was more excited at the prospect of the contest: "An important event in the football world today will be the first appearance of the Australian team of rugby league footballers at Rochdale. The tourists have had 10 days in which to get acclimatised... although it is unlikely that (they) will be fully tested until they meet the Lancashire County team at Warrington a fortnight hence."

The report was less certain of a surprise Hornets win: "Their task ought not to be unduly severe considering the form shown last Saturday by Rochdale Hornets, who suffered defeat on their own ground at the hands of St Helens Recreation."

Named in the Kangaroos side were two players who would have a significant future impact at the Athletic Grounds: New South Wales centre Cec Fifield and Queensland's second row powerhouse Vic Armbruster. With 8,000 in the Athletic Grounds, double the previous week's attendance, the Australians "gave a spirited exhibition of clever and resourceful football", outpacing – and eventually out-gunning – a gutsy Hornets by 36–3. Trailing only 13–3 at the break, Hornets stuck to their task gamely before running out of steam. The Kangaroos scored 18 of their points in the last 11 minutes.

Despite the heavy defeat, Hornets drew recognition for their efforts: "... tackling at times like demons and getting no reward." The same report noted how Hornets bossed the scrums: "I doubt if [Australia] will ever scrummage like the Rochdale players did. [They] packed too loosely and the scrummage on many occasions collapsed in its entirety."

"The home players were clearly masters of this art, and occasionally caused trouble by their dribbling powers. The Kangaroos did not show any great liking for these tactics and few of their players relished the job of going down for the ball."

Indeed, Hornets' try came from centre Halton, who dropped the ball onto his foot to dribble it past Aussie full-back McMillan and into the in-goal to score. In addition, Hornets full-back Gowers showed enough to be selected to play for Lancashire against Australia two weeks later.

As the Australians moved on to beat York 32–11 the following week, Hornets went back into league action at Leigh; going down 27–11 despite a brace of tries from Halton. It was another two weeks before Hornets picked up their first win. Overall, the first half of the season was an up-and-down affair, winning seven of the 15 games to sit a heady 15th, exactly half-way, in a 28 team league: a 16–5 win over fourth placed Oldham on Boxing Day, backing up a 5–5 draw at Bramley on Christmas Day, a highlight.

After Christmas was a very different picture. Of the 20 games played, Hornets could only muster six more wins – slipping to 22nd in the league with a win percentage a fraction over 40 percent. Off the field, Hornets' directors had the Australian tourists to thank for the club's £188 15s 8½d profit – the financial rewards from the tour game and for hosting the historic 4th test match sufficient to nudge the balance sheet back into the black.

Despite the profit, the board was unhappy, saying: "... we have to report that the season has not been a good one in many respects." Citing the slump in league form, the lack of points scored, poor attendances, and an even larger amount blown on local juniors who didn't make the grade, the directors reached out: "We appeal to shareholders and the public generally in order to enable us to build up a team worthy of our town."

The following season, however, it was one of the town's most famous daughters that would step up and help the club, In January 1931 – hot on the heels of the making of her first film, *Sally in Our Alley*, Gracie Fields was one of the country's biggest stars of stage and screen. Renowned for her altruism, she was happy to lend Hornets her crowd-pulling powers when she visited Rochdale to play a week of charity shows.

Heralded as a 'personal triumph', her shows drew packed houses to The Hippodrome and she was greeted by crowds everywhere she went in the town. But when the time came for her to make her appearance at the Athletic Grounds, the weather intervened. *The Stage* wrote: "Her one disappointment was that she was not able to wear the football suit she had had made in the Rochdale Hornets colours to kick off in the match on Saturday, because of the blizzard which caused the match to be postponed." Gracie promised to return to Rochdale before the end of the season – and she was as good as her word. Just two weeks later, Gracie did the honours at the rearranged Wakefield game.

A Tuesday afternoon crowd of 3,000 braved bitterly cold wind and sleet to see Gracie Fields lead out the teams clad in a fur coat and Tommy Woods' international cap. Once in the middle of the heavy pitch, she shed her coat to reveal a red, white and blue jersey, white shorts, 'football stockings' and boots. She announced: "I'm going to do this job gradely."

Despite putting plenty of power behind her kick, the ball only went a few yards - but she got involved again when she insisted on joining the Hornets front row at the first scrum. According to *The Stage*, she jokingly complained that "... the men in the scrum did not squeeze me much..."

The game couldn't really follow Gracie's performance. Played in increasingly 'severe weather' that made the conditions 'very trying for the players', the referee stopped the game six minutes from time with Wakefield leading 11–0.

Hornets' directors said of the day: "Our thanks are due to Miss Gracie Fields. Although her effort did not prove a success this was due entirely to the inclement weather, and no-one regretted the fact more than Miss Fields herself. It was a splendid act on her part and we are very grateful to her."

It can be argued that helping draw 3,000 people to a snow-bound Athletic Grounds on a Tuesday afternoon was more of a success than she was given credit for. Indeed, the event attracted national publicity and provided a flicker of relief in a season that threatened to see the club crushed by the weight of its financial burden.

On Monday 9 March, the board met to consider a detailed report into the club's financial position. The report revealed a bank overdraft of £1,500, loans to directors of £1,300 and unpaid debts of £800. With eight of the remaining 12 games to be played away from home, the liabilities at the end of the season were forecast at over £4,000.

Facing such an onerous position, the board dropped a bombshell: a decision to place all of the players on the transfer list and to offer the Athletic Grounds up for sale. It seemed extreme, but Hornets' chairman Mr J Bright Clegg denied that the board was bluffing. He said that they felt that that they could not carry on any longer on the support they had received during the last few seasons.

Painting a bleak picture, he warned that, unless there was some indication that better support would be forthcoming, there would be no alternative other than for the club to go out of existence at the end of the season. The board's plan was to play their matches until the end of the season to "give the public an opportunity to offer better support".

Bright Clegg said that the directors felt that they should not to be called upon to put up any more money and if the town didn't want rugby league, then it could not have it. Now, he said, it was up to the public.

42

Gracie Fields tossing up before the game with the team captains, George Nepia of Streatham & Mitcham (left) and the Rochdale skipper. The Londoners won 15–0. (Courtesy Alex Service)

One journalist revealed that it had been 'common knowledge for some time' that Hornets financial position was serious, but that "... none of the supporters had any idea that the club had gone so far behind financially as to cause the directors to make these decisions."

Having kept supporters in the dark and blamed the Rochdale sporting public for its lack of support, one report pointed out that, despite threatening to sell all of the club's assets "... the directors have not made any decisions regards calling a town meeting." So much for engaging the public. It was anticipated, though that the Hornets Supporters Club would 'take some action'.

It also seems that the Rugby League was also kept out of the loop. Secretary John Wilson said that, although League officials had known for some time that the Rochdale Hornets club had been doing badly, they had "... no information regarding the latest development."

With regard to the transfer of players, Wilson was at pains to point out that a club could only dispose of its players so long as it was a member of the Northern Rugby League, and that the League Committee "... would not allow a club to sell the whole of its players and then walk out of the league."

The Lancashire Evening Post summarised the whole sorry affair: "The Hornets have not had a good playing season, but the town is such an old rugby centre that it can hardly be imagined that interest has got so small that a revival is not possible. The fact that the decision of the directors defers the threatened demise to the end of the season is rather hopeful and gives the opportunity to the enthusiasts to formulate a scheme to remedy the present situation."

As anticipated, Hornets limped to the end of the season – ultimately winning just 10 of their 38 games. Despite reporting a profit of £324 11s 3½d, the accounts make difficult reading – a 'considerable loss' only avoided due to a £1,000 'gift' from an anonymous donor – the equivalent of £67,000 in 2021.

Some detective work from the local press revealed Hornets director George Close as the individual responsible. Described as "a patron of the various sporting activities of the town", Close had made his money as a director of a company that developed and ran cinemas across Lancashire – including Rochdale's plush Rialto, on the corner of Milnrow Road and Drake Street. As well as a local movie tycoon, he was a rugby league man at heart. A Hornets director since the 1926–27 season, he was also the president of the Rochdale District Junior Rugby League, president of the East Lancashire Rugby League, president of the Hornets Supporters' Club and president of the Lancashire Federation of Rugby League Supporters Clubs. His donation, he said was "... to be used in the best interests of the club..."

The board were fulsome in their gratitude: "It is very pleasing to record the magnificent gift of £1,000 by our director Mr GA Close. But for this gift it is doubtful whether we should have been able to fulfil all our engagements." His reward was his unanimous election to the position of Honorary President. Meantime, Hornets supporters had mobilised and were reported to be carrying on with their scheme of house-to-house collections which had raised £46 – the equivalent of £3,100 today.

Having found their 'financial remedy' sitting in the boardroom, it was much further afield that Hornets looked for the man on whom they would pin their ambitions for playing success.

From the small farming community of Meerschaum Vale, near Lismore in New South Wales, Louis Victor Armbruster was a country football prodigy. Described by his junior club of Mulumbimby as 'tall, tough and talented', he was the complete rugby league forward, equally at home at lock (loose forward) or in the second-row.

Recognised for his forceful running, ball handling, the ability to slip out passes when surrounded by defenders and an uncanny knack of reading and fielding opposition kicks, 'Vic', as he was known, went on to become a dominant force in Australian representative rugby league: clocking up the rare triple honour of playing for New South Wales, Queensland and Australia.

He won his only NSW cap at the age of 20 in 1922's single interstate clash, the youngest player in the historic match which saw Queensland beat New South Wales for the first time since 1908. Vic was so impressed with the Maroons' performance that he wrote to Toowoomba Valleys coach Duncan Thompson to say he was thinking about a move North. Thompson later said: "I couldn't get him to Toowoomba quick enough."

Having moved to Queensland in 1924 to play for Valleys, Vic's abilities caught the eye of both the Toowoomba representative and Queensland state selectors. Armbruster went on to play in the all-conquering Toowoomba Competition rep. side of 1924–25 that beat Sydney premiers Souths, Brisbane, Ipswich and representative sides including New South Wales, Victoria and New Zealand. More impressively, Vic played in the famous tour match between Toowoomba and England in 1924, where the "Galloping Clydesdales" won 23–20. He went on to play 42 times for Queensland – 26 of them against NSW. Between 1924 and 1930 he also played 24 times for Australia – in eight test matches and 16 tour games.

Armbruster's international career began in the second Ashes test of 1924. He followed that up with a try in the Kangaroos third test win in Brisbane. He played all three tests against England in 1928 and was one of the first forwards chosen for the 1929–30 Kangaroos tour.

Hailed as one of the finest back-rows ever to wear the green and gold, Armbruster played in Australia's second row when international Rugby League history was made at the Athletic Grounds in January 1930.

After the scheduled three match series had ended all-square, one win each and a draw, the Rugby Football League took the unusual step of arranging a fourth test match against the Kangaroos. They selected Rochdale as the venue.

A press campaign was waged against the proposal to stage the additional game, but it went ahead on 15 January 1930. The Kangaroos lost the decider 3–0 with England's try from Stan Smith coming six minutes from time.

This unprecedented fourth test ensured that the Australian tour of 1929–30 started and ended at the Athletic Grounds – which gave the Rochdale rugby league public two opportunities to see Victor Armbruster in action.

The Hornets board was clearly impressed as, in 1931, Armbruster again departed for England. This time to wear red, white and blue of Rochdale Hornets. On 25 July, Hornets received a cable from their agent in Brisbane that he had secured the services of Vic Armbruster and that he would leave for England on the first available boat. A trip that would take about 40 days.

OGDEN'S CIGARETTES

V. ARMBRUSTER (ROCHDALE HORNETS)

Left: Australian rugby league legend Vic Armbruster crossed the world to captain Rochdale Hornets. Back home he represented New South Wales, Queensland and Australia. He also led a Toowoomba representative team to victory over the British Lions in 1924. (Rochdale Hornets Heritage Archive) Right: A cigarette card of Armbruster.

One report read: "Armbruster, with the possible exception of Treweek, was the outstanding forward of the last Australian touring team and was a first choice for the test matches. He has represented Queensland in state matches and Australia in tests for a number of years, but is young enough to do great service for the Hornets." Young enough? At 29, he was approaching his peak as a forward and his signing sent a signal of intent to every other club.

Having already signed flying Queensland winger Cec Aynsley, the addition of a bona-fide Australian Rugby League legend gave Hornets a potent mix of pace, power and quality. But it's pertinent to ask how a club that just four months earlier was claiming penury could afford to sign star names from the other side of the world? Given that player wages had actually gone down by over £100 on the previous season, it's fair to assume that the cost of the imports was being borne off the books.

A clue can be found in a single line from the shareholders report for the 1931–32 season: "We have to thank again our Honorary President Mr GA Close for providing at his own expense two of our most prominent players."

Armbruster made his Hornets debut on 19 September 1931. In the firing line was a shockingly bad Bradford Northern side en-route to their fourth consecutive wooden spoon.

In the previous three seasons in which Bradford Northern finished bottom of the League, they won just 21 times in 123 league games, including a miserable 29-game losing run. Even the partisan Yorkshire press feared the worst for Bradford. "At Rochdale where the Hornets will play Armbruster, the Australian tour forward, Bradford Northern, about whose future there is anxiety again, seem doomed to another defeat," wrote *The Yorkshire Post*.

The Leeds Mercury made similar predictions: "The Hornets will have Armbruster, that fine Australian forward, in their pack for the first time. If Armbruster can do for the Rochdale forwards what Aynsley has done for the backs, it will not be too long before the Hornets are climbing the table. At all events they are likely to be too strong for the Northern side which has been so generous in its concession of points so far."

They were right. Supercharged by the presence of their Australian stars, Hornets scored nine tries to one in a 35–5 flogging of the hapless Yorkshiremen. *The Yorkshire Post* described Bradford as 'overwhelmed' by Hornets, with Vic Armbruster named as helping turn Hornets from 'a mediocre team to a brilliant one'.

The remainder of the first half of the season was less straightforward once Hornets started playing the league's big guns. But there were noticeable signs of improvement, in both results and the style of Hornets' play. Seven wins and two draws from 19 games saw Hornets sat in 18th place at the turn of the year – but their home form was good, losing only once at the Athletic Grounds after the arrival of Vic Armbruster – a one-point defeat to Halifax. Eye-catching results included a 17–8 win over Oldham and an impressive 12–12 draw at Wigan.

In the second half of the season, Hornets delivered 12 wins from the 19 games played, lifting them to 12th place, their first top half finish in five years. But the improvement in Hornets' situation led to a rift between the directors and George Close, sparking rumours that he'd walked away from the club.

While Close admitted that he had not been actively associated with the Hornets for several weeks, he denied rumours that he had resigned from the presidency, saying that it was his intention "simply to slide out". Close maintained that he was still interested in the welfare of

Hornets, but that, in the weeks during which the club had been doing better, he had been side-lined by other directors and placed in a position of "mere figurehead". When asked for their side of the story, the Rochdale Hornets directors decided "not to make any statement".

But the fans did speak up. A report from 8 December 1931 said: "The supporters of Rochdale Hornets Football Club are anxious that the reported discussion between Mr GA Close and the directors should end and that all should work for the benefit of the club."

George Close remained as president and a director until the end of the 1932–33 season, at which point he "... found himself at variance with the other members of the board on the question of policy and resigned his position on the directorate".

The subsequent 1933–34 season saw a dip in Hornets' fortunes. On the field the team slipped back to finish 17th in the league. The Annual Report said: "We once again anticipated our team making better progress in the league table, but unfortunately they seldom rose to the occasion. At times they did quite well, but more often than not were very disappointing..."

Off the field, the club tabled a loss of £609 16s 9d, blaming bad weather for poor gates and 'bad luck' in a Challenge Cup draw that saw Hornets lose 6–5 at Hull in the first round. The board's plan to improve matters was to appoint Vic Armbruster as player-manager. For three years, Armbruster had been Hornets most outstanding player and, given the chance to shape the team in his own style, the board anticipated "... a more successful season and [we] expect he will receive every support both from the players and followers of Rugby League football."

But before he even began, the board added a caveat. "We are very disappointed with the results of our appeal to the members to apply and pay for their season tickets for next year at once. We recognise that our team requires strengthening in several departments, but this cannot be done without money, and unless this is forthcoming our new manager will not be able to build up the team as he desires."

It proved a prophetic statement. Within a year, Vic Armbruster and fellow Queenslander Cec Aynsley announced they were to return home to Australia. Armbruster made it clear that the lack of finance had been a serious handicap in his efforts for the club. The press said: "No-one was more keen to see Rochdale attain great heights in the game than Armbruster, but the difficulties confronting a team manager are many if the money is not available to aid progress. Armbruster is a likeable personality and a thorough sportsman and with the right support would, I am sure, have filled the part with success."

But the year was about to get much worse. On the morning of 8 September 1935. the main stand, dressing rooms, press-box, telephone room, directors' refreshment rooms and club offices were completely destroyed by a raging fire.

The fire was discovered some time after 6.30am by a newsagent on his delivery round and reported shortly after 7.45, when a message was called through to Rochdale police. Two fire engines and a van containing extra equipment were rushed to the Athletic Grounds. It was not known how the fire started, but it was already burning furiously at the Milnrow Road end when the fire brigade arrived – and it quickly became obvious that the task of fighting the fire was a hopeless one.

Despite there being three hydrants on site at the Athletic Grounds, the water pressure was so low that the fire brigade had to lay hose for a quarter of a mile in one direction and almost as far again in another. Eventually, every part of the grandstand was burning so fiercely that, on the pitch side, people couldn't get within 50 yards due to high winds fanning the blaze. The flames were so fierce that the heat bent the iron floodlight poles around the greyhound track and scorched the pitch. Within an hour of the outbreak, all that remained were the walls and a handful of steel pillars that formed part of the stand's underlying structure.

In the club office was a safe that contained the £91 takings from the previous evening's game against Wigan as well as other cash, the ledger and the club's bank books. Once the fire had burnt out, the safe was retrieved from the debris. On opening it the money and the other documents were found intact. The only other assets to survive were one set of playing jerseys that had been sent away for numbering.

One report said: "The Rochdale directors had a meeting this morning and the chairman Mr AE Ashworth said that the match with Halifax on Saturday will be played – and they wanted to appeal to their supporters to rally round." Hornets lost the game 13–0.

The same report pointed out that: "The loss is covered by insurance." The payout, reported in the annual accounts, came to £4,000.

There was much talk in the press about the Hornets directors immediately making plans for a new grandstand - and the mayor and his predecessor, Councillors Parker and Ashworth, opened a fund for the rebuilding of the club's stand. It raised a 'handsome donation' of £486 12s 7d. The new stand was designed to seat 1,300 people – 190 feet long, almost 30 feet deep and with a roof overhanging by over 20 feet to cover the enclosures below. Construction would take six months. In the meantime, the club erected benches in the Railway Side stand to accommodate members and grandstand regulars.

Unfortunately, three months into the new stand's construction, a January gale tore the roof off the Railway Side stand, hurling debris onto the railway line behind and leaving supporters exposed to the elements.

The new main stand was officially opened for the Liverpool Stanley game on 7 March 1936 by the Mayor, GJ Parker. Hornets lost 12–5. A line in the accounts states that 'at the season's end the balance of the contract for the erection of the new stand came to £1,265 5s 6d plus some unaccounted expenses such as architects' fees.'

Despite poor attendances and a fall in gate receipts of £828 4s 7d, the accounts show a profit of £168 13s and 7d for the season. Ahead of the 1937 AGM, George Close returned to offer himself as a director, only to withdraw his nomination at the meeting. However, at the unanimous request of the sitting directors he was co-opted onto the board. Despite Close's return, the 1937–38 season was a miserable one. Hornets sank to 25th in the league with only nine wins from 36 games. Having flogged junior side Glasshoughton 50–2 in round one of the Challenge Cup, they crashed out at St Helens Recs in round two, 18–10. The Lancashire Cup was no better. The team fell at the first hurdle, 18–3 at Leigh. And, for good measure, Oldham won the Infirmaries Cup at the Athletic Grounds.

By January 1938, Hornets were – again – deep in the financial mire. *The Lancashire Post* broke the news: "There is real danger that Rochdale Hornets, one of the oldest rugby league clubs, will have to close down at the end of the season. It has been decided by the directors to call a meeting of shareholders to decide whether it is worthwhile continuing the club."

Jack Williams, Hornets' record try scorer with 107 from 1931 to 1937. (Courtesy Jim Stringer)

The directors called the meeting for Thursday 20 January, citing 'poor gates' as the reason for their financial position; the previous week's game had yielded receipts of only £87. It was strongly mooted that the club would have to close before the end of the season "... unless rugby supporters are prepared to back the club so that the directors can pay their way."

At the meeting the directors revealed the depth of the financial hole that the club was in: £3,000 owed to creditors and £6,000 owed to debenture holders. (In simple terms debenture is effectively a long-term unsecured loan to an organisation that becomes repayable on a set date and is paid back at a guaranteed rate of interest. They usually have a term greater than 10 years – and are only backed by the word and the reputation of the issuer.)

Chairman A Ashworth said the club simply had no money with which to carry on the club. The board also revealed that they'd received an offer from a mystery London-based greyhound racing 'syndicate' for the purchase of the ground, its stands and other assets. The scant details were put to the shareholders for consideration.

Director FW Greenwood said that the amount being offered by these "certain gentlemen" would enable the directors to pay-off the debenture holders and the creditors – and still leave a surplus with which to continue the club. In return for selling, the syndicate would grant the club a lease on the ground so that they could continue playing there. The shareholders gave the board the green light to continue negotiations and report back at a later date.

By the end of the following week, the sale to the syndicate looked increasingly likely. A statement from the directors said: "Owing to the inability of the Rugby League to come to our financial assistance, the directors are reluctantly compelled to open negotiations for the sale of the company's fixed assets." Within 24 hours of the statement, the press began reporting the deal as done. "Rugby League Club Becomes Tenant Instead Of Owner" shouted the headline in T*he Liverpool Echo*. "London Syndicate takes over Hornets' ground after League refuses a loan."

"The sale of their spacious ground to a London Syndicate, means that in order to meet their liabilities the directors – with the sanction of the shareholders of the company – have decided to become tenants instead of owners of the ground. The club will have an option upon the ground for the purposes of football and ... are simply realising on their greatest asset."

But it was a premature assumption. Behind the scenes negotiations with the largest debenture holders secured their approval to ask the others if they would increase the value of their loans from £6,000 to £10,000. The theory was that raising £4,000 would enable the directors to pay off their trade creditors and have sufficient balance left over to continue running the club. While this action secured the club's ownership of the Athletic Grounds, it merely pushed concerns about repaying a now bigger debt further into the future.

By the end of the season, the club reported a significant loss of £1,172 14s 11d, with over £300 owed to players and officials. At the AGM there was a proposal passed to reduce the size of the board to the constituted minimum of eight directors. George Close didn't make the cut, but by then he was in deteriorating health.

George Close died age 63 on 5 June 1939. The Club's annual report carried the following notice: "The Directors deeply regret the recent death of Mr George A Close, Life Member, whose generous services have been of great value to the Hornets over many years."

Indeed, in the parochial world of rugby league, it was curiously fitting that it took a cinema mogul to see the bigger picture. In addition to luring top Antipodean talent to the Athletic Grounds, George Close's connections across the Atlantic led him to offer opportunities to Canadians Sid and Roy Gaunt and Ken Fleming, who had all been playing the Union game in British Columbia. Without his vision – and his financial backing – Hornets' struggles looked set to continue.

And with Britain on the brink of another devastating war, success seemed further away than ever.

References:

The Bioscope - Wednesday 22 August 1928

Athletic News - Monday 29 July 1929

Hull Daily Mail - Saturday 15 June 1929

Athletic News - Monday 19 August 1929

Hull Daily Mail - Wednesday 4 September 1929

Lancashire Evening Post - Friday 6 September 1929

Yorkshire Post - Monday 9 September 1929

Hull Daily Mail - Monday 9 September 1929

Western Daily Press - Thursday 12 September 1929

The Stage - Thursday 5 February 1931

Lancashire Evening Post - Wednesday 18 February 1931

Halifax Evening Courier - Wednesday 18 February 1931

Yorkshire Post - Wednesday 18 February 1931

The Stage - Thursday 26 February 1931

Halifax Evening Courier - Monday 06 April 1931

'A Centenary of Rugby League 1908 - 2008 - The Definitive Story of the game in Australia', Ian Heads/David MIddleton 2008

Halifax Evening Courier - Saturday 25 July 1931

Yorkshire Post - Saturday 19 September 1931

Leeds Mercury - Saturday 19 September 1931

Halifax Evening Courier - Saturday 12 December 1931

Halifax Evening Courier - Saturday 6 April 1935

Halifax Evening Courier - Wednesday 18 September 1935

Yorkshire Post - Thursday 19 September 1935

Bradford Observer - Friday 10 January 1936

Lancashire Evening Post - Tuesday 11 January 1938

Liverpool Echo - Wednesday 12 January 1938

Hull Daily Mail - Wednesday 12 January 1938

Leeds Mercury - Friday 21 January 1938

Halifax Evening Courier - Thursday 27 January 1938

Liverpool Echo - Saturday 29 January 1938

Bradford Observer - Friday 21 January 1938

Halifax Evening Courier - Wednesday 2 February 1938

Rochdale Observer - Wednesday 7 June 1939

bbc.co.uk - nation on film: "Boom to Bust - The Decline of the Cotton Industry" - 24 September 2014

cottontown.org: Crisis in the industry

"Leisure in an Industrial town - A case study of Rochdale Lancashire, 1880–1939" - P.T Wild. 1985

"Rochdale Retrospect: Towards the Centenary of the Borough" - R.P. Taylor. 1956

Rochdale Hornets Report and Accounts 1929

Rochdale Hornets Report and Accounts 1930

Rochdale Hornets Report and Accounts 1932

Rochdale Hornets Report and Accounts 1933

Rugby League Review: "Rochdale Athletic Grounds" - 4 October 1949

7. 1948 to 1958: The weight of expectations

After the deprivations of the Second World War, the country threw itself headlong into a period of inventiveness, optimism and a renewed spirit of hope. The future was bright and anything seemed possible.

Similarly, the years bookended between Hornets' two Challenge Cup semi-final appearances in 1948 and 1958 are considered in club folklore as a golden period of big crowds, star players, champagne football and success. An influx of Australians created a sense of ambition on a grander scale; players who would become 21st century club legends forged reputations in Hornets teams that brimmed with internationals. But collective memory is a fickle thing.

With an increasing number of players called-up to fight and the Athletic Grounds commandeered for recruit training, Hornets had dropped out of the wartime Lancashire League. A 12–4 defeat against Salford at the Athletic Grounds on 11 May 1940 heralded what the board described as "...the barren war years."

Re-forming the club in the immediate aftermath of war was a struggle. For the 1945–46 season, the Hornets board committed to resuming fixtures, but had to hurriedly assemble a team from the few older pre-war players still on the books and "any others we could afford to sign". After a five year break, a scratch Hornets side including eight players from a Barrow armament works team travelled to face a Hull Kingston Rovers outfit packed with their pre-war stars. Hornets went down by a commendable 14–5.

To compensate for the lack of quality, Hornets went for a player-manager with huge experience. 35-year-old Stanley Brogden had enjoyed a glittering pre-war career; stints as a lynchpin at Huddersfield, Leeds and Hull FC saw him win 15 England and 16 Great Britain caps. He moved from The Boulevard to the Athletic Grounds for 'a huge fee', but the task was clearly too great.

Just nine wins and a draw from 36 games saw Hornets finish 24th in a 27-team league. Brogden was stood down as coach. With him able to focus on playing, the board believed they had "the nucleus of a team at the Athletic Grounds which will hold its own with the majority of clubs." They also had a plan: to appoint an experienced former player as trainer-coach, and to give the club a strong local foundation, having "... all the players living in the town, or within reasonable distance of it..."

On 25 May 1946, in *The Manchester Evening News,* below job ads for a cellulose sprayer, machine operator and a shorthand typist, appeared the following: "Rochdale Hornets Football Club Ltd, Athletic Grounds Rochdale – Full-time Trainer-Coach-Groundsman required. Applicants should state age, experience and salary required, and forward copies of two recent testimonials to the above address not later than Saturday 8 June 1946. Envelopes to be endorsed 'Application' G Halligan, Secretary."

The successful applicant was 42-year-old former Swinton loose-forward Fred Butters, but under his guidance 1946–1947 was even more disappointing. Having failed to agree playing terms for the season, Brogden was placed on the transfer list at his own request at a fee pf £600. In January 1947, he left to join Salford. The transfer caused a rift in the board that saw one director resign. On the field, things were no better. With wins hard to come by, one report said: "Rochdale Hornets are not impressive at the moment and do not appear to be anything like the team one expects..." Another said: "The young Hornets are lacking a little in experience."

In a season that included a run of 14 straight defeats, Hornets finished next to bottom of a 28 team championship with just nine wins from 36 games. They didn't fare much better in the cups: dumped out of the Challenge Cup in the first round, 24–2 over two legs by Widnes, battered by an aggregate score of 81–9 over a two-legged first round of the Lancashire Cup by Wigan; and losing at home to Oldham in the Infirmaries Cup, 14–8.

The directors saw falling attendances as part of a 'chicken and egg' situation. They said: "It was not a case of support falling away because of lack of success on the field. The support right from the start of the season was such that the question of meeting current expenses was foremost, and no surplus accumulated at any time for speculative buying of players."

The following season seemed to herald a change of fortune. Boosted by the recruitment of a 'reliable pack of forwards' modest progress was made in the league, 11 wins and two draws in 36 games saw Hornets finish a heady 22nd in a 28 team championship. But inspired by 'special bonuses for cup wins', that saw the club's wage bill increase by £1,400, they showed much more eye-catching form.

Having nicked the Law Cup by a point at Watersheddings, 18–17, a fortuitous run in the Lancashire Cup saw Hornets progress to the semi-final. A first round 23–7 aggregate win over Lancashire Amateurs, followed by a bye in the quarter finals saw Hornets lose 27–3 to reigning league champions Wigan in the semi-final at Central Park.

But it was in the Challenge Cup that Hornets made a major mark. Round one was a two-legged affair against amateurs Pemberton Rovers. Hornets won 13–0 at home and 11–0 at Central Park. Round two was a 3–2 nail-biting win at home to Belle Vue Rangers.

Despite *The Yorkshire Post* predicting that Keighley's 'forward mastery' and ground advantage would make them 'good enough to beat the Hornets' in the quarter final, Hornets came away from Lawkholme Lane with a narrow 6–4 win; two tries to two penalties, convincing enough.

The Bradford Observer said: "If ever a pack won a game, it was the Rochdale six at Keighley. They began by winning nearly every scrum and then, in the loose, Fearnley, Rothwell and Oxley over-shadowed their opposite numbers for the rest of the game."

"Keighley were disappointing, but on the play, Hornets were the better team and well deserved the honour of assuring Lancashire equal representation in the semi-finals."

In a repeat of the earlier Lancashire Cup semi-final, Hornets faced Wigan at Swinton's Station Road, on 3 April 1948. By the date of the semi-final, Wigan were already storming to the top of the table – and were racing favourites to get to Wembley. Indeed, one Wigan bookmaker offered odds of 3,000 to one against a Hornets victory. But Hornets' cup run had been built on stern defence – they had gone all the way to the semi-final without conceding a try and weren't going to Swinton just to make up the numbers.

On the day, the attendance of 26,004 was lower than anticipated due to a Wigan Corporation bus strike causing the cancellation of 27 supporter buses. Having lost the toss, Hornets played the first half into a strong wind.

The 1948 Challenge Cup semi-final Hornets team. (Courtesy *Rugby League Journal*)

The first quarter was tight, Wigan's only real chances coming from two missed penalties. Wigan took the lead with a 22nd minute try. Another try round the blind-side of a scrum gave Wigan a 6–0 half-time lead. Hornets started the second half full of fight and should have closed the gap, but Gummer lost control of the ball over the Wigan line and the chance was gone. With both sides exchanging missed penalties, the game was finally sealed when Wigan grabbed a late converted try to give them an 11–0 win.

Reports describe the game as "A stern, robust struggle in which Hornets, although lacking the skill of Wigan in attack, presented a solid defence." Despite the defeat, there was anticipation that this against-the-odds cup run that ended one step from Wembley glory would provide a springboard for Hornets to kick-on.

With their £1,300 share of the Challenge Cup semi-final receipts, the club turned a profit of £1,498 18s 10d, with gate receipts almost doubling and ticket receipts increasing from £749 to £900. And Hornets' cup exploits were reflected in the gates. Support at home matches was up on previous years – peaking with the Hornets versus Oldham Easter fixture that pulled in a crowd of 10,000 to the Athletic Grounds.

With expectations raised, all eyes were on the following year's Challenge Cup draw. The first round of the 1948–49 Challenge Cup was to be played across two legs and Hornets were drawn against a star-studded Huddersfield in what *The Yorkshire Post* described as 'an easy looking tie'.

However, Hornets produced the shock of the weekend with a major upset at Fartown, where a young Hornets team outplayed a Huddersfield side featuring 10 internationals. One report describes how Huddersfield "... lacked the team spirit of the youthful Hornets who, inspired by a deserved interval lead, subdued all the Fartowners' recovery efforts." Hornets keeping Huddersfield tryless to win 5–2.

Ahead of the second leg, *The Manchester Evening News* was critical of the two-leg system, stating that "Huddersfield, regarded in Yorkshire as the strongest challengers to Lancashire's best..." had had their cup hopes 'saved' by opportunity of a second leg. "Rochdale Hornets provided the biggest sensation last week when they led Huddersfield at Fartown – 'spotting' then upsetting the Yorkshiremen's style."

They went on: "The 'two leg' system has many critics, but none can deny that it has created a very intriguing position and this will be reflected in the big crowds attracted to grounds tomorrow." And they were right.

On Saturday 19 February, 22,227 spectators packed into the Athletic Grounds, the club's best gate for more than 25 years, to see if Hornets could produce a second consecutive cup upset. Spurred on by the large crowd, Hornets tight defence restrained Huddersfield's best efforts, but it couldn't last. Playing what was described as 'sparkling football', the Fartowners produced three tries to take the tie beyond Hornets' reach. Hornets did have chances, though – two three-man overlaps were blown when Winstanley opted not to pass, and Hornets' kicker Peter Gronow missed seven penalties.

Despite exiting the cup in round one, the win at Fartown – and the sizeable turnout at home – hinted that Hornets had the potential to take on the big clubs. But even this hint of success would come at a price. While gate receipts and season ticket sales were slightly more than the previous season, in an attempt to improve the playing strength of the side, the board had spent £2,535 in transfer and signing fees – £1,500 more than in the previous year – to deliver a modest improvement in performance. 12 wins, three draws and 21 defeats could still only secure a 22nd place finish in a 29 club league.

Chairman Wilfred Kershaw had loftier plans, saying: "The ambition is to see the team in the upper half of the Rugby League table, capable of bringing to Rochdale again one of the major trophies." In the inaugural issue of the annual Supporters' Club newsletter, 'The Hornet', he laid responsibility for the club's future success firmly at the feet of supporters. "Quite frankly the road we took in 1945 by restarting football at the Athletic Grounds after the war has not been an easy one. Support has not justified heavy expenditure on transfer fees, but the best has been done with the limited means, and progress has been made."

Kershaw continued: "There is a poser for all who are concerned with the workings of a Football Club. The impatient supporters say: 'Get a winning team and the support will come.' The officials say: 'Give us the support and we will get the team.' As a board we are being as ambitious as possible on moderate gates. We promise that our enterprise will keep pace with growing support. So to the Rochdale Public I say: 'It is your move now'."

Despite the previous year's investment in players, the 1949–50 season was a shocker. Of 36 matches and five cup games played, Hornets won only five and drew three, finishing third bottom of the league. Their scoring record was the worst recorded in post-war football, avoiding the smallest ever points-for total, 200, set by Liverpool Stanley, by just two points.

With crowds down to an average of only 3,500, gate receipts had collapsed from £10,590 in 1948–49 to £6,467 15s 3d. Season ticket sales had also slumped from £1,086 to £748 5s. And Hornets' dealings in the transfer market had been a disaster. The net effect of a large turnover of player transfers was that the club paid out £1,261 6s 6d more than it received. Their only good piece of business being the signing of former Vine Tavern amateur Ted Cahill from Liverpool Stanley for £1,000.

Having swallowed a £2,089 16s 9d, loss, their worst in the post-war period, Hornets needed an innovative plan to bring the crowds flocking back along Milnrow Road. At the end of the 1949–50 season, the board took what they believed to be one of the most ambitious steps in the club's history; they approached Australian Cec Fifield to become Hornets' Manager-Coach.

Cec Fifield had an impeccable rugby league pedigree. He'd played representative football for Australia and New South Wales and in the NSWRFL Premiership for Western Suburbs, Balmain and Canterbury-Bankstown. He had experience of the English game too, having played 224 games for Hull FC. He'd been to Rochdale before. As a tourist with the 1929–30 Kangaroos, he played in all four tests against England – breaking his ankle in the controversial series-deciding fourth test at the Athletic Grounds.

In addition to bringing his experience, he was briefed to select several young Australian players to help strengthen the team. But this was a tricky process. In 1947, the Australian Rugby League Board of Control had imposed a ban on international transfers to prevent wealthy English clubs luring their best players, so Fifield had to look into the union game.

He selected Tom Duffy, Wally Ellean, Cec 'Babe' Kelly, and Reg and Ron Stanford: all of whom were, at the time, junior rugby union players, although they had played rugby league as teenagers. They left Australia by boat at the end of July 1950.

However, on 10 July, at the request of the Australian Board of Control, The Rugby League Council in England imposed an embargo on English clubs signing Australian rugby union players who had previously played league. As such, the five Aussie lads arrived in Rochdale on 1 September 1950 to find themselves thrown into the midst of an international incident that would rumble on for over a year.

At a Rugby League Council meeting on Thursday 7 September, it was decided that they would not be allowed to play for Hornets that weekend. Having played rugby league before moving to rugby union, the Australian Board of Control refused to give them clearance certificates. Hornets appealed that they had signed these players before the latest ban was introduced.

In response, the Rugby League Council referred the appeal to the Rugby League Tour Committee, who had responsibility for all international affairs. They were due to meet the following Tuesday, 12 September, in Manchester. Hornets were instructed to send club representatives, all five players and Cec Fifield to face the committee.

It was a long meeting. The Rugby League Tour Committee took four hours to decide that Hornets' five Australians were not barred from British rugby league under the terms of the recent ban. RFL Secretary Bill Fallowfield said that the Committee's decision was unanimous. They had decided that the players were amateurs and that, according to League by-laws, the registration of amateur players is allowed for one season. But this was far from the end of the matter.

In response, a 'strongly worded' protest from the Australian Board of Control was discussed at a Rugby League Council meeting on Tuesday 19 December. The protest contended that, although the players had been attached to rugby union clubs when they were signed, as they had previously played league, the RFL should have insisted on the production of clearance certificates before accepting their registrations.

The Australian Board of Control also stated that they had no intention of issuing clearance certificates for the Hornets players because they regarded their move from league to union as a ruse to evade the 1947 poaching ban.

The Rugby League Council stood by their previous finding and asked their Australian counterparts to accept the position as it stood. Though they did assure them that they were willing to consider any suggestions that the Australian Board of Control might make regarding signing restrictions.

This came back to bite Hornets in February of 1951. By now the whole situation was attracting national media attention. *The Daily Mirror* reported: "Reg and Ron Stanford, former Sydney Rugby League players who have already played for Rochdale Hornets without permission from the Australian Board of Control have now been refused official clearances to play in England. The English Rugby League will re-open the case against the Stanford Brothers at the (RL) Council meeting at Manchester on Thursday."

Hornets Chairman Wilf Kershaw was livid: "We went before the Rugby League Council in October and we were found 'not guilty'," he said. "We do not think it right to stand trial twice. The rules say that we can sign an Australian rugby union player but not a rugby league player. We contend that the Stanfords were rugby union players."

At the subsequent Rugby League Council meeting it was announced that the Australian Board of Control had now refused to issue clearance certificates for all of Hornets Australian players. Having agreed to consider suggestions from the Australian Board of Control on signing restrictions, the Rugby League Council submitted the case to the board of appeal and asked Australia to send representation.

Representation came in the shape of a cable that read: "The Australian Rugby League Board once again wishes to protest emphatically against the attitude adopted by the English Rugby League over players now participating in English football with the Rochdale Club. The players concerned were formally registered by the New South Wales Rugby League and the board protests strongly against the English league not carrying out the terms of the ban, as agreed by both countries in 1947. The board views with great concern the attitude of the English League."

As the 1950–51 season ended, the positive impact of Hornets' Australian influx could be seen on the field and on the books. Hornets finished the season in 22nd place with 14 wins and a draw from 36 games. Crowds, gate receipts and season ticket sales had almost doubled, with the club turning round the previous year's £2,089 16s 9d loss into £1,797 10s 3d profit. Plus, emerging star full-back Ted Cahill was called-up to play for Lancashire against Cumberland at Barrow. Writing in *The Hornet* Cec Fifield described it as a season of "contrasting experiences". He went on: "There have been handicaps in the way of getting on with the job of making the Hornets the team I would like to see, but we must take a long view and have patience."

October 1950: Cec Fifield's Hornets' team includes controversial Australian signings Ron Stanford, Wally Ellean and Cec 'Babe' Kelly. This is the side that ended Wigan's 21 game winning run by 10–6. (Rochdale Hornets Heritage Archive)

On the morning of Saturday 2 February 1952, Hornets supporters work to clear the pitch of snow and ice ahead of the game against Halifax. (Rochdale Hornets Heritage Archive)

With a new season to look forward to, the club's wrangles with an intransigent Australian Board of Control were far from over. Hornets directors stated that a "… reply from the Australian Board of Control which has been asked to grant clearance papers to the club's five young Australian players is awaited." When the reply came, the news wasn't good.

The Australian Board of Control maintained that the Rugby League had broken their transfer ban and, in May 1951, a meeting of the Rugby League Council in Manchester declared that, 'after months of sniping by the Australian Board of Control they would not re-register the players for the forthcoming season unless clearance certificates were issued.'

Fast-forward four months and, with the 1951–52 season imminent, there had been no progress. It is reported on 8 September that Hornets were notified by the Rugby League secretary that the Australian Board of Control refused to lift the ban on the five players.

Hornets demanded a meeting with the Rugby League Council and released an angry statement describing the situation as "… arbitrary in the extreme, the situation being aggravated by the fact that permission to play the five men was given in September 1950 and withdrawn in May this year. The board are prepared to stand by their action in engaging the players, and will ask for the fullest investigation on the highest possible level into the whole matter."

By the end of September, the RFL had received a cable from the Australian Board of Control reiterating their refusal to issue clearance certificates. Settling the issue would require an element of international diplomacy. Sir Edwin Airey, the chairman of the Rugby League made a 'personal request' of Mr Harry Flegg, Lancashire-born chairman of the Australian Board of Control, to use his influence to help "iron out a difficult situation".

In response, the Australian Board of Control agreed to meet on Thursday 18 October to "… reconsider the case of Australian players with Rochdale Hornets who have not been allowed to play football this season because of the ban imposed by the agreement between the Australian Board of Control and the Rugby League."

After 13 months of bitter wrangling, slanging and stonewalling, 'The Rochdale 5' were granted clearance to play 'legitimately' in England. *The Yorkshire Post* reported: "Following the appeal made by Sir Edwin Airey, Chairman of the Rugby League Council, the Australian Board of Control at a special meeting today has granted permission for Rochdale Hornets to play the five Australians for whom no clearance certificates were secured. The Rochdale Secretary Mr RL Jones on behalf of the club, sent Sir Edwin a telegram of appreciation."

The Hornet reported that the five players had kept up their training continuously throughout the embargo and that they recommenced playing on Saturday October 20th: Ron Stanford and Cec Kelly in the first team at Keighley; Reg Stanford, Wally Ellean and Tom Duffy in the 'A'-team against Salford at the Athletic Grounds.

Ironically, within hours of learning that he was eligible to play again, Cec Kelly was informed that he had been selected to play scrum-half for Other Nationalities against France at Hull on 3 November.

Amid all the wrangling, Hornets did find time to take on the touring New Zealand side at the Athletic Grounds. On Tuesday 18 September 1951, the Kiwis came to town with ten test players in their side. What looked like a hard task was made harder with Hornets missing all five of their banned Australian imports and Teddy Cahill.

A crowd of 4,500 saw Hornets produce a shock start, taking the lead within a minute from a Lord penalty from 40 yards. Hornets' aggressive, spirited play in the early exchanges shook the Kiwis, who soon found themselves further behind: a break by Booth backed up by Kelly, who found space to send Ward in by the flag. For good measure, Lord kicked a great goal from the touchline to extend Hornets' lead. Just before the break New Zealand fashioned a scrappy try after gathering a loose ball. Hornets leading at half time 7–3.

The second half saw a more assured Kiwis take the game to Hornets. On 50 minutes a break saw the ball pass through hands for an unconverted try. A penalty two minutes later edged the Kiwis in front 8–7. Hornets came close to hitting back when winger Redford kicked ahead only to be obstructed on his run by a New Zealand defender, then Booth tried to bullock in from close range only to fumble the ball over the line.

With only five minutes remaining Hornets went in search of the killer blow, but their adventure ended in disaster. Harassed on the touchline, Booth looked to offload the ball inside - only for the Kiwis wing to intercept and run 40 yards to score. The conversion took the score to 13–7.

With only a minute remaining, Hornets were awarded a penalty for offside; Lord landing a long-range penalty to make the final score Hornets 9 New Zealand 13. After the game, the club hosted the Kiwis at a formal post-match dinner and dance at the Town Hall – the players seated alternately, Hornets and Kiwis. As a thank you, the Kiwis sang a Maori song and performed their Haka for their Rochdale hosts. The report and accounts showed that the event lost £200 – the tip, it seems, of a financial iceberg that threatened to sink the club.

On 17 January 1952, with the club £1,200 in debt, a crowded meeting at the Pioneers Hall on Lord Street brought a vote of no-confidence against the directors. It was passed by 172 votes to 110 and the board resigned en-masse. Chairman Wilfred Kershaw had already resigned the previous month because he claimed that the board was uncooperative with him as chairman. It was also revealed that, due to the financial state of the club, the Supporters and Shareholders' Association had been paying the players wages and travelling expenses for several weeks.

In addition, the Supporters Association had not only paid outstanding tax accounts of £450, the phone bill and the rates, they also bought £1,400 worth of debenture stock that they knew the board could not afford to redeem, and waived the 6.5 percent interest payable. An extraordinary gesture.

At the meeting a temporary board was elected to manage the club's affairs. The next day, their first act was to confirm publicly that Fifield remained in full control of the team and its direction. But within a month, interim chairman, and former Hornets player, James Lindley and his new board made three changes to the side to face Cardiff, which Hornets lost 8–4. Having undermined Fifield's authority, they released him from his contract just 72 hours later.

Lindley said: "There is nothing personal in our decision, and remuneration until the end of April, when Mr Fifield's agreement expires, will be paid." The new board also announced they were talking to Warrington about a £1,000 offer for centre Ron Stanford.

The shareholders were up in arms, demanding an extraordinary general meeting to question what they saw as an over-stepping of the interim board's remit. One shareholder said: "Their job was to get a new permanent board elected, not sack the manager and arrange the transfer of the club's best player."

However, despite the anger of shareholders, at the EGM on Tuesday 18 March 1952, a new board of directors headed by Lindley was duly elected. Former chairman Wilfred Kershaw was given a life membership in recognition of his long service and his role in restarting rugby league in the town after the war.

However, the issues behind the scenes were already affecting on-field performances; a report on a defeat at Widnes stated emphatically: "The financial and administrative worries at Hornets' club has had a most unsettling effect on the players."

Hornets ended the season sixth bottom with just 10 wins from 36 games. In their first annual report and accounts, the new board blamed the team's poor performance on the Australian ban, injuries and the 'shocking weather'. In April, they placed an ad in the regional press reading: "PLAYER-MANAGER-COACH required for season 1952–53, plus playing terms – apply the secretary."

In the summer of 1952, Hornets announced the appointment of 34-year-old Welsh international centre Norman Harris as player-coach. Released by Leigh for a 'fairly small fee', Harris had enjoyed a stellar rugby union career before switching to league, joining Oldham after the war and then Leigh three years later.

The board's hope was that a player-coach would be able to exert more influence over a youthful team, but one of the first things he had to contend with was Cec Kelly's request to be placed on the transfer list. The influential Australian playmaker was listed at £2,000 and sold to Wigan ahead of the new season.

In order to give Harris the chance to build a competitive team, the board appealed to the public of Rochdale to lend the funds needed to finance the purchase of new players. In September they launched a scheme that asked fans to subscribe in units of £5. The plan was to set aside £100 from each game's gate receipts to repay the loans. But less than a week later, the club announced that they wouldn't proceed with their £5 loan scheme because match receipts at the time indicated that they would have enough money to buy the players they needed without borrowing.

Within a month, the club posted the following small-ad: "Rochdale Hornets Football Club require a secretary who must be capable of dealing with all matters relating to accounts to balance sheet, also all usual secretarial matters including correspondence, wages, PAYE, weekly budgets, preparation for board meetings etc. without supervision. Must be prepared for evening work and to travel at weekend."

The season started poorly. Player-coach Norman Harris broke his foot and Hornets were winless until the end of October. But a string of wins against Castleford, Workington, Widnes and a 27–5 thrashing of Warrington gave fans renewed hope, though the new board's forecast that the team would finish in the top half of the league looked decidedly ambitious. What was recognised, though, was Hornets' desire to play attractive rugby. A report in *The Runcorn News* after the win at Widnes said: "If this Rochdale Hornets are a bottom four side then the league has a false bottom... one can make a sporting acknowledgement of the superiority of the Rochdale side and congratulate all concerned on the way it has recovered from a depressing start."

"On this showing Rochdale are a strong well-balanced side, not over endowed with speed, but making up for that with fast handling which at times reached the best Huddersfield standards."

Thirteen wins and three draws saw them finish 22nd in a 30 team Championship. But turning improved performances into profit remained a challenge, with the accounts for the year stating that "... strengthening the playing personnel and an increase in wages due to winning more matches..." led to a season's loss of £1,447 14s 1d.

It seems like fans were frustrated too. In his address to the Supporters' Association at the end of the season, James Lindley said: "Much publicity has been given regarding players wanting and asking to be placed on the open-to-transfer list, unfortunately this has been true. A word of advice for spectators; if one of the players temporarily loses his form, don't for heaven's sake catcall or jeer at him, he realises probably more than you he is below form, and such treatment will not improve his game, but will do much towards making him dissatisfied and requesting his release from the club."

The 1953–54 season was a high-water mark, when Hornets looked most likely to break into the elite of the British game, with Hornets players gaining representative honours on a regular basis

Australian utility forward Wally Ellean was selected for other Nationalities against Wales, France and England. Welshmen Bernard McNally and Eynon Hawkins called up together to represent Wales versus France. McNally was also selected for the Rest of the World' versus France. However, the stand-out player was Edward 'Teddy' Cahill. Teddy began his career in 1945 playing for Vine Tavern in St Helens. After just half a dozen games, he was snapped up by Liverpool Stanley. After 75 games for the Championship's perpetual basement club, Hornets paid an eyewatering £1,000 to bring him to the Athletic Grounds, where he quickly built a reputation as a classy attacking full-back. And in 1953–54 he was at the peak of his powers. Selected twice for Lancashire, against Yorkshire and Cumberland, he forced his way into the England side that took on France and Other Nationalities.

His performances caught the eye of the Great Britain Lions selectors and he was invited to play for Whites versus Reds in a Great Britain tour trial match at Station Road on 10 March 1954. He kicked one goal in a 20–14 defeat, but was the unanimous choice as Great Britain's full-back for their tour of Australia and New Zealand.

In Australia, Teddy played eight tour games for Great Britain, kicking 14 goals – form that saw him selected for the second test in Brisbane. However, in the run-up to the test he suffered a badly twisted knee in a game at Rockhampton and had to return home for treatment.

While Teddy Cahill was grabbing the headlines in the region's sports pages, it was a signing from Australia that was about to put Hornets on the front pages of the national newspapers. On Monday 23 November 1953, Hornets announced the signing of Wally McArthur. Widely vaunted as the fastest player ever to pull on a Hornets shirt, Wally McArthur was an Australian sporting phenomenon. He was lightning fast and an absolute points machine. In his local Adelaide competition, he racked-up 900 points in three seasons playing for Semaphore. Indeed, he ended his career there before departing for Rochdale with a Grand Final win in which he scored a try and four goals.

Left: Australian sprint sensation Wally McArthur takes on the Blackpool defence in front of a huge Athletic Grounds crowd. Hornets won 37–8. (Rochdale Hornets Heritage Archive)

It was as a sprinter that he'd made his name. At the age of 14 he ran the world's fastest 440 yards for his age group and went on to become South Australia's Under–19 100 and 220 yards champion. Despite an attempt to exclude him because of his ethnicity, he won the National Under–19 100 yards title, but was then denied selection for Australia's 1952 Olympics team. Australian Journalist John Pilger claims it was discrimination due to his indigenous heritage. Wally turned to professional sprinting and was unbeaten in his first 10 races, but he was drawn to rugby league and its inclusive attitude.

He rapidly became one of the state's leading league players. Semaphore went unbeaten for two seasons, with Wally voted the state's fairest and best player in 1952. The following year he was selected for South Australia against Western Australia, and won the man-of-the-match award. Paul Quinn, a former Hornets player living in Adelaide, saw Wally's potential and was appointed by the club to open negotiations about a possible move to Rochdale. It was a tricky situation to navigate. Australia's ban on international transfers was still in place - and Hornets were already on the authorities' radar after the notorious Cec Fifield incident three years previously.

So, instead of applying to go to Rochdale to play rugby league, Wally 'decided' to fly halfway round the world to a Northern mill town to complete his engineering apprenticeship. Once his move for 'work reasons' was agreed, it was casually mentioned that he might be interested in having a few games for Hornets as well. The Australian Board of Control rubber-stamped the move and, on Thursday 19 November 1953, 19-year-old Wally McArthur boarded a plane for England. In his pocket a four-year contract that promised him £250 per year, plus match fees and a return ticket to Australia.

On his arrival, *The Daily Mirror* had doubts about his cover story. Beneath the headline 'Their new man is too busy to work' they wrote: "When Wally McArthur left Australia for England last week he had two ambitions – to play rugby league football for Rochdale Hornets and continue his career as an engineering apprentice. But Wally has shelved the work idea temporarily. First priority was to warm up his football and get into Rochdale's team as soon as possible. So early yesterday morning, instead of looking for a job, he was down on the Rochdale ground."

Hornets secretary C. Wilson was optimistic: "If all goes well, McArthur's first match will probably be against Salford at Rochdale on December 12th." Chairman James Lindley said: "Wally is the nicest lad I have ever met, we hope to make him very happy with us."

Indeed, he did make his debut against Salford, scoring three goals. He played another 17 times that season and his athletic prowess, raw speed and penchant for spectacular tries hinted at so much more to come. Former Hornets timekeeper Ray Myers said he was so fast "he could catch pigeons".

Under new Hornets manager-coach Joe Warham, Wally opened the 1954–55 season with a points-scoring blitz against Blackpool Borough: three tries and eight goals smashed the club's points scoring record. However, his bigger impact was to be seen on the terraces over the coming weeks. The first seven games of the season drew an incredible 75,689 spectators, the first time in the club's history that Hornets home crowds averaged more than 10,000. The average for the season would be 8,852.

Beyond that point, Wally began to struggle. There was much conjecture about whether coming from junior rugby to the hard-knock English rugby league had proven too big a step; whether he was getting enough ball with enough space to work his magic; and whether the expectations on his shoulders were too great for a young man a long way from home.

None of this was helped by club officials whispering to the local paper that some supporters had been telling Wally that he 'would be better off somewhere else'. The final straw came when Wally's fiancée Marlene came to join him in Rochdale and they married. From the outset he'd said in the national press that Marlene was coming to join him once he'd settled in. But the Hornets directors denied saying they'd find the couple suitable accommodation.

The rift became bitter. Wally disenchanted at his treatment; the club accusing him of attitude problems. In January 1955 he asked for a transfer. They put the fastest man in rugby league on the transfer list at £2,500. His last game for Hornets was an 'A' team game away to Liverpool City.

With the Challenge Cup transfer deadline looming, a move to league leaders, reigning champions and Challenge Cup holders Warrington broke down over an agreement on providing a flight back to Australia. On 1 February, two hours ahead of the transfer deadline, Wally made the 'most unexpected' move to Blackpool who had only joined the league at the start of the season and were in the market for a big name to boost their attendances. They were also rock bottom of the division.

Over the next two years he moved again, first to Salford, then to a high-flying Workington Town who spectacularly crashed to 20th in the table. Wally had had enough of England. In August 1959 he applied to the RFL for a clearance certificate that would let him play professionally in Australia. Workington rejected the request, claiming he had not fulfilled his obligations to the club. Wally returned to Adelaide, but the clearance certificate he needed never arrived. He never played professional rugby league again.

Hornets ended the 1954–55 season on a high. 20 wins and three draws from 36 games saw them finish 12th, the top half finish that the board had craved for so long. But Wally McArthur's departure felt like a talisman lost. There's a sense that the momentum gained over the previous years had begun to falter: that this was a club playing at its limit. Indeed, the club would wait 18 years for its next top-half finish.

The following season Hornets "… fell away considerably after a bright and successful start…" due to injuries, a loss of form, and a lack of reserves to fill first team spots — consequently crashing back to 20th in the league. The club had also begun to lean, again, on the Supporters' Association for financial assistance to undertake essential ground improvements. It fell to chairman James Lindley to reassure fans that "… in the last three or four seasons we have solved many problems and although I believe that we are on the right course there are still many more problems to be solved."

But the board were sending contradictory messages. James Lindley said "We are well aware of the weaknesses in the team but we are not going to be pitchforked into panic buying and I repeat what I have said many times when I say that any new players who do come to the Athletic Grounds will have to be better than the ones already on the books."

The report and accounts for the 1955–56 season showed a loss of £1,523 16s 7d, with the "… policy of the board in strengthening the playing personnel…" listed as one of the main reasons behind the loss. Having fallen eight places in the league, there must be questions asked on their 'strengthening policy'.

Clearly 'club policy' was a divisive topic that James Lindley saw fit to address: "Often the public do not see eye to eye with official policy, but they can rest assured that the directors are doing and will continue to do their very best for the well-being of the club." However, the shareholders didn't 'see eye to eye with official policy' either. At a subsequent AGM, the shareholders instigated a major change in team selection policy, whereby control of all team matters was to be handed over by the board to team manager-coach.

In the early stages of the 1956–57 season, it looked like it had worked. A young, inexperienced Hornets team raced away to second in the table, with the best away record in the league. They were in the top four well until late November, but the momentum could not be maintained. Hornets faded away to finish 16th with a 50:50 record of 19 wins from 38 games, and their stuttering form heralded what was described in the club's report and accounts as an 'alarming fall in attendances'. The figures don't lie, the average attendances for a five year period are:

1952–53: 5,781	1955–56: 7,460
1953–54: 8,792	1956–57: 4,378
1954–55: 8,852	

Looking for a reason, Wally McArthur came in 1953–54 and left halfway through 1954–55. The figures don't lie – he was box office. But it was the refusal of James Lindley's board to fulfil the promises they'd made to him that led to his departure.

Lindley tried hard to paint a positive picture: "On the whole the Hornets have given spectators value for money, and our assets in the way of players offset to some extent the poor financial position." In terms of addressing the season's loss of £1,121 0s 7d, the board "… set themselves against selling players to tide us over this period…" and called for the public to rally round, stating that it was "… the duty of followers of the Rugby League code in the town to play their part in encouraging the team and officials by their attendance at the Athletic Grounds."

With expenditure outstripping revenue for the duration of his board's five year tenure, Lindley needed to find new revenue streams. The Small Lotteries and Gaming Act, 1956 presented such an opportunity. The new act legalised the running of small lotteries by societies, for charitable, sporting or other purposes. "The present period is one bringing new hope," he said, "By the legalising of small lotteries, the Supporters Club have organised a scheme which should benefit the Hornets materially."

At the AGM, Lindley and his vice-chair G Halligan stood down. Newly co-opted director Arthur Walker offered himself for election. Within a year he was chairman. Described in some quarters as 'a flamboyant character', Arthur Walker was a cosmopolitan sporting polymath - always looking beyond rugby league's traditional boundaries for exciting sources of new talent. One of his first 'explorations' was in the emerging Italian Rugby League. Founded in 1950 by a group of rebels discontent with the policies of the Italian rugby union, officials, players and clubs launched their own competition (sounds familiar?), supported by the Rugby Football League. In November 1957, Arthur Walker welcomed Treviso halfback Ferdi Sarterato to the Athletic Grounds.

As the union game considered itself a strictly amateur sport at the time, he faced persecution by Italian rugby union authorities on his return, which meant that Hornets couldn't register him under his own name. In a stroke of genius, Hornets christened him 'Ferdi Corsi' after the famous Corsi brothers. As he was to play a key role in Hornets' last shot at Challenge Cup glory, it is only fair that here he gets recognition for his contribution under his real name.

Sarterato made his first team debut on 1 February 1958 away to Hull Kingston Rovers. Also making his debut that afternoon was Wiganer Jim Parr, who'd spent a year playing at Whitehaven. Having completed two successful trial games in the 'A' team, his £600 transfer fee was paid by the Supporters Club.

Hornets beat Rovers 17–12 at Craven Park that afternoon with tries from Reg Bailey, Ray Buxton and Norman Short plus four goals from Les Jones. On the way home the team bus stopped off for a few drinks and to watch the televised draw for the following week's Challenge Cup first round.

In the same establishment Hornets found the previous season's league runners-up Hull FC, on their way back to Humberside following a victory at Keighley. Star-studded Hull were again riding high in the league and, much to their amusement, they were drawn at home to play the lowly Hornets.

"The scoreboard won't be big enough!" shouted Hull hooker Tommy Harris across the pub. Jim Parr responded "We'll see Tommy, we will see". And Jim Parr was right.

A last minute try from Ray Buxton secured an against-the-odds 16–13 victory over the high-flying Airlie Birds at a snowy Boulevard. In front of a partisan crowd of 15,987 the Hornets forwards dominated the feared Hull pack all afternoon. Buxton also scored Hornets other touchdown, with Les Jones kicking five goals. Given that Hull would be crowned Rugby League champions at the end of the season this was a genuine giant-killing act.

Captain George Parsons leads Hornets out for the 1958 Challenge Cup semi-final against Wigan at Swinton. Despite a heroic effort, Hornets went down 5–3. (Rochdale Hornets Heritage Archive)

Hornets chairman Arthur Walker (left) welcomes Treviso half-back Ferdi Sarterato to Hornets. To avoid issues with the Italian Rugby Union, Hornets registered him as 'Ferdi Corsi', named after the famous Corsi Brothers. Sarterato scored Hornets' only try in the 1958 Challenge Cup semi-final. (Rochdale Hornets Heritage Archive)

Such was the impact of that victory that, in the following week's match programme, Hornets announced that messages of congratulations had been received at the club from far and wide, including a telegram from all aboard HMS Ark Royal which was on manoeuvres in the Mediterranean.

Hornets were first out of the hat in the second round draw, but it was only on the Wednesday that their opponents were confirmed following Bradford Northern's victory over Bramley in a tie that had previously been postponed due to snow.

With another tough battle to come, Hornets arranged an additional daytime training session on the Wednesday before the Bradford game, followed by a club night out to see Aladdin at the Palace Theatre in Manchester.

On Saturday 22 February, Bradford were duly dispatched at The Athletic Grounds 11–8, thanks to a Norman Short try and four Les Jones goals. The quarter-final saw Hornets drawn at home against Yorkshire Cup finalists York. Two Norman Short tries and a Les Jones goal Hornets edged out the visitors 8–5 to secure the club's first Challenge Cup semi-final for 10 years. In a case of sporting déjà-vu, it would be against Wigan at Station Road.

On 29 March 1958, heavy rain had persisted all morning in the North West, which didn't bode well for a fast, open game. With 28,597 spectators packed into Station Road for the Challenge Cup semi-final, the rain eased off just before kick-off.

Hornets had been unchanged throughout their cup run, but come the day of the semi-final the team had one enforced change. Star prop Bill Hanson had been injured a couple of weeks earlier and was replaced in the Hornets' line-up by 30-year-old former Warrington prop Ken Livesey. With Hanson not fit in time for the semi, Livesey kept his place in the side. Against a Wigan team that boasted international class players from one to 13, the Hornets team on the day was: Teddy Cahill, Ray Buxton, Les Jones, Norman Short, Ferdi 'Corsi' Sarterato, John Chisnall, Johnny Fishwick, Ken Livesey, Ray Dagnall, Alan Scholes, George Parsons, Reg Bailey, Jim Parr.

The first half was a tight, full-blooded affair with Hornets refusing to yield to the favourites. Wigan were reduced to 'bull-at-a-gate barging to get clear' and Hornets had 'the answers to all the ordinary-looking Wigan moves'. The teams exchanged unsuccessful penalties, and a high tackle on Teddy Cahill left him dazed and struggling, but Hornets remained resolute. Even the legendary Billy Boston was kept in his box by some hard-hitting defence. One report said: "Boston wandered far and wide in search of an opportunity, but Rochdale were most unwilling collaborators ... Buxton tackled Boston brilliantly as the winger was gathering pace for an all-out assault on the line." A 37th minute penalty edged Wigan in front and, in a rare moment of lucid play, Ashton and Sullivan combined giving Wigan a try out wide. Half time Wigan 5 Hornets 0.

The second half reverted to stalemate. The heavy pitch turning the match into a forward battle, leading to long periods of very little cohesive progress from both sides. Just before the hour mark, Hornets' cogs clicked, Johnny Fishwick fed Ferdi Sarterato in for a deserved Hornets try. Les Jones' conversion attempt drifted agonisingly wide, leaving Hornets chasing the game in the last quarter. One report said that Wigan "never found a way to kill off Rochdale", but they clung on to claim their sixth visit to Wembley.

Hornets opened the new Railway Side stand extension on Saturday 27 September 1958 for Hornets 'A' versus Barrow 'A'.
(Rochdale Hornets Heritage Archive)

It was Ferdi 'Corsi' Sarterato's last appearance in a Hornets shirt. He returned to Italy an evangelist for rugby league. Two years later he played two games for Italy against the Kangaroos, in Padova and his home town of Treviso. Jim Parr went on to play 223 games for Rochdale Hornets, scoring 13 tries.

The semi-final was far from a classic. SH Yates wrote in *The Liverpool Echo*: "I saw Wigan qualify for Wembley by beating Rochdale Hornets with as grim and unexciting a display of Rugby as could be imagined." Another report summed up Hornets' disappointment: "A great display against the odds is small compensation for the Hornets which went down by a paltry two points, just a goal away from the glamour of Wembley and its trimmings."

Just a goal away. Again, so close and yet... Indeed, the great question remains: if Hornets had won either of the two Challenge Cup semi-finals they played over this period, would it have changed the trajectory of the club? Would the money, the media exposure – the 'trimmings' – have ignited a new hope of cup finals, silverware, big crowds and a place among the game's elite who built dynasties through the 50s and 60s that helped secure their futures. Were the two cup semi-final defeats bigger opportunities lost than just the chance of a trip to Wembley?

Hornets ended the 1957–58 season in 19th place and recorded a loss of £1,323 4s 7d. It would be another nine seasons before they would finish above 20th.

As their fans have learned over the years, it's the hope that kills you in the end.

References

Manchester Evening News - Saturday 25 May 1946
Manchester Evening News - Friday 25 October 1946
Bradford Observer - Monday 15 March 1948
Derby Daily Telegraph - Saturday 3 April 1948
Bradford Observer - Monday 14 February 1949
Manchester Evening News - Friday 18 February 1949
Yorkshire Post - Monday 21 February 1949
Bradford Observer - Wednesday 20 February 1952
Daily Mirror - Thursday 21 February 1952
Yorkshire Post - Saturday 20 September 1952
Rochdale Hornets Football Club Report and Accounts 1946–47 to 1957–58
The Hornet 1948–49 to 1957–58
Daily Mirror Friday 20 November 1953

Daily Mirror - Wednesday 25 November 1953
Daily Mirror - Friday 27 November 1953
Liverpool Echo - Wednesday 19 January 1955
Yorkshire Post and Leeds Intelligencer - Wednesday 2 February 1955
Liverpool Echo - Monday 31 March 1958
Runcorn Weekly News - Wednesday 2 April 1958
A Centenary History of the Rochdale Hornets Football Club Company Ltd: R. Fletcher - 1971
The Glory of Their Times: Crossing the Colour Line in Rugby League: P. Melling, T. Collins - 2004
http://wigan.rlfans.com/news.php?readmore=1366
www.loverugbyleague.com: "Wales face Italy for the first time" - 30 September 2010

8. 1961: Vinaka Fiji

Fiji is a small group of islands bathing in the tropical marine climate of the Southern Pacific Ocean. The total population of Fiji is around 800,000 people. Its two largest islands – Vanua Levu and Viti Levu – are home to 87 percent of them. They are surrounded by hundreds of smaller islands with populations ranging from 10 to 500 people.

Beyond the beautiful tourist resorts dotted around the island, three-quarters of Fijians live on Viti Levu's coasts, either in the capital city of Suva or in smaller urban areas such as Nadi (pronounced 'Nandi') where the airport is located, or Lautoka, where sugar-cane is the main industry. Temperatures in the cool season average 22°C. Fiji is also 10,000 miles from Rochdale. Literally half a world away.

Unsurprisingly, given its spirit of adventure, the story of how Fijians crossed the world to play rugby league in a Lancashire mill town has been told and retold so many times that it has become shrouded in club folklore.

There is, in fact, a great deal of unsubstantiated speculation around precisely when Hornets' chairman Arthur Walker first saw the Fijians play. What is indisputable is that Walker's vision brought the Rochdale-Fijian connection together.

Walker was not just Rochdale Hornets' chairman, he was a shrewd businessman and well-connected, both in- and outside rugby league. With the personality of an entrepreneur, plenty of energy and access to cash, he was a man of big ideas.

The commonly told story is that Walker saw Fiji play Australia in Sydney when he was down-under with the Great Britain touring side, and that was where he had the idea of bringing powerful, athletic Fijian players to Rochdale. A couple of sources that refer to him as 'Hornets Chairman' have that date as early as 1954 – but as Walker didn't join the Hornets board until two years later, that seems unlikely.

Great Britain did tour Australia in 1958, but Fiji didn't play the Wallabies in Australia that year. It does seem possible that Walker saw the Fijians play a year earlier. In July 1957, en-route back to the UK after the Rugby League World Cup in Australia, Great Britain stopped off in New Zealand to play the Kiwis as part of a combined Great Britain / France XIII. Also in July 1957, the Fiji rugby union side began their tour of New Zealand.

However that first encounter came about, Walker noticed two players who looked and played so differently than the rest of the Fijian team. The sheer size, speed and character of these two individuals was overwhelming – as if he were watching adults playing against a group of children.

One of them was Orisi Dawai, a ball handling centre with tremendous vision and strength. Dawai was a double international. He'd represented Fiji as a sprinter and high-jumper at the 1950 Empire games in Auckland and from 1954 he was a regular in Fiji's national rugby union side. Between his two sporting careers, Dawai served for two years with the Fijian army in Malaya.

His speed, ability to read the game and unselfishness in the interests of his team, saw him made captain of Fiji on rugby union tours of New Zealand in 1957, Tonga in 1958 and Australia in 1961.

The other player to catch Arthur Walker's eye was a six feet four inches, 17 stone flying winger called Josefa Levula, a Fijian sporting superstar blessed with electrifying pace. Levula emerged as a unique sporting talent in 1951, when 3,000 fans packed Suva's Buckhurst Park to watch Suva and the Northern District contest the national rugby final. Suva had won the trophy for 10 straight years, but 21-year-old Levula scored four tries to break their decade of dominance in Fijian rugby union.

In the same year, he toured with the Fiji rugby team to New Zealand where he scored two tries in a 21–14 victory over the New Zealand Maori. His performance saw him chosen as one of the year's best five players by the *Rugby Almanack of New Zealand*, they described him as: "... a great wing three-quarter, we believe the world's best."

Across the Tasman, when Fiji played Australia, his extraordinary ability was also recognised by the Australian press. On seeing him in full flight, The *Brisbane Courier Mail* dubbed him the 'Flying Fijian'. They wrote of the "... phenomenal stride and speed of the Fijian Rugby Union team's six feet two inches winger, Joe Levula... (the) speed of Levula over 220 yards is reputed to be near the Olympic record class." And he went on to prove them right.

In February 1954, Levula became the first Fijian to finish on the podium in the Australian Athletics Championships. During the heats of the 100-yard dash he blasted home in just 9.72 seconds. In the final, he was only beaten by seven-times Australian 100 yards champion Hector Hogan. Levula also produced a bronze medal performance over 220 yards. A month later, Hogan equalled the world 100 yards record.

On home soil, in a local Fijian athletics competition, Levula bettered his Australian performance, winning the 100 yards in a blistering 9.47 seconds. By 1954, Levula was serving in the military in Malaya and his achievements on the track had caught the attention of legendary American Olympian Jesse Owens, who was in Malaya with the United States Information Service. Owens won the 1936 Olympic 100 metres gold medal with a time of 10.3 seconds, but he'd heard of a Fijian who ran the 100 in under 10 seconds, and he wanted to meet the man who could run faster than himself. Owens engineered a diversion to the small town of Batu Pahat where the Fijian contingent was based just to meet Josefa Levula.

Capped 17 times by Fiji's rugby union side, Levula was renowned for running over the top of opposing wingers rather than round them, his sheer size and power proving too much for his opponents. The *Fiji Sun* described Levula's distinctive playing style: "His high-stepping action was allied to an aggressive temperament." It described facing him as: "... the thunderous approach of a menacing figure whose eyes burned like the light of an express train." It was this intensity that made Arthur Walker determined to bring Fijians over to England to play rugby league for Rochdale Hornets. But he came up against a problem.

Walker's interest came at a time when the Paramount Chief of Fiji Ratu Sukuna did not allow Fijians to leave the country. He believed that Fijians belonged to Fiji and they were forbidden from going overseas except for educational purposes. Even then, they had to return home at the end of their studies. But when Ratu Sukuna passed away in 1958, it opened the doors for the people of Fiji to explore the world.

In early 1961, Walker took the bold move of placing an advertisement in the *Fiji Times*, inviting rugby players from the Pacific to come and play rugby league for Rochdale Hornets.

One of the first responses came from the long-time Fijian national captain Orisi Dawai. Dawai requested that he would only travel to England if his cousin could join him in the UK. His cousin? Jo Levula. How could Hornets say no?

Coming from a country where rugby union was tantamount to a religion, leaving to go and play professionally in England was a big thing for the people of Fiji, and the pair were given a heroes' send-off when they left. By September of 1961, the impending arrival of the two Fijians was making headlines across the UK too: "Fiji RU Players Arrive Next Month" shouted The *Coventry Evening Telegraph*. "Two Fiji Rugby Union players, Orisi Dawai and Joe Levula, who were recently signed by Rochdale Hornets Rugby League informed the club by cable today that they will arrive in England early in October." The news was received less favourably by the Fiji Rugby Union, who slapped the pair with a life ban.

The pair arrived at Manchester Airport on Friday 13 October 1961, met by Arthur Walker himself. Whisked to face the press at the Athletic Grounds, Jo Levula modestly claimed to be 'something of a goalkicker'. When challenged to show off his skills, he landed two kicks from 30 yards – in his bare feet! Orisi Dawai said: "We are looking forward to our stay in Rochdale and hope that we settle down into the side as quickly as possible. It is very cold, but not as cold as we expected it to be."

With jobs as storemen lined-up, Levula and Dawai signed four year playing contracts at £4 10s per week plus a £6 bonus for every win, making them Fiji's first professional rugby league players. The following day they watched their very first game of rugby league as Hornets took on Wigan at Central Park. Hornets went down 20–6, Billy Boston scored two tries for Wigan.

A week after their arrival, the pair made their 'A' team debuts at home against Liverpool City. The game ended in a 14–14 draw, with the Fijians scoring all of Hornets' points between them. Dawai crossed for a try and Levula scoring a try and four goals. 1,525 curious Rochdalians came to see history made; it was five times the normal size of an 'A' team crowd.

Levula and Dawai played with so much finesse and strength that they made the game look easy, and *The Rochdale Observer* marvelled at the Fijians' "unorthodox tactics", which "delighted spectators, with Dawai on the right often finding Levula on the left with his long passes."

The Hornets versus Blackpool match programme from 28 October said: "Joe Levilla and Orusi Dawai (sic) made their debut on Saturday with the 'A' team and received a great ovation from the crowd. How very nice of the 1,500 crowd to turn up and make them feel at home. Many thanks to the 'A' team for playing so well with them, enabling them to score all the points. These two boys will travel to Blackpool today (on 'A' team duty) to get really fit before they are launched in the first team."

The two made their much awaited first team debuts on 11 November 1961 at home against Whitehaven. This time, the match programme spelled their names correctly: "Our Fiji players Joe Levula and Orisi Dawai are playing today. This is the first time in the history of rugby league that any Fijians have played in senior rugby in this country. These lads like an encouraging shout, and these very nice boys deserve everything you can give them." The game ended in a 6–6 draw, Hornets had led 6–2 at the break.

Left: The original two Fijians, Joe Levula and Orisi Dawai arriving in England and being met by Hornets officials. (Courtesy *Rugby League Journal*)

BBC television rugby league commentator Eddie Waring interviews (left to right) Orisi Dawai, Laitia Ravouvou, Joe Levula and Vote Drui at a snowbound Athletic Grounds. The contrast between Fiji and Rochdale could hardly have been greater. (Rochdale Hornets Heritage Archive)

Joe Levula (left) and Hornets director Alan Ellis prepare to push over a pile of pennies for charity at the Old Clock Face pub on Toad Lane, Rochdale in January 1962. The pennies were collected for the Leonard Cheshire Home at Honresfield House. Interestingly, before Honresfield House became a care home, it was owned by Sir Alfred Joseph Law MP, the donor of the Law Cup.
(Rochdale Hornets Heritage Archive)

Joe Levula, Voate Drui and Orisi Dawai were joined by Litai Burgolevu and Gideon Dolo as their South Sea Serenaders group captivated audiences throughout the Rochdale area.
(Rochdale Hornets Heritage Archive)

Despite their low-key start, the Fijians created a buzz around the town. Spectators were excited to watch a new style of open rugby being played at the Athletic Grounds and fans would even turn up on training nights, eager to get a glimpse of these now famous Fijians. Even fellow players were starstruck when they saw them practicing goalkicks, especially in their bare feet.

As Levula and Dawai settled into life in Rochdale, the people of the town took them to their hearts, admiring how they acted both on and off the pitch. Hornets made sure they were well looked after, putting them up in a house at 305 Milnrow Road – a stone's throw from the Athletic Grounds. Taking care of them was the family of former Hornet Tommy Woods, his wife Leah made sure everything they needed was catered for. Over time, the house was to become a 'refuge' for all Fijians coming to Rochdale. And, by the end of January 1962, another two were already on the way.

In his programme notes, Arthur Walker announced their impending arrival: "Two new Fiji forwards have been signed and this was only made possible by the donation of £1,000 from the Supporters' Club and, unless the public rally round us and give us better support this is the last signing we can possibly expect. We are steadily losing £100 per week."

The two Fijian forwards were a tough, rugged utility called Voate Drui and a six feet six inches giant of a man named Laitia Ravouvou. Both had unique playing styles: Drui was like a rampaging bull, but had slick ball-handling skills. Ravouvou had a laid-back approach to the game, but would constantly terrorise the opposition with his defence and attack. He'd also played international rugby union in the same Fiji side as Levula and Dawai.

The new signings – along with Levula and Dawai's wives Lavinia and Margaret – embarked on their journey on Wednesday 31 January. They arrived at Heathrow late on the Thursday evening where they caught a connecting flight to Manchester, arriving in Rochdale on the morning of Friday 2 February. "They will be in the main stand at Saturday's match" chirped the previous week's programme notes. Presumably jetlagged.

Hornets supporters and the Fijians' Newbold neighbours chipped-in to make the players and their wives as welcome as possible. An appeal to help make their house more homely received what the club described as 'a magnificent response'. The programme notes from 3 February said: "We take this opportunity to thank everyone concerned who have worked to get the house ready this week and also to thank everyone who has given gifts to help completely furnish the house for these Fijians so they can all be together."

"We received gifts of bedding, a three piece suite, kitchenette, hall stand, carpets, two single beds, three sideboards, an extra couch and all kitchen utensils. One hardy supporter has brought them groceries. Thank you all very much."

As previously, interest in the two new Fijian players was high, with another bumper crowd of over 1,000 watching their 'A' team debuts in a defeat against Salford. Ravouvou made his first team debut on 24 March 1962, a 23–10 home defeat against Swinton. Drui had to wait a little longer, making his debut the following season on 22 September 1962 in a 22–7 defeat at Oldham.

Regardless of results, the four Fijians became local celebrities. From being invited by *The Rochdale Observer* to draw the winners of the weekly Young Readers' Club birthday competition to being interviewed by Eddie Waring at a snow-bound Athletic Grounds for the BBC's *Sportsview* programme, their presence in Rochdale created great interest.

The four became six with the arrival of Litai 'Big Ben' Burogolevu and Gideon Dolo for the 1962–63 season. Both had potential, but their opportunities were limited to 'A' team rugby. Conversely it was Hornets' seventh Fijian signing who, arguably, left the biggest impact on people's memories.

At six feet three inches and weighing in at over 16 stones, Apisai Toga (pronounced 'Tonga') arrived in Rochdale on 24 January 1964, signed on the recommendation of his step brother Ravouvou. Like Dawai and Levula before him, Toga was a Nadi rugby union product. Coupling a rampaging, no-nonsense attitude with his creative skills, he was cut out to become the star of the show.

One of seven rugby-playing brothers, Api – as everyone called him – was not just a gifted footballer, but a prodigious athlete. The very best of an emerging generation of Fijian rugby talent, he represented Fiji in the first South Pacific Games in 1963. His departure to play rugby league in Rochdale was bitterly mourned by the Fiji Rugby Union.

In a rugby union puff-piece condemning rugby league's 'weakening of its player potential' the union-sympathetic *Pacific Islands Monthly* wrote: "Understandably, although Fiji was happy that its image was enhanced in Britain, it was not so happy at the efflux of several fine representative players. One who went to England was Apisai Toga, a great man physically and a great forward on the field. In the North he did as much as anyone to enhance Fiji's image as a sporting country."

It just happened – in their eyes – to be the 'wrong' sport. Indeed, they placed the blame for opening Fiji's door to the 'scourge' of rugby league firmly on Hornets: "Fiji lost some of its finest union players to Rochdale Hornets and other North-of-England clubs, some of them as a direct result of an advertisement published in Suva by the Hornets' manager inviting Fiji players to come to Lancashire for attractive wages."

Apisai Toga made his Hornets debut on 15 February 1964 in a 15–8 home defeat against Workington Town. He became an instant favourite with Hornets fans, who loved his blockbusting playing style. He soon formed an explosive second row partnership with Ravouvou, and with Drui now a regular in the team, Hornets had a formidable pack.

By August 1964, Jo Levula's time at Hornets was over. After 80 appearances over three successful seasons in which he scored 37 tries and 207 points, he requested a transfer, unhappy at being left out of the pre-season Law Cup game.

A few days later – on the same day that Oldham's Johnny Noon agreed terms to become Hornets' new player-coach – officials from the newly reformed Bradford Northern travelled to Rochdale and signed Levula for a fee of £1,500. Only a week after his departure, it looked like Apisai Toga might just follow him to Odsal, after what Bob Fletcher in his centenary booklet describes as 'a difference' over money.

The Rochdale Observer explained the 'Toga Situation': "When the first of the Fijians were signed by the Hornets they were an unknown quantity, and Hornets took a risk. The Fijians agreed to play for Hornets and, in return, Hornets agreed to pay their return fare to Fiji. In addition, they were guaranteed a £10-a-week job."

"All agreed to these terms except Toga. He only signed professional forms which made him a player for life. Each season, however, each player signs playing forms, and this season Toga refused the terms. He asked for an exorbitant fee." The 'exorbitant fee' being £1,800.

A report from 27 August says that Bradford had: "... agreed terms for Hornets' dissatisfied forward Apesai Toga (sic), who refused to sign for the Rochdale club because the £1,800 signing-on fee he demanded was not forthcoming."

We can find no record of how the issue was settled, but Arthur Walker did say: "I think some people got at him and that he listened to a lot of bad advice from a lot of people."

Over the next three years, Toga's direct, destructive style made him one of the most respected second rowers in the English game. By the end of the 1966–67 season, he was one of the hottest properties in world rugby league and his growing value exceeded Hornets' willingness to pay.

Back in Fiji, Bob Godfrey, an Australian working for an airline at Nadi airport took an interest in Apisai's career and suggested he try his luck in Sydney. Api initially had conversations with South Sydney Rabbitohs, but they could not reach an agreement. That's when St George moved in – offering Hornets £2,000 (£30,000 in 2021) for him to move to Kogarah Oval.

Toga left Hornets in May 1967 having played 98 games and scored nine tries. As the first Fijian to play rugby league in Australia, Toga attracted a great deal of media attention and his barnstorming style established him as a popular fan-favourite. In his second season he was joined at St George by his brother Inosi and the pair soon gained cult-like status amongst the red-and-white faithful.

At the end of the 1972 season, Toga had returned to Fiji to visit his family. Shortly before he was due back in Australia he went swimming and cut his foot on some coral. He returned to St George for pre-season training, unaware that he had contracted Tetanus.

Just four days after returning to Australia, Api was running between Inosi and Steve Edge during a training session at Carrs Park, Kogarah when he collapsed. He was rushed to hospital with seizures, but died of the infection on 30 January 1973. He was 27 years old.

During his five seasons with St George, Toga played 38 games in reserve grade, 65 in first-grade and scored nine tries. An all-action giant on the field, he was described by all who knew him as the perfect gentleman off it.

His brother Inosi Toga says that Api saw the opportunity to play in England as a chance to mature and develop his game – and that he often spoke of how playing for Hornets in the cold, the wet and the mud of an uncompromising competition gave him the harder edge he needed to become a world-class footballer.

In the early 1960s the British Army was struggling with volunteer recruitment after the abolition of National Service. From Fiji, '212 Soldiers for the Queen' – 200 men and 12 women – enlisted in the British Army and would serve with distinction across the world in places as far-flung as Malaya, Germany, Northern Ireland and The Falklands. The 212 were required to come to the UK to complete their Army training. Among them was Mike Ratu.

Swapping Fiji for the depths of an English winter was something of a shock. Having arrived at Heathrow, he had to travel to Catterick in North Yorkshire where it was −2°. He had never been so cold – and he'd never seen snow. He recalls sitting down, shivering in the camp's mess, wrapped in as many blankets as he could put around him.

Through the window he could see some of his comrades out in the freezing cold, smoking. Mike says: "I went outside shouting at them 'What the hell are you doing smoking. Put them out!' It was only then that I could see that the 'smoke' coming from their mouths was the air. It was that cold."

It was while they were training at Catterick that Mike Ratu and other members of the 212 began visiting Rochdale at the weekends to meet Jo Levula and Orisi Dawai – two Fijian sporting legends. Mike says: "Years before, back home in the Fijian villages, people would gather round the radio listening to the Fijian national team play rugby. Whenever Orisi and Jo's name were mentioned, everyone jumped up and started screaming."

"They were definitely the biggest and most famous sporting icons of that era and it was a privilege to be able to meet our heroes."

Even though (at 30 years old) Joe and Orisi were a lot older than many of the 212 Soldiers, they were very accommodating to all visitors to their Rochdale home. Mike describes the meetings: "Orisi, being slightly older than Jo, played the father figure to all visiting Fijians. Whatever decisions needed making, it was always Orisi who had the final word. That was the culture of village life in Fiji. Wherever we were, whether we were sorting out problems, arranging places for people to stay or organising social events, respect to the village elders was paramount."

The gatherings at the house were the first steps the Fijians took in putting down roots in the town and building a community. Socialising was an integral part of the Fijian lifestyle in Rochdale – so much so, that some of the Hornets contingent, along with regular Fijian visitors, formed a musical group playing a variety of South Sea Island music.

Members included Hornets' Joe Levula, Voate Drui and 'Big Ben' Burogolevu along with regular visitors Fred Mua, Joe Kamanalagi, John Ravetali, Joe Saukuru and a Tongan called George Masi. Rochdale musician Tony Vasco completed the line-up.

In contrast to its Lancashire surroundings, the sound of paradise went down well in Rochdale and beyond. It even made international headlines. *Commonwealth Magazine* wrote: "The Fijians have added to their earnings - and to the fun they get in life - by forming a band, the South Sea Island Serenaders ... whose Pacific rhythms are popular all over the North of England."

Entertaining people at local pubs and social clubs, they would sometimes play at several different venues each night and fans would get up and sing alongside the band. It certainly created an atmosphere which the locals enjoyed and helped forge bonds between the Fijians and Rochdalians.

By 1964, Mike Ratu was based with the Royal Signals in Gloucestershire – and playing for Stroud Rugby Union Club's 1st XV. When the Fijian national rugby union team toured Wales and the South West that year Ratu, with his Fijian connection, was selected to play against the touring side.

The assistant manager and coach of the tourists was a Fijian sporting icon called Pat Raddock. Pat was also one of Ratu's old school teachers at Queen Victoria School back home in Fiji. Word had already got around about Ratu's strong tackling technique and powerful, direct running, so Pat made contact with Orisi Dawai, knowing that Mike Ratu had visited Rochdale with other friends of the 212.

He recommended that Ratu should have a trial with Hornets and the club agreed, giving him a run in the 'A' team on a Friday night at Swinton. This was followed by a first team trial the following Monday against Oldham, playing under the name A.N. Other.

Suitably impressed, Hornets signed Mike Ratu on 16 September 1965. His full debut came exactly a month later against the New Zealand tourists. The programme for that day references Hornets' pioneering recruitment history: "Traditionally, we have always been well to the forefront in introducing Commonwealth players into the side." The Hornets team against the Kiwis featured Ratu, Toga and Drui and battled to a creditable 10–4 defeat in front of a crowd of 7,075.

Two weeks later, the same three Fijians appeared for Hornets in the Lancashire Cup Final against Warrington at Knowsley Road. En-route to the final, Hornets had won 14–9 at Blackpool, 4–0 at home against Swinton with two goals and had convincingly stuffed Leigh 19–0 in the semi-final, with Toga scoring a try.

The 1965 Lancashire Cup Final was the first time the fixture had been played on a Friday evening, and its first time under floodlights. The programme for the game describes Hornets' Fijian contingent:

- Apesai Toga (sic), a second row forward, aged 24, 6ft 1in, 16st. A Fijian, who has been with the Hornets for over 2 years. A man of extraordinary strength and very difficult to stop.
- Voate Drui, forward, aged 26, 5ft 10in, 15st. Has played many games for Hornets with whom he became a member of the playing staff 4 years ago
- Mike Ratu, winger, aged 21, 6ft, 13st. Another Fijian - one of several on Hornets books. Signed from the Stroud (Gloucester) R.U. Club in recent times.

One match preview identified the Fijians as a real threat to Warrington, recognising how Hornets had: "... harnessed the power of strapping Fijian forward Apesai Toga (sic) to such an extent that Hornets supporters now rate the Fijian as one of the strongest and most dangerous attacking forwards in the game."

"Toga has developed into a very fine forward and it will take some effective tackling from Warrington to [stop] the six feet two inches 16 stone giant. He is a big favourite with Rochdale fans this season, who have coined the catch phrase 'We have a Toga in our pack' and it could have a significance which Warrington can hardly afford to ignore."

The article continues: "Another capture from the amateur code is Fijian winger Mike Ratu, a strong runner and sound tackler who was leading try scorer with Stroud R.U. Club last season."

On the eve of the final, *The Liverpool Echo* wasn't expecting a classic, they wrote: "On paper, there have probably been more attractive looking finals..." In retrospect, Hornets fans would probably agree: they lost 16–5 in front of an incredible crowd of 21,360. All Hornets' points were scored in the first half by Graham Starkey with a try and a goal.

In the following year, Hornets had floodlights of their own. They were switched on by Rochdale MP Jack McCann ahead of Hornets' game with Huddersfield on Saturday 24 September 1966. It was a major investment for the club, with the installation of lights costing

£8,750, £5,500 of which was provided as a loan by the Rugby Football League. Hornets won the game 9–4 in front of 3,912 supporters.

The last of the original wave of Fijians to play for Rochdale Hornets was Jonetani Kucuve. Like Mike Ratu before him, Kucuve was a winger – and a soldier from the 212. He signed at the start of the 1970–71 season, but only played a handful of first team games for the club.

Mike Ratu maintains Rochdale's connection with Fiji that spans the generations. Mike married a Rochdale girl and still lives in the town. His son Emon emulated his father and played for Hornets in the 1990s after a stint at Swinton. His grandson Michael became the third-generation Ratu to pull on a Rochdale jersey when he signed in 2013, having played with Leeds, Hull KR, Halifax and Swinton.

Fijian legacy

The influx of Fijian talent in the 1960s had an impact in Rochdale that went beyond rugby league. Having created a centre of Fijian culture for players of both rugby codes, the influence of those first pioneers has pervaded the town's sporting and social landscape ever since.

In the 1970s, Old Rochdalians RFC, now Littleborough Rugby Union Club, opened their doors to a new wave of Fijian players including Freddy Mua, Watisoni Rogose, Sisa Matadigo, Adama Rokotuni and former Hornet Mike Ratu. Along with them they brought their children – second generation Fijians growing up in Rochdale. Michael and Emon Ratu, Karl and Andrew Rogose, Phillip and David Rokotuni all played mini rugby at the club. This helped to keep Fiji in Rochdale's sporting spotlight – and strengthened the town's growing Fijian community.

As always, the social aspect was important. At the end of each season, Old Rochdalians would host a game which involved big names like Joe Levula and other Fijian rugby players taking on their 1st XV. This was followed by an 'Island Nite' - an evening of traditional Fijian ceremonies including dancing, singing, fire walking and the drinking of Kava.

Kava, or Grog as it is commonly known, is Fiji's national drink – a mild narcotic made from the roots of the Yaqona plant which are crushed into a pulp then dried. The resulting powder is then wrapped in a linen towel then soaked and squeezed in a bowl of water. Served in coconut shells, Kava looks – and initially tastes – like dishwater. First it makes your tongue go numb, but after a few cups the world seems a much better place.

More than an end of season event, it was a 'homecoming'; a social gathering that drew Fijians from all over the country – including the Fijian Ambassador who would arrive at the Club near Hollingworth Lake in a diplomatic car, followed by his security detail. Not only did the event bring in Fijian soldiers serving in the UK, over the years it was attended by the Fijian Prime Minister – and by singer Tanita Tikaram who has Fijian heritage.

In 2008 the Australian Fijian Rugby League Association played a four-match tour of England. As a mark of respect to those early pioneers, they based themselves at the Flying Horse Hotel in Rochdale. The week they arrived, it snowed. The entire squad was seen outside Rochdale Town Hall having a snowball fight. It was the first snow that many of them had ever seen. One of the tourists, Netani Suka stayed on in the UK, playing rugby league locally. He played in trials for Rochdale Hornets, but visa complications prevented him signing for the club.

Rochdale's Fijian connection was a major factor in the town being allocated the Fiji versus Ireland game at the 2013 World Cup. In the run-up to the game, a scratch Rochdale Hornets side took on the Bati in a warm-up match, going down 70–0 to a Fijian side packed with world-class NRL talent. In the World Cup, Fiji beat Ireland 32–14. The attendance of 8,872 set a ground record for rugby league. Fiji's legendary Captain Petero Civoniceva said of his time in Rochdale: "We have just been blown away by the reception we received since we've been here. We have learnt about the history we have here and it's something to be proud of. When we went to city hall, it was pretty emotional."

Playing at the end of a stellar international career; Civoniceva said that he would confirm his retirement from rugby league by leaving his boots in the UK when he returned home. He chose to leave them in Rochdale.

In the last 10 years, Rochdale's rugby league community has seen a resurgence in Fijian players. After the World Cup, Hornets signed Fiji International Ryan Millard for the 2014 season. Ben Komai Naulumata at Rochdale Mayfield played one game for Hornets under Bobbie Goulding and scored a try. He was followed by Jo Qaniuci via the Rochdale Cobras, whose club badge incorporates a Fijian palm tree, and Seta Tala who came through via Hopwood Hall College. And, when Hornets won the 2016 League One Championship final in Toulouse, they had Jo Qaniuci and Michael Ratu in the side.

Sixty years after Orisi Dawai and Jo Levula made their journey here, the UK`s largest and most active Fijian Association is based in Rochdale. Ensuring that there is a corner of not only Hornets', but Rochdale's history that will be forever Fiji.

References

worldrugbymuseum.blog: "Historic Rugby Internationals: Australia v Fiji, 1952" - 4 November 2019

Fiji Sun: "The Rise Of Joe Levula" - 14 March 2013

Fiji Sun: "Rochdale Welcomes Australian Fijians" 7 Dec 2008

thestar.com.my: "A word of praise from athletics legend Jesse Owens changed this Malaysian's life" - Saturday, 21 Jul 2018

The Fiji Times: "A long-term affair" - 22 October 2016

Coventry Evening Telegraph - Monday 11 September 1961

Liverpool Echo - Saturday 14 October 1961

Commonwealth Magazine: "Giants from Fiji make name in British Rugby" - undated.

Total Rugby League: "The remarkable story of Rochdale's Fijian pioneers" - 14 April 2020

Newcastle Evening Chronicle - Thursday 27 August 1964

Rochdale Observer 9 September 1964

Rugby League World: "Big Ap and Little Ap" - 27 March 1968 (Australian publication)

dragons.com.au: "Dragons Honour Apisai Toga"- 2 Jun 2016

Pacific Islands Monthly (Vol. 44, No. 3): 'Deaths of Island People' - 1 March 1973

Rochdale Rugby League Heritage: "Meeting Mr Toga" - 29 June 2015

Liverpool Echo - Saturday 23 October 1965

Liverpool Echo - Saturday 30 October 1965

skysports.com/rugby-league/news/12054/4614502/a-warm-welcome - 10 December 2008

loverugbyleague.com/post/civoniceva-blown-away-by-rochdale-reception - 29 October 2013

The 1965 tour to France

Selection de l' Aude loose-forward Pierre Escourrou looks to avoid Hornets hooker Kevin Ashcroft and winger Frank Hope in the game at Carcassonne on 29 May 1965.
(Both courtesy Mary Murgatroyd)

Kevin Ashcroft spots a gap in the Selection de l' Aude defence in the game at Carcassonne.

A poster for Hornets' French tour game against Racing Club Saint-Gaudinois Comminges XIII (Saint Gaudens) on 6 June 1965, described as a 'Grand International Match of Rugby League'

Cover of the programme from Hornets' game against an Aude Select XIII on 29 May 1965.
(Both courtesy Mary Murgatroyd)

Action from the 1960s and 1970s

Tom Pimblett (far right) flies down the wing at the Athletic Ground for Rochdale Hornets against Warrington. Malcolm Price is far left; Hornets' captain Graham Starkey is to the left of Tom. Warrington's Parry Gordon is also running back to cover.
(Courtesy Tom Pimblett)

Rochdale Hornets line up for a pre-season photo shoot with the moors in the distance. Tom is far right on the front row. Others in the back row include: Mick Mooney [far left], Peter Birchall [third from left], Eddie Tees [sixth from left] Ken Roberts [fourth from right] and Henry Delooze [third from right]. Ken Tighe is far left on the middle row. (Courtesy Tom Pimblett)

Hornets take on Blackpool Borough at home. Blackpool's Billy Boston is tackled by Hornets' second-rower Alan Hodgkinson. Tom Pimblett, who scored twice in the game, is next to him on the right. On the far right is another former Wigan player, Ray Ashby. Ashby and Boston had both been capped by Great Britain, and Alan Hodgkinson later became a British Lions tourist, so three British Lions played that afternoon. Billy Boston had a couple of seasons at Blackpool after he retired from Wigan.
(Courtesy Tom Pimblett)

9. 1971: Myler

In August 1961 Hornets tabled a loss of £10,819, blamed principally on a 31.6 percent year-on-year fall in attendances and a corresponding decrease in season ticket sales. A £10,816 donation from the supporters' club just about offset the loss and the board "... regretted that such a fine effort can merely be used to subsidise the existence of rugby league in Rochdale."

The 1961–62 season echoed the downbeat mood of the club's financial performance: just nine wins from 36 league games saw Hornets finish 24th, with first round exits in both the Challenge and Lancashire cups. It set the tone for the decade to follow. Despite the flair of their Fijian contingent and tour games against the Kiwis and the Kangaroos, Hornets spent most of the 1960s treading water.

Between the 1961–62 and 1970–71 seasons, Hornets won only a third of their competitive games in all league and cup competitions – Challenge Cup, Lancashire Cup and BBC2 Floodlit Trophy. In that period, they only made it past round one of the Challenge Cup twice and, despite getting to the Lancashire Cup Final in 1965–66, a 16–5 defeat to Warrington at Knowsley Road, they managed only another two Lancashire Cup wins.

The table doesn't lie; during those 10 seasons, Hornets' highest league finish was 18th – finishing 20th or lower in the league on the nine other occasions. Chairman Arthur Walker had a plan, though. At the end of the 1969–70 season he quit to head-up the new board at Oldham.

His replacement, Ted Stockley, was a brief appointment, passing away soon after taking the chair. Stepping in to replace him at the Athletic Grounds was former Hornets prop Alan Ellis. Having joined the club immediately after the Second World War, Ellis's first team appearances had been limited so he went back to the amateur game, returning to Hornets as a director in the late 1960s.

He was appointed chairman at a real low-point. After a game against Barrow yielded receipts of less than £60, Ellis said: "It didn't cover the cost of the programmes." The 1970–71 season that followed was a disaster. Amid player disaffection, falling crowds and some frankly awful performances, Hornets crashed to 25th in the league with just nine wins from 34 games. It was an ignominious way to celebrate the club's centenary.

On 24 April 1971, almost 100 years to the day since the club's formation, *The Rochdale Observer* was relentless in its scathing criticism. It wrote: "There have been campaigns when fewer points have been collected, but never have the terraces been so deserted, never has the spirit been lower and not since the 'bad old days' immediately after the Second World War, has there been as much concern for the future."

"For the diehard it has been a nightmare of a season with discontent running from top to bottom. The result has been the loss of over 600 supporters a week and a financial crisis the directors seem unwilling to talk about."

Indeed, the directors were held squarely responsible for the whole sorry situation; at fault for not pulling the players together to get to the root of the creeping discontent that ate away at the season; at fault for their knee-jerk firing of coach Derrick Schofield after a narrow

13–7 Challenge Cup defeat at Warrington; at fault for not scotching rumours that the club was somehow awash with cash to sign new players when no such money was available.

If the board had told the public about the true financial picture much earlier, that might have drawn more sympathy towards the club. As it was, the board held off revealing the truth about the club's dire circumstances, by which time people had grown tired of waiting for any kind of news and had begun to vote with their feet.

The Rochdale Observer was stunned at their behaviour: "The directors must never forget that they are where they are because of the shareholders and their first duty is to them. In times of stress they must be willing to give up much spare time to try and help the club out of difficulties. Not every member of the board can claim to be doing that, unfortunately."

Despite a combined £2,700 annual rent from the speedway and the petrol station at the Kingsway end of the ground – and a £500 donation from the Supporters Club – Hornets were £2,000 into their bank overdraft and owed £2,500 to other creditors. The situation was described as 'serious'.

After a home game against Blackpool yielded a gate of just £87, £13 short of the players' wage bill, chairman Alan Ellis painted a bleak picture: "On top of that we had to pay the referee, the two touch judges and the police. There are officials' wages as well. There's only one way we can go from here and that is up. We cannot go any lower."

Ellis knew that if Hornets were to break out of their rut of mediocrity, it needed a big change. And, in 1971, names didn't come much bigger than the Great Britain captain, Frank Myler.

Frank Myler was a supremely gifted rugby footballer. After only a handful of 'A' team games, he made his senior debut for Widnes at the age of 17 against Liverpool City at Naughton Park on 27 December 1955 and scored two tries. Over 13 seasons he played 367 first team matches for Widnes, including a Challenge Cup Final at Wembley in 1964, in which he scored a try in the Chemics' 13–5 win over Hull Kingston Rovers.

He played 20 times for Lancashire and made his Great Britain debut in 1960 against New Zealand at Odsal. GB won 23–8 and Myler scored a try. At the end of the 1966–67 season, the unthinkable happened. The Chemics were short of forwards and short of cash. St Helens offered £6,000 plus forwards Ray French and Dave Markey in exchange for Myler, an offer Widnes couldn't refuse. Myler was sold to St Helens.

Frank went on to make 144 appearances and score 46 tries during four seasons at Knowsley Road, in which he played an integral role in creating Saints' brand of fast, open rugby. He capped an outstanding 1969–70 season with a Harry Sunderland Trophy-winning man-of-the-match performance in the Saints' 24–14 victory over Castleford in the League Championship Final.

Already a Great Britain tourist to Australia and New Zealand in 1962 and 1966, he captained of the 1970 Rugby League Lions to tour Australia and New Zealand. Great Britain lost the first test in Brisbane 37–15, the only defeat of the tour. They hit back with a stunning 28–7 victory in front of over 60,000 in Sydney, clinching the Ashes with a 21–17 victory in the deciding test on 4 July 1970, making Myler the last Great Britain captain to win the Ashes. For good measure, Myler also skippered the Lions to a three test whitewash of the Kiwis. In total, Myler played 24 tests for Great Britain between 1960 and 1970, nine as captain.

Hornets coach/captain Frank Myler takes on the Hunslet defence at the Athletic Grounds on 8 April 1972 (Rochdale Hornets Heritage Archive)

Hornets chairman Alan Ellis (left) was forced out by Littleborough haulier Jack Grindrod (right) in 1973. Ellis never forgave his former friend. (Courtesy Jim Stringer)

And, just when the Australians had had enough of Frank Myler, in November 1970 he steered Saints to a resounding 37–10 victory over the touring Kangaroos at Knowsley Road.

Described as 'a natural footballer with an intense will to win' and 'a shrewd tactician with electric pace', his experience at the highest level of the game was second to none. So, when Alan Ellis heard that St Helens were prepared to release Myler, he seized the opportunity. In May 1971, Ellis and secretary Fred Kershaw headed for Widnes Golf Club, where they persuaded the 32-year-old Myler to come to Rochdale Hornets as player-coach.

In his first training session, Myler made two observations on the squad he'd inherited: the forwards lacked size and the backs lacked pace. With a modest budget, Myler went shopping for players. And with the Ashes-winning captain at the helm, Hornets suddenly had pulling power.

First stop was former Great Britain captain, Bill Holliday. Lured away from Swinton to become Myler's skipper, he was signed in a deal done at Manchester docks where he worked as a ship's electrician. Close behind came 1966 Great Britain tourist Willie Aspinall, signed from Warrington, then Lancashire County three-quarter Brian Glover arrived from St Helens.

Myler knew the depth of the talent pool at St Helens and who wasn't really getting a chance to show their capabilities. Peter Gartland and Bill Sheffield were kicking their heels in the 'A' team at Knowsley Road. Former Saints youngster John Butler had gone to Keighley after his deal at Knowsley Road fell through at the last minute, but he never really settled at Lawkholme Lane. He was transfer listed initially at £6,000, then at £4,000. Frank Myler drove a hard bargain and Butler joined Hornets for £1,000.

Within weeks, Myler's influence was obvious, with the press predicting that Hornets would: "... certainly upset some of the big guns this season...". One report read: "Frank Myler, Hornets player-coach and former Widnes, St Helens and Great Britain star is doing an excellent job of shaping Hornets into a formidable force. There is no doubt that Myler has quickly become a strong favourite with the Hornets crowd. His team are playing some exceptionally good football and will be difficult to beat."

Nowhere was that more noticeable than in the BBC2 Floodlit Trophy, where Hornets picked off some of the game's biggest names. A first round, two-legged tie saw Hornets spank Oldham 42–18 on aggregate. Round two brought Hornets a trip to the Willows where they dispatched Salford in a shock 17–15 win. In round three, Myler masterminded a narrow 6–5 victory over his old club Widnes.

Despite Hornets' good form in the competition, no-one anticipated their 30–8 hammering of Hull FC in the semi-final. Waiting in the final was Myler's former team St Helens. However, by now, Hornets were being taken very seriously: "That splendid win by Frank Myler's Rochdale side [over Hull] has again emphasised that they could spring a surprise on Saints at Knowsley Road," wrote *The Liverpool Echo*.

"Rochdale's win also means a return to St Helens for a number of former Knowsley Road men including of course former skipper Frank Myler. The others include winger Brian Glover, forward Bill Sheffield and scrum half Peter Gartland."

"The build-up to this final comes with both sides scoring some exceptionally good wins, [and] sets the stage for a really grandstand finish. Both teams play the fast, open brand of football and they look certain to have a night of supreme football entertainment."

The final, however, was anything but open. A crowd of 9,255 braved heavy rain to see a game dominated by tough defence on a heavy glue-pot pitch. With both sides struggling desperately to find a crucial opening, Saints' Kel Coslett and Hornets' Joe Chamberlain exchanged penalty goals in the first quarter. Despite Myler's constant probing, another Coslett penalty gave Saints a narrow 4–2 lead at the break.

The second half was in much the same vein. Myler tried everything he knew to conjure-up the one break that would unlock the game, but it never came. With Hornets' defence also refusing to be breached, it took a further two Coslett goals to win a tryless Final 8–2. Despite the defeat, Frank Myler's Hornets had shown that they could go the distance with the best in the game.

Impressively, in his first season, not only did Frank Myler steer Hornets to the Final of the BBC2 Floodlit Trophy, Hornets also won 21 of their 34 games to finish eighth, their highest league position for 58 years, to secure a place in the Championship play-offs. More importantly, his brand of exciting rugby increased gates by 150 percent.

On St George's Day 1972, eighth placed Hornets beat ninth placed Wakefield 18–13 to set up a return match at Knowsley Road against a St Helens side that hadn't lost at home for eight months. Another close encounter was predicted, but, for Hornets, the absence of their talismanic stand-off due to injury proved too great a handicap to overcome. The Hornets went down 17–5 to end a transformative season in which Frank Myler had played in 33 of Hornets 48 games.

The 1972–73 campaign was one of consolidation, with Myler adding more experience to his side. Goalkicking former England and Lions rugby union star Tom Brophy was signed from Barrow; loose-forward Tony Halmshaw became Hornets' record signing from Halifax, a record broken within weeks when the club paid £7,000 for the enigmatic back-row forward Terry Fogerty.

For Myler, though, his playing days were almost over. After 17 years, the bumps and strains of week-in, week-out rugby league were proving harder to shake off. Having scored eight tries from 15 starts, plus one from the bench, Frank Myler selected himself at stand-off for the final game of his career on 7 January 1973: Hornets versus Salford at the Athletic Grounds. Salford nicked it 13–11.

However, Myler's influence remained clear. League doubles over Hull KR, Barrow and Oldham, a 22–8 pasting of Wigan and a 7–7 home draw with Leigh followed by a 12–5 win at Hilton Park established Hornets as a team to be wary of. Ending the season with 20 wins from 34 games, Hornets finished 11th on points difference to give them another run at the Championship play-offs.

A first round 14–10 win at high-flying Salford teed-up a trip to league leaders Warrington. The Wire still smarting after Hornets had handed Alex Murphy's side a shock 17–5 league defeat at Wilderspool a month earlier. Warrington gained revenge with a 16–9 win, but more importantly, with the league split at 16th to create two divisions, Hornets found themselves in the top flight of rugby league.

With Myler confined to the bench for the 1973–74 season, he needed a stand-off to steer his side round the park. His solution was to turn John Butler into a world-class number six. His improvement caught the press's attention: "... signed from Keighley as a loose forward,

Myler has switched him very successfully to stand-off half and he is turning in some outstanding displays." Having made that same transition early in his career, Myler poured every last drop of his experience into Butler. This transformed his game and got him selected for the 1974 Lions tour of Australia and New Zealand, where he played in 18 matches.

While Hornets' league form was pretty ordinary, in the Players No.6 Trophy they looked like serious contenders. Myler masterminded an impressive campaign, built not on champagne rugby, but on hard-working, gritty defence. In the first two rounds, Hornets disposed of Huddersfield and York without conceding a try. Leeds came to the Athletic Grounds in the quarter-final and Hornets limited their opportunities to produce a shock 7–5 win, through a massive last minute drop-goal from Bill Holliday, dug out of the touchline mud from almost half-way. The semi-final saw Bramley swept aside 14–2.

A hotly contested Final was anticipated, with Hornets seen as a genuine threat to an all-star Warrington side. Though the in-form Wire were tipped as favourites, the final was expected to pose a genuine challenge. One journalist wrote: "Hornets are one of the most improved sides of recent seasons and a key man in that revival is Frank Myler, ex-Widnes, St Helens and Great Britain star who is doing a super job of welding Rochdale into one of the game's most powerful teams."

Created in Frank Myler's image, John Butler had become Hornets' major attacking threat, scoring five tries on their run to the Final. He was seen as the player who made Hornets tick and was expected to give Warrington's experienced stand-off Alan Whittle a run for his money. Myler's astute eye for forwards hadn't gone unnoticed either: "Warrington's strong pack will find they have their work cut out against a Rochdale set strengthened with such signings as Tony Halmshaw, Terry Fogerty and Bill Holliday." Indeed, Fogerty was considered so important that the board flew him back from his holiday for the game.

On Saturday 9 February 1974, a convoy of Ellen Smith's coaches headed to Wigan's Central Park to see a rare Hornets appearance in a major cup Final. On a heavy pitch all the early pressure came from Warrington. Hornets' defence conceded a penalty for Whitehead to give the Wire a 2–0 lead. Hornets responded well; a right wing run by Norman Brelsford followed by a trademark break from John Butler were both held-up just short. On 13 minutes, Whitehead stretched Warrington's lead with another penalty, but Hornets dug-in.

With the half-hour mark approaching the Warrington pressure finally told; prop Nicholas bumping off two tacklers to score. Whitehead adding the extras for a 9–0 lead. And things got worse for Hornets. John Butler had taken a knock and was struggling with a hip injury.

With Warrington ending the half strongly, Myler needed his side to hang on to the break so he could get his charges into the dressing room and regroup, but with just two minutes remaining Warrington centre Noonan forced his way through a tiring Hornets defence to give his side a 12–0 half-time lead. The Hornets fans in the 10,047 crowd were shattered to see Hornets emerge for the second half without Butler. But after just three minutes of the second half, Hornets belied their loss. The ball moved swiftly through hands to squeeze Norman Brelsford in at the corner. A dubious second try from Noonan was converted by Whitehead to stretch the Wire's lead to 17–3, but Hornets went wide again; this time Dave Taylor scored. Bill Holliday kicked the goal from the touchline and, with half an hour left, Hornets fans' optimism was reignited.

Left: Hornets captain Bill Holliday (8) leads the team out for the 1973-74 Players No.6 Trophy final against Warrington at Central Park. He is followed by Norman Brelsford (2) David Taylor and John Butler (6). Hornets lost 27–16. (Courtesy Jim Stringer)

Below: A Rochdale team group from 1974. Back: Tony Halmshaw, Henry Delooze, Bob Welding, Bill Holliday, Peter Birchall, Alan Hodgkinson; centre: Bill Sheffield, Jim Crellin, Norman Brelsford, Peter Clarke, Bill Aspinall, Rod Tickle; front: Stuart Whitehead, Tom Brophy, Peter Gartland, John Butler, John Hammond, Ray Harris. (Courtesy *Rugby League Journal*)

But Rochdalian hearts were broken when Warrington landed a double whammy in the six minutes around the hour mark. Converted tries from Bevan and Whitehead left Hornets chasing down a 27–8 deficit in the last quarter. Hope flickered briefly when Norman Brelsford raced 40 yards to score, but Warrington restricted Hornets to a last-minute consolation try from Tom Brophy; Hornets went down 27–16. A report in the *John Player Yearbook* said: "Rochdale players quietly took the losers' medals, knowing that they had given of their best. Even a man as professionally dedicated as Frank Myler could not ask for more than that." Hornets' reward for reaching a major final? A much needed £2,500 - in cash!

It was a good result in another good season. With 13 wins and two draws from 30 games, Hornets finished 10th, a place above Wigan, to cement their place in the First Division. Indeed, the team looked set to kick-on in the 1974–75 season when Myler dropped a bombshell. With two businesses to manage, and no longer able to exert direct influence on the course of games, he stood down as Hornets coach.

He said: "I had enjoyed my spell at Rochdale immensely and the string to my bow as player-coach was fine, but the part of coaching where I had to sit helpless on the bench unable to do anything if the lads were playing poorly was frustrating. I had no thought of becoming a manager or coach ... and after 19 years in the game ... I'd had enough."

Just like that – after three incredible seasons – the Myler era was over. His biggest legacy at Rochdale was to raise expectations. He gave supporters a three-year glimpse of what could be possible – big name signings, international caps, cup finals, slick rugby – and set the standard against which Hornets coaches would be unrealistically measured for the next 20 years. The fact that his name is still spoken in reverent tones 50 years later, underlines the impact he had on the club. Indeed, when Hornets supporters elected their all-time team in 2015, Frank Myler was far and away the most popular choice of coach.

Frank Myler's arrival in 1971 coincided with the arrival in the Hornets boardroom of wealthy Littleborough haulier Jack Grindrod. But the success Myler delivered on the pitch hid off-field acrimony that caused a rift in the board. Alan Ellis had been instrumental in getting Jack Grindrod to join the board, but proved to be his downfall. In May 1973 *The Rochdale Observer* described "... a bloodless battle in the boardroom" with one faction firmly against the other following Jack Grindrod's nomination of Peter Morgan for a seat on the board.

It continued: "After three tedious shareholders meetings peace was declared, but not before Mr Grindrod replaced Alan Ellis as chairman, leaving one faction of directors ruefully licking their wounds." Ellis remained as a director, but never forgave his former close friend.

References

Rochdale Hornets Report and Accounts 1961 to 1967
Rochdale Observer Saturday 20 March 1971
Rochdale Observer 24 April 1971
Liverpool Echo - Monday 1 November 1971
Liverpool Echo - Saturday 11 December 1971
Liverpool Echo - Wednesday 15 December 1971
Liverpool Echo - Friday 28 April 1972
Liverpool Echo - Saturday 2 February 1974
Rochdale Hornets v Hull: Programme Notes Wednesday 30 October 1974

John Player Yearbook 1974–75
Rochdale Observer – 9 May 2009.
www.telegraph.co.uk: 'Frank Myler, Great Britain rugby league captain who led them to their last Ashes victory' - 22 April 2020
www.saintsrlfc.com: 'FRANK MYLER – A TRUE GREAT OF RUGBY LEAGUE' - 28 March 2020
A Touch of Class - The Frank Myler Story: Maurice Bamford, 2010
Rugby League Journal - Issue 70, Spring 2020

10. 1975 to 1979: The yo-yo years

In October 1974, Myler was replaced by former Hornet Graham Starkey, who had been coaching at Wigan. A scholar of the game, Starkey was a coaching innovator. As coach of Oldham three years previously, he'd pioneered the concept of the pre-match warm-up and had taken the, then, unusual move of watching games from the stand because he could get a better view of play. At Central Park he'd become the first Wigan coach to insist that the coach should pick the team. Starkey is seen now as a coach ahead of his time, but in 1974 he had huge shoes to fill and an equally large burden of expectation.

He started his tenure impressively, delivering wins against Wakefield Trinity and Leeds. Three wins from the next four games followed, but any optimism of remaining in Division One was dealt a hammer blow when injuries to scrum-half Peter Gartland and loose-forward Tony Halmshaw sent Hornets into a tail-spin.

Yorkshire county centre John Hughes and goalkicking full-back John Maloney were both signed to add some attacking firepower – Maloney was Hull FC's second-highest ever points scorer – but wins were few and far apart.

A 10–9 Easter Monday defeat at Warrington effectively put paid to Hornets' First Division survival hopes. The result was made more bitter by the fact that the Wire snatched victory courtesy of a 'ghost goal' that appeared to pass outside the uprights. Hornets finished the 1974–75 season next to bottom of the First Division with just eight wins from 30 games and were relegated.

Through the summer of 1975, all the talk coming out of the Athletic Grounds was of 'instant success' in the Second Division and a swift return to the top flight, but a 29–2 home thrashing by Oldham in the Law Cup indicated that some recalibration of expectations might have been required.

The 1975–76 league season started with a home game against Blackpool Borough, who had ended the previous season 3rd bottom of the Second Division. Hornets could only manage an unconvincing 7–7 draw. The *Rochdale Observer* described it as "... an abysmal start..."

A 5–2 win over Leigh at Hilton Park eight days later raised hopes, but they were dashed the following week when Hornets crashed out of the Lancashire Cup, losing 22–10 to Workington. Hornets' see-saw form continued. A 22–10 win at Blackpool helped erase some of the opening-day embarrassment, only for Hornets to slip-up at Halifax a week later, going down 23–14.

The Players No.6 Trophy offered some respite, only for injury-hit Hornets to crash 33–10 away to Hull KR. Hornets fans hoped for a bounce-back response from their side. Instead, Hornets stumbled to a 2–2 draw against a "woefully weak" Workington Town. Next up, a Floodlit Trophy preliminary round tie against reigning First Division Champions St Helens.

Given Hornets' stuttering form, fans clearly anticipated a hammering and only 805 people showed up. Those fans present were rewarded for their effort with an inspirational performance; Hornets faded late in the game to lose 15–7.

Instead of seeing the performance as an augur of potential, the Hornets board saw it as one defeat too far. At the following night's training, Graham Starkey was invited to step into the boardroom, while 'A' team coach Henry Delooze ran the players through their drills.

Reports suggest that chairman Jack Grindrod had a frank exchange of views with Starkey, but firing him with two years to run on his contract would have been a costly move. "We had already had discussions with Graham twice this week and asked him to strengthen the side," said Grindrod. "We told him that money was available, but he didn't come up with any answers, so we asked him if he wanted to resign. Graham said he wanted to think about it for a couple of hours and he left the club saying he would telephone back. This he did and told us that he wanted to resign from the position as coach."

A frustrated Starkey interpreted events somewhat differently: "I had already met the board twice in the week, but we could not agree on a matter of policy. When I was called in on Thursday night I was asked to resign. So I resigned. I don't want to add anything further than that because it would only start a slanging match."

Jack Grindrod clearly had thoughts of recreating the magic formula of the Myler era: "We will advertise the vacancy and wait for the results. It is too early to say who will get the job, but we could be looking for a player-coach to take over." Meanwhile, the board asked Henry Delooze to take charge of the first team until a suitable Myler-clone could be found.

That weekend Hornets welcomed 'a very nondescript' New Hunslet to the Athletic Grounds and crashed 15–11, having led 7–2 at half time. *Rochdale Observer* reporter Stan Townsend was scathing in his criticism: "It's difficult to pin-point one specific reason for the Jekyll and Hyde performances Hornets are handing out weekly, simply because there are so many areas of the game in which the team is falling down. Planned moves are scarce, backing up is poor, passing inaccurate and finishing is terrible." Stand-in coach Delooze summed the performance up in a single sentence: "We were pathetic."

Off the field, the names of potential coaches began to circulate around the club - all of them snugly fitting the Frank Myler template of top-flight playmaker turned player-coach. Kel Coslett (St Helens), Chris Hesketh (Salford), Doug Laughton (Widnes), David Hill (Bradford) and Ray Batten (Leeds) were all considered suitably experienced.

Jack Grindrod kept his cards close to his chest. "We haven't decided what course to take," he said. "It will depend on the board meeting as to how we go about it." But with a Friday night game at Whitehaven to plan for, preparations were left with Henry Delooze, who was now in charge of managing both 'A' team and first team affairs.

Described as a 'highly mobile' loose forward and 'a useful goalkicker', Henry Delooze began his professional rugby league career with Warrington, going on to make 53 appearances for the Wire between 1960 and 1966. He then moved to Barrow and played for them at Wembley in their 17–12 defeat to Featherstone Rovers in the 1967 Challenge Cup Final, where he uncharacteristically missed three first-half penalties. He signed for Hornets in September 1967 and made his debut on 20 September against Salford at the Willows.

The *Rochdale Observer* had Delooze down as a potential outsider for the Hornets coaching job, recognising that: "... his knowledge of the game is unquestionable and he has the right straight-talking no-nonsense approach the team needs to drive them through the present crisis..." Delooze underlined his credentials by coaching Hornets to victory at Whitehaven.

In the boardroom, though, the directors only had eyes for a top-class player coach. With a list of applicants including "... players with recent international experience..." Jack Grindrod confirmed that a player-coach in the Myler mould was what was needed at the Athletic Grounds. An announcement was promised within a week.

As October ticked over into November, the AGM came around, with the board facing questions about the lack of action in finding a coach. There had been reports that the fee being asked for transfer-listed loose forward Tony Halmshaw had been slashed in an attempt to hasten his sale, get him off the books and create surplus cash to entice a player-coach. However, there was still no sign of an appointment.

At the AGM, which, at 23 minutes was one of the shortest on record, Jack Grindrod shrugged off shareholders' concerns about the coaching situation. "The matter is well in hand", he said. "We have decided to put back the final selection for a few weeks in view of the excellent performance of the team last weekend."

Two things had become clear during Delooze's temporary charge. He clearly had the ability to get the players working as a unit. More importantly, while the Hornets board was busy flirting with household names like Kel Coslett and Doug Laughton, Delooze really wanted to be coach of Rochdale Hornets. Jack Grindrod confirmed it, saying: "... Henry Delooze has made it known that he wants to be considered for the position [so] we must give the situation chance to develop."

No sooner had Delooze been confirmed as a candidate than Hornets lost 15–6 at lowly Huyton. Delooze was gutted. "We were diabolical," he said. "This defeat won't have helped my chances of staking a claim for the coaching job one bit."

As Hornets looked no nearer to appointing a big-name player coach, Delooze felt he was treading water. With no mandate to make major changes, it was difficult to plan ahead thinking that the next game could be his last. Through his obvious frustration, the fans could sense his concern that the board's procrastination was affecting morale within the squad. "I hope I am given the chance," he said, "but most of all the directors need to name someone quickly for the players' sakes. This game is all about team spirit and you have to get the players in the right frame of mind before they go out on the field."

Certainly, it is clear how Delooze would have struggled to gain the confidence of the players when he hadn't yet been given full control. And he was even beginning to doubt his own abilities as a coach, saying: "I was overlooked when Frank Myler packed in and, if it happens again, I might consider moving on."

Despite the stasis in the boardroom, Henry Delooze prepared Hornets for a trip to South Leeds to take on New Hunslet. a phoenix club born out of the ashes of the original Parkside-based club. Having sold their ground for £300,000 in 1973, the Hunslet board had simply divvied up the proceeds among their shareholders and wound up the club.

With New Hunslet now playing at the nearby Greyhound Stadium, games there brought a list of challenges for visiting coaches. The small heavy pitch reduced the potential for fast, open rugby; the greyhound track between fans and the field contributed to a lack of atmosphere; the pitch itself was surrounded by a chain-link fence - and players could often be seen picking up dog faeces from the pitch before kick-off. If all of that wasn't disconcerting enough, the ground also sported American Football style 'tuning-fork' goal-posts.

It was hardly surprising that Hunslet had gone unbeaten at home. Despite this litany of potential obstacles, Hornets turned in an exhibition of controlled rugby to produce a shock 19–12 win, courtesy of tries from Mick McLaughlin, Warren Ayres and Steve McGiffen.

Twenty four hours after the Hunslet victory, the Hornets board announced the new coach. After weeks of promising a 'new Frank Myler' they gave Henry Delooze the job. Almost immediately the board began backing away from their original plan. "At first, when Graham Starkey left, the idea was to go for a player-coach," said secretary Fred Kershaw. "But recent events have brought about a change of heart. We have offered Henry the job and it is in his hands now."

Despite wanting the job, Delooze was cautious about accepting the role. Myler and Starkey had both been offered three year contracts, whereas he had been asked to take the job until the end of the season, with his position being reviewed then.

"Obviously, I have to look at the situation very carefully," he said. "I want the job, but what I have to think about is for how long will I be in charge? I don't want to put my head in a noose and then find the floor has been taken away come the end of the season, if we do badly."

While Henry Delooze wrestled with his decision, there was much wrangling off the field too, with reports of a boardroom split that put Jack Grindrod's control of the club in jeopardy. Grindrod, due for re-election the following month, moved quickly to dispel any talk of a rift: "As far as I am aware there are no moves afoot to get me out. Of course, we have differences of opinion, that can be expected on any board, but this doesn't mean that we are split down the middle."

There was speculation in the press that the six man board comprising Jack Grindrod, Roy Hindle (vice-chair), Alan Hindle, Ray Taylor, John Leeson and Tom Mercer was finding it difficult to agree on "certain matters" when a three-versus-three vote created a stalemate.

Hopes of solving the situation were raised when a 'local businessman' offered his nomination for the board at the AGM several weeks earlier, but he backed out only hours before the meeting for 'personal reasons'. Having denied a split, Grindrod said: "At this very moment we are making moves to co-opt someone to bridge the gap." Unfortunately, the unnamed party was unable to join the board due to 'other commitments'. When pressed further on whether his place as chairman was at risk, Grindrod shrugged off the suggestion: "If I don't get back into office I will have to think very seriously about my position at Hornets, but I don't think that will occur."

Two weeks after Jack Grindrod's denial of a rift, director Tom Mercer resigned from the board. His departure was surrounded by whispers of a 'clash of personalities'. He'd sat on the board for less than 12 months.

Grindrod was adamant that the resignation was, like so many others, for 'personal reasons' and he waved away rumours that the pair had not seen eye-to eye for some time. "Like any board, we have our differences of opinion on certain matters, that is only natural," he said. "But to say that we were at each other's throat is just not true."

Despite his protestations that Mercer had walked out for reasons known only to himself, Grindrod was quick to refute any ideas that other resignations would follow: "As far as I am aware no-one else is contemplating resignation. If there are to be any more, the people concerned have not declared their intentions to me." He was also at pains to deny that the resignation had anything whatsoever to do with his pending re-election as chairman at the upcoming AGM.

When pressed further on whether any particular issue had sparked the resignation, Grindrod pushed back: "Not as I know of, you will have to ask Mr Mercer himself. If he wants to make a comment, then that's up to him."

It's clear that this flippant suggestion was intended to shut down any discussion. But Tom Mercer came back all guns blazing. Quite simply, the 'personal reason' that he left the board was that he couldn't stand Jack Grindrod and that he could no longer serve the club under his chairmanship.

Interestingly, Mercer used exactly the same phrase that Graham Starkey had used when asked about the details of his resignation: "I don't want to start a slanging match, but I do want to clear up a few points made by the chairman."

Mercer explained how his fractious relationship with Jack Grindrod began before he even joined the board: "About nine months before I was elected, the possibility of my being co-opted was discussed, but I was told later that Mr Grindrod declared that he would resign if this took place."

He went on: "During the time I have been on the board, I have made many attempts to bury past differences with the chairman, but to no avail. There have been several heated arguments between us, both inside and outside the boardroom, culminating in a very ugly scene on the team coach coming back from Whitehaven..."

"Mr Grindrod has since apologised for the incident." Despite every other director asking Tom Mercer to reconsider his decision, he maintained that he couldn't continue on the board while Grindrod was chairman. A fortnight later, Jack Grindrod was re-elected to the chair, given a unanimous vote of confidence by the same directors who had pleaded with Mercer to stay.

On the field, Hornets were gaining momentum under Henry Delooze, but gates at the Athletic Grounds had almost halved. Interestingly, the reason appeared to be on their doorstep. By December 1975, a multitude of terraced streets that had fed Newbold's main artery of Vavasour Street were demolished to make way for a new social housing scheme. Garden Street, Bilberry Street, Windmill Street, Basil Street, Grafton Street, Jackson Street and many more, including the once bustling Vavasour Street itself, all razed to the ground, leaving Hornets' traditional catchment area a wasteland. And the people who lived there? Gone – scattered across the borough and further afield.

The Rochdale Observer contemplated the devastating impact on Hornets: "There must have been a good contingent of supporters who lived in the vicinity and have opted to stay away from home games because of the travel across town. Before they just had to walk a few hundred yards, whereas now they might have to catch a couple of buses."

"With over 20 streets, possibly with an average of 50 houses per street, being demolished, it could mean that somewhere in the region of 5,000 people have been moved from the area. If, say, an average of one in five was a Hornets fan, that totals 1,000. Take away the possibility that one in five still makes the trip and a figure of 800 comes out as an estimate of the fans missing at home games because of the upheaval. A chilling thought."

Indeed, even when the new housing was built, replacing 5,000 people who had grown-up with Rochdale Hornets in their community with 5,000 'incomers' with no affinity with rugby league, never mind Hornets, and you can imagine the scale of the challenge of having to effectively replace 800 'lost' supporters.

And who could blame the dispersed fans for missing games? Four bus journeys costing half as much as your admission to the game made watching Hornets a costly business. And travelling an hour each way, on public transport, on a Sunday, was hardly an enticing prospect for fans weaned on leaving home at quarter to three for a 10-minute stroll up Milnrow Road.

What was certain was that people would rather watch a winning team, and results suggested that Henry Delooze had turned the tide. Despite injuries to Tony Gourley (bruised hip), Terry O'Neil (broken jaw), Wally Jones (broken hand) and Tony Allen (knee ligaments), December 1975 saw Hornets run into their best form of the season. After a shaky start, they were now being (prematurely) talked about as potential outsiders for promotion. Certainly, Delooze had made his side not only difficult to beat, but also capable of finding ways to win.

Nowhere was this more obvious than over a tricky Christmas period. Hornets took three points from a possible four with a tenacious 10–9 win against Leigh and a gritty 7–7 draw at Barrow, all achieved without scoring a single try. In the New Year the wins kept coming. Having already won at Whitehaven, victory at Workington secured a rare Cumbrian double as the players began to believe in their abilities.

Delooze's no-nonsense approach resonated well with the senior players. His shrewd additions of Wally Jones and Dave Hawley added some real quality to the side and, against the odds, Hornets found themselves as shock candidates for a promotion place.

With the top four promoted, and Barrow odds-on favourites for the top spot, Hornets found themselves fighting for one of the remaining places with Workington, Leigh and Hull. Coming into the last weekend of the season, the battle for the top four was tight and the maths were simple. Hornets had to win at York to go up. If they lost, Hull would take their place. The season, which had begun in such disappointing style, would be defined by these 80 minutes.

Going to Clarence Street was never the easiest of trips, made more difficult on this occasion by York's inclusion of the legendary Neil Fox at loose-forward. York set off at a torrid pace and, with Fox pulling the strings, dominated the first half to lead 8–2 at the break.

At half-time, a limping Tony Halmshaw was replaced by Alan Robinson. The second half was just minutes old when Warren Ayres skipped through two tackles to send him galloping into space; prop Alan Hodkinson in support to take the inside pass and score under the posts. Maloney was on target with the conversion, the gap now one point.

Then, in the 52nd minute, came one of the most (in)famous moments in Hornets' club folklore. Out of nowhere, a flare-up at a play the ball saw Neil Fox swing a wild kick at Hornets hooker Peter Clarke. With Clarke laid out receiving "extensive attention", referee Stan Wall had no alternative but to send Fox off. Intervention by a touch judge then saw Clarke follow Fox up the tunnel.

Closer investigation suggests that the incident was craftily choreographed by Clarke himself. Having spent the first 12 minutes of the second half niggling the former Great Britain

100

loose forward, the wily hooker needed something that would really push Fox's buttons. Speaking about the incident many years later, Fox said: "I felt a boot up my backside, and I wasn't going to let it go."

For Peter Clarke, getting sent off was an occupational hazard. For the squeaky-clean Fox, it was the first sending off in a long and distinguished career. Hornets' loss of Clarke was an inconvenience, but Fox's dismissal was devastating for York. Without his leadership they crumbled, and Hornets took total command.

Penalised for stealing the ball, York were pushed back to their 25 yard line. Mick McLoughlin set up the play, Wally Jones created the gap, finding Warren Ayres in support to outpace the cover and give Hornets the lead. John Maloney added the extras.

And it was Ayres who shattered not only York's hopes of victory, but the promotion hopes of Hull FC as well. Having launched a huge touch-finder, he sent Alan Robinson on a blockbusting run that ended with Tony Gourley touching down. Maloney added the conversion. In the closing stages, a McLoughlin drop-goal settled Hornets nerves and, with York in disarray, Hornets hit them with a late sucker punch when Alan Robinson produced a fine individual try. Maloney's conversion sparked wild celebrations among the travelling Hornets fans.

Hornets returned to the top flight as runners-up. Peter Clarke received a one-match suspension for his part in the Neil Fox incident. And, given the way Henry Delooze's tenure began, promotion at the first attempt was validation of his credentials as a more than capable coach. All round, a job well done.

Hauling Hornets back into the First Division had come at a cost. With attendances down by over 1,000 on the previous season, Hornets' gate revenue had fallen by almost £7,000. Season ticket revenues were also down by £1,000. This shortfall was compounded by the need to pay 19 win bonuses, a sum estimated at £10,000.

On the expenditure side, the club spent £6,000 on transfer fees, with the rates, heating and lighting bills leaping by £1,000. Total outgoings for the season were £57,233, an increase of around £12,000 on the previous year.

Despite a £15,719 profit from the VP lounge, Supporters Club donations of £2,572 and £31,500 from lottery and Stock Car returns, the club made a loss of £8,917.48. Club secretary Fred Kershaw said: "It has only been due to the efforts off the field that we are able to produce what the club feels is a good statement of accounts... but there is little chance of us surviving if we have to face another year such as the one we have just witnessed."

Having secured promotion, the board and Henry Delooze sat down to discuss which players would be retained for the forthcoming tilt at First Division survival. Rather than introduce wholesale changes, they retained all but three of the squad that got them promoted. They also introduced the best of the club's younger players, including goalkicking full-back Chris Storey, scrum-half Tony Allen and Great Britain Colts players Steve Kurtianyk and Jeff Brearley.

Delooze had also added some hard-nosed experience since his appointment in the shape of Wally Jones, Dave Hawley and Mick Henighan, augmenting a seriously talented pack already containing Alan Hodkinson, Tony Gourley, Tony Cooke and Alan Robinson. In the backs he signed Featherstone centre Dave Hartley, utility player John Rawlinson and added

Blackpool flyer Jimmy Johnson on the wing. Hopes were high that this mix of youth and experience could give it a real dig in the top flight.

Ahead of the season, Delooze took a young side to Watersheddings in the Law Cup and, despite some teething troubles, came away with a creditable 21–21 draw. Full-back Chris Storey came away with damaged ribs and an appointment at the hospital for x-rays.

The first benchmark of Hornets' progress came at Widnes in the Lancashire Cup. Despite going down 25–13, they competed well against the 'Cup Kings' and hopes were high that Hornets would spring an upset when Widnes visited the Athletic Grounds a week later in the BBC2 Floodlit Trophy preliminary round. As it was, Widnes sneaked a narrow 5–2 win, but Hornets looked capable of competing with the best in the game.

The league season started with a visit from St Helens and Hornets stunned the First Division by holding off a late Saints surge to win 24–21. Hornets then travelled to Odsal, minus first-choice half-back Mick McLoughlin. He was joined on the injury list by Tony Gourley who had a recurrence of a shoulder injury. Shored up by 'A' team players, Hornets crashed 15–7 in a drab affair that saw Mick Henighan and Dave Hartley limp from the field injured.

Next up, an injury-hit Warrington came to the Athletic Grounds with a virtual reserve team. Ahead of the game, Hornets utility back Gordon Baker pulled up in training with a pulled hamstring. Delooze drafted in 20-year-old forward Steve Kurtianyk as cover. Hornets lost 21–14. The *Rochdale Observer* described them as 'a shambles', full-back Norman Turley was the architect of Warrington's win, kicking a makeshift Hornets side all over the park.

As the injuries continued to pile up, the defeats kept coming. A 31–24 loss at Featherstone saw prop Dave Hawley and second rower Tony Cooke join the casualty list. In the week before the trip to Castleford, centre Steve McGiffen was ruled out with a foot injury. A Hornets side made up of 'A' teamers and patched-up regulars lost 37–26 at Wheldon Road.

Jack Grindrod voiced his frustration: "We're really up against it at the moment regarding injuries and, bar going out and signing a complete set of forwards there is little we can do." There was little that Hornets could do at the Willows either; Salford ran riot to win 33–6.

Hornets were now in dire straits, to the point where Colts (Under-19s) and 'A' team games were being postponed due to the number of players being drafted up a grade to cover the first team's injury crisis.

In response, the board called round every club they could to see which players were available to help stem the tide. But there were few takers. One group of Yorkshire-based players under consideration would only come if Hornets picked them up and brought them to training! Desperate, the club arranged a minibus.

Having lost eight straight games, Henry Delooze's decimated side faced Widnes at home. Circumstances suggested that the Chemics would win easily, but Hornets put up a brave show to lose narrowly 11–5.

While Delooze had been battling for weeks to name 15 fit players, the directors had formulated a plan to address the crisis. On Tuesday 16 November Hornets chairman Jack Grindrod and club secretary Fred Kershaw drove to Henry Delooze's Warrington home and sacked him. It was exactly 12 months to the day after he took over from Graham Starkey.

At first Delooze was philosophical: "We have just not been getting the results and I am the obvious person to blame, since it is the coach who always bears the brunt in a situation such as this. But I feel injuries have played a big part in Hornets being bottom of the pile."

Back in Rochdale, Hornets' directors revealed former St Helens captain and Welsh international Kel Coslett as the club's new player-coach. Secretary Fred Kershaw said: "The directors feel this is the only way we can cure the current situation. They feel the best way is to have someone on the field to dictate and Kel Coslett is their choice."

Behind the facade of professionalism, Delooze was crushed. The *Rochdale Observer* wrote emotively on the fallout: "While new coach Kel Coslett busied himself with the affairs of organising Hornets training sessions, deposed coach Henry Delooze smouldered in the background trying to hide his feelings of hurt..."

Delooze's regret was palpable: "I haven't a clue what I'm going to do with myself yet. I complete 10 years with the club next year so I am able to apply for a benefit." To add insult to injury, the board told him that they'd honour the remaining five months of his contract if he stayed as a player. "Whether or not I will take up the challenge and stay with Hornets as a player is something I have yet to decide," he said. "Obviously I have some hard thinking ahead of me in the next week or so."

Like the loyal pro he was, Delooze reported for training with the 'A' team just 48 hours after receiving the bombshell. But when it came to it, he couldn't face playing reserve rugby for the club he'd coached just a week before.

New coach Kel Coslett was a Bynea boy - a valley village deep in Welsh rugby territory. As one of Wales's rising stars he looked set for a glittering career in the union game. By the age of 20, he'd played for top sides Llanelli and Aberavon and won caps against England, Scotland and France in the 1962 Five Nations Championship.

Later that year, Coslett came home from an afternoon shift at the steelworks to find St Helens directors Lionel Swift and Basil Lowe sitting in his front room. "To be honest," he said, "I didn't even know where St Helens was... but I was confident in my own ability, so I signed not knowing the difference between both codes."

In the 1962–63 season, Coslett played in every game for St Helens, scoring in all but one of them. The next season, he cemented his place in the side. But his third season at Knowsley Road was cut short after just three games when he broke his leg - against Rochdale Hornets.

With his full-back spot taken by Frank Barrow, Coslett's only way back into the side was to reinvent himself as a loose-forward, and he became the keystone of Saints' outstanding pack for the next decade, setting club records for most appearances (531) and points (3413).

Coslett also captained Saints to two Challenge Cup Final wins at Wembley. In 1972, in a 16–13 victory over Leeds, he kicked five goals and won the Lance Todd Trophy. Then in 1976, Saints beat Widnes 20–5. This one was very satisfying after the media had dubbed the Saints team 'Dad's Army', due to the numbers of players in the side aged over 30.

The plan beyond that season was for Coslett to retire from playing and join Eric Ashton's coaching staff, the intention being that he'd be groomed as Ashton's eventual replacement. Hornets had tried to sign Coslett as player-coach 12 months earlier as a replacement for Graham Starkey, but felt that Saints' demand for a £4,000 fee was too much. Now, effectively 'retired' from playing, the asking price was only £1,000. With designs on carving himself a coaching career, Coslett felt that the Hornets job was "too good to turn down".

His first task was to prepare a Hornets side for a trip to Wigan. Having consulted captain Alan Hodkinson and 'A' team coach Peter Gartland on selection, they had a near first-choice pack available for the first time in weeks. Coslett picked himself at loose-forward.

Inspired by his presence, Hornets ran Wigan close, eventually going down 31–21. The turning point was Hodkinson's sending off for a high tackle on Green Vigo, which earned him a two match ban.

Slowly, but surely, wins started to come and Hornets hauled themselves off the foot of the table, overtaking Leigh, Oldham and Barrow. Most notably, a trip to Naughton Park to play Widnes the week before the Chemics were due to play their third successive Challenge Cup Final produced a shock 12–9 win that gave Hornets an outside chance of First Division survival.

However, the maths was not in their favour. With three games to play, Hornets sat fourth bottom on 20 points, above them were Workington on 25 points. It meant that Hornets had to win all of their remaining games, against Castleford, Hull KR and Wigan, and Workington had to lose all theirs, against Widnes, Wakefield and Featherstone.

Coslett understood the magnitude of the task in hand: "If we win all three games it will be a tremendous achievement. Here we are, having won our last four matches, possibly going to finish on 26 points, which accounts for half of our fixtures as wins, and still heading for relegation."

In the first of the three games, Hornets belied their league position to turn-over third-placed Castleford 14–10. But the cheering had hardly died down before news started coming through that Workington had beaten Widnes at Naughton Park. Despite a brave turnaround of the season, Hornets were, again, relegated into the Second Division.

The last game of the season, at home to Wigan, goes down in Hornets' history as their inaugural sponsored game. For the sum of £250 George Holt Builders' Merchant of Walkden became Hornets first ever match sponsor.

The first half was hard to watch. Neither side able to crack the other's defence: 0–0 at half time. The second half was hardly better. Hornets only response to two Wigan tries, one converted, was two John Maloney goals. Hornets ended a frustrating season with a whimper, going down – in all senses – by 8-4.

The £50 player-of-the-match award was presented by Mr BS Langton - director of match sponsor George Holt Ltd. It isn't recorded who won the award.

Despite relegation, Kel Coslett was quick to confirm that he was staying with Rochdale Hornets: "I'm not the type of person to leave a sinking ship. The club, the players and most of all the fans have been tremendous in the past months and I have every confidence we can win our place back in Division One next year."

"We have some very good youngsters coming along who will blend well with the matured players next season."

For one of those 'matured players' the season ended with exciting news. Club captain Alan Hodkinson was selected for Great Britain's World Cup tour of Australia and New Zealand, but it wasn't an experience he enjoyed.

Left: In 1977, Alan Hodkinson became the most recent Hornets player to be chosen for a Great Britain tour. (Courtesy Jim Stringer). Right: Kel Coslett during his time at St Helens (Courtesy Alex Service)

He wasn't selected to play against Australia, New Zealand or France and, of the 12 games played, he only started in four and was a substitute in a fifth. To his disappointment, he was the least-used player in the touring squad.

"The tour was a flop as far as I was concerned" he said. "I haven't a clue why I didn't get the chance to play in the international games. I was fit enough and trained as hard as anyone on tour." The selectors claimed they were 'not fully convinced' of his fitness after he'd taken a knock to the ribs in a testimonial game before the tour, but Hodkinson refuted this. "If they thought that, then I could understand missing out on the first couple of games, but I thought they might have given me a run out against Australia in the match prior to the final."
"Even after we had been beaten twice by the Aussies, they still chose the same team again against New South Wales, which was a full international side, and left me on the bench. I'm just glad to be back home again," he said.

As he didn't play in any of the international games, Hodkinson did not receive a cap for playing for his country. Looking back, it's a shame that Alan Hodkinson couldn't take more away from his Great Britain tour experience. He wouldn't have known it then, but he had the honour of being the last Hornets player to be selected for Great Britain. And that's something to be proud of.

Back at Hornets, both chairman and coach were bullish about Hornets' chances of a quick return to the First Division. Jack Grindrod was happy to put his money where his mouth was, offering lucrative terms that were, for a change, accepted without quibble or negotiation by the players. He said: The terms we have offered them are as good as they were in Division One - plus an added incentive to take us clear of Division Two."

The board debated long and hard about passing on the potential cost of the promotion bid to supporters by increasing the price of watching games. After a three and a half hour board meeting it was decided to fix the price at the gate at 60p and reduce the price of season tickets to £7 for general ground standing, £9 for main stand seats and £8 for the main stand paddock.

Coslett was sure about his side's chances of promotion: "I expect us to be top of Division Two by Christmas," he said. "If we play to our strengths, keep away from major injuries and go out with confidence every time, I can't see any side in Division Two beating us."

His prediction looked good in the early outings. Having overcome Oldham 14–5 in the Law Cup and battered Barrow 27–5 in the Lancashire Cup, Hornets looked a well-drilled, hard-working unit. The second round of the Lancashire Cup brought the mighty St Helens to the Athletic Grounds and Hornets produced a great performance to grab a shock 4–4 draw.

In a game where defences were to the fore, no tries were scored. Hornets points came from drop-goals from Tony Halmshaw and Tony Wainwright and a Chris Storey penalty. Saints' only reply was two penalties from Pimblett. The replay took place at Knowsley Road 48 hours later, this time Saints proved too strong, winning 16–5. But Hornets had set the bar for expectations.

The 1977–78 league season began with a series of wins that were big on effort, but light on entertainment. First up, a straightforward enough 18–5 win over Huyton, followed by a gruelling 7–5 beating of Whitehaven in the relentless Cumbrian rain. An error-strewn 10–5 victory over the Gallant Youths of Batley teed-up a no-frills 20–10 win at Halifax.

A comfortable, if uninspiring, 15–1 win against Whitehaven came next; then a workmanlike 20–5 win at Blackpool. The *Manchester Evening News* wrote: "Promotion seeking Rochdale will have to play a lot better than this if they are to go back up this season." Despite the lack of showmanship, Hornets fans were happy. Six wins from six and their side sat top of the Second Division.

Next up were Halifax and, after weeks of slugging out wins, Hornets leapt into life to deliver the most convincing win at the Athletic Grounds for 40 years. Hornets were relentless, ripping into Halifax from the first whistle, tries arriving at regular intervals and each was cheered more wildly than its predecessor.

After 40 minutes of top-class football, Hornets led 30–3 at the break. The second half was slightly less of a parade, but Hornets steamed in another 19 points to win 49–8. The tally was impressive: 11 tries including a hat-trick each for Jimmy Johnson and Kevin Ashcroft, plus a brace for Tony Wainwright. Eight goals and a try for Chris Storey. Hornets were top of the Division and playing like champions. It was a day to savour.

Through October and November, the wins kept coming, Keighley, Blackpool, Batley, York and Huyton were all brushed aside to complete a run of 12 straight league wins. The run was ended in a shock 17–16 home defeat to Doncaster, but normal service was resumed a week later with a convincing 14–5 win at Oldham on Boxing Day. Oldham's only try came at the death, described as "fluky" after Oldham appeared to have lost possession.

It was a merry Christmas for Hornets: spent in pole position at the top of Division Two just as Kel Coslett had predicted. The new year began in much the same vein: a magnificent team performance to beat second-placed Leigh by 12–9. The League table that week showed that, from 15 games, Hornets had scored 262 points and conceded just 88.

A 23–13 victory at Swinton continued Hornets' winning streak, but an 11–8 home defeat to promotion rivals Barrow heralded a run of eight games in which Hornets could only muster four wins. During the same period Leigh won six times and Barrow seven and both of them secured wins over Hornets, 18–12 and 16–8 respectively.

With four games remaining, and having dominated the competition from the outset - Hornets found themselves in third place behind Leigh and Barrow. While the Second Division Championship looked to have slipped from their grasp, Hornets had to beat Huddersfield at home to secure promotion.

Kel Coslett, who had missed three games with back trouble, selected himself to play. In a game of this magnitude, Hornets needed their general to lead from the front. And what a performance he gave; dictating play, distributing the ball, driving his side forward. Two moments of Coslett's handling magic set up a brace of tries for the uncatchable Warren Ayres. The coach capped a virtuoso display by landing seven goals from seven attempts, including two touchline efforts.

With two tries from Jimmy Johnson plus Tony Wainwright's audacious 40 yard show-and-go score from acting half, Hornets were simply too good for Huddersfield, running out 29–7 winners and securing promotion.

The run-in for the top spot went down to the wire, with both Leigh and Barrow dropping points. Hornets ended unconvincingly too, a low-key 13–2 win at Doncaster, followed by a 15–7 defeat at York. The season ended with Hornets coming back from 15–2 down to beat Huddersfield 18–15 at Fartown. Sadly, too little too late for Hornets' championship chances.

After 26 gruelling games Leigh, Barrow and Hornets all ended with 42 points from 21 wins. The final places were decided on points difference, with champions Leigh on +303, runners-up Barrow on +287 and Hornets in third on +237.

Promotion to the First Division proved a costly business, as 21 win pay-outs from 26 games swallowed most of the club's profits. With bonuses and extras, the players' wage bill of £33,166.10 was an increase of almost £10,000 on the previous year. There was also a £10,000 outlay on new players. The cost of rates, heating and lighting also rose by £1,000 to £6,495.

Gate receipts increased by £5,000, but the main revenues came from off-field activities. The lottery and bingo brought in £9,000. Rents from the Amoco garage, the visiting Circus and fairground, plus the Stock Cars amounted to £9,000. The takings from the VP lounge also totalled £9,000.

In the end, £5,000 in Supporters' Club donations was needed to push Hornets into the black, as the club tabled a profit of £2,221.42. The Supporters' Club also generously stood the £500 cost of laying concrete terracing in front of the Hornets Nest Bar.

With Hornets back in the top flight at the first attempt, staying there was Jack Grindrod's priority: "We firmly intend to stay in Division One next season at all costs," he said. The actual cost was revealed to be a new player budget of £20,000 (the equivalent of £100,000 in 2021). The fact that the club didn't actually have £20,000 didn't worry Grindrod in the slightest: "We will have to find the money somehow," he said. "We realise it is essential the club stays in Division One this time. To come back down again could prove disastrous."

Having announced his retirement from playing, Kel Coslett began writing up his shopping list. First on it was a ball-playing prop to replace himself. Second was a specialist hooker to replace the retiring Kevin Ashcroft. As for the rest of the pack: "We need at least two, maybe three new top-class forwards for next season," he said.

To clear the decks for an influx of new players, Coslett had also decided which players wouldn't figure in his future plans. Terry Fogerty, Mick Henighan, Granville Hoyle, Colin Simkins and John Rouski were all transfer listed at much reduced fees; Les and Ray Harris were released and long-serving winger Norman Brelsford was offered a free transfer after his request to leave after 10 years' service. Tony Pratt, who had only played one game all season, was also scratched from the register.

One controversial close-season announcement was that, this time, Hornets fans would have to pay the price of the club's success, with admission prices increased by a third from 60p to 80p. Season tickets in the main stand seats were increased to £14, ground tickets to £11 - and 'boys' tickets were priced at £1.50. "Cheap at the price," declared Jack Grindrod.

The increase came about after a decision taken at the Rugby League's AGM in Blackpool to increase the minimum price charged for all league games. "There was a consensus of opinion at the meeting that the game was being undersold and I am inclined to agree," said Grindrod. "Considering other sports demand in excess of £1 to go through the turnstiles, rugby league must be one of the cheapest forms of entertainment left."

Despite the fact that he'd pledged to conjure up £20,000 to keep Hornets in the First Division "at all costs", Grindrod outlined the financial state of the club. "Let's get our facts in perspective. It takes a tremendous amount of finance to run a club in this day and age. It is not just a matter of paying the players either winning or losing money, there are the added costs of rates, heating, lighting, laundry etc. which have to be met every year – and every year those costs go up."

"Last season for instance, our outgoings were astronomical because we were paying winning money almost every week, but the gates were the lowest for many, many years. It remains to be seen just what the damage is from that season in Division Two."

While Kel Coslett and the board set about bringing in new players, there was one long-established part of the Athletic Grounds landscape on its way out; the hill – upon which sat the famous Hornets scoreboard. One of the most recognisable landmarks in the game, the hill was sacrificed to create space for new Stock Car pits.

Secretary Fred Kershaw was distinctly unemotional about the loss of the ground's distinctive feature: "The present system for the Stock Cars, that of using the car park facilities behind the main stand, is not satisfactory. We feel they would benefit better if they made their approach to the track from the scoreboard end." Or, more accurately, the end where the scoreboard used to be.

In an attempt to put a positive spin on such a dramatic change, Kershaw said: "It's all part of our plans to give the ground a facelift for the return to Division One." On the plus side, the sale of the cinders from the hill raised £2,963.

Other plans for the return to the top flight included new playing terms. Players were asked to consider £40 for a home win, £45 for an away win, with an additional pence-per-point bonus. The terms were an increase of £10 per man on the previous season's deal – the bonus scheme an additional 20p per point.

The early omens for the 1978–79 season were not good. In the Law Cup, the traditional barometer for expectations of the season ahead, Hornets were embarrassed, losing 26–8 to an Oldham side that would finish in the bottom half of Division Two.

But Hornets confounded the naysayers with a shock draw at Knowsley Road in the Lancashire Cup, a 77th minute drop-goal from Tony Wainwright secured a 14–14 draw with St Helens. The replay took place at the Athletic Grounds just three days later. Once again Hornets sprung a shock, but this time it was St Helens who needed the late drop-goal to salvage an 8–8 draw.

After the final whistle, both sets of players remained on the field anticipating extra time. There was a great deal of discussion between coaches, match officials and club secretaries over the protocols in place in the event of a second draw. But it soon became clear that no-one had anticipated the possibility of a drawn replay.

In the end, it took a phone call to the Lancashire Committee who, co-incidentally, were meeting at Swinton on the same night, to get confirmation on how the tie would be settled. The decision was to play a second replay on neutral ground 48 hours later. The venue chosen was Central Park. Unfortunately, a third game in six days against St Helens was a game too far for a leg-weary Hornets who lost 28–9.

The three games in a week also gave Kel Coslett a major injury headache. Ahead of the opening league game at Widnes, Hornets had full-back Steve Prime, both wingers, Jimmy Johnson and Paul Longstaff, and both centres – Tony Wainwright and Mick McLoughlin, on the treatment table. Missing four first team regulars, Hornets lost 39–5.

The line-up against Hull KR the following week included two un-named triallists. Lining up for the Robins were Clive Sullivan, Alan Agar, Roger Milward and David Watkinson. Against the odds, Hornets lost narrowly 21–15. Triallist hooker Terry Langan handed his international counterpart Watkinson a lesson, winning the scrums 13–3. Hornets signed him up.

Defeats against Widnes and Hull KR were enough for full-back John Maloney. He told Jack Grindrod he was quitting the game altogether: "I have to consider my wife and family. For the past 12 years they have seen very little of me at weekends because of my involvement in the game." Kel Coslett's assessment was brutally direct: "Naturally I am very disappointed that he has decided to finish. I thought he had more character than to give up that easily."

The following weekend Hornets went to Leigh. Billed as 'The Battle of the Minnows', Hornets lost 10–3. *The Rochdale Observer* described their performance as "atrocious", "inept", "shocking" and "hopeless". Forwards Charlie Birdsall and Alan Bailey joined the injury list. Disappointed at his repeated selection as a substitute, prop Tony Gourley hit the club with a transfer request, saying: "If I am not good enough to be in the 13 who take the field, then I would rather be with another club." John Maloney added: "I have played my last game for Hornets, but I still feel I have a couple of good seasons left. There just doesn't seem to be any progress made from last season and the way it looks at the moment Hornets are heading straight back to Division Two."

Maloney was sure where the blame lay: "The board seems to be sitting on the fence. It is obvious the team needs a player of Kel Coslett's ability because there is no-one dictating play. I am not prepared to play again until they find someone."

His comments clearly got to Jack Grindrod who snapped back: "Some people seem to think that we are sitting on the fence and not making any moves to buy players, but I can assure them that we have been very active in the past few weeks."

"What we don't intend to do is spend money on players who are no better than those already on the books. We have done that in the past and look where it has got us. As far as signing a ball-handling forward, I have made approaches to three players who are not on the transfer list and each time we have been turned away."

With increasing ripples of disquiet in the camp, Hornets travelled to Salford in the Player's No.6 Trophy. Ironically, they were systematically dismantled by former Hornets playmaker John Butler as Salford won 25–7. Hornets' only try came in the 77th minute.

Back in the league, a 33–5 defeat at St Helens didn't really help matters, and things went from bad to worse when the previous season's player-of-the-year, Tony Cooke handed in a transfer request. His "personal" reasons for wanting a move? "I'm not happy with my form and I feel a change of clubs could do me the world of good."

On 15 October, Hornets finally produced their long-awaited first win of the season: a dour game that bore all the hallmarks of a potential defeat. Having led 8–5 at the break, Hornets had to come from behind to beat Barrow 13–9. But a win did little to quell the dressing room; Jimmy Johnson and John Rawlinson joined a list of 14 players in dispute or wanting transfers.

The situation became so severe that Kel Coslett was forced out of his seven-month retirement for the forthcoming game against Leeds. His signing of maverick Welsh international half-back Paul Woods also lifted spirits, as Hornets produced a miracle 11–9 win over the Loiners. Coslett rolled back the years with a commanding performance.

Through November, Coslett's influence paid off as the wins began to come: 33–5 against Featherstone; 10–9 over Huddersfield in the BBC2 Floodlit Trophy and, most impressively, 7–3 over third-placed St Helens. But the run-up to Christmas brought four straight defeats, including two losses in 48 hours, to leave Hornets fourth bottom of the First Division.

January fell foul of an arctic winter, with successive postponements creating a backlog of five games. The only respite came at the Willows on 27 January. Ahead of the game, Hornets announced that Salford had signed Tony Gourley for £10,000. Without him, Hornets grabbed their first away win of the season, 13–4.

The edge was taken off the celebrations because injured second rower Wally Jones announced that he'd be handing in a transfer request as soon as he was fit. Laid-up with a broken arm that required surgery, Jones was upset that the club had "shunned" him and his family: "No-one from the club came to see me or ask my wife if she was coping all right. Kel Coslett came one night, but after that no-one came near. After the shabby way the club has treated both my wife and myself, there is no way I want to play for them again."

Into February, the weather got worse with more postponements and the storm in the Hornets dressing room continued. First Chris Storey asked for a move and was listed at £3,000. Then Brett Garside and John Manning, two of the club's most promising prospects, made in transfer requests after being left out of the 'A' team. They were followed by Tony

110

Wainwright, who said: "I've been getting very despondent lately. The training facilities, the club's trouble with Wally Jones and now the sale of Tony Gourley has made me unsettled."

With players falling like dominoes, Jack Grindrod had a clear idea what was behind the disquiet. He blamed the weather. "The main reason for the unrest is that players are becoming frustrated at not being able to play," he said. "They train regular as clockwork on Tuesdays and Thursdays, only to find that the weekends are blank because of the weather. It seems that one way they can let off steam is by deciding to find another club." Grindrod's conclusion? "Once the weather breaks and we can get back to normal I feel that players will be too involved in the fixture programme to let these tensions get the better of them."

By the end of February, Hornets had not played a home game for 84 days. A 15–0 Challenge Cup win over Second Division basement side Batley heralded a return to action, but the revised First Division fixture list forced Hornets to play eight games in April to make up the backlog. The next seven games brought just two wins: a bruising, bad-tempered 17–9 win over Workington and a tryless 6–2 victory over Wigan, played in monsoon conditions.

The run of defeats included a disputed 11–10 Challenge Cup loss to St Helens: a painfully narrow margin decided by an awful refereeing decision. Somehow, he interpreted Harry Pinner's blatant loss of possession as a ball-steal by Warren Ayres. The resulting penalty proved the difference. Ayres' take on it? "A diabolical decision, I just couldn't believe it."

On 8 April, Hornets' bad luck would strike decisively, bringing one moment that would determine their fate for the next decade. Bradford Northern were the visitors. In their side were Great Britain trio Keith Mumby, Alan Redfern and Len Casey. Kel Coslett picked the strongest Hornets side in months and included himself at loose-forward.

With Coslett at the helm Hornets started brightly, taking an early lead. But, following a text-book tackle on Bradford's man-mountain Ian van Bellen, Coslett didn't get up. The stretcher was called for. Kel Coslett's game, his season and career were over; his knee-cap shattered. Despite leading 7–5 at half time, Hornets struggled without him and lost 16–8.

The absence of Coslett's authority was the theme for the rest of the season. In the last nine games, Hornets won only once. With three games left, the survival equation became impossible to solve. To stay in the First Division, Hornets needed to win all three games by an overall margin of 60 points, and the team above them, Salford, had to lose all three of their games. Hornets lost the next three games, conceding 72 points and scoring only 19.

With just eight wins from 30 games, Hornets were dumped back into the Second Division. Newly appointed club secretary Malcolm Lord tried hard to sound resolute: "We'll be back," he said. "There will be a determined effort to bounce back in one season."

There would be no quick return this time. Seven days before the new season was due to start, Kel Coslett resigned, saying: "I just couldn't see any future at Rochdale. I was disappointed with the results and annoyed at the attitude of some of the players. My pride won't allow me to continue with a team that is beaten week-in and week-out. I have never been used to it and defeat is something which I find hard to accept."

Hornets finished the following season seventh in the Second Division. The Yo-Yo years – and Hornets' tenuous grasp on First Division status – were well and truly over.

References

Rochdale Observer 11 October 1975
Rochdale Observer 1 November 1975
Rochdale Observer 5 November 1975
Rochdale Observer 8 November 1975
Rochdale Observer 12 November 1975
Rochdale Observer 29 November 1975
Rochdale Observer 6 December 1975
Rochdale Observer 17 December 1975
Rochdale Observer 14 April 1976
Rochdale Observer 17 April 1976
Rochdale Observer 5 May 1976
Rochdale Observer 10 July 1976
Rochdale Observer 31 July 1976
Rochdale Observer 14 August 1976
Rochdale Observer 18 August 1976
Rochdale Observer 25 August 1976
Rochdale Observer 28 August 1976
Rochdale Observer 1 September 1976
Rochdale Observer 8 September 1976
Rochdale Observer 8 September 1976
Rochdale Observer 25 September 1976
Rochdale Observer 29 September 1976
Rochdale Observer 8 October 1976
Rochdale Observer 13 October 1976
Rochdale Observer 16 October 1976
Rochdale Observer 20 October 1976
Rochdale Observer 27 October 1976
Rochdale Observer 17 November 1976
Rochdale Observer 20 November 1976
Rochdale Observer 24 November 1976
Rochdale Observer 27 November 1976
Rochdale Observer 5 December 1976
Rochdale Observer 16 April 1977
Rochdale Observer 20 April 1977
Rochdale Observer 23 April 1977
Rochdale Observer 27 April 1977
Rochdale Observer 9 July 1977
Rochdale Observer 23 July 1977
Rochdale Observer 13 August 1977
Rochdale Observer 31 August 1977
Rochdale Hornets match programme v Leigh 1 January 1978
Rochdale Observer 1 April 1978
Rochdale Observer 5 April 1978
Rochdale Observer 8 April 1978
Rochdale Hornets match programme v Huddersfield 9 April 1978
Rochdale Observer 22 April 1978
Rochdale Observer 26 April 1978
Rochdale Observer 20 May 1978
Rochdale Observer 5 July 1978
Rochdale Observer 6 September 1978

Rochdale Observer 13 September 1978
Rochdale Observer 23 September 1978
Rochdale Observer 27 September 1978
Rochdale Observer 30 September 1978
Rochdale Observer 11 October 1978
Rochdale Observer 14 October 1978
Rochdale Observer 18 October 1978
Rochdale Observer 21 October 1978
Rochdale Observer 25 October 1978
Rochdale Observer 25 October 1978
Rochdale Observer 28 October 1978
Rochdale Observer 1 November 1978
Rochdale Observer 8 November 1978
Rochdale Observer 11 November 1978
Rochdale Observer 15 November 1978
Rochdale Observer 18 November 1978
Rochdale Observer 22 November 1978
Rochdale Observer 29 November 1978
Rochdale Observer 13 December 1978
Rochdale Observer 16 December 1978
Rochdale Observer 3 January 1979
Rochdale Observer 10 January 1979
Rochdale Observer 20 January 1979
Rochdale Observer 27 January 1979
Rochdale Observer 3 February 1979
Rochdale Observer 7 February 1979
Rochdale Observer 10 February 1979
Rochdale Observer 14 February 1979
Rochdale Observer 17 February 1979
Rochdale Observer 28 February 1979
Rochdale Observer 3 March 1979
Rochdale Observer 7 March 1979
Rochdale Observer 10 March 1979
Rochdale Observer 17 March 1979
Rochdale Observer 21 March 1979
Rochdale Observer 24 March 1979
Rochdale Observer 28 March 1979
Rochdale Observer 31 March 1979
Rochdale Observer 4 April 1979
Rochdale Observer 7 April 1979
Rochdale Observer 14 April 1979
Rochdale Observer 18 April 1979
Rochdale Observer 21 April 1979
Rochdale Observer 25 April 1979
Rochdale Observer 28 April 1979
Rochdale Observer 2 May 1979
Rochdale Observer 5 May 1979
Rochdale Observer 9 May 1979
Rochdale Observer 16 May 1979
Rochdale Observer 12 May 1979
Rochdale Observer 19 May 1979
Rochdale Observer 25 August 1979
Rochdale Observer 2 January 1980

11. 1980: Decline and fall

Hornets began the 80s mired in a financial crisis. In November 1980, just three months into the new season, chairman Jack Grindrod gathered the players together at a training session to tell them that the board was looking to cut costs by £600 per week (equivalent to £2,500 in 2021).

The first team was asked to take a £10 cut in their winning money; 'A' team players were asked to accept that their winning pay would be cut to £10; and all players were informed that training would be reduced to one night a week, except prior to cup games.

Almost inconceivably, Hornets also transfer-listed their talismanic prop Alan Hodkinson, in his benefit year, for £20,000. His eventual move to Wigan smacked of selling off the family silver. Grindrod told The *Rochdale Observer*: "The recession is beginning to hit us in many ways. We are not making the same returns from our off-field activities."

Plan-B was to seek a merger with Rochdale AFC. Grindrod said: "It was suggested to me that it might be a good idea for Rochdale Hornets and Rochdale Football Club to merge under one roof. I have had loose talks with Rochdale's co-chairman John Faulks, who agreed it could be worth looking at, but that is as far as it went." A month later the plan was shelved.

Hornets had started the season in decent form. Despite first round exits in the Lancashire Cup and John Player Trophy, both away, at Wigan and Leigh respectively, Hornets had picked up nine league wins in the first 14 games.

In the ninth of those wins, Hornets made history, becoming the first side to defeat the newly formed Fulham RLFC at Craven Cottage. In front of a crowd of 6,162, and roared on by a big following from Rochdale, a brace of tries from Sammy Gilmore, one from Graham Gorvin and a trademark try from Henderson Gill blew Fulham off the park. Norman Turley hit five goals and a drop-goal; and even winger Ian Holland chipped in with a drop-goal. It was close to the perfect performance, but after that the season deteriorated.

Hornets followed their remarkable result in London with five straight defeats. A win against Huyton gave brief respite, but it preceded three more consecutive losses. Narrow wins over Swinton, 12–10, and at Huyton, 20–19, raised hopes for the run-in, but Hornets only mustered one more victory from the remaining four games, beating Doncaster 33–13.

Hornets ended the season 10th in the Second Division with 13 wins from 28 games. After the triumph at Fulham, Hornets managed only four wins in 15 games. At the end of the season, Hornets sacked Paul Longstaff, appointing Terry Fogerty as his successor.

1981 was also the year in which Hornets featured in *Another Bloody Sunday*, a Yorkshire Television documentary on the travails of a Doncaster side in search of its only win of the season. Hornets' appearance focused on the previous season's desperate 11–3 win over Doncaster in the first round of the Challenge Cup. Hornets' 10 minutes of fame provide a fascinating, insight into the game and the club as it was then. Compared with the game we watch today it looks bleak, broke and brutal. The first phase of the 1981–82 season was disrupted by the exit of key players. In pre-season, prop John Glover departed to Whitehaven for £15,000. Three games in, Hornets lost towering prop Sean Hoare, to Fulham for £30,000.

The programme from Hornets famous win at Craven Cottage in January 1981, the first time the publishers of this book had seen Fulham lose. (Courtesy Peter Lush)

The following month saw a bidding war between Wigan and St Helens for crowd favourite and flying wing wizard Henderson Gill. After seven games, and three tries, Wigan secured his signature for £30,000.

By the time Hornets played Bradford Northern in the John Player Trophy in October, they had won three out of their eight league games and banked £75,000: a pretty good return. However, in the programme notes for the Bradford game, the board was in less than celebratory mood: "The directors are as sorry as you that we have had to be on the wrong side of the transfer market in the past few weeks. But few fans have realised just how serious the financial position was becoming at the Athletic Grounds."

Anyone thinking that an influx of £75,000 would solve the club's problems was wrong: "The money which has come in from the sale of Henderson Gill, Sean Hoare and John Glover has gained us a respite, but we must warn Rochdale that this is only a respite, not a permanent solution."

Once again, the board put the onus on supporters to turn things around: "What we must do now is build up a good side and bring back the crowds who have been missing in the last few seasons. It is up to you to support us. Terry Fogerty will do the rest, we hope."

Three wins in the next four games was encouraging; 8–3 at Huyton, 13–6 against Blackpool and 9–4 against Batley. But then Hornets went on a run of four straight defeats, the last of which, a 10–3 home defeat to Dewsbury, saw coach Terry Fogerty resign 20 minutes after the final hooter. He declared it: "The worst team performance I have ever seen." Assistant coach Dick Bonser was handed the reins on a caretaker basis for the remainder of the season.

From March, Hornets were in free-fall. Just three wins from 14 games saw them slide down the table to finish 5th from bottom with just 10 wins from 32 games. At the end of a disappointing season, hopes of better times were briefly raised when Hornets announced plans to create a 'Super Stadium' sports complex on the Athletic Grounds site. It was to be developed in conjunction with the Council and Rochdale AFC, who were in dire straits having had to apply for re-election to the Football League after finishing 89th of the league's 92 clubs.

The idea of turning the Athletic Grounds into a 'Super Stadium' was not a new one. It was first mooted in February 1966 after the Hornets board, headed by Arthur Walker, wrote to

Rochdale Corporation to see if they were interested in developing the site as a community stadium. The move was prompted after the Rugby Football League wrote to all clubs suggesting they investigate the possibilities of wider community use of their grounds.

Alderman Cyril Smith was the Mayor of Rochdale at the time and he said that the Corporation was 'quite enthusiastic' about the possibility of a sports centre at the Athletic Grounds: "... providing the Corporation can be satisfied there is a need for such a thing."

The Rochdale Observer reported that the Town Clerk's department would set up a team to investigate the potential of developing the Athletic Grounds "... not only from a local point of view, but from a regional one." Alderman Smith anticipated that the report on the proposal would be presented "... in three to four months." In the end nothing happened and the idea was quietly dropped.

The 1982 version, with plans for an all-weather pitch, all-seated stands and a sports hall for public use, was reported to be Rochdale Council's preferred project in a bid to attract £1m of funding from the Government's Urban Development Grant Scheme. In order to apply for funding, the Council was compelled to bid against 42 other local authorities. Nothing came from the application, but the conversion of the Athletic Grounds into a 'Super Stadium' would remain a recurring concept.

With another season to prepare for, Hornets needed a coach. After pursuing former Great Britain and England forward George Nichols as a potential player-coach, Hornets finally appointed Bill Kirkbride to the role. With a long and distinguished playing career in the UK and Australia, Kirkbride had a good pedigree as a coach. Having taken Wakefield Trinity to Wembley in 1979, he went on to coach York to a Second Division championship in 1980–81, so he looked like a good fit to make Hornets competitive.

But, despite an opening day win at Huddersfield, Hornets struggled to get into their stride. With only three more wins from the next 15 games, the first half of the season was short on excitement. A narrow 14–11 New Year defeat at Swinton set the tone for the remainder. Indeed, on the last day of January, Hornets visited Crown Flatt and slugged out a quite literally pointless 0–0 draw with Dewsbury

Around the same time, Bill Kirkbride stepped down as a player after suffering his fourth concussion of the year. It left him with a selection quandary as his most likely replacement at prop, Brett Garside, had been suspended for 10 weeks after being sent off playing amateur rugby league on a permit, which allowed a former professional to play in the amateur game. His punishment was made up of four weeks for kicking, five weeks for abusing the referee and one week for refusing to leave the field.

Hornets battled on and shone in March when they didn't lose a single game, beating Doncaster, Whitehaven, Huyton and Blackpool. But the resurgence was brief. Hornets ended the season with a run of six games without a win to finish 13th of 17 clubs with 10 wins from 32 games.

The club had a frugal build-up to the 1983–84 season, signing only one player, scrum-half Brian Hughes, from York for £2,000. He proved an astute and durable acquisition, going on to become the only player to appear in every one of Hornets' 37 league and cup games. The season started poorly with only one win in the first eight games. But even though wins came sporadically, the form of second-row John Stapleton caught the eye. Scoring with

115

steady regularity, he became Hornets' go-to strike player with a hard, fast, direct style that was pretty much unstoppable at close quarters.

While the first half of the season was hit-and-miss, the second half was a struggle. A run of 10 games with only a solitary win tested the reserve of even the most patient Hornets fan. Hornets ended the season with three straight defeats – at Huyton, Halifax and Kent Invicta – to finish 12th with 13 wins from 34 games.

The story of a very ordinary season was the extraordinary strike-rate of Stapleton, returning 21 tries from the second row to finish top try scorer by some distance. He also contributed a single drop-goal, in a 31–27 win against Swinton. Having attracted attention, Stapleton was put on the transfer list in the off-season. He was signed by Swinton.

Hornets started the new season with a run of six games in which they only won once. Bill Kirkbride had seen enough and handed in his notice. In a bizarre move, local businessman Jim Smith offered to invest £50,000 in the club if Hornets replaced him with Alex Murphy. They didn't. They appointed prop Charlie Birdsall as caretaker coach, and the transformation was immediate. Hornets went on a seven match run in which they lost only once and Birdsall was given the job on a permanent basis. The next game Birdsall delivered a stirring 9–9 draw against Salford.

But a disappointing 32–6 Boxing Day defeat at Blackpool heralded a series of games in which Hornets struggled to string together back-to-back wins. The low-point was a 25–0 home hammering by Fulham on a Wednesday night that drew just 222 spectators. The home game the following Sunday against Whitehaven fared marginally better with a crowd of 248.

Hornets ended the season much as they'd started it, a five game run in which they eked out a single victory. It came on the last day of the season, 9–8 at Mansfield, a Billy Platt drop-goal the difference. Despite what felt like a frustrating season, Hornets finished 12th, one place below the once mighty Wakefield Trinity on points difference. Of greater concern was the collapse of the crowds to worryingly unsustainable levels. And off the field, there was turbulence in the boardroom.

On 3 March 1985, Hornets held a 'two-in-one' AGM. Having failed to submit accounts in 1983, it was intended to put the 1983 and 1984 accounts in front of the shareholders in order to bring the club's reporting up to date. The 1983 accounts showed a loss of £22,323. The accounts for 1984, somehow, declared a profit of £1,178. Also on the agenda was the election of directors: the five incumbents all up for re-election and the introduction of a new candidate, former Hornets Under-17s and Colts coach Fred Wood.

The 32-year-old Wood was cut from different cloth to his fellow candidates. Unlike the other traditional, self-made local business types, Wood was a sales executive at Applied Micros, a computer company based in Warrington. He brought a younger perspective, a professional corporate attitude and the sense of an exciting digital future.

The resignation of directors Tony Higham and David Walker 'due to increasing pressure of work' made Wood's election a formality. He said his aim was: "To use my business expertise in selling Hornets to the public. I want to get round the local schools and encourage the game there too." His first innovation was to give away hot cross buns to the first 300 fans through the turnstiles at the Good Friday game against Bridgend.

Seen here receiving a sponsorship cheque from Carcraft owner Frank McKee at the Athletic
Grounds, Hornets chairman Fred Wood (R) had big plans to take Hornets all the way
to the top flight. Hornets fell just short of promotion and Wood was ousted from the club.
(Courtesy Jim Stringer)

The first act of incumbent chairman David Ratcliffe was to resign, forcing the election of a
new chair. Also citing 'increasing work pressures' as his reason for standing down, Ratcliffe
said "The position is an extremely demanding one and needs at least 25 hours of devoted
time every week in order to do it properly. I can't afford that amount of time any more, but
I intend to carry on as a director to help the club in its uphill battle."

The meeting at which the chairman should have been elected was postponed due to
director Jack Grindrod's attendance at a Rugby League Council meeting, but when the
Hornets board finally elected its chair, it was Grindrod who got the nod from his fellow
directors. Grindrod was a domineering character. He had previously been Hornets' chairman
for 12 years, after his ousting of Allan Ellis in 1971, and his election was seen as a return to
old-school values that harked back to the halcyon days of the early 1970s. But it didn't take
long before it was revealed that everything in the Hornets boardroom was far from rosy.

In June, the club was hit with a financial hammer-blow. In the wake of the Bradford City
fire disaster, Hornets were slapped with a 600 percent increase in the cost of its fire insurance

for the main stand. Previously £1,900, the club faced a bill of £11,500 that it simply couldn't afford to pay. Jack Grindrod was staggered by the size of the premium: "Quite honestly, I can't see how we can afford to pay it," he said. "We have been given 30 days in which to pay or our current policy is out of date. We are still covered by a separate public liability policy that takes in all kinds of accidents, but it might mean that we have to function without a fire policy."

Grindrod denied that the stand, with its plastic seats and wooden benches, was a fire hazard, because "The roof is made of asbestos…"

The insurance bill arrived just as the promotor of Stock Car racing at the Athletic Grounds departed, taking with him the £10,000 of revenue that the racing contributed to the club. Grindrod was incredulous: "We are being asked to find a further £10,000 in order to renew our insurance against fire. Put that alongside our costs to insure the VP Lounge, Nest Bar, lottery office – and also the rates – and we have a bill of more than £22,000. That's more than our gate receipts for a full season."

"If this club is to function as a professional outfit next season, we must receive some financial assistance from somewhere." Much like he had in 1980, Jack Grindrod called a meeting of the players and asked them to 'mull over' reduced playing terms for the forthcoming 1985–86 season, with a promise that they would receive a 'merit bonus' if the team finished in one of the promotion places. According to The *Rochdale Observer*: "No agreement was reached."

As June progressed, the storm clouds darkened over the Athletic Grounds. With the club's overdraft reportedly stretched to 'well over £100,000', news of the club's parlous financial state led to a rash of rumours circulating in the town. They included that the club was about to fold, that Hornets were in merger talks with the Dale and that there was a mysterious group planning a takeover. Most concerning was the unconfirmed news that the club was prepared to relinquish its professional status and join the amateur ranks.

The *Rochdale Observer* wrote: "Hard though it may be for the directors to decide which way to turn and what route to take in order to keep rugby league alive in the town [we are] suggesting that they 'come clean' and tell the folk in Rochdale what they need to know."

"The least they deserve is to find out what is going on behind the scenes at the Athletic Grounds in order that they can make an effort to help the club through its biggest ever crisis." Jack Grindrod kept his cards close to his chest. He said: "The club's vice-chairman Alan Hindle and myself have discussed the situation in detail and we feel we could have a solution to the problem, but that is all I'm prepared to say at the moment."

He added: "A board meeting has been called so that I can put certain options on the table. Once they have been discussed we shall call a meeting of the shareholders to put them in the picture and let them decide which option we should take." Amid the financial wrangles, there were also signs of a split in the boardroom. After quashing the rumour that the club would join the amateur ranks, Grindrod admitted that the option had been discussed: "We talked about that subject briefly at last week's board meeting, after which one of the directors felt it necessary to divulge it to the press. That will also be discussed on Monday night."

It also emerged that a 'ginger group' was buying up as many shares as they could get their hands on in order to launch a takeover bid. Grindrod seethed: "A member of the board is believed to be involved with this although I refuse to name who it is."

He was perfectly clear, though, that he had no intention of giving up control of the club: "What I would like to advise is that, even if they manage to acquire an amount of shares, they cannot be passed on officially without the board's authority and they won't give it. So my advice to shareholders is that this is not the right time to sell."

On the rumour of a possible merger with the Dale, he offered a curt "no comment". The date for the shareholders meeting to determine the future of the club was set for Thursday 18 July. Ahead of the meeting, the board broke cover. In what appeared to be a confusing cry for help, Hornets sent an SOS letter to Rochdale Council asking for their support in a proposed merger with the Dale. The Council's chief executive, John Towey, made as much sense of it as he could: "I am told that an informal extraordinary general meeting of Hornets shareholders has been called on Thursday 18 July. A discussion on the financial difficulties facing the club will take place."

"The meeting will also consider whether there is support for an approach to Rochdale Council and to Rochdale Football Club for a scheme which could ensure the continuation of rugby league football in Rochdale. When the request is received by the council it will go to the appropriate committee."

The scale of the crisis was eye-watering. On top of the £11,500 insurance bill and the lost £10,000 of stock car revenue, it was revealed that Hornets were £80,000 in the red and that the balance sheet was expected to show a £30,000 trading loss for the year.

Jack Grindrod said: "All the facts will be put to the shareholders. One of the options they will have to consider is that we join forces with the soccer club. That would, in effect, wind-up rugby league at the Athletic Grounds and mean moving to Spotland." To the long-suffering Hornets fans, such a move across town was unthinkable.

In the run-up to the meeting there was little respite for Hornets. On Sunday 30 June the club fell foul of a burglary that caused several thousand pounds worth of damage that the club could ill-afford to cover. The thieves stole the PA system, the contents of the freezer, all the club's balls and a large quantity of lottery tickets. Less than a fortnight later the club was hit again, this time thieves caused £350 worth of damage breaking in through the roof to take another 8,000 lottery tickets. Jack Grindrod suggested that "someone with a grudge against the club could be mounting a vendetta."

The day before the EGM it was revealed that four 'Rochdale businessmen' were poised to stage a takeover bid. Their spokesman was new director Fred Wood. He said: "We will be asking the board to resign en-bloc to save the embarrassment of confronting the shareholders. If the group is given control of the club, they will close the door to a possible merger with Rochdale Football Club."

Nicknamed 'The Gang of Four', the consortium was named as David Russell, managing director of Farouche Kitchens; Ian Whittles, owner of a Rochdale firm; Alan Brennan and former Hornets caretaker coach Dick Bonser. The EGM was direct and to the point. The 'Gang of Four' asked the board to step down. The board agreed to resign if the new group could raise £150,000 by the following Tuesday. The shareholders ratified that agreement giving the consortium four days to raise the cash.

Speaking for the group, Fred Wood said that the £150,000 would include an extended bank loan, sponsorships and the promise of backing from JW Lees brewery. He went on: "There will be no need for another extraordinary meeting because of the flexibility shown by the shareholders. They obviously feel we can raise the funds asked for by Tuesday."

In addition to boardroom wrangling, the 'Super Stadium' concept was back on the table. Shareholders at the meeting were told that the British Amateur Rugby League Association (BARLA) had made an audacious 'take it or leave it' offer of £180,000 for the Athletic Grounds, with the aim of turning it into a centre of excellence to house its national squad and stage all of its major finals. The stadium's facilities would also be offered to local schools.

The deal was that BARLA would buy the entire Athletic Grounds site then lease the playing area back to Hornets at £1,000 per year. BARLA's Maurice Oldroyd said: "Our offer is to Rochdale Hornets regardless of which board is in control." But the offer would only be on the table for seven days. "I must stress that we cannot wait too long for a reply," said Oldroyd. "We have the ability to use money at our disposal to buy land. We want to produce a stadium of excellence for the public to share and if Rochdale want to take advantage of that we are prepared to enter into immediate negotiations." Fred Wood said that, if given control of the club, the consortium would 'proceed to continue negotiations with BARLA'.

Local rugby league journalist Stan Townsend canvassed hard for acceptance of the deal: "Given the BARLA offer, and couple it with the money that the 'incoming board' have said they could raise, it would put Hornets on Easy Street for a long time to come. The idea of having a 'super stadium' within the town is one which must whet the appetite of the sporting public of Rochdale."

Within a week, Jack Grindrod's board had agreed to stand-down and hand over the running of the club to the takeover group. However, it wasn't the clean and simple transfer of power that the takeover group wanted. While agreed in principle at the EGM, the handover did require ratification at a shareholders meeting on 1 August, at which Jack Grindrod, Alan Hindle, Rudy Howarth and John Leeson would present their resignation letters. The remaining director, Fred Wood, would then seek shareholder agreement to join the new set of directors.

Jack Grindrod wasn't prepared to go quietly. In one last petulant swipe at the shareholders, he said: "Our solicitors advised us not to resign until this group of businessmen put some hard cash forward. So far all we have seen is paper money in the form of guarantees."

"It's promises, promises, promises as far as we can see, but that is all. If the shareholders want to accept that then be it on their own heads. This is not sour grapes. The directors are only concerned with the club's future. But it seems we can go no further and that the shareholders want us out."

One thing that was certain was that the BARLA deal was dead in the water. Fred Wood said: "I have had further talks with Maurice Oldroyd and told him that we would be prepared to enter negotiations which could mean them sharing our facilities. But they want to own the ground lock, stock and barrel. We are not prepared to do that."

He went on: "The ground is the one asset we intend to hold onto at all costs and from the meeting with the shareholders last week, we got the impression that they don't want to sell it either."

With just four weeks to the start of the 1985–86 season, club secretary Keith Mort, acting on behalf of the incoming board, informed the players that, once the boardroom wrangles were sorted out, they would be offered the same money as the previous season, effectively doubling the 'unagreed' offer made by the outgoing board. The offer was accepted and the players began pre-season, a month later than planned.

Almost immediately the new board-in-waiting began having conversations with 'top players' with a view to them signing, pending the successful ratification of the takeover. Lined up were Castleford forward Andy Timson, listed at £10,000, Doncaster full-back Kevin Harcombe (£10,000) and Warrington centre Ian Duane (£15,000). The incoming board had also lined-up Wigan's Cup Final prop Brian Dunn at £18,000, and top Kiwi forward Mike Kuiti. Fred Wood was bullish: "We are not doing this just to impress people, we really want to get a top class side together."

But all of the deals remained dependent on the 'incoming board' carrying the vote at the shareholder's meeting. The *Rochdale Observer* was decidedly unexcited at the prospect: "It's a case of Hobson's Choice for the shareholders, who have little option but to give the new men a chance."

Then, just a week before the vote, David Russell of Farouche Kitchens pulled out of the consortium. He was hurriedly replaced by local solicitor Bill Goodwin and the takeover group made clear that their plan to run the club would go ahead. At the meeting, Hornets' shareholders took just 20 minutes to ratify the takeover. They also made it clear to the new board that they would not 'sell out' to BARLA. The first act of the new board was to appoint Fred Wood as club chairman and as its representative at all Rugby League Council meetings.

Wood said: "When I joined the board in March this year, I believed I could bring something new to Rochdale Hornets. I never dreamed it would be a 'new' board. The events of May, June and July were right out of *Man at the Top* and *Dallas*", two 1980s television dramas about corruption, nepotism and lies.

With a summer of Machiavellian politics over, it was a relief for everyone to return to rugby matters. With a dynamic new board having spent £60,000 on new players, and having lined up half a dozen exciting Australian and Kiwi players, expectations and season ticket sales for the forthcoming season were high.

In the run-up to the start of the season, Hornets claimed three victories in friendlies against Castleford Lock Lane, the Rochdale amateur town team and Runcorn Highfield, the latter in appalling conditions in front of a crowd of just 400. Disappointed at the attendance, Fred Wood said: "Let's just hope the spectators get behind us for Sunday's home game against Whitehaven."

In an attempt to recoup some of their huge investment, the club increased the admission from £1.80 to £2. They also introduced an extra charge of 50p for fans wanting to sit in the main stand.

121

With the Antipodean contingent not due to arrive for two more weeks, Hornets' team for the opening weekend had a bit of a makeshift look to it, with half-back Mark Sanderson at loose-forward and an un-named triallist at centre.

In his programme notes, Fred Wood oozed confidence: "The atmosphere at the club is at an all time high. Success and First Division rugby are the main aims for this season, achieve that together and the Hornets' greatest years are yet to come." Hornets lost 10–5 in front of a crowd of 810, with all of their points coming from the boot of Kevin Harcombe with two penalties and a drop-goal. Not quite the revolution fans were expecting.

A scratchy 16–10 win at Carlisle a week later settled nerves a little ahead of Hornets' home Lancashire Cup tie against a Widnes side packed with household names. Ahead of the game Hornets signed a household name of their own, Steve Nash. The 37-year-old former Salford, Featherstone and Great Britain scrum-half had been retired for over a year after suffering a broken jaw and a damaged eye. But coach Charlie Birdsall had talked him into 'helping Hornets out on a match-to-match basis'. Regardless of the circumstances, it was a signing that made people sit up and take notice.

The Widnes game wasn't the massacre that many envisaged. Hornets turned in a gutsy, hard-working performance to go down just 17–6, outscored by only two tries to one; the margin stretched by four goals from Mick Burke and a drop-goal from Wilf George.

The following week Hornets blitzed Doncaster 52–13 in a 10-try pummelling that saw winger Phil Edge grab four tries. In the line-up were two exciting Australian prospects, Phil McKenzie from Illawarra and North Sydney's Greg Austin. Flying to join them were Greg's brother Tony Austin, a prop from Manly and Derek Shaefer a utility back from Mullumbimby, one of the oldest rugby league clubs in Australia, founded in 1909.

On the back of four straight wins, Hornets went to Sheffield, where Tony Austin and Derek Shaefer made their debuts. Hornets battered the Eagles 40–12, with Austin and Shaefer grabbing a try each, but it was a tragic day for Derek Shaefer whose season was ended by a horrific broken leg that sent shudders through the crowd.

Despite the setback, the wins kept coming, with 12 straight victories rocketing Hornets into promotion contention. During that run Hornets' cause was boosted by the arrival of top-class Kiwis Mike Kuiti and Phil Bancroft. Hornets' comedy credentials were also improved when comedian and local nightclub owner Bobby Ball joined the board. His Braces Nightclub name was emblazoned on the front of the shirt as he took up a role "... assisting in promoting the Athletic Grounds as an entertainments centre."

A two point defeat at Workington was dismissed as a blip and the blow of a 29–8 Boxing Day home defeat by Leigh was cushioned by a crowd of over 4,000. But, as the season went on, wins became harder to come by. Through February and March Hornets managed only two wins from seven games, and the departure back to New Zealand of Kuiti and Bancroft left a huge hole at the heart of the side.

Off the field an acrimonious rift in the boardroom between chairman Fred Wood and his vice-chair Ian Whittles also proved unsettling. In early March Wood had announced that Whittles was no longer a director of the club. When Whittles went on holiday, Wood co-opted Len Stansfield onto the board as his replacement. On his return from Tenerife, Whittles appeared at a game, but didn't sit with the other directors. "I didn't want to sit next to Fred

Wood," he said. "But I will be attending the next board meeting on Wednesday to clear up the idea that I am no longer on the board."

Needless to say, Wood saw things differently: "If Ian Whittles turns up at Wednesday's board meeting, he will not be allowed through the door. Mr Whittles could call himself a director, he could also call himself Father Christmas if he likes, but as far as we're concerned, he is not a member of the board any longer."

Things got worse when Hornets had a much publicised visit from the bailiffs looking for payment of an unpaid tax bill of over £20,000. Fred Wood put out the now obligatory plea for fans to support the club in bigger numbers. He said: "This season hasn't gone the way we hoped it would for various reasons, one of which is that we'd hoped for gates in excess of 2,500. We said at the beginning we needed to have a certain figure to break even. That unfortunately has not been achieved."

With eight games to play Hornets sat fifth in the table, one place below the promotion spots and a solitary point behind Wakefield who were fourth. However, the season that started with such optimism fell apart in the last month with a run of five straight defeats including a 22–6 mauling at Blackpool and an embarrassing 19–18 home defeat to Keighley in which Hornets threw away an 11-point second-half lead. Having seen enough, coach Charlie Birdsall quit saying: "I just felt I could do no more with the players". He was replaced by Eric Fitzsimons and Steve Nash in a caretaker capacity.

Two home wins in the last two games were too little too late. Hornets finished fifth, two points outside the top four. Whitehaven finished in fourth place with a worse points difference, but having beaten Hornets home and away.

In his programme notes for the last game of the season, Fred Wood set a solemn tone. "I have been wrong on several accounts this season," he wrote. "The major one being we did not get the promotion to the First Division that we anticipated. The reasons why will be the subject of long deliberation over the next few weeks by the board."

It can be seen from his words that Wood knew that his had been an all-or-nothing takeover and that failure would herald yet more change in the boardroom: "My message to you all (possibly my final one as chairman) is that this club will not go back to the dark days of previous years, we are hell bent on giving you a winning, successful side and no amount of knocks will deflect us from that task."

Despite encouraging words from Fred Wood about 'building for the future', the team was picked apart. Phil McKenzie was signed by Widnes, Greg Austin by Salford. Phil Bancroft stayed in New Zealand where he picked up two Kiwi caps and went to play for the Haswell Hornets instead. Mike Kuiti came back to the UK four years later to play for Leeds.

Despite much paper talk about Hornets interviewing Kiwis coach Graham Lowe and Illawarra Steelers boss Brian Smith for the vacant coaching job, the reality of the club's financial situation was, once again, deeply concerning.

Despite Wood's caginess about the scale of the loss incurred over the season, The *Rochdale Observer* speculated that it could be the club's worst ever financial return. Wood said: "We have yet to go through the balance sheet, but it looks like an even bigger loss than last year for several reasons. One is the number of players signed during the season and the other is the way the attendances fell away during the last few months of the season."

The club called an EGM for 8 July to outline its financial position to the shareholders. When notification of the AGM arrived, it delivered a horrendous double-whammy. Not only had the club's debts more than doubled to £250,000, the letter contained a proposed Extraordinary Resolution that shook shareholders to the core. It asked them to vote in agreement that "... the company cannot, by reason of its liabilities, continue its business and that it is advisable to wind-up the same and that the Company be wound up accordingly. That Mr John Herbert Priestley of Queen Street Sheffield and Mr Peter Lomas of High Street Manchester act as joint liquidators for the purpose of such winding up."

Just 10 months after the old board were ousted because of the club's financial plight, Hornets fans once more found themselves staring into the abyss. And, again, it looked like responsibility for the club's future had been abdicated to the shareholders.

A week before the EGM was due to take place, it was revealed that Fred Wood's plan to survive liquidation was to transfer all of the club's assets into a new company called Tri-Shield Ltd. which would pick-up where the liquidated Rochdale Hornets left off. It was at this point that the Rugby Football League stepped in and refused permission for the transfer to take place.

Wood was incredulous: "The shareholders would have had the majority of control in the new company," he claimed. "The hope was that we could protect the club's assets in the transfer."

"The move to block it by the Rugby League Council may be a setback for the time being, but there are other avenues we can take. I can't reveal what they are right now, but the shareholders will know all about our plans at next week's meeting."

However, at a board meeting on the very next day, Wood was forced to step down from the chair. A statement from the board read: "At a meeting on the Thursday 3rd of July 1986, the directors felt it could be in the best interests of the club if Mr Wood resigned as chairman. Following a vote of the directors, Mr Wood resigned. Mr Leonard Stansfield was subsequently elected chairman and assumed his responsibilities immediately."

Reports suggest that the board thought that Wood was too much of a loose-cannon: accused of making decisions, breaking stories to the media and even signing players without the knowledge of, or consultation with, his fellow directors.

Their statement said that: "Mr Wood will remain a director for the present." But when he was removed from his role as the club's Rugby League Council representative, it was apparent that he was living on borrowed time. The shareholders meeting felt like a case of déjà-vu. Firstly, the Super-Stadium card was played: this time hopes being pinned on the creation of a new stadium set within a shopping complex somewhere 'further along Kingsway'. Then the 'mystery consortium' was brought to the table by former Chairman Jack Grindrod: this time, a trio of 'local businessmen' prepared to raise cash, but unwilling to be named. Then came a call for the board, except Len Stansfield, to resign so that the mystery men could reveal themselves and put themselves up for election. At which point, the board adjourned the meeting, had a brief conversation, came back and said 'no'.

Len Stansfield said: "The directors felt it would be wrong to opt out at this stage. It would be like deserting a ship in its hour of need." Indeed, this was a very dark hour and the need was great. Barclays Bank had first claim on the Athletic Grounds, owed £120,000 by the club.

Brewery JW Lees was owed £28,000, the Inland Revenue was owed £20,000. With other creditors also queuing up to be paid it was calculated that, if the club sold all of its assets, it would be £54,000 short of clearing its debts.

By the end of July, Fred Wood was gone. The other directors said they felt it would be in the best interests of the club if he left. Wood said: "I believe that had I not resigned there was a section of the shareholders who were prepared to call an extraordinary meeting to vote me off the board."

The only other board member to stand down was Bobby Ball. Playing a summer season in Bournemouth, he said that he could not give the time needed to be a 'good club director'. By the time the AGM came around in August, Hornets' board had been pursuing every potential avenue to increase revenue. The opportunity to reintroduce Stock Car racing at the Athletic Grounds had gone down badly with local residents who complained about the noise, so the club endeavoured to negotiate a grant from the council, in return for them surrendering their Stock Car licence.

There was a pop concert where it was hoped 5,000 people would attend, but only 500 turned up. A promoter from Bury showed interest in bringing greyhound racing back to the Athletic Grounds on a 15 year deal worth £100,000. But despite initial plans for a £400,000 upgrade to the stadium and its facilities, the idea never left the drawing board.

Hornets even offered to sell the Athletic Grounds to the council and lease it back from them. The Council said they'd give the plan 'serious thought', and came back with a valuation of just £310,000.

The shareholders did sanction the board to offer its creditors 15p in the pound as a 'deposit' against monies owed, with monthly payments thereafter until the debts were cleared. The creditors accepted the proposal and the liquidators were stood down.

The club's spokesman said: "All we are concerned about is trying to look for ways of keeping rugby league alive in Rochdale. We have a large asset that is worth a lot of money and it needs to be used."

Hornets' cause wasn't helped when the club was slapped with a £1,000 fine, suspended for a year, after an incident at the Barrow home match the previous season where a spectator assaulted the referee. The club said: "Any further incidents of crowd misbehaviour would result in the fine having to be paid immediately. We would hope that supporters are aware of that."

With a new season imminent, coach Eric Fitzsimons was seeking to bolster his squad of kids, amateurs and old-campaigners with four quality Australian imports. Prop Gerry Byrom and half-back Mark Harrigan both came from Sydney's Western Suburbs Magpies; stand-off Darren Thompson and prop Craig Purcell from the Collegians club in Wollongong. In order to get the four to the UK, Hornets launched 'Aussie-Aid', an appeal to supporters and sponsors to raise £1,600 to fund their airfares. The club had hoped to pay the fares itself, but the money it had set aside was used to pay a hefty water rates bill.

The 1986–87 season was a good one. Boosted by the class of their imports Hornets finishing fifth with 19 league wins from 28 games. After a mixed start, a run of seven straight wins launched them into the Premiership play-off places. The first round was a comfortable 30–18 win over Doncaster at Tattersfield in which prop Brian Dunn scored a hat-trick in front of an attendance of 2,543. This gave Hornets a trip to Elland Road to play Champions Hunslet in the semi-final.

The biggest Hornets following for many years made the trip over the Pennines only to discover that coach Eric Fitzsimons had opted for the experience of his 38-year-old assistant coach Steve Nash at scrum-half over in-form half-back Mark Dobson. Nash had only started three games all season. Despite trailing just 10–8 at the break, Hornets collapsed in the second half, eventually crashing 32–8.

By August 1987, the mythical Super Stadium plan was back on the table. The programme notes for the season opener against Runcorn Highfield said: "Progress on the eventual construction of a super all sports stadium has been a little slower than we had originally anticipated, nevertheless it is progressing and we hope to conclude the final agreement shortly. The present intent is that we will play the whole of this season at the Athletic Grounds and then move away for approximately two years. Our temporary home has not been finalised yet, but we hope to remain within Rochdale."

But in October all hopes of Rochdale Council developing the Athletic Grounds into a Super-Stadium were gone. Having declared the deal 'a dead duck', Hornets turned their attention to negotiating the sale of the site to property developers. Hornets initially entered into negotiations to sell the Athletic Grounds to a consortium including Intercity Property Group and Bovis Construction for between £1.5 and £3 million, depending on planning permission. Claiming to be 'on the verge' of signing the deal with Intercity/Bovis, Hornets were linked immediately with a move across town to share with 'crisis torn Rochdale FC at Spotland'.

By early December the contract had been sent to the club's solicitors for the details to be ironed-out. Given that Hornets' board had been meeting the wage bill out of its own pockets for some weeks a sale couldn't come soon enough, but the Christmas break delayed progress.

Come the first week in January a major announcement on the future of the Athletic Grounds was anticipated within days. And it was clear that this was no longer just an opportunity to save Rochdale Hornets. *The Rochdale Observer* described it as a "... multi-million pound plan to save the rugby league club and Rochdale AFC..." But when an announcement came just four days later, it revealed that Hornets had pulled out of the Intercity/Bovis deal and had begun negotiating terms with another developer.

It was reported that the Intercity/Bovis deal fell through after the developer tried to change the terms of the contract at the last minute. Hornets' solicitor had advised the club against the deal because the new clauses indicated that, after the initial payment, they would have received nothing until the ground development was completed, waiting potentially for years before the balance of cash was paid. With debts of £360,000 and an ongoing loss of £400 a week, waiting was something that Hornets could not afford to do. The final nail in the coffin of that project was Rochdale Council rejecting the Intercity/Bovis planning application.

The deal with the new developer promised money up-front and regular payments as development progressed. It was worth "in excess of £2.5 million". Hornets wasted no time in submitting a planning application.

Rochdale FC chairman Jim Marsh didn't waste any time either, engaging his Hornets counterpart Len Stansfield in 'informal talks on the future of both clubs'. With the Dale deep in 'a desperate financial mess', Marsh admitted that their attempts to find interested investors had received 'no response' and that the football club needed 'a miracle' to stay in the Football League.

The Rochdale Observer wrote: "Both sides remain tight-lipped about a Hornets takeover of Spotland, but it now seems obvious that a fairy godmother is unlikely to appear to Rochdale FC now that the pantomime season is over." There was, however, already a great drama surrounding the nature of any Hornets cash-injection into the ground of their ailing football neighbours.

There was press conjecture that the Dale would want to see the ground remain in their hands, with Hornets buying a share of Spotland with enough cash to put the football club back in the black. In return they would get a long-term lease with a low-rent. But it was clear from the outset that Hornets wouldn't pay off the Dale's debts simply to become tenants at the stadium.

Amid the speculation, *The Rochdale Observer* reinforced the importance of the deal to the continuation of professional football of both codes in the town: "One thing is obvious: both clubs must share facilities and costs or both seem certain to go to the wall."

On 16 January 1988 Hornets announced that they had concluded negotiations to sell the Athletic Grounds to Wright Properties Ltd of Hull. Representatives of both parties presented a planning application to Rochdale Council. A club statement said: "This is the culmination of many, many months of frustrating negotiations. We all feel extremely satisfied that after many ups and downs we now have finally reached an agreement which gives the club an absolutely superb deal." But it all depended on Rochdale Council rubber-stamping the planning application. A club spokesman said: "This deal is the only viable scheme which will salvage a future out of the financial wreckage at the Athletic Grounds.

At a special meeting of shareholders on 10 February, shareholders were told that Wright Properties had already paid a non-refundable £30,000 deposit and that, once all debts were cleared, Hornets would have enough left over to build a 'modest purpose-built stadium' and put £1 million in the bank." The sale was ratified by 37 votes to two.

The deposit allowed the club to settle outstanding debts to Ellen Smith Coaches, Norweb, British Gas, North West Water, British Telecom and Filaspun, who supplied the Hornets club ties. Hornets remained cagey on a move across town, a spokesman saying: "Whether we go to Spotland is up to the soccer club board. We have our problems, they have theirs." Across town, the football club's problems looked pretty severe: debts estimated to be 'in the region of £300,000' and a record trading loss for the year.

Programme notes from the Keighley defeat on 6 March said: "The sale of the ground has naturally gone quiet due to legal formalities and we would hope you bear with us. As the shareholders agreed, nothing further can be said until we are given the go ahead and it is a matter of patience to wait and see if our final game at the Athletic Grounds will indeed be Oldham on Good Friday."

Hornets decided to make the game an all-ticket affair. Having held a record crowd of 41,831 for the 1924 Challenge Cup Final between Oldham and Wigan, the venerable old ground had a safety restricted capacity of just 5,000. And Hornets were anticipating a sell-out. Good Friday 1988 fell on 1 April. Fate, it seems, has a sense of humour.

Neil Cowie looks to offload in the last game at the Athletic Grounds, 1 April 1988. In support Graham Idle (left), Terry Mellor (centre) and Andy Ruane (right.) (Courtesy Jim Stringer)

Given the emotions of the day and the niggling uncertainty surrounding the sale, the day had the air of a wake about it. Images from the game show a ground that had long since seen better days. Once considered the finest stadium in Lancashire, the Athletic Grounds had become a crumbling, unloved shadow of its former self.

The visitors for its swansong were a very good Oldham side en-route to the Second Division title. It was 94 years since Hornets first played Oldham on the Athletic Grounds, a two-tries to nil victory in front of 15,000 people. But, on this day, the odds were long on Hornets producing a romantic end to their Athletic Grounds story. This derby was the Roughyeds' seventh match in a 15 game run in which they lost only once. They would finish the season with just four defeats.

In the programme notes, the board seemed resigned to the inevitable: "The main topic of conversation throughout the season has been the sale of the Athletic Grounds and at the time of going to press for this final programme of the season the situation remains unresolved."

"If we are watching our favourites from a new venue next year the nostalgia of the Athletic Grounds will remain in some hearts for ever. So savour what could be your last look at these familiar surroundings and remember the good things in rugby league witnessed in this stadium."

As anticipated, Oldham proved far too strong. With no hint of sentimentality, they swept Hornets aside, scoring 11 tries to win 58–6 in front of 3,260 fans. Popular Australian half-back Aaron Sawyer etched his name in history as the last Hornets try-scorer at the Athletic Grounds. His try was converted by Gary Hitchen, who became the last Hornets points-scorer on their famous old ground. At the final hooter hands were shaken, photos taken and last looks quietly lingered over. Fans stood in 'their spot' – in silence – long after the players had left the field.

A month later, the Athletic Grounds suffered its final indignity when a fire destroyed the central section of the main stand, causing £100,000 worth of damage. It was uninsured, the club unable to meet the £50,000 premium.

What the fire did do was confirm the Oldham game as Hornets' last at the Athletic Grounds. Chairman Len Stansfield said: "We cannot play at the Athletic Grounds because the stand could well be condemned and that would mean that we could no longer use the dressing rooms, boardroom or offices underneath."

"The priority now is to find a place to play next season. We have not discounted the possibility of playing at Spotland." In the end, the last season at the Athletic Grounds was a long, relentless slog with little for the faithful to cheer. After beating Barrow 6–4 in the Challenge Cup on 31 January, Hornets didn't win another home game. They managed just a solitary away win all season, 11–10 at Carlisle.

Hornets finished third bottom with just 10 wins from 28 games. In doing so they scored the second fewest number of tries in both divisions with 52, just one more than basement club Batley, an average of less than two tries per game.

Planning permission was granted for Wright Properties to build a new Morrisons store. What was once expected to become a Super-Stadium would become a supermarket. Rochdale Hornets, who had battled against financial ruin for most of their history, prepared for the next chapter of their history with £2.6 million in the bank.

From the proceeds of sale of the Athletic Grounds, Hornets used £400,000 to purchase a 47.5 percent shareholding in Denehurst Park (Rochdale) Ltd, also known as 'The Stadium Company', a property management company formed to take over the ownership, development and management of Rochdale AFC's Spotland Stadium.

The other shareholders in The Stadium Company were Rochdale AFC (47.5 percent) and Rochdale Metropolitan Borough Council (5 percent). The plan was that its revenue would come from rents paid by both sporting clubs and any income brought in through other commercial ventures.

Ultimately, it was a deal that worked for all parties. The cash injection pulled the Dale back from the brink; Hornets had an equal share in a stadium with lots of development potential. And, with their club debt-free and cash-rich, Hornets' long-suffering fans prepared for a move across town with expectations of a brighter future.

References

Rothmans Rugby League Yearbook 1981–82
Rothmans Rugby League Yearbook 1982–83
Rothmans Rugby League Yearbook 1983–84
Rothmans Rugby League Yearbook 1984–85
Rothmans Rugby League Yearbook 1985–86
Rothmans Rugby League Yearbook 1986–87
Rothmans Rugby League Yearbook 1987–88
Rochdale Observer - 15 November 1980
Rochdale Observer - 6 March 1985
Rochdale Observer - 16 March 1985
Rochdale Observer - 23 March 1985
Rochdale Observer - 3 April 1985
Rochdale Observer - 8 June 1985
Rochdale Observer - 15 June 1985
Rochdale Observer - 19 June 1985
Rochdale Observer - 22 June 1985
Rochdale Observer - 26 June 1985
Rochdale Observer - 28 June 1985
Rochdale Observer - 9 January 1988
Rochdale Observer - 13 January 1988
Rochdale Observer - 16 January 1988
Rochdale Observer - 23 January 1988
Rochdale Observer - 27 January 1988
Rochdale Observer - 30 January 1988
Rochdale Observer - 6 February 1988
Rochdale Observer - 13 February 1988
Rochdale Observer - 20 February 1988
Rochdale Observer - 6 April 1988
Rochdale Observer - 7 May 1988
Rochdale Observer - 14 May 1988
Rochdale Hornets v Whitehaven Programme Notes 1 September 1985
Rochdale Hornets v Blackpool Borough Programme Notes 8 December 1985
Rochdale Hornets v Huddersfield Programme Notes 7 May 1986
Rochdale Hornets v Oldham Programme Notes 1 April 1988
Minutes of Rochdale Hornets RLFC Board Meetings October 1987 - November 1998

12. 1990: Never a dull moment

In June 1989 Hornets sacked coach Jim Crellin. They had finished ninth in the Second Division with 15 wins from 28 games. A month later they appointed former Man of Steel Allan Agar, who'd coached Featherstone Rovers to a famous Challenge Cup Final win over Hull FC just six years earlier.

Sitting on over £1m in cash following the sale of the Athletic Grounds, Hornets and their new coach went on a spending-spree. They brought in Widnes scrum-half Andy Sullivan for £20,000, Kiwi Dean Lonergan (fee undisclosed), Warrington prop Tony Humphries for £30,000 and Castleford forward John Blackburn for £20,000. To cap it all, the club shattered its record transfer fee, paying Widnes £75,000 for prop Mike O'Neill.

Under Agar, Hornets hit the ground running, starting the season with a run of eight straight victories, including some real fireworks on 5 November, a record-breaking 92–0 home win over Runcorn Highfield. The 16 tries scored were shared among eight try-scorers, with Martin Hall, Logan Edwards and Mark Lord scoring hat-tricks. It was a good day for stand-off Steve 'Ticker' Turner too; he broke Hornets' goals in a game record with 14 and he also scored a try to weigh in with a personal tally of 32 points.

As the victories kept coming, all eyes were on the impending Boxing Day clash with Oldham. The Roughyeds had run neck-and-neck with Hornets at the top end of the table all season and, with Christmas less than a month away, the pressure became palpable as both of the fierce derby rivals sought any sliver of advantage in their push for promotion.

Oldham approached the game distracted by three consecutive rounds of the Regal Trophy. Hornets had a wobble with two out of character defeats: a 36–22 Regal Trophy first round defeat against Sheffield, played on a Friday night at Halifax's Thrum Hall, and a lacklustre 25–18 home loss to Bramley, the only home league defeat of the season.

Come Boxing Day Spotland was packed. 8,061 fans, a Rochdale Hornets record for the ground, were crowbarred in to see the Second Division match of the season. The atmosphere was electric. Advantage in the promotion race was at stake, as were the bragging rights, in the most meaningful A627M derby for many years.

With just seven minutes gone, Hornets were in front: Andy Sullivan fed Dean Lonergan into space near halfway. The giant Kiwi bolted downfield, sold Oldham full-back Hyde an outrageous dummy and crashed in to score. John Woods slotted over the touchline conversion to give Hornets the lead.

The early loss of Karl Marriott with a leg injury forced Hornets to shuffle their pack a little and, as Oldham began to apply some defensive pressure, they dragged themselves back into the game. McAlister converted his own try just before the quarter and added a penalty five minutes later to edge Oldham ahead.

As the game became increasingly tight, both sides bombed golden opportunities to score, but with the half-time hooter imminent, John Woods hit the gas to outstrip the Oldham defence and score out wide. Hornets ahead at the break 10–8.

In the second half, Hornets unleashed an onslaught. An aerial bombardment by Andy Sullivan had Lord and Hyde in all kinds of trouble; the forwards ripped-in, repeatedly forcing turnovers. One such tackle saw Atkinson cough up the ball; Mark Lord and John Higgins combined to take Hornets upfield where Neil Cowie produced a wonder pass to give Paul Gamble a clear run to the line. Steve 'Ticker' Turner added the extras to extend Hornets' lead. Ticker was on target again with a penalty on the hour to give Hornets a 10 point buffer.

Victory was sealed with 10 minutes remaining. Another steepling Andy Sullivan bomb; Hyde flapping and fumbling; Paul McDermott on hand to scoop up the ball and score; Turner with the conversion. Hornets fans in full voice; Oldham fans heading for the gates in droves. A late, late Oldham try by Lord was scant consolation for the visitors, but this was Hornets' day. One of the most memorable of the Spotland era.

Hornets line-up on the day was: Chris Myler, John Higgins, Mark Lord, Mark Nixon, Karl Marriott; John Woods, Andy Sullivan; Paul Gamble, Martin Hall, Neil Cowie, Dean Lonergan, Tony Humphries, Paul McDermott. Subs: Steve Turner, Bob Marsden.

Bar an irritating defeat at Ryedale York and a narrow 22–16 loss at Widnes, the second half of the season echoed the first. A run of six straight wins culminated in Hornets travelling to Swinton needing a win to get promoted.

On a sunny Sunday afternoon, a sizeable and very noisy Hornets following made the trip to Station Road to see their side cruise to a 37–16 victory that sparked a post-match pitch invasion and joyous celebrations. Hornets turned in a near flawless performance that left Swinton chasing shadows. It was also the game in which lynchpin scrum-half Andy Sullivan, who had laid-on dozens of tries for his team-mates, scored his only try of the season.

In the two games after promotion was secured, Hornets went on a points spree, scoring 52 against Keighley and 70 against Trafford Borough to set-up a final day showdown at Watersheddings to decide who finished second.

Having been outstanding all season, Hornets saved their worst performance of the season for last, crashing to Oldham by 30–2. But John Woods's penalty made all the difference as Hornets snatched second place from Oldham's grasp on a single point of points difference. In a memorable season, Hornets won 24 of their 28 league games.

In preparation for life in the top flight, Hornets signed scrum-half Neil Holding from St Helens for £50,000, hooker Ian Gormley from Salford at £60,000, Gold Coast Chargers half-back Bob Grogan and, via Chorley Borough, Kiwi half-back Stu Galbraith, both fees were undisclosed.

Hornets' first season back in the top flight since 1978–79 was a disaster, but it had started so well. The first league game was at sunny Wakefield. A large and noisy Hornets following had turned out to see their team compete with the best in the British game. After 10 minutes, winger Mark Viller dived in by the flag to give Hornets a 4–0 nil lead. Briefly, the Hornets fans believed that, just maybe, they belonged at the top table. But it was a short-lived celebration.

By the final hooter, Wakefield had scored seven unanswered tries, each converted by former Hornet Kevin Harcombe, to win 42–6. Hornets' only other contribution came from two Myler drop-goals. It was the first defeat of many.

Hornets eventually broke their duck seven games into a 26 game season: a 19–12 victory over Bradford Northern that would turn out to be their only win of the season. Despite

Hornets' quite abysmal league form, fans took some respite from a run in the Regal Trophy that saw them go all the way to the semi-final.

The first round was a perfunctory 30–10 defeat of Saddleworth Rangers. Round two saw Hornets travel to Tattersfield on a Wednesday night in December where they overcame Doncaster 14–10 in near Arctic conditions. The draw for round three produced a trip to Castleford, where a masterclass in game management from Colin Whitfield and a cheeky Neil Holding drop-goal saw Hornets produce a shock 19–14 win.

Hornets travelled to Headingley for the semi-final with confidence, having beaten Bradford in the league. But, on the day, they couldn't find a way through a stingy Bradford defence, eventually going down 13–2 in front of the BBC television cameras.

Having briefly shown what they were capable of, Hornets' return to league action heralded a run of 16 straight defeats, broken only by a narrow 14–10 win over Second Division Chorley in the Challenge Cup. With the slide clearly out of his control, coach Alan Agar took the unusual step of resigning at half-time during a 30–16 defeat at Sheffield. His assistant Brian Juliff took temporary charge the following week at Castleford, a 42–0 defeat. Scrum-half Neil Holding was then appointed player-coach for the last 11 games of the season, but the damage had been done.

Hornets ended the season rock-bottom of the Stones Bitter Championship, 14 points adrift of next to bottom Sheffield with a points difference of −595. More notably, Hornets returned to the Second Division having spent more than a quarter of a million pounds on transfer fees over two seasons.

Having been ignominiously relegated from the top flight, new Hornets coach Stan Gittins wasted no time in trading the costly players signed for the abortive First Division campaign for players better suited to his direct, no-nonsense ethos. Neil Holding went to Oldham in exchange for Australian half-back Brett Clark and former Great Britain tour centre Ronnie Duane. Then he did a deal that sent Mike O'Neill to Leeds and brought powerhouse Kiwi loose-forward Mike Kuiti back to Hornets. He was joined in the pack by explosive Samoan international prop Paul Okesene.

Just ahead of the season's start, Wigan swooped to sign Neil Cowie for £60,000, with a further £15,000 on his international debut. Gittins went for an experienced replacement, former Warrington forward Bob Eccles.

It's fair to say that Hornets proved steady if unspectacular in an eight team second division where teams played the other clubs four times. But, once again, they shone in a cup competition, this time the Lancashire Cup.

Hornets brushed aside Third Division Highfield 34–13 in round one, but provided the giant-killing highlight of round two, beating First Division Salford at Spotland. Hornets left the Red Devils stunned with a dominant first-half performance, going in at the half-time with a 21–0 lead. Despite Salford's best efforts after the break Hornets stood firm, running out 25–18 victors. The semi-final draw fell in Hornets' favour. St Helens drew Wigan. Hornets drew Carlisle at home; a tie which pitted Paul Okesene against his brother Hitro in a true battle of the giants. But it was Paul's day. Hornets swept past Carlisle with a clear 19–6 win to reach their first Lancashire Cup Final for 26 years.

Awaiting them in the Final was a star-studded St Helens side packed with internationals, but Hornets produced one of the most courageous performances the competition has seen, twice having Saints on the ropes only for them to scramble back into the game.

The shock was on after 13 minutes when Mike Kuiti and Colin Whitfield combined up the narrow left edge for Ronnie Duane to crash in and score. Saints grabbed a try from Veivers, but Hornets hit back with a moment of magic: prop Bob Marsden broke in centre field and drew Saints defenders to him. Darren Abram looped round to take the offload, skating into space to score from 40 metres. Colin Whitfield hit the extras; Saints reeling. A Bishop try for Saints brought them back into contention, but the Hornets fans in the 9,269 crowd could hardly believe their side's 10–8 half time lead.

Saints went ahead for the first time just five minutes after the break when Bishop found Veivers with a neat pass. Their next try was hotly contested, both on the field and on the television commentary. Hornets had the feed at a scrum close to their own line. As Steve Gartland bent to collect the ball, Saints prop Mann broke early, kicked the ball from Gartland's fingertips and dived in to touch down. Referee David Campbell, in charge of his first major final, pointed to the spot, surrounded by angry Hornets.

Hornets hit back, though. First a long clearing kick towards Saints full-back Tanner was chased by Paul Okesene. Just as Tanner gathered the ball, Okesene hit him like an express train, leaving him splayed-out on the Wilderspool turf. Hornets pushed forward, Bob Marsden this time feeding Mike Kuiti in to score. Hornets back in the chase at 20–14. Despite throwing everything at Saints, Hornets couldn't engineer an opening. In response, Veivers rolled back the years to produce a slick pass that sent Mann in for the deciding try.

The game ended on a sour note as Saints' half-back Paul Bishop was sent off on the hooter for stamping on Brett Clark in the last tackle of the game. Despite the defeat, Hornets had shown that they were a side prepared to work hard, dig-in and play some expansive rugby when the opportunity arose.

Hornets ended the season a comfortable fifth in the Second Division with 12 wins and two draws from 28 games and looked in a good position to kick-on. It was a season in which change on the field was echoed by changes off it. The March 1992 AGM saw shareholders elect a new director, who became a distinctly different style of chairman.

Programme notes for the Carlisle game on 1 March 1992 – Hornets won 44–14 – announced a new addition to the Hornets board, accountant Bob Tattersall: "An executive with sportswear giants Reebok is a new face on the Hornets board, replacing secretary Paul Reynolds. Robert Tattersall, who lives close to Spotland, is well known in local sporting circles." Tattersall's experience in corporate finance with a leading sports brand felt like a good fit. Within weeks of his appointment, Hornets players began running out in new Reebok boots and a Reebok advertisement appeared in the programme. It had the air of a 'brand endorsement' about it. It felt modern and professional, the sort of thing a top flight football team would do.

Bob Tattersall's focus, though was on the business. He said: "If the company is to remain in business for the foreseeable future it is imperative that strict financial controls are put and kept in place."

French Connection: Hornets prop Cliff Eccles drives into the Treize Catalan defence in a John Player Cup tie on 8 November 1992. Hornets beat the French championship finalists elect 32–16.
(Courtesy Jim Stringer)

Reebok executive Bob Tattersall joined the Hornets board with plans to implement strict financial controls and stabilise the club. But his methods fell foul of the 'old guard', who used their shareholding power to force through a vote of no-confidence in one of the most contentious meetings in the club's history. (Courtesy Jim Stringer)

135

He was also an advocate of building stronger relationships with supporters, recognising the need to keep spectators involved and aware of what was happening at the club. On match-days he would walk around the ground chatting with fans, listening to their comments, engaging with their concerns. More radically, he was an advocate of making shares in the company more readily available to those who wanted them.

Hornets began the 1992–93 season in style, winning 10 of the first 14 league games. For good measure, they also thumped top French side Treize Catalan 36–16 at Spotland in the Regal Trophy. In the new year, January was a month of upheaval. Four consecutive away games delivered four straight defeats that saw Stan Gittins sacked. He was replaced by former Parramatta reserve-grade prop Peter Regan who'd cut his coaching teeth at a number of clubs in the NSW Country competition. The first challenge he had to contend with was Hornets selling his first-choice hooker Martin Hall to Wigan for £35,000.

Through February and into March, Hornets' form improved; four league wins from five games had confidence on the up. But off the field a storm was brewing. Over the season it became clear that Bob Tattersall's prudent, accountable management style had rattled a few cages amongst some sections of the shareholders. A year after his appointment some of them sought a return to the old order. An Extraordinary General Meeting was called by a group of shareholders for Monday 15 March 1993. Their motion? A vote of no confidence in the board and the subsequent removal of its members.

The move polarised the shareholders: those who saw Bob Tattersall's board as a break from past failures and a positive force for radical change and those who craved a return to a more traditional style of management. Ahead of the EGM, Tattersall was forthright in the defence of his approach: "Since I joined the board in 1992, I have attempted with my colleagues to put in place a solid administration base in order that the company can run its affairs in a business-like manner." He went on: "It has taken us the last six to eight months to get the company stabilised and in a position where aggressive and prudent management can take advantage of the golden opportunity provided to the club by the new facilities at Spotland and the appointment of a new coach."

His philosophy was simple: sort out the commercial side and then replenish the board by co-opting business-people with specific areas of expertise. He said: "We need to be electing new people and not re-electing directors tainted by recent failures to control the financial aspect of the club."

The group standing for election against Tattersall's board planned to reduce the club's financial deficit by £175,000 by cutting staff costs – primarily player contracts – and funding a 'Team Development Account' from "... transfer fees received, a new fixed term endowment and revenue from special projects." They also planned a new lottery with the aim of recruiting 'between six and seven thousand members' which they said would generate £3,000 of revenue per week.

The EGM saw the unfolding of one of the most contentious events in the club's history. The first part of the no-confidence proposal required a series of votes on the removal of individual directors; the second part required a series of votes to install new directors proposed by the group standing for election.

The first motion had the room on edge. It asked that chairman Bob Tattersall be removed as a director. On a show of hands its defeat looked like a formality: 25 for, 34 against. However, there came a call for a poll vote: a vote where voters' individual shareholdings – and any proxies they might hold – are counted. With individuals in the minority holding blocks of up to 100 shares, the tables were turned. The motion to remove Bob Tattersall was passed by 1,656 to 1,125.

The motion to also remove Len Stansfield went much the same way. And, when the motions to appoint Ray Clarke, Jim Crellin, John Nicholson and Paul Reynolds were similarly defeated on a show of hands, the anger in the room grew as each vote was overturned following a call for a poll vote. There was no doubt, this was a coup that no-one saw coming.

Amid allegations from the floor of 'undemocratic procedures', uproar ensued as the voices of ordinary fans with small shareholdings were silenced by the influence of legacy shareholders, including some who never came to games or showed even the remotest interest in the club.

Despite surviving the power-grab, sitting vice-chairman Tom Ashworth and director Dennis Turner resigned on principal. Club doctor Gordon Ratcliffe also resigned in protest at the voting procedures, saying he could not work with the new board. Bob Tattersall described it as: "an utter disgrace which goes against the rules of natural justice."

The fallout was bitter: the letters page of *The Rochdale Observer* full to overflowing with the disappointment of ordinary fans. They called the vote 'a betrayal', 'a stab in the back by idiot shareholders', a 'return to the old brigade', 'a giant leap backwards' and 'entry through the back door'.

Given the strength of feeling among rank-and-file supporters, Hornets general manager Ian McMahon was concerned about the impact that any potential supporter protests would have on the players at that weekend's game against Swinton. He said: "If everyone can transfer the passion with which they have fought off the field over the last couple of weeks into backing the players, then I am sure that the players will respond positively."

Hornets lost the Swinton game 25–14, with protests mostly confined to some low-key booing of the directors. After the game, McMahon was forced to deny that the club had used 'heavy handed' tactics to prevent supporters raising their voices in protest at the way in which the board had taken control. Amid accusations that stewards had been sent onto the Wilbutts Lane terrace to intimidate fans into silence, he said: "We sent the stewards around the ground at the end of the match because we had been told there might be an attempt to stage a demonstration on the pitch."

In the wake of the EGM, Bob Tattersall too spoke of the use of intimidatory tactics: "We attempted to break down the barriers that existed between directors and the fans and had made inroads into it ... I feel that the time is right to release shares to the supporters of the club. I was warned that if I didn't conform or withdraw, I would be removed from office, which subsequently happened."

He continued: "I know who was behind it, so do the people who were at the shareholders meeting and that is the problem with the present structure of the company where people have accumulated shares over a good number of years and can exercise power in a way that may not always be in the best interests of the club..."

After the EGM Hornets stuttered badly: four straight defeats evidence enough that the off-field traumas had affected the playing side. Despite the upheavals, Hornets battled hard to finish fourth in an eight team Second Division. That secured a place in convoluted Divisional Premiership play-offs that saw Hornets pitched against Third Division champions Keighley Cougars. Riding high on the crest of the Cougarmania wave, Keighley brought a huge following to Spotland, but it was the Hornets fans in the 2,457 crowd that had the last laugh as Peter Regan's team swept past the Cougars in a thrilling 26–18 victory that left Hornets just 80 minutes from Old Trafford.

However, glory was to elude Hornets as Third Division runners-up Workington produced a shock 30–16 win in front of a large and boisterous travelling support amongst the 4,025 crowd.

Hornets prepared for the 1993–94 season by putting a whole host of players on the transfer list. Leading try and points scorer Steve Gartland was listed at £50,000, Cliff Eccles at £70,000, Karl Marriott and Ian Gormley at £35,000 each and Paul Reynolds (player, not director) at £10,000. There was some other player movement too; Matt Calland joined Featherstone for £30,000, Mike Kuiti joined Oldham, and Hornets exchanged winger Adrian Belle and utility forward David Chrimes for Oldham's goalkicking centre Martin Strett. It was all very disconcerting.

The season started with a bang, a 64–8 pasting of Highfield in which winger Jason Green scored a hat-trick. But by October Hornets had slid to five consecutive defeats and, just six weeks into a new season, Peter Regan's short, but popular, reign as Hornets coach was ended, leaving the club looking for its sixth coach in three years.

Despite having ended the previous season a comfortable 4th in an eight team second division, Hornets finished more than a dozen points behind the front-runners Featherstone and Oldham. Now they were looking for the man who could turn them into serious challengers. They chose another Australian: Steve 'Gibbo' Gibson.

As an exceptionally gifted, attacking fullback, Gibbo's playing ability was not in question. Fast, skilful and inventive, he'd enjoyed a successful career at Salford and had developed cult status amongst adoring fans at The Willows. They loved how he played and they loved his approachable, likeable, cheeky personality, happy-go-lucky, quick-witted and always with time for a chat and a joke.

Steve Gibson was born in Allora, a tiny rural town on the Darling Downs in South-Eastern Queensland, with a population of 1,223. He had five rugby league-playing brothers and four sisters. He started playing at Allora Junior Rugby League and later played senior club rugby for Wattles in the neighbouring town of Clifton.

In 1984 he gained selection for the Queensland Country side that toured New Zealand. That same year he scored the winning try in an 18–16 success for the Toowoomba Clydesdales representative side over the touring Great Britain Lions, though he modestly says that was one of his worst ever matches. Gibbo then had a season with Norths in Brisbane followed by two seasons with Souths Magpies when an opportunity arose for him to play in England.

In 1993, Steve Gibson, an affable Australian full-back became Hornets' player coach. He built a hard-working team around a core of local players that could compete with the best in the game. (Courtesy Jim Stringer)

With a couple of weeks of the Australian season remaining Gibbo was approached by a scout, and just three weeks later a deal had been agreed with Salford. He arrived in England in the late summer of 1987. Gibbo admits: "It all happened very quickly."

As part of his contract at Salford, Gibbo was given a car. The first thing he did was to drive to London 'the long way round', taking in all the sights and getting lost many times en-route. Nobody believed that he'd actually driven there and back, but a 500 mile round trip was nothing for someone used to the vast open spaces of Queensland.

Living so far from home meant that keeping in contact with friends and family back in Queensland had its challenges. Fortunately, a friendly journalist let slip to Gibbo that the press box at the Willows had international phone access. Being a good teammate, he informed his fellow Australians about this. One Christmas, there were a dozen Antipodean players queuing to use the phone line, which, once discovered, wasn't well-received by the club. Gibbo kept his head down, his good form giving him a degree of protection from any serious punishment, but Australian Tony Rampling and Kiwi Mark Brooke-Cowden were sacked for the misdemeanour.

It was during his time at Salford that Gibbo met Iain 'Corky' McCorquodale, who was the club's 'A' team coach. Corky had enjoyed a long and successful professional rugby league career himself, predominantly with Workington and Fulham, where he was renowned as an ace goal-kicking winger. An Oldham schoolteacher who did so much for the game in the town at all levels, Corky would often lead the training sessions at the Willows and he had an easy knack of making players feel relaxed and confident.

Though different in personality, Gibbo and Corky's rugby philosophies were similar. Corky's mantra was "keep it simple, make it quick" and, like Gibbo, he encouraged open, attacking, improvised play. When they came together at Hornets, training centred on ball-work. Gibbo loved 'tick and pass' and he was always captain and first pick. He also loved practising outlandish moves that he would occasionally try in games, one favourite being a flick kick over the defence with the back of his heel.

When legendary Australian international full-back Garry Jack arrived at The Willows in 1993, it was a cue for Gibbo to move on. At the time Hornets had an interest in Salford's Martin Birkett and director Jim Crellin went to watch the classy Cumbrian centre play.

However, Gibbo had an outstanding match and, within a week, he'd accepted the job as Hornets' player-coach. He'd represented Salford with distinction, scoring 73 tries. In 1991 he was rated the best full-back in Britain and he also holds the record of being Salford's longest serving overseas player.

Gibbo's only prior coaching experience hadn't ended well. While at Salford he was asked to run a community coaching session with local schoolchildren. He playfully gave a youngster a kick, which landed him in hot water. Gibbo joked: "I never denied kicking the kid, but what was I supposed to do? He passed the f***ing thing forward!"

The appointment, championed by Jim Crellin, was almost an act of provocation towards some of the other board members. To say there wasn't harmony in the boardroom would be an understatement. Though the decision was, initially, heavily criticised by the 'old brigade', former chairman Peter Rush remains a huge Gibson fan: "Gibbo was a very welcome signing, one of the bravest players we've had. He was fast, strong, intelligent - the best guy I ever worked with as chairman. He had a huge personality, a great leader and really was a true 'man of steel'."

Indeed, Gibbo was smart enough to recognise that he needed help with the coaching aspect of his role and, like all coaches, he wanted to put his own backroom team together. On Gibbo's departure from the Willows, Iain McCorquodale wrote to him sending his congratulations on securing the Hornets job. Corky recalls that he hoped it wouldn't appear too obviously as a letter of application for the assistant's job, although that's exactly what it was and it had the desired effect.

Gibbo recalls, "I needed guidance obviously. I needed help and I needed to bring in new ideas." Corky provided the perfect support. Gibbo made an outstanding start in his role as player-coach. After five consecutive losses before his arrival, he delivered three straight wins, against Bramley, Dewsbury and Blackpool, and scored in each one, returning five tries from three games. It ensured that his cult status quickly transferred from Salford to Spotland.

Gibbo's abiding memory of the make-up of the squad he and Corky developed was the high number of local Rochdale lads and near-local Oldham lads. Gibbo remembers proudly: "We turned Hornets into a local club, with all the boys from Rochdale at the heart of it."

Looking back, the number of lads from those two towns who played first team rugby was exceptional. Emon Ratu, Karl Marriott, Paul O'Keefe, Steve Turner, Steve Gartland, Rob Hall, Martin Kay, Vinnie Miller, Chris Churm, Martin Bunce, Steve Mawdsley, Sean Whitehead, Neil Flanagan, Michael Farrell, Tony Hilton, Paul Higginson, Gareth Pratt, Chris Coop, Craig Diggle, Craig Mort and Chris Hilton were all regular first-teamers under Gibbo.

One benefit of a Hornets team consisting of so many local lads was the regular positive post-match team bonding sessions around the hostelries of Rochdale, which were great for morale. Many of the Oldham lads in particular had their special idiosyncrasies after a pint or two. Martin Kay and Neil Flanagan, both former Great Britain youth internationals and fine products of Oldham St Annes, had a penchant for dispensing of their clothing at any opportunity. Steve Mawdsley, former Saddleworth Rangers, BARLA tourist and a very sensible banker by day, took great delight in starting the night by doing press ups on his way to the first pub ... face-down in the biggest puddle he could find. He would regularly arrive at the bar with his clothes dripping wet as if it were the most natural thing in the world. Emon Ratu was also a fan of continuing his exercise regime during a night out. His particular favourite was star jumps in the back of black taxi cabs, much to the driver's astonishment.

The strong presence of local players was, in many ways, financially driven with most having been picked up economically from the local amateur ranks. Corky's network and knowledge of amateur rugby league, particularly in Oldham, was very strong. In addition, Hornets had other Oldham rugby league stalwarts Ray Clark and Chris Deakin with great local experience. Because of those links, Oldham St Annes, Saddleworth, Fitton Hill and Waterhead all proved fertile supply grounds.

And what could be better than a Hornets team with a core of tough, tight-knit Rochdale lads? This engendered a desire to perform and huge will to win. No player embodied this sentiment more than Karl Marriott. Karl, a former Great Britain youth international, was fast, strong, aggressive and skilful. He made other players raise their games through his own single-minded commitment to the cause. "Nobody is going to take the bread from my babies' mouths!" he would say in the dressing room before a game and everyone knew what was expected of them.

No more so than in the 15–8 win against high-flying London Crusaders on 2 January 1994 in which Karl scored a try and took the man-of-the-match award with a typically swashbuckling performance. The game was the first of a 10-game run in which Hornets won eight, including memorable victories against Huddersfield, 42–8. and away to champions-elect Workington.

Workington were en-route to promotion, runaway league leaders, with the likes of Des Drummond, Ged Byrne, Phil McKenzie, Brad Hepi and James Pickering in their side. However, Hornets had some class too. Gibbo particularly remembers former Queensland State of Origin player Cavill Heugh having a blinder in the shock 37–12 win at Derwent Park. He was always able to tell in the first few tackles of a game whether he was up for it or not. And, on this day, Cavill Heugh was at his finest.

Workington just could not contain Hornets, with try-scoring performances from Cavill Heugh, Steve Gartland (2), Ian Bates, Richard Pachniuk and Vinnie Miller, who scored a length of the field try following a Gibson break from his own goal line.

At the end of Gibbo's first season in charge, Hornets finished exactly halfway in a remodelled 16 team Second Division with 18 wins from 30 league games; 20 from 35 in all competitions. Despite limited funds, Gibbo and Corky continued to make some shrewd signings. Having brought in a former Salford contingent of David Fell, Wayne Reid and John Gilfillan, they turned their sights to the other side of the Pennines.

Castleford's former-GB prop forward Keith England was a great signing for Hornets, leading by example every week. The coaching duo decided, as away wins in white rose county had proven hard to come by, they needed some additional Yorkshire influence. Bradford Northern's heavyweight prop Paul Grayshon was brought in with the intention of addressing this imbalance.

Corky says, "I really liked Graysh. He was a good player, from a good family and we could get him at a good price. He was a big bloke and when we went to summer rugby I asked the board for a new kit, mainly to help Graysh. The shirts were so thick you could hardly breathe in them!"

"I asked for something a bit lighter in weight and colour - and it was just about the only time the board was unanimous! Director Paul Reynolds told me 'We are not changing those shirts under any circumstances!' Eventually we got Paul's son Mark, the club kit-man, to talk his dad around and everyone could breathe again."

Rochdale's own Steve 'Ticker' Turner takes on the Keighley Cougars defence at a sunny Spotland in 1995. In support, another Rochdale product, Chris Hilton.
(Rochdale Hornets Heritage Archive)

Mark Reynolds also used to run on with the sand for the kickers on match-days, but he wore his heart on his sleeve and would often let his feelings be known to the officials. Corky remembers that it didn't always help Hornets' cause: "Mark used to wind up the touch judges with his colourful language and partisan behaviour, which didn't always serve us well."

In a local derby against Oldham, a team that Reynolds especially hated, Corky tried to use a bit of psychology to temper his enthusiasm. He pulled him to one side just as the match was starting and told him: "I've heard Great Britain are looking for a new kit man. They're considering a shortlist of four and your name's one of them. But you just have to calm yourself down. Imagine being on duty in an international match at the Sydney Cricket Ground. You can't go running on screaming and abusing the officials. Mark said 'I'll stop it as of this moment'."

Corky recalls, however, that: "... the game had only been going about 10 minutes and he was at the side of the pitch screaming as usual. He then came up to the dugout, head down, and said to me: 'I don't suppose I'll get that job now.'"

Hornets kicked off the 1994–95 season in style with another good win away in Cumbria, beating Barrow 48–22 on a scorching August day. Iain McCorquodale recalls how he did some extra practice with recent half-back signing Chris Churm the day before the game: "I asked Churmy to stay back and we practiced chipping the ball over a defender, me, and re-gathering. In the Barrow game Chris was on a hat-trick and made a break with just the full-back to beat. 'Chip him!' I shouted. Chris attempted a chip, but instead kicked the ball straight into the full-back's face, breaking his nose and knocking him cold. I'm just glad it wasn't me!"

In the next match, Hornets entertained Keighley, who were still riding the wave of 'Cougarmania'. The division's big spenders were coached by Corky's arch-rival, and fellow Oldham school teacher, Phil Larder. "I was desperate to win this game against Larder", recalls McCorquodale, "but unfortunately I missed the game as I was on a school trip to France. With 10 minutes of the game remaining, I called the club from France to ask the score. Nobody could tell me the score, they were all too busy counting the money from the bumper gate receipts from the hordes of travelling Keighley fans. I had to hold on for 10 minutes. It cost me a fortune. And we lost, 30–16." Indeed, the attendance of 2,304 was Hornets' biggest gate of the season.

In the most memorable game of the campaign, Hornets drew all-conquering Wigan away at Central Park in the second round of the Regal Trophy and gave the reigning World Champions a torrid time. Hornets were trailing by just one score with 13 minutes remaining, but then came disaster. Australian second-row Brian McCarthy was given a red card for poleaxing Henry Paul, falling victim to the Kiwi's incredible step and change of direction. Playing a man short, Hornets were unable to prevent Wigan from blowing-out the scoreline, eventually going down 34–12.

Wigan fielded a star-studded team, including Shaun Edwards, Andy Farrell, Martin Offiah, Gary Connolly, Va'aiga Tuigamala and former Welsh rugby union international Scott Quinnell on debut, but this was the perfect example of how a Steve Gibson-inspired team with a core of local players could raise their game and compete with the very best in the game. To put Hornets' performance into perspective, in the semi-final and the final, Wigan beat Castleford 34–6 and Warrington, 40–10, by bigger margins.

Buoyed by the experience, Hornets went on to win their next seven matches. A 25–18 stumble at Hunslet was followed the following week by another influential red card. This time, chief play-maker Wayne Reid was sent off in an 18–12 Challenge Cup defeat at Ryedale-York. It was the only red card of Reid's career. The defeat signalled a change in fortunes as Hornets slipped to two home defeats to Batley and Bramley.

The 1995–96 campaign saw a truncated Centenary league campaign of just 20 rounds designed to facilitate the switch to summer rugby. The new league featured big-hitters like Salford, Featherstone, Widnes and Hull FC, who'd all missed the cut for Super League.

Hornets' win–loss ratio weakened to 10:12, but there were still some big scalps taken, including a 14–10 Regal Trophy shock win away to Hull KR and 54–20 mauling of Hull under the Spotland lights. The latter saw Chris Churm (3) Karl Marriott (2) and Steve Gibson among the try scorers as a rampant Hornets handed the Airlie Birds a lesson in fast, clinical football.

Before the home match against Andy Gregory's Salford in September 1995, the Salford vice-chairman, Danny Gray, presented Gibbo with an Honorary Life Membership of his former club. Gibbo was really fired-up for this match and the players knew how important this was for him. After a pulsating game Hornets scored to go 27–26 ahead with less than a minute on the clock. From the re-start Salford kicked long and the ball was sailing harmlessly over the dead ball line on the full. But Hornets' Australian second row Matt Ryan, who had been in sparkling form, attempted unnecessarily to catch the ball and knocked it forward.

With seconds remaining, Hornets dropped out from under their posts. Heartbreakingly, Salford scored just as the hooter sounded to steal victory. Everyone was devastated knowing the importance of this match to Gibbo, not least his compatriot Matt Ryan. Gibbo agonised that this would have been the sweetest victory of his career. He really meant it too. Alas, it was not to be.

Hornets finished a creditable eighth, with only Huddersfield scoring more points in the bottom half of the division.

The first season of summer rugby league was to be the last for Gibbo and Corky in charge at Hornets. Just two wins in the first dozen games, and one of those against amateurs Thatto Heath, forced the Board's hand and Gibbo was let go in May 1996. Before that though, Hornets produced a performance under Gibbo that typified the team at that time and which will remain long in the memories of supporters.

Hornets drew St Helens at home in the 5th Round of the Challenge Cup. Saints would go on to be inaugural Super League Champions and also win the Challenge Cup at Wembley that year. Rarely that season were they pressed as Hornets pressed them that day. Saints kicked off and immediately pinned Hornets on their own line, forcing a turnover and exerting the pressure everyone expected from a team packed with internationals. However, Hornets hit back. Hard. A jolting tackle from Emon Ratu regained possession for Hornets on their own line and a couple of drives took them 20 metres upfield.

The next play stunned Saints. The ball found Wayne Reid at second man. Reid was blessed with the ability to open up the meanest of defences and he hit the hard running Ratu with a lovely delayed pass to release him into open space. The Fijian remained composed; crossing the halfway line he slipped the ball back to Reid supporting on the inside.

As full-back Steve Prescott approached to make the tackle, Reid picked out Chris Churm in support and Churm raced away from 40 metres to score the opening try of the game. For nine whole minutes, Hornets were going to Wembley.

Hornets continued to go toe-to-toe with Saints and scored further tries from Vinnie Miller (2) and Adam Greenwood, following a brilliant break and looping, speculative pass from Flanagan. In the end Saints ran out 58–20 victors, but it was another example of how this team of local lads, bolstered by some wily experienced pros, had the belief and the ability to compete with the best in the country.

The lasting legacy of Gibbo's Rochdale Hornets is that fans still fondly speak of a brand of entertaining, attacking rugby created in the image of the man himself. Some great wins, some near misses, but certainly, never a dull moment.

Daily Mirror rugby league correspondent Gareth Walker says: "Watching Steve Gibson's Rochdale Hornets team was much like watching the player himself - exciting, unpredictable, and capable of beating almost anybody on their day."

"You often didn't know what to expect when you turned up on match day, but if the team clicked, the likes of Richard Pachniuk, Chris Churm, Gibson himself, Vinnie Miller and my own personal favourite Wayne Reid could combine for specular tries."

"One in particular always lived in the memory. Reid split a defence through the middle and faced the full-back with a support player on either side. He then dummied the straightforward, sensible right to left pass and flicked the ball in the opposition direction to his other supporting man for the try. It was a move that I tried countless times to recreate on playgrounds, without much success. It epitomised the Steve Gibson and Iain McCorquodale era – free-spirited, off-the-cuff and innovative."

There may have been no trophies and no titles, but this period in Hornets history delivered many positives: a competitive, local-based team, relative stability and a fantastic understanding and mutual appreciation between players, staff and supporters.

Indeed, when the club produced a souvenir plate of Hornets legends to commemorate the game's centenary, it chose Steve Gibson from the modern era to be immortalised in crockery.

Two Tragedies

Tragedy struck twice in 1998 as two Hornets players died just 57 days apart. Karl Marriott was the embodiment of rugby league in Rochdale. Having progressed though the junior ranks at Mayfield, he represented the Rochdale Town Team at Under–16, Under–17 and Under-19 level. He also achieved higher representative honours playing for Lancashire at Under–17 and Under-19. In the summer of 1989, he achieved the highest honour of his amateur career, chosen for the BARLA Young Lions tour of Australia.

On his return from the tour, Karl signed for Rochdale Hornets, although he'd already made one appearance as a triallist off the bench in the last game played at the Athletic Grounds. He made his full debut against Workington at Spotland on 22 October 1989 and scored a try in a 50–24 Hornets win. Two weeks later he scored a hat-trick in Hornets' record 92–0 demolition of Runcorn Highfield.

In the 1989–90 season, he scored seven tries to help Hornets gain promotion to the First Division, but he had his best spell with the club under Steve Gibson when, despite a couple of injuries, he scored 28 tries over four seasons.

Fearless, hard-working and completely committed to the Hornets cause, Karl was in line for a well-deserved testimonial with the club when tragedy struck. On Friday 30 October 1998, Karl returned home after training and complained of feeling unwell. Shortly afterwards he collapsed. Karl was rushed by ambulance to Rochdale Infirmary, but attempts to revive him were unsuccessful. He was three weeks short of his 29th birthday. The coroner determined that he'd died of heart failure.

The club, the town and the game were shaken. *The Rochdale Observer* headline dubbed him: "A Hornets folk hero." Chairman Ray Taylor said: "He was a super lad, a Rochdale Hornets man through and through". His team-mate Steve Turner echoed that sentiment: "He could have signed for a few clubs, but he always stayed loyal to Hornets."

The day after his death, a minute's silence was observed ahead of the Great Britain versus New Zealand test at Huddersfield. Great Britain prop and former team-mate of Karl's at Hornets, Neil Cowie wore a black arm-band in memory of his friend. Tears were shed by the Hornets contingent in the crowd.

Karl Marriott made 156 appearances for Rochdale Hornets over a 10 year period. He scored 48 tries and a single drop-goal for a total of 193 points.

Roy Powell was a rugby league legend. Having played 226 games for Leeds, a further 123 for Bradford and over 60 games for Featherstone, he was one of the most respected forwards in the game. Also, he played 19 times for Great Britain and played in 10 Great Britain tour games. The pinnacle of his international career was playing in the Great Britain side that defeated Australia at Wembley in 1990.

Renowned for his work-rate and unquenchable appetite for defence he was the player that good coaches built their sides around. After his stint at Featherstone, Roy Powell moved to Mount Pleasant where he helped Batley to win the inaugural Trans-Pennine Cup. But there was great concern when he collapsed and swallowed his tongue in the final, the swift actions of referee Steve Nicholson and the medical staff saving his life. He had suffered a similar incident nine years earlier, while playing for Leeds.

Roy had spent most of his career playing alongside his lifelong friend Deryck Fox. They'd played together at St John Fisher school in Dewsbury, at Bradford, Featherstone and Batley, as well as for Great Britain. Fox became coach at Hornets in May 1998 and, when he looked to strengthen his side for the forthcoming 1999 season, he turned to his oldest and most reliable friend to be his playing assistant coach.

However, Hornets fans would never get to see this genuine world-class player wear the red, white and blue. On 27 December 1998, Hornets were in pre-season training at Oulder Hill School when Roy collapsed after a standard training drill. His team-mate Mick Coult, a fully trained fire-fighter, worked on him until the ambulance arrived, but Roy could not be revived. He was 33 years old.

References
Rothmans Rugby League Yearbook 1990–91
Rothmans Rugby League Yearbook 1991–92
Rothmans Rugby League Yearbook 1992–93
Rothmans Rugby League Yearbook 1993–94
Rothmans Rugby League Yearbook 1994–95
Rothmans Rugby League Yearbook 1995–96
Rochdale Observer Saturday 13 March 1993
Rochdale Observer Wednesday 17 March 1993
Rochdale Observer Saturday 20 March 1993
Match Programme: Hornets v Swinton 21 March 1993
Rochdale Observer Wednesday 24 March 1993
Rochdale Observer Saturday 27 March 1993
Rochdale Observer - 4 November 1998
stevericketts.com.au: "FLASHBACK: DECEMBER 1998" - 28 December 2018
independent.co.uk: "Obituary: Roy Powell" - 1 January 1999
yorkshireeveningpost.co.uk: "Heavy Woollen derby's a tribute to former Leeds Rhinos' 'Mr Reliable', Roy Powell" - 26 December 2018

13. 2000: Turmoil

The nation saw the arrival of a new millennium as a time for confidence and optimism. Everything that came before was considered 'so last century' and everything ahead felt like a bright future of hope and opportunity just waiting to be seized.

Hornets began the new era with two coaches called Steve, both of whom walked out on the club. Sydney-born Steve Linnane was what could be called a 'complex character'. A prodigiously talented half-back, in his debut season with St George in 1985 he was the NSWRL's top try scorer, Dally M Rookie of the Year and played in the Grand Final.

Linnane's promise was brought to a shuddering halt in August 1987 when he was suspended for 20 weeks by the NSWRL judiciary after being found guilty of gouging Penrith Panthers' Greg Alexander and his replacement Doug Delaney. The act was described in the Australian *Daily Telegraph* as "... perhaps one of the most notorious fouls in the game's history...". Linnane is reported to 'have almost pulled Alexander's eye out'.

He stayed with St George for another three years until he was sacked after an incident at the St George Leagues club in the off-season. Linnane was then picked-up by Newcastle Knights, but after one season he moved up the Hunter Valley to become player-coach at Kurri Kurri Bulldogs.

Linnane transformed the Bulldogs from perpetual also-rans to three-time premiership winners. Their 1993 Grand Final win was the club's first premiership since 1945. Linnane said it was more special than anything he'd achieved at St George. To date, they haven't won another since he left.

Clearly showing promise as a coach, Linnane quit as player in 1996 to become Newcastle Knights' reserve-grade coach. And in December 1999 he left to take the reins at Rochdale Hornets. The acquisition of a promising young Australian coach sparked excitement among supporters, but the honeymoon was a short one. Linnane's first game in charge was at home against Oldham in the Law Cup on 27 December. It seemed that everyone in the ground except Linnane knew the significance of winning the Law Cup, but he just saw it as a pre-season trial game. By chopping and changing the team over the 80 minutes, Hornets stuttered and struggled to find any real rhythm, eventually going down 23–20.

At a 'meet the fans' forum three days later, the first question from the floor was "Did no-one tell you how important it is to beat Oldham, regardless of the fixture?" The following weekend, Hornets began the Northern Ford Premiership season with a 42–14 home defeat at the hands of Leigh. Not the best of starts.

More impressively, Hornets did make a rare foray to the fifth round of the Challenge Cup. Having beaten The Army 66–6 in round three, Hornets thrashed Oldham 30–14 in the following round to set up a trip to the Boulevard to face Super League side Hull Sharks.

No-one realistically expected Hornets to spring a cup shock, but Hornets fans amongst the 3,982 crowd watched through their fingers as their side shipped 15 tries from 10 individual try scorers to crash to a record 82–10 defeat. Hornets' points on the day came from a try apiece for Steve Wilde and Danny Wood, with Wood adding a conversion.

As winter warmed into spring, Steve Linnane was found guilty of using foul and abusive language to a match official following Hornets' home defeat by Widnes. He was fined £500, £350 of which was suspended to the end of September. As it turned out, the fine suspension had a longer shelf-life than Linnane did. In June 2000, he resigned to replace Martin Hall as Gary Mercer's assistant at Halifax.

Hornets battled through to the end of the season finishing 13th out of 18 clubs, winning 10 of their 28 games. Amid great fanfare, Steve Deakin was appointed as Linnane's replacement in August 2000. Deakin had built a reputation as career 'Number Two' – assistant to John Kear when Sheffield won the Challenge Cup in 1998 and assistant coach at Halifax, Oldham and Keighley.

Hornets gave him the opportunity to show what he could do as a head coach. Deakin showed his gratitude by walking out on a two-year contract to return to Keighley just two weeks before the start of the new season, leaving Hornets in the lurch. He was never forgiven by fans for what was seen as a betrayal and it earned him the nickname "Sneakin' Deakin".

Given the unrest of the previous months, Hornets next coaching appointment needed to bring reliability, stability and an understanding of the culture of the club. In November 2000, the board looked to one of its own success stories, former hooker Martin Hall.

Signed as a 21-year-old from Oldham in 1989, Hall went on to play 107 games for Hornets and was in Hornets' promotion side of 1989–90 and their subsequent campaign in the top flight in 1990–91. In 1992 he was snapped-up by Wigan, and he went on to win pretty much every honour available in the game. In 1994 he played against Brisbane in Wigan's stunning 20–14 World Club Championship win. The following year he scored at Wembley as Wigan thrashed Leeds 30–10 to win the Challenge Cup in the first final to employ in-goal judges. He also won two consecutive Regal Trophies.

Over a five year spell in which Wigan won four Championships, Hall played 149 games for the Cherry & Whites. He gained international recognition too, with nine Welsh caps - including three games at the 1995 World Cup. After Wigan he had short stints in Super League at Castleford, Halifax and Hull FC, before joining Halifax as Gary Mercer's assistant coach. Speaking in the *Manchester Evening News*, Hall said: "I wasn't there long, about five months, but with Gary playing I had a lot of hands-on control. I cut my teeth there really. That short experience led me to believe that I could take a coaching job if I wished."

At the heart of Hall's appointment was the belief that he could steady the Hornets ship, but Hall stated that his first priority was to bring success to the club which gave him his first real chance as a player and as a coach. "To be brutally honest, I wouldn't have applied for any other job in rugby league other than the Hornets job because of my background at the club ... it was Rochdale Hornets, their directors and coaching staff who gave me a real chance, and I'll always be indebted to them."

Despite only having taken over a fortnight before the season started, Martin Hall turned Hornets into the Northern Ford Premiership's surprise package. After a slow start in which they lost five of their seven opening games, Hornets clicked in February to go on a run of 21 league games in which they lost only twice. This surge in momentum catapulted them from a lowly 16th to snatch 3rd place from Oldham on points difference, courtesy of a 26–10 win at Batley on the last day of the season.

Their reward was a trip to second-placed Widnes in the first round of the play-offs. There was a great deal of interest in Hornets' progress given that the final was due to be played at Spotland. The game at Widnes was a mammoth battle. Early tries from David Stephenson and Darren Robinson gave Hornets an early 14–6 lead, but Widnes clawed their way back into the game and scored in the last minute of the first half to be 22–14 up at the break.

Hornets started the second half with a bang, a converted Robinson try after just two minutes got them back to 22–20. The game then became a tense arm-wrestle. With just 15 minutes to play, Widnes regained the advantage with a try from Long. The Vikings secured the win on 70 minutes when Cantillon took a quick tap to score a dubious try before Hornets' defence was set.

Hornets had the last say with a late Paul Owen try, but went down 34–24. Thankfully, the play-off format gave Hornets a second bite at the cherry, a home tie against Hull Kingston Rovers. Buoyed by the performance at Widnes, Hornets were in no mood to let Hull KR off the hook. A 15th minute Sean 'Tommy' Cooper try gave Hornets the lead. Despite the visitors' dominance they struggled to break down a determined Hornets defence, their only reward a Walker try on the half hour that saw the sides locked at 4–4 at the break.

Three Hornets tries in the third quarter from Marlon Billy, James Bunyan and Danny Wood gave Hornets what looked like an unassailable lead, but two very late tries from the Robins pulled them within range. Victory was confirmed by a Danny Sculthorpe drop-goal. Hornets won 21–14 to secure a home semi-final against Oldham.

Having started the season in disarray, Hornets found themselves 80 minutes from a home grand final and with a genuine shot at promotion to the promised land of Super League. The magnitude of the game was palpable and a febrile crowd of 4,153 saw Hornets wade into Oldham from the outset. Tries in the first 10 minutes from Danny Sculthorpe and Sean

Cooper gave Hornets a racing start. An Oldham try from Brennan closed the gap, but three more tries from Darren Robinson, Matt Calland and Marlon Billy had Hornets in complete command. Four goals from Rich gave the half the veneer of a contest as Hornets led 24–12 at the interval.

Hornets began the second half in similar vein. A try and two goals from Danny Wood stretched their lead, a penalty from Rich Oldham's only response. After 67 minutes Hornets led 32–14. And then came disaster.

Oldham's player-coach Mike Ford re-emerged from the bench to turn the game on its head. A converted Casey try on 68 minutes looked like consolation for Oldham; a converted McNicholas try three minutes later had Oldham within four points: Hornets suddenly clinging to the ropes. With six minutes to play Ford fed Henare into space to score. Rich levelled the scores and Hornets were reeling. A carbon-copy try for Henare and a Ford drop-goal for good measure broke Hornets hearts; Oldham back from the dead to win 39–32.

Despite the gut-wrenching end to the season, there were plenty of positives. Marlon Billy smashed Hornets' 66-year record for tries in a season with 31; Danny Wood scored over 300 points; and, in Danny Sculthorpe, the club had unearthed a ball-handling prop with an exquisite kicking game.

In 2002, Hornets again proved serious challengers in the Northern Ford Premiership, winning 19 out of 27 games to finish third. And it was a long slog, a 35 game season – 27 league, six national cup and two Challenge Cup games – that began on 2 December and ended for Hornets on 22 September.

The season was defined by what amounted to a running battle with Oldham, in which Hornets held the narrowest of advantages. As an appetiser, Hornets had kicked off the season by winning the Law Cup by 27–14. Hornets then came up against their fiercest rivals in the National Cup at Ashton United's Hurst Cross ground. Hornets stole the game 14–13 with tries from Sean Cooper and Matt Calland plus three goals from Danny Wood.

The first league meeting also took place at Hurst Cross, Hornets again narrow winners, this time 28–24 with tries from Paul Owen (2), Warren Ayres, Matt Calland and Iain Higgins plus four goals from Danny Wood. The return bout at Spotland was another tight affair. Hornets squeaked home 18–17 with tries from Casey Mayberry, Richard Pachniuk and skipper Paul Smith.

A third place league finish and a top nine play-off guaranteed Hornets a week off in round one and home advantage in the elimination semi-final. Oldham only sneaked into the top nine on points difference with a win at Keighley on the last day of the season. The first round of the play-offs sent them to fourth placed Hull KR where they pulled off a shock 19–11 win to become Hornets' opponents at Spotland a week later, the fifth and final act in what had been a gripping season-long drama.

Given the close intensity of the previous meetings, the 2,573 in attendance anticipated a heart stopping thriller. What materialised was something else entirely. Hornets shipped converted tries to Barber and Sibson in the first 15 minutes. Barber added a penalty to give Oldham a 14–0 lead at the break. The second half was a war of attrition, but it was Hornets who cracked in the 65th minute: Barber scoring and converting his own try for 20–0.

A converted Matt Long try with 60 seconds remaining was barely consolation for Hornets, who had beaten Oldham four times in the season, but lost the one that really mattered.

Hall's third season at the helm established Hornets as a force in the newly branded National League 1. Thirteen wins from 18 games secured another third place finish, six points clear of Hull KR who were fourth. En route, the second-row partnership of Paul Smith and Dave Larder weighed in with 35 tries and Mick Nanyn broke the club record for points in a season.

This was a season in which a Hull KR side now coached by Steve Linnane proved hard to shake off. Having been edged out 27–20 in round four of the Challenge Cup, Hornets gained revenge in the league winning 29–18 at Spotland. More impressive was the 33–18 victory at Craven Park in which Ian Watson and Radney Bowker ran the Robins ragged.

When the play-offs came around, Hornets narrowly saw off the challenge of Whitehaven in a 40–38 nail-biter at Spotland. Hornets led all the way from a try by Jon Roper in the 10th minute, but were chased hard by Whitehaven until the game was sealed by a 75th minute Dave Larder try.

Over on Humberside, Hull KR had beaten Oldham to set up a titanic battle for Hornets with the Robins. The first half was nip and tuck. Hull KR opened the scoring, but Hornets roared back with tries from James Bunyan, Mick Nanyn and Dave Larder to secure a narrow 18–16 lead at the break. Second half pressure from Hull KR saw them edge ahead on the hour, but a Matt Calland try and the boot of Nanyn put Hornets back in contention.

With the score locked at 26–26 with less than a minute left, Ian Watson lined up what would have been the match-winning drop-goal. Spotland held its breath. Watson's kick was charged down by Stott, the loose ball gathered by former Hornet Latham Tawhai and he sent Parker on an 80-metre sprint for the winning try that left Hornets' fans in stunned silence.

Hallmark of the season was a steady consistency that saw Martin Hall voted the National League One coach of the year. Having sat fourth after the opening weekend, Hornets never slipped below third place. And for one glorious week in May, following a 60–6 humbling of the Rams at Dewsbury, Hornets sat top of the table. But, despite a third consecutive third-place finish, crowds over the season stubbornly averaged just over 1,000, a fall on the previous year.

Without doubt Martin Hall had taken Hornets from plucky underdogs to genuine contenders, but it had come at a price. While Hornets played attractive, winning rugby, the impact of paying regular winning money and the failure to convert success into bigger crowds meant that expenditure was far greater than revenue.

Still smarting from the play-ff semi-final elimination, the club descended into a close-season marred by an unsavoury barrage of public spats, infighting, financial horror-stories, resignations and mud-slinging that set a new low for the club's reputation in the town. Underneath the provocative headline "HORNETS HANDOUT", *The Rochdale Observer* reported that Hornets were in negotiations with RMBC for a loan of £50,000 to rescue the club and 'guarantee the future of professional rugby league in the town'.

By mid-October, stories that the club had failed to meet player contract payments had begun to surface. Scrum-Half Ian Watson said: "We were due to get our wages on Wednesday [15th], but were then told it was going to be the 20th. It's now been changed to the end of the month. The players are devastated ... we are all worried about paying our mortgages."

Chairman Ray Taylor was adamant that the situation would be sorted out 'soon'. "It's obviously disappointing that we've got to the end of a long, hard season and the gate receipts haven't allowed us to pay the players. We haven't missed a payment to them all year and we've just stumbled at the final hurdle." Amid rumours of an impending player exodus, Hornets supporters struggled to get any clarity on what looked like a deteriorating situation. And the calling of an extraordinary general meeting of the shareholders while coach Martin Hall was on holiday didn't augur well.

Described at the time as 'at his wit's end', Taylor was forthright on the scale of the crisis: "The club is in deep trouble and the board now feel the time has come to make everyone aware of the situation. We would also like to inform the shareholders of the proposed council loan and the difficulties we have faced in securing an outcome. We can't go on not paying our bills. Lots of people have helped us out in the past, but we can't keep asking the same people."

The Rochdale Observer reported that the club's balance sheet revealed nearly £500,000 of debt. Despite the desperate situation, October's EGM had the air of rearranging the deckchairs on the Titanic. The board's proposed solution to mitigate Hornets' spiralling financial crisis was to issue one million new 50p shares with the optimistic intention of raising £500,000.

In addition, there was debate among the 45 shareholders present around the value of the club's shareholding in the Stadium Company. In a desperate attempt to raise cash, the club had offered a proportion of its shares to RMBC – who held a 5 percent shareholding in the company. The Council had offered 30p per share, an offer considered derisory by the board. In response the shareholders backed the club's valuation of £2 per share and mandated the board to not consider any offers under that amount.

The board also spent a significant amount of time refuting the size of the amount owed to the Stadium Company. In a dispute fought out on the front and back pages of *The Rochdale Observer*, the council claimed that the club owed £70,000; Rochdale AFC claimed the sum was £80,000. The Hornets board maintained that the actual debt was 'considerably less', somewhere between £10,000 and £20,000.

At the end of the meeting, many shareholders pledged cash to alleviate the financial pressure. Club secretary Paul Reynolds said: "Provided those pledges stack-up in the next two or three days then I'm confident we will be able to confirm to Martin Hall he can go ahead and make playing plans for the coming season."

Turning pledges into cash quickly was important. The club intended to use it to settle two pressing debts: Hull KR were still owed their share of a split gate from the play-off game two months earlier, and the players still hadn't been paid. But Reynolds' message of hope was tempered by a note of caution: "We might still go to the wall. No-one knows at this point."

Within a week of the meeting, Hornets became the target of a hostile takeover by stadium company partners Rochdale AFC, who made an audacious and highly public move to take control of the club. Announced in a statement on the Rochdale AFC's website, the soccer club's financial director, and director of the Stadium Company, Graham Morris claimed the bid was to 'guarantee the future of rugby league in Rochdale'.

An offer of £105,000 was made with the intention of running Rochdale Hornets as a subsidiary of Rochdale AFC. The plan was to use that money to pay off the Inland Revenue and other outstanding debts. Morris said: "We informed the current board that we would offer a genuine commitment to the club and remove current financial restraints that are in place. The thinking behind it was it would guarantee both sets of management would then work together and head in the same direction."

The Hornets board rejected the offer, calling it 'derisory'. They simply saw it as an attempt to regain de facto ownership of the stadium. Paul Reynolds said: "What they were trying to do was get the ground back for £100,000. With our assets totalling over £1m, we thought it was rather a cheap buy-out." But it wasn't the only takeover bid in town.

On 4 November, coach Martin Hall had contacted Ray Taylor proposing the possibility of a 'takeover and rescue plan' which would "... cement both the short and long term survival of Rochdale Hornets". In the proposal, Hall revealed that he and an anonymous consortium had a plan to trade out of the debt, provide sufficient finance to get the club through the close season and a business plan to ensure profitable trading and sustainable growth over two years, regardless of on-field performance.

After two weeks of discussions, on Friday 21 November the consortium submitted its formal proposal, including their terms, the first of which was the resignation of the current directors 'with immediate effect'. The consortium made it clear that they required a response by 'no later than 5pm on Saturday 22 November'.

In a response dated 22 November, Hornets' board pointed out that any decision on the proposal would need to be put in front of an EGM of the shareholders and that the club would send notices 'early this coming week'. There was also a request to meet with the consortium and its advisors to address several aspects of the proposals which required 'further clarification'.

In a telephone conversation between the board and the consortium, both parties agreed to extend the deadline to 5pm on Sunday 23 November. A fax from the consortium at 3.50pm on Sunday afternoon ramped up the urgency; making it clear that if there were no 'unequivocal acceptance' of the proposal's terms by 5pm then the offer would be withdrawn.

It stated that, while appreciating the need for shareholders to ratify the board's decision to rescind control, they saw the lack of a response as 'stalling tactics' in order see the offer withdrawn or amended in order to reduce the personal liabilities of the directors.

At 5pm a response from Ray Taylor asked for an extension to the deadline because he was unable to contact three other directors and the club's advisors. In his response, Taylor pointed out that he was 'not able to make a unilateral decision'. At 9.30pm on Sunday evening, the proposal was withdrawn, with the consortium's mystery financial backer unprepared to wait any longer.

Despite the offer of an extension to his contract, the events surrounding the failed takeover convinced Hall that he could no longer work with the board. He was certainly not prepared to continue as coach if they remained in place. Hall said: "The club is in turmoil, the playing squad is falling to pieces, the club debts are spiralling out of control and nobody there seemed to have any answers. I have spent far too much time and effort at the club and I don't want to see it die."

"After we agreed an extension to the deadline, we eventually received a fax from the chairman, which did not lead us to believe that we were any closer to a resolution."

Secretary Paul Reynolds countered, claiming that the board required a meeting with its advisors to address 'legal problems' with the proposal and that any answer would have to wait until after the weekend. The board did, though, state their willingness to resign immediately subject to ironing out the issues.

Hall's departure from the club heralded a mass exodus of the majority of the playing squad, leaving only two players contracted for the forthcoming season. Hall was followed out of the club by director Peter Rush who left in protest, claiming he'd 'fully backed' Hall's takeover bid and that the board's statement about their willingness to resign "... was in no way representative of discussions I was involved in." However, minutes from the board meeting on Saturday 22 November show that Rush and the other directors had voted unanimously that, if the club's advisors were satisfied that the proposals were bona fide, the board would, in fact, resign.

The purpose of the Special General Meeting on 15 December was, ostensibly, to ratify the new share release. But that was an administrative formality. What people really wanted to discuss was the failed takeover bid. When pressed on why they had rejected what looked like a way out of the financial mire, the board said that they hadn't rejected the bid, they'd merely asked for a seven-day deadline to formalise the legalities.

It was pointed out that there were several reasons why the club couldn't just hand over control. The board asked the consortium's advisors to meet the club's advisors, but the consortium wasn't prepared to do that. The board was also advised that they shouldn't agree to a deal that required them to sign over the club to anonymous people. Plus, the loan from the council had been agreed on a specific basis, but the consortium wanted to use it for another purpose.

Throughout this tumultuous period, Ray Taylor was critical of Rochdale Metropolitan Borough Council (RMBC), who he saw as unwilling to help. He compared RMBC to their counterparts at Oldham Council who had sponsored the Roughyeds for £60,000 a season for two years: "We haven't had a brass farthing from Rochdale Council. If we had the same help as Oldham, we wouldn't have a problem. We offered the council some of our shares in the Stadium Company 18 months ago and we still haven't had a satisfactory response."

However, when a response came, it was scathing in its criticism of Hornets' directors. It arrived in the form of a letter from Councillor Paul Rowen, former leader of RMBC, leader of the Liberal Democrat Group and former chairman of the Denehurst Park Stadium Company.

He wrote: "Without proper financial backing and control, the team will get nowhere. Hornets as a business is insolvent and if that fact is not faced up to in the next few weeks, the Inland revenue will ensure Hornets are a thing of the past. The only people responsible for this sorry state of affairs are the board of directors, and it's time for them to go."

He continued: "I'd like to see Rochdale Council working with Hornets to develop rugby in the town. However, like the majority of Councillors there is no way I'm prepared to lend a penny to the current board. I've seen at first hand the *Walter Mitty* denial of facts of the likes of Paul Reynolds."

He concluded on how Hall's consortium could have been a 'fresh start' for professional rugby league in the town. "Heaven knows," he wrote, "they could not be any worse than this present bunch." *The Rochdale Observer* gleefully splashed Rowan's letter on its back page. On the same day, Hornets revealed the appointment of Bobbie Goulding as their new coach.

Bobbie Goulding was the archetypal 'wayward genius'; a potent mix of talent to burn and a very short fuse. He made his senior debut at 16 and became the youngest ever Great Britain Lions tourist at just 18. Between 1988 and 1998, he was the 'enfant terrible' of rugby league, combining mercurial skill, a deadly kicking game and a precarious disciplinary record at Wigan, Leeds, Widnes and St Helens. Beyond that he had short stints at Huddersfield, Wakefield, Salford and Leigh.

His unconventional creativity also saw him play 17 times for Great Britain and five times for England. His career included two Challenge Cup wins, a Regal Trophy Final and the 1995 World Cup Final. He was the also the leading points scorer on Great Britain's 1996 tour and, the same year, became the highest points scorer in one game for Great Britain with 32 points versus Fiji.

Goulding's arrival at Hornets was a real left-field move. Other than a stint coaching his local community club, Widnes St Marie's, he was unproven as a coach, and he had not played professionally since he'd left Leigh a year earlier.

However, there was a sense that, at that moment in time, Hornets and Goulding needed each other. Chairman Ray Taylor was absolutely delighted. He said: "I can see the way forward for this club now, because he will ignite interest in the town." For Goulding it was a chance for redemption. "He wants to rebuild his reputation in the game and sees us a vehicle to do that." said Taylor.

It was reported that, in order to prove his commitment, Goulding would do the job 'on a voluntary basis' and 'without a salary'. Goulding's first challenge as a coach was to assemble a squad on a far smaller budget than his predecessor had. Still fighting financial fires on several fronts, Ray Taylor outlined the scale of the challenge: "We've slashed our playing costs this season. If we can take £50,000 off that bill and find £50,000 in extra revenue we will have turned the thing around by £100,000. We will have turned a loss into a profit and I think we will do that this year."

As Goulding set about recruiting a squad from scratch, the spectre of the club's growing historical debt was a worrying presence. "We are trying to keep past creditors happy. It's a harder job than most realise," said Taylor. "Not only are we having to fund this season, but we are trying to pay off debts. Every time we get a bit of money somebody wants it."

Goulding, though, was canny with his signings, compiling a team of amateurs, academy players, student internationals, journeyman pros and lads with a point to prove. The early omens looked promising as Hornets were edged out of the Law Cup at Oldham by just two points and delivered a Challenge Cup third round 60–24 thrashing of Russian side Dynamo Moscow. But a Challenge Cup fourth round trip to Warrington – Hornets sacrificed home advantage to set-up the inaugural game at the Halliwell Jones Stadium – saw Hornets pummelled 80–0.

Ray Taylor looked on the bright side, saying: "The £20,000 from the Warrington match gave us a welcome lift." However, it heralded a run of 10 games in which Hornets only won once. Indeed, they were the only League One club not to progress to the second phase of the Arriva Trains Cup.

Slowly, though, Bobbie Goulding's influence took effect. Five straight wins in August lifted Hornets off the bottom of the table. Among them a stunning 44–18 flogging of a star-studded Leigh at Hilton Park that had the travelling fans absolutely bouncing. Incredibly, with just two games remaining, they were still within reach of the play-offs. But it wasn't to be.

Hornets ended the season having defied the odds, finishing eighth of 10 clubs with seven wins and a draw from 18 games to stay in League One. Goulding's impact was palpable. His enthusiasm had reignited the club, and it was recognised by the wider game. Michael Platt was voted National League One Young Player of the Year, veteran Tommy Hodgkinson was named in the All Stars team and Bobbie Goulding ended his first season as a professional coach nominated for Coach of the Year.

2005 was a season of mixed fortunes. Hornets grabbed sixth place and the final play-off spot, and their nine wins from 18 games included landmark victories over Halifax and Castleford in which Bobbie Goulding's leadership proved the difference on both occasions.

The Halifax game was a thriller with a sting in the tail. A Chris Giles try after just five minutes gave Hornets an early lead, but three in reply gave Halifax a 16–6 half-time lead. The first 20 minutes after the break were tight, but two quick-fire tries after the hour from Goulding and Andy Saywell put Hornets back in the hunt. Halifax's only response were a penalty and drop-goal to give the visitors a narrow 19–16 lead.

With a minute left on the clock, a Halifax error 10 metres from their own line gave Hornets the feed at the last scrum of the game. In front of the massed Halifax fans, Bobbie Goulding produced a moment of absolute magic. Reeling away from the back of the scrum, he drew defenders towards him, before slipping the sweetest of short balls to Radney Bowker to score under the black dot and win the game.

Castleford's season in National League One was their first outside the top flight since their entry into the RFL in 1926. They came to Spotland on a steaming hot July afternoon, top of the table and undefeated in their first 10 league games, racing favourites not only to win the game, but tipped as near certainties to make an instant return to Super League.

However, Bobbie Goulding had other ideas. It took only five minutes for Hornets to take charge. Radney Bowker produced a grubber kick, Chris Campbell pouncing to score; Goulding off the touchline with the conversion. A quick response from Castleford drew the scores level, but Goulding continued to lead from the front, his dazzling kicking game pinning the Tigers deep in their own half for long periods.

Knowing the importance of any advantage, Goulding slammed home a drop-goal to restore Hornets' lead. But it was short lived: Reid scoring a dubious try to edge Castleford in front 10–7. A 23rd minute Goulding penalty pulled Hornets closer and, when Castleford were snagged offside at the restart, he gratefully drilled home the penalty from halfway.

Castleford's only other chance of the half came when Shenton looked certain to score, but was nudged into touch by Chris Campbell. Hornets were ahead 11–10 at half time. The second half was barely five minutes old when a converted Davis try gave Castleford a five point lead, but Goulding again took charge.

From a scrum, he hoisted a high kick towards Shenton, who spilled the ball under pressure from Chris Campbell and Andy Gorski. Campbell slipped the loose ball to Sam Butterworth who scored with his first touch. Goulding added the extras and, with 23 minutes to play, Hornets led 17–16.

On the hour Castleford's Bird hit Mark McCully with a cheap shot and Goulding's immediate retribution earned him a 10-minute breather. But Hornets stood firm as Castleford ran out of ideas. Goulding left the field three minutes from time with a standing ovation and a bicep injury that finished his season.

Hornets only lost twice more that campaign. Castleford went on to lose three more games, which allowed Whitehaven to pip them to the League Leader's trophy. By the season's end, Hornets' small squad was battered, bruised and threadbare. The trip to third placed Hull KR in the play-offs saw them travel without a recognised scrum-half; hooker Dave McConnell acted as stand-in. Conversely, the Robins had in-form half-back James Webster in their team and it proved too great a difference.

Hornets crashed 45–4 at Craven Park to end an otherwise successful season. Andy Gorski was their only try-scorer. Bobbie Goulding's influence was again recognised with a National League One Coach of the Year nomination, but the many highs of the 2005 season were tempered by the loss of two major figures.

In April, Hornets lost long-standing chief executive Paul Reynolds. Having initially helped run the Hornets Nest Bar at the Athletic Grounds in the 1970s, Reynolds was appointed Hornets secretary in 1984 and co-opted on to the board two years later. In 1988 he was heavily involved in the sale of the Athletic Grounds and the club's move to Spotland. He became chief executive at Hornets in 1995.

Then, In October, Hornets lost talismanic chairman Ray Taylor. Taylor first joined the Hornets board in 1969, stepping down in 1981 to devote more time to his family. He returned to the board in the mid–1990s and became chairman in 1995. For his services to the game, he was made president of the RFL in 2002 and a Life Member of the RFL. He also served on the RFL Council, the game's governing body.

Bobbie Goulding said he regarded Ray Taylor as a father figure and praised him for being a 'coach's chairman'. At the funeral, Goulding carried the coffin alongside club captain Andy Gorski, Danny Sculthorpe, Phil Farrell, Paul Owen and Richard Varkulis.

A month later, Goulding resigned, citing 'frustration with the club's financial difficulties' and the inability of Hornets to compete financially with the leading clubs in National League One. A *Guardian* report said that his hopes of building a squad to challenge for promotion to Super League had suffered 'a series of blows', with the decision of Wakefield Trinity's Australian utility Julian O'Neill to accept a better offer from Leigh 'proving the last straw'.

References

The Canberra Times: "Linnane, Lance: How justice is seen to be done" - Friday 14 August 1987

The Canberra Times: "Linnane's at Home" - Sunday 17 March 1991

dailytelegraph.com.au: "Rugby league at its worst: Cheap shots, squirrel grips and biting" - 17 March 2017

newcastleherald.com.au: "Linnanes Revive Old Glory" - 19 September 2019

http://news.bbc.co.uk/1/hi/sport/rugby_league/695028.stm - 29 March, 2000

thetelegraphandargus.co.uk - 22 July 2000

Manchester Evening News: "One of Hornets' favourite sons is a man with a mission" - November 2000

League Express Rugby League 2001–2002

League Express Rugby League 2002–2003

Rochdale Observer 13 September 2003

Rochdale Observer 18 October 2003

Rochdale Observer 25 October 2003

Rochdale Observer 29 October 2003

Rochdale Observer 1 November 2003

Rochdale Observer 8 November 2003

Rochdale Observer 26 November 2003

Rochdale Observer 10 December 2003

independent.co.uk: "Goulding named as Rochdale coach" - 3 December 2003

news.bbc.co.uk: "Goulding joins Hornets"-
3 December, 2003

Rochdale Hornets Special General Meeting
15 December 2003 Shareholder Notes

Gillette Rugby League Yearbook 2003–2004

Gillette Rugby League Yearbook 2004–2005

Gillette Rugby League Yearbook 2005–2006

Rochdale Observer 24 April 2004

Rochdale Observer 4 May 2005

Guardian.com: "Goulding gives up on handicapped Hornets" - 18 November 2005

14. 2008: Downfall

Hornets' 2007 National League One season had been a disaster. Three wins from 18 games saw Darren Abram fired, leaving assistant coach Shaun Gartland with the unenviable task of seeing out the season. Despite his best efforts, the damage was already done. Hornets only avoided finishing bottom because Doncaster had been docked points for going into administration. Hornets bade farewell to National League One with a humiliating 106–0 home defeat by Castleford on the last day of the season.

In search of on-field salvation, the board turned to prodigal coach Bobbie Goulding. A statement said: "Bobbie has approached us and at a time when the board is feeling a little low it was a terrific call to take. It shows the high regard Bobbie still has for the club and I know he would be a very popular choice with supporters." Behind the scenes, though, there was good reason why the board might have been 'feeling a little low'.

In December 2007, the club was served with a winding-up order by HM Revenue and Customs for non-payment of a PAYE bill. To stave off the order, the bill had to be settled, but the only asset of any value was the club's 45 percent shareholding in Denehurst Park (Rochdale) Ltd, which was valued on the balance sheet at £200,000.

For years successive boards had been offsetting losses against this valuation, but it had become increasingly impossible to balance the books. Desperate times called for desperate measures and, on 27 March 2008, Hornets went cap-in-hand to the RFL for a loan of £120,000, with interest accruing at 5 percent per year. In return, Hornets offered its shareholding in the stadium company as security against the loan.

One of the conditions of the loan was that Denehurst Park (Rochdale) Ltd had to deposit Hornets' share certificates with the RFL, along with a signed, undated transfer form which would allow them to take immediate ownership if Hornets defaulted on the loan. The loan was reported to be £7,000 short of the club's tax bill, but Hornets' directors had committed to make up the shortfall. It was agreed that repayment of the RFL loan would start in 2009. This coincided with a new Sky TV deal that increased the funding for National League clubs.

It wasn't the first time that Hornets had used their shareholding to get them out of a financial hole. Hornets had used their shares as collateral against a £50,000 loan from Rochdale Metropolitan Borough Council in 2004. That loan was settled in April 2008, specifically to remove any potential impediment to the RFL loan. Hornets CEO Peter Whitehead said: "I believe the directors have commercially done a good job for this club in that the situation for monies owed is as good as it's been for a long time and better than it's been many times in recent years. Now that this issue has been settled, we can concentrate on the business side and playing side."

Goulding's second coming didn't have the same impact as his first as Hornets coach. The first couple of months of the 2008 season were mixed. With National League Cup, Challenge Cup and National League Two fixtures, Goulding delivered six wins from 11 games.

A run of seven straight defeats in all competitions, culminating in a 52–8 home flogging by Gateshead Thunder, left Hornets third from bottom. The board had seen enough.

159

Bobbie Goulding during his time at St Helens. (Alex Service)

A club statement said: "It is with real disappointment that Rochdale Hornets announces its decision to terminate the contract of coach Bobbie Goulding with immediate effect." The decision hit Hornets captain James Elston hard. He had a close relationship with Goulding and disagreed publicly with the decision. In *The Manchester Evening News* he said: "I feel it's a big mistake because the reason the players are at the club, and I think I can speak for everybody in the team, is because of Bobbie Goulding. In the past couple of weeks we have not performed and the players have let Bobbie down."

"If anything, it's us who should be facing the consequences and not Bobbie. He couldn't have done anything more for us." The board's reaction was swift. Goulding was replaced by Darren Shaw and James Elston was packed off to Dewsbury Rams. In the next game, Hornets thumped York City Knights 44–10.

Shaw set about addressing the squad's deficiencies, signing Australian trio Jono Muir (second row), Paul Rolls (half-back) and Janan Billings (hooker), along with former St Helens and Widnes back Chris Giles. Hornets also signed Leeds Rhinos' winger Leroy Rivett.

The season was transformed as Hornets went on a late run of five straight wins, which put them into the play-offs. Hornets' last game of the regular season was away to York City

Knights. York were player-coached by Paul and David March, two wily campaigners. Regardless of the score, Hornets would return to York in the elimination play-off.

In an ordinary game, Hornets were losing 40–22. David March had turned in a virtuoso performance at loose-forward, but on 75 minutes, was sucked into a squabble by Hornets prop Dave Best. In the ensuing fracas, March aimed a head-butt at a Hornets player. Referee Dave Merrick showed him the red card. In the melee that followed, Paul March argued with the referee and was also sent off. Hornets lost 40–26, but won the psychological battle.

By the time Hornets returned to York two weeks later, both of the March brothers had been suspended for three games. Without them York were rudderless and Hornets took full advantage, winning 26–12, with Leroy Rivett scoring two tries in a man-of-the-match performance.

The next match in the play-offs saw Hornets visit Keighley. The first half was one-way traffic as the Cougars racked-up four converted tries. Hornets' only response a converted Martin Ainscough try. A try by Carl Sneyd on the hooter gave Hornets a glimmer of hope, sending them in at the break 24–10 down.

The second half was a complete reversal of fortunes. All Keighley could muster was a solitary penalty goal as Hornets ran riot. Three tries in the opening six minutes of the half from Ian Sinfield, Dave Cunliffe and Chris Giles had the Cougars reeling. Sinfield broke Keighley hearts with six minutes remaining when he went in for his second. Cue mayhem among the delirious travelling Hornets fans. Having come up on the blind side, Hornets were suddenly serious play-off contenders and their victory at Lawkholme Lane set up a mouth-watering Elimination Final against the old enemy, Oldham, at Boundary Park.

Oldham started brightly, grabbing an early lead through tries from Melville and Langley. But Hornets finished the half stronger, with converted tries from Paul Alcock and Janan Billings, plus a penalty from Carl Sneyd, to give Hornets a narrow 14–12 lead. Unfortunately, the second half was 40 minutes too far for Darren Shaw's side; Oldham produced a second half blitz, with 26 unanswered points and ended Hornets' Grand Final dreams.

Off the field, the summer of 2008 saw the resignation of Hornets CEO Peter Whitehead on health grounds. "My blood pressure's too high," he said. "the job itself is stressful." Having been in post for 14 months, he said: "The most challenging part of running a rugby league club is trying to keep the finances in order, and trying to generate enough income to pay all the bills and wages and everything else that goes with it."

"If we got 1,500-plus supporters for every home game there wouldn't be any financial trouble, but we don't, so the commercial side of Hornets is forever looking at new ways to increase the income. The club is not entitled to the support of the town without earning it, but I think it earns it. It's been going 137 years, it would be a tragedy if this club wasn't here." But, within months of his departure, Whitehead's worst fear would soon become a reality.

On 6 November, the club was holed below the waterline when it was hit with another winding-up order from HM Revenue & Customs, this time for an unpaid tax bill of £55,489. From here, it was only ever a matter of time before it sank without a trace. And things moved very quickly indeed. Facing a High Court hearing on 14 January, the winding-up order was not only an issue that required an urgent response, it would also become the catalyst that saw the full scale of Hornets' financial plight dragged out into the daylight.

The club announced an emergency shareholders' meeting for Monday 1 December 2008 and urged all shareholders to attend. Former chairman David Vining, director Norman Halsall, and chief executive Ken Oldham planned to discuss forming a working party to look at the ways forward for Hornets, expressions of interest and support for the club. Oldham said: "This has been a busy time for us, but we are confident that if we stick together, with our supporters and sponsors, we will get through. We are currently working with the Rugby League on a plan of action."

The meeting also had to address the double resignation of chairman Martin Shenton and his wife Karen Reynolds who was vice-chair. The pair stood down amid allegations of nepotism from Dave 'Nosey' Parker in his *League Weekly* column two weeks previously.

Parker's article suggested that kit-man Mark Reynolds, Karen's brother, and his son Gavin Reynolds had been made club directors. The article said Gavin had been made financial director. An anonymous club spokesman explained that Gavin was not a director, but that he had been helping the club supply accounts and cashflow forecasts to the RFL. The spokesman did say that Mark had been co-opted onto the board to take over from Martin Shenton as director of rugby, in good faith and 'out of necessity'. The board believed that recruiting new directors was a condition of complying with RFL's requirement for the submission of a business plan for the 2009 season. They believed that they were unable to sign players until they had done so.

The appointments had attracted attention due to the board side-stepping the protocols of its own constitution. Despite an admission in *The Rochdale Observer* that they were aware of the need to call an AGM and consult shareholders over the appointment of new directors, the club spokesman said: "We did appoint Mark and Gavin to assist with the running of Rochdale Hornets without referring to the shareholders. We did not, in our opinion, have the time to consult with the shareholders and do not believe we acted with anything other than in the best interests of the club."

On 22 December, long-standing director Norman Halsall resigned. In a meeting with concerned supporters a few days earlier, he'd thrown the keys to the Hornets office onto the table and walked out stating: "If you want it, you can have it."

Amid the turmoil, coach Darren Shaw and assistant coach Paul Anderson had not been paid and faced a difficult Christmas. In desperation they reached out to independent supporters' association, The Hornets Nest-Egg, for help. Two days before Christmas, representatives of the Nest-Egg met them and paid them out of their funds. It was clear that events were out of the club's control.

At an EGM on Monday 12 January, shareholders were told that if the club did not go into administration their club would be wound up at the High Court 48 hours later. Shareholders voted unanimously to put the club into administration. Having already met with administrators, club officials submitted the necessary paperwork the following day.

On 23 January 2009, The Rochdale Hornets Football Club Limited (incorporated 1 August 1906) was placed in the hands of the RFL's approved administrators, O'Hara's of Batley. The game was well and truly up. According to O'Hara's, Hornets owed trade & expense creditors

£28,250, employees £14,250, the Yorkshire Bank £5,000, £94,434 in unpaid tax and national insurance contributions, £95,000 in unpaid VAT and £120,000 to the Rugby Football League. In addition, there were £282,758 in unpaid directors loans on the books. To add insult to injury, the club had taken £8,000 in season ticket sales and hospitality box deposits which were now lost. Total liabilities: £647,692. There was also the unresolved matter of £69,442 owed to the Denehurst Park Stadium Company.

Upon the club's dissolution, the RFL took ownership of 45 percent of The Stadium Company. The administration process, which included the sale of the club's remaining assets, raised just £23,457.77, all of which was swallowed up in administration and legal fees. Creditors didn't receive a penny. Meanwhile, the incumbent board was scrambling to find a way to keep the club alive.

Rochdale AFC announced their interest in stepping in to preserve the Hornets name. Hornets CEO Ken Oldham said: "We are talking to the football club about forming a new company but it won't be a merger. There would still be two separate companies, but the football club may have a director on the new board."

Behind the scenes, the RFL was working on a solution too. An RFL spokesman said: "We are talking to a couple of groups who might be interested in working with the club going forward." As it had done so often in the past, the club's survival would lie with its supporters.

References

Gillette Rugby League Yearbook 2008–2009

manchestereveningnews.co.uk/sport/rugby-league/goulding-keen-on-hornets-return–999242

manchestereveningnews.co.uk/sport/rugby-league/captain-goulding-sacking-is-a-mistake–955649

yorkpress.co.uk/sport/yorkcityknights/2311535.knights-boss-to-wield-axe-after-heavy-hornets-loss/

Oldham Chronicle 1 December 2008

manchestereveningnews.co.uk/sport/rugby-league/focus-the-key-for-abrams-men–993758

manchestereveningnews.co.uk/sport/other-sport/retirement-beckons-as-peter-says-au–961159

manchestereveningnews.co.uk/sport/rugby-league/rfl-loan-to-stave-off-wind-up-order–949559

manchestereveningnews.co.uk/sport/rugby-league/hornets-board-in-resignation-offer–973962

manchestereveningnews.co.uk/sport/rugby-league/directors-stand-down-from-hornets-board–974646

rochdaleonline.co.uk/news-features/4/sport-news/17422/hornets-league-opener-in-jeopardy

theguardian.com/sport/2009/jan/13/rochdale-hornets-administration-rugby-league

Rochdale Hornets Football Club Co. Ltd: "Abbreviated unaudited accounts for the year ended 31 May 2007" - June 2008

Companies House Form 395: "Particulars of a mortgage or charge" - 27 March 2008

yorkpress.co.uk/sport/yorkcityknights/matchreports/3619625.knights–40-rochdale-hornets–26/

news.bbc.co.uk/sport1/hi/rugby-league/7595898.stm

Guardian: "Rochdale Hornets face financial crisis ahead of new season" - 13 Jan 2009

Rochdale Online: "Hornets league opener in jeopardy" - 9 December 2008

Rochdale Online: "Hornets to enter administration" - 13 January 2009

news.bbc.co.uk: "Hornets voted into administration" - 13 January 2009

The Gazette Office Public Record: "Petitions to Wind Up (Companies) - Notice L–58657–491864" - 6 December 2007

Companies Form No.395: "Particulars of a mortgage or charge" - 31 August 2004

Companies Form 403a: "Declaration of satisfaction in full or in part of a mortgage or charge" - 3 March 2008

Companies Form No.395: "Particulars of a mortgage or charge" - 27 March 2008

Administrators Document: Form 2.23B "Notice of result of meeting of creditors" - 3 April 2009

Administrators Document: Form 2.35B "Notice of move from administration to dissolution" - 20th January 2010

Denehurst Park (Rochdale) Limited, Report and Unaudited Accounts, Year Ended 31 May 2008

15. A new hope: The birth of a Co-operative Club

"Or watch the things you gave your life to, broken,
And stoop and build 'em up with worn-out tools:"

Rochdale Hornets entered 2009 at death's door, with all hope seemingly lost. The club's entry into administration and the sheer scale of the debt had tainted its reputation. Breakdowns in relationships with the governing body, local media, Rochdale AFC and supporters had created an increasingly toxic environment swirling with rumours, allegations and threats. Any anticipation of a late reprieve was tempered by the football club announcing a potential interest in taking over the Hornets.

The first suggestion that the club could have a future came in the shape of a phone call from Hornets' commercial manager, Debbie Troops, on the afternoon of 6 January 2009 to supporter Mark Wynn, who was also chair of the Hornets supporters team Rochdale Swarm.

Troops had just taken a call from the Rugby Football League (RFL) proposing supporter ownership as a way of saving Rochdale Hornets and she asked Wynn if he knew of a group of fans who might be willing to take on the running of the club.

Wynn suggested to Troops that there might be an interest among supporters. His first call was to Jim Stringer, chair of the Hornets Nest-Egg, an independent Rochdale Hornets Supporters Group that had raised over £35,000 since its formation in 2003. Over six years, the Nest-Egg had invested the majority of its funds in shares in the club. Shares that were now worthless.

Throughout the turmoil, the Nest-Egg had worked hard to keep its members abreast of developments at the club. This included a series of ad-hoc meetings at The Baum on Toad Lane, which, aptly, sits next door to the Rochdale Pioneers Museum, birthplace of the modern co-operative movement.

The backdrop to this early activity was that everybody knew that the clock was ticking. With the first game of the season pencilled in for Sunday 15 February, it would require a huge amount of work in a little over a month if the club were to be saved. Over 6 and 7 January, Stringer pulled together a working group of Nest-Egg members who had expressed an interest in getting actively involved in supporting the club. In parallel, the RFL appointed experienced club administrator Steve Ferres as its advisor to a potential Hornets fan group.

Mark Wynn rang Ferres to confirm that there was definite interest in the idea of supporter ownership and a meeting was arranged for the evening of 8 January. The John Milne Pub in Milnrow was chosen because it was easy to find from Junction 20 of the M62. Ferres insisted that all matters had to be discussed in total confidence. He felt that, due to the acrimony, in-fighting and mistrust around the club, an open dialogue wouldn't be helpful at such an early stage.

The Hornets supporters at the initial meeting with Steve Ferres were: Brian Belfield (lottery volunteer), Julie Clarke (Nest-Egg secretary), Geoff Hurst (Nest-Egg member), Jim Stringer and Mark Wynn. They were joined by Charlie Fairbank, a Rugby League Supporter from Wakefield with an interest in supporter involvement and co-operative ownership.

Lifelong Hornets supporter Peter Walker was also part of the working group, but was unable to attend.

The initial meeting had an air of intrigue about it. Steve Ferres was already waiting for the group when they arrived, sitting in a corner alcove "away from prying eyes and ears." His opening remarks painted a dark picture of the state of the club. He made it clear that, as things stood, the RFL saw no credible offer on the table to take on the running of Rochdale Hornets. The chances of survival, he said, were a lot less than 50:50.

He then confirmed that the RFL would like to propose that Rochdale Hornets reform as rugby league's first supporter-owned and operated club. Ferres made it clear that the RFL appreciated that this would be a huge undertaking for a group of supporters with no experience in running a professional rugby league club. To make things even more challenging, as a prerequisite of playing in the RFL's competition, the supporters would have to produce a bond of at least £75,000.

He also said that if the supporters raised the money and could demonstrate their commitment, he would oversee the project. To assist the group in the administration and operation of the club, he said that he'd lined up someone he referred to as 'The Driver': a business expert who would keep the project moving and on-track. He refused to say who this 'Driver' was at this point in discussions, saying that until the group showed commitment and provided evidence of its ability to raise the £75,000 bond, there was little chance of progress.

Ferres's immediate priority was a business plan. He gave the working group a list of tasks to pull together into a proposal that would demonstrate their vision and desire to take things forward. When Ferres left the meeting there was a sense of both excitement and foreboding. The weight of responsibility felt among the group – knowing that the future existence of Rochdale Hornets lay, potentially, in their hands – was palpable.

The morning after, Jim Stringer emailed the working group with the key points for the business plan. It covered every aspect of running a rugby league club, from management structure, match day operations and cost & revenue projections to marketing, community development and fundraising. What had felt like an impossible idea was suddenly very real indeed.

While all this was going on, the Hornets board had called an emergency EGM at Spotland Stadium on Monday 12 January 2009 to discuss the proposal that the existing club be wound up and that a new club would be formed under the ownership of Rochdale AFC. Supporters group the Hornets Nest-Egg was now one of the club's more influential shareholders. Given the short notice of the EGM meeting, it was important that the views of its members were taken into account and that they agreed a voting position.

Stringer arranged an impromptu gathering of Hornets Nest-Egg members on Sunday 11 January, at which the idea of Rochdale AFC taking over Hornets was discussed at length. The almost universal opinion among members was that the football club would simply run the club down in order to regain full ownership of Spotland Stadium and that any such proposal be opposed.

The meeting was attended by Paul Ormerod, a Rochdale-born, London-based economist, who asked a series of searching questions about investment in a new club and how much might be needed to make it happen. In the aftermath of the meeting, Paul Ormerod and Jim Stringer exchanged correspondence around the potential for a new club. In confidence, Stringer shared the RFL's proposal about a supporter-owned Rochdale Hornets. Ormerod liked the idea and offered to put up the £75,000 bond needed to take the idea forward. Ormerod then arranged to meet with Steve Ferres to discuss the proposal and demonstrate both his willingness and ability to provide the necessary capital.

At the EGM on 12 January, the Rochdale Hornets board announced that if the club did not go into administration, it would be wound up at the High Court. Shareholders supported the action unanimously. They also announced that there had been discussions with the football club about them taking over Hornets. The plan was for a joint board, but with members of the incumbent Hornets administration running the day-to-day aspects of the club. Several years later, Andy Kelly, a director at the football club at the time said, although he had tried, he couldn't get anyone interested in joining a new board to support Hornets.

Certainly, in some parts of the room it was felt that the club was in denial about how precarious its future was, especially given the nature of the discussions that the RFL were having with the supporters' working group. Over the next few days, a flurry of emails, phone calls and meetings took place as the idea of a supporter-owned club, began to take shape.

Paul Ormerod – now part of the working group – met with the person Steve Ferres had referred to as 'The Driver'. The person in question was Sam Greenwood, director of a Rossendale-based company called SponsorBank, which specialised in finding sponsorship and kit deals for grassroots sports teams. The working group were reassured that Greenwood and his fellow-director Allistair Carmichael came highly recommended by Ferres and had passed due diligence by the RFL.

Jim Stringer too had had a lengthy conversation with Greenwood about SponsorBank's role. Greenwood said he would use his own people to provide marketing and admin support to the new club, and that he was keen to support a fan-led initiative based on co-operative principles that would attract community funding. Greenwood also confirmed that he was happy to play a day-to-day, hands-on role in the background "... steering the ship in the right direction...".

It was a whirlwind. In just seven days from the first meeting with Steve Ferres, the working group had, through the generosity of Paul Ormerod, secured the investment it needed and had in place the support of a management company recommended by Ferres on behalf of the RFL. The working group had its initial meeting with Sam Greenwood and Allistair Carmichael at their base in Waterfoot on Tuesday 20 January. In the background, Rochdale Hornets as we knew it continued to plot its course into administration, with *The Guardian* running an article claiming that the club owed at least £310,000 pounds to multiple creditors.

On the playing side, head coach Darren Shaw had done a miraculous job of holding his squad together through the weeks of uncertainty, but the now national news of Hornets' imminent demise had alerted other clubs to the potential availability of players. Conscious that his squad was at risk of being picked apart, Shaw approached Jim Stringer to see if the Hornets Nest-Egg could make a contribution to help keep his squad together, but its bank account by now was nearly empty. In the meantime, Paul Ormerod and Steve Ferres had met with Shaw and explained that a new ownership model was being put together, that the culture of the club would have to change, and that previous wage expectations simply couldn't be continued if any new club were to be sustainable.

The ailing club's move into administration was now confirmed for Friday 23 January. However, in what appeared a bizarre move to many, the board was still talking about Hornets playing Leigh in a pre-season friendly in what appeared to be a last-ditch attempt to save the club via the shared gate money from the match. Needless to say, the game never took place. By now, the flow of information being processed daily became a tidal wave. As first point-of-contact for the Hornets Nest-Egg, Jim Stringer was shouldering the majority of the communications burden. This could range from budget breakdowns for the RFL and legal documentation for Supporters Direct to change-of-status information for the bank and even requests for cash from the club.

Indeed, just three days before the club went into administration, he received a request for £250 to cover that week's training expenses. Over time these requests had become increasingly regular, but having paid the coaching staff's wages over Christmas, the Hornets' Nest-Egg's coffers were bare.

With so much going on, it cannot be understated how frenetic the atmosphere was surrounding the new club project. Desperately trying to save Rochdale Hornets in semi-secrecy proved challenging, with rumours, misinformation and, at times, downright lies circulating about the club. When Steve Ferres met with the Football Club to discuss the situation and inform them that the RFL's preferred option was for the supporter-owned model, the rumour mill went into overdrive. Former Hornets chairman David Vining said that he'd heard a rumour that the Hornets Nest-Egg was taking over the club. Staff at the stadium had heard that the Stadium Company was about to go into administration, that the football club would buy it back and kick Hornets out.

Discussions with the Stadium Company had revealed some major issues. Primarily, it was laden with debt and close to bankruptcy itself. As such, the Stadium Company wanted the £80,000 owed by the 'old' Hornets club or they wouldn't sanction a 'new' Hornets playing at Spotland. Paul Ormerod stepped in to try and unpick the mess, as both sides waited for the other to blink.

Amid a furious round of meetings, emails, calls and texts the working group, which now included Walter Tann, continued to pull together the rest of the business, with Ormerod maintaining a keen eye on budget and cashflow forecasts.

One unexpected challenge was the fighting of misinformation, speculation and, from some quarters, open hostility. With the rumours now getting louder and more bitter, the working group's priority was staying focused on the possibility that salvation was at hand. To head off any further conjecture and take control of the narrative, the decision was made to go public as soon as possible.

Two weeks after the meeting at the John Milne, a press release was drafted to get the news into the public domain: Rochdale Hornets would reform as a supporter-owned co-operative. Jim Stringer sent the press release out to Hornets Nest Egg Members on the evening of 26 January. Subsequent releases were sent to coincide with the print schedules of the *Rochdale Observer* and rugby league trade papers. In his email to confirm to the working group that the press release had been sent, Stringer said that his hand was shaking as he pressed send on what was a momentous leap of faith in the both the history and the future of Rochdale Hornets.

A meeting with the members of the Hornets Nest-Egg was arranged for the following day. A meeting was also lined up with the playing, coaching and backroom staff. The meeting with the Hornets Nest-Egg members was one of relief. The members had been staunchly loyal and wonderfully generous over six difficult years. Without their backing this whole process would have stalled. Now, there was a mix of enthusiasm and apprehension as members looked to enter the unknown as a fully fledged co-operative.

The meeting with the players and backroom staff was and unusual affair to say the least. Telling people who had stood by the club that their contracts with the 'old Hornets' were null and void, and that they would be offered significantly reduced terms was never going to go down well.

After training, the working group, players, coaches and backroom staff all packed into a dressing room at Oulder Hill School. The lack of space meant that the majority of the players all sat on the floor. In a scene reminiscent of an old Western, Jim Stringer – chair of the Hornets Nest-Egg, de facto chairman of the working group and, by default, chair of the new co-operative – joined them on the floor to go through what the new club would look like.

One of the key challenges for the working group was the setting up a of a new company and governance structure. The Hornets Nest-Egg had always been a supporters fundraising group and not a Supporters Trust in the legal sense. As a vehicle for allowing supporter-ownership, it had to become an Industrial and Provident Society, an entity that must work for the benefit of the community that it serves and which must operate within a strict legally-binding constitution governed by the Financial Conduct Authority (FCA).

A lengthy process that would usually take weeks had to be completed by 31 January if the new club were to start the new season. This made getting the new club registered as a co-operative somewhat problematic. Again, this was something that no-one involved had any experience of. Thankfully the RFL had been working with Supporters Direct, an organisation set up by the British government to help supporter trusts secure greater accountability and democratic representation within sporting organisations. Having been primarily focused on football clubs, Supporters Direct were very keen to extend their reach into rugby league.

With Paul Ormerod travelling for work, Jim Stringer and Walter Tann working in Manchester, Julie Clarke en-route to a training course and Supporters Direct's Jacqui Forster heading for London, the only opportunity to get all of the necessary signatures on the documentation in time to hit the submission deadline required a 6.30am meeting at Manchester Piccadilly railway station.

In the rush to complete the registration, Supporters Direct registered the new club's name as 'Rochdale Hornets Rugby Football League Club Society Limited' instead of 'Rugby League Football Club'. It was of little consequence. The full 'business name' would never appear on the badge and it took fans one step closer to having a Rochdale Hornets to support again.

However, one curve-ball that wasn't anticipated was having to fight for the right to play under the Rochdale Hornets name. In 2009, the trading name of 'Rochdale Hornets' still belonged to the now defunct Rochdale Hornets 1906 Ltd. On consulting its solicitors, the working group was required to petition the shareholders of the defunct Rochdale Hornets for permission to use the name and they had to agree in a majority to relinquish the name.

Acting on behalf of the administrator O'Hara's, Clarion Solicitors contacted the defunct Hornets shareholders on 24 of February with a resolution to allow the new club to use the name 'Rochdale Hornets'. Incredibly the shareholders rejected the resolution, leaving the new club without the necessary majority. Given that the new club had to start the season with a name, there were two options available.

The first was to drop the Hornets part of the name, and there were suggestions on the table to do that. The second was to retain the 'Hornets' suffix as that was the most marketable element. Given the acrimony surrounding the formation of the new club It was felt that adopting the name Hornets Rugby League was the lesser of two evils until such time the new club could reinstate its full name.

Having taken legal advice on how the club might return the name 'Rochdale' to the badge, the working group was advised that a period of two years would be considered sufficient for the rights of the defunct company, now not trading, to lapse. So, for the first two seasons, the club would have to play under the name Hornets Rugby League.

Contrary to the rumours that the new club rejected the name Rochdale as an attempt at a rebrand or as a snub to the town, it was, in fact, a practical temporary solution that fulfilled a legal requirement. Disappointingly, even several years later, some would continue to peddle this myth in an attempt to discredit the people involved.

Indeed, it was absolutely crucial to everyone that the new club built solid community links after decades of disinvestment and neglect. Like the original founders, creating a 'club to represent the whole town' was always a priority, especially as the co-operative had a constitutional obligation to do that. What had been the working group had now become, ahead of the inaugural election of officers, the co-operative's Steering Group. Having formed a new business, the next test was the steep learning curve of running a rugby league club and working towards the 'new' Hornets first game as a co-operative club, away at local rivals Oldham in the pre-season Northern Rail Cup. But the local derby was put on ice, postponed due to the weather.

That meant that the new Hornets took to the field for the first time against Barrow in the Northern Rail Cup on 15 February 2009. The team on that day was: Chris Giles, John Gillam, Mick Fogerty, Casey Mayberry, Craig Johnston, Martin Ainscough, Martin Gambles, Dave Best, Liam Grundy, Paul Raftery, Wayne Corcoran, Ian Sinfield and Mark Brocklehurst. Subs: Sam Butterworth, Martin McLoughlin, Andy Smith, Andy Isherwood.

The first half was a tight affair. Hornets went behind to an early try from Barrow centre Bell. But Hornets hit back to take the lead. The new club's first try came from Mick Fogerty after seven minutes. He was followed six minutes later with a try from Chris Giles. Both tries were converted by Wayne Corcoran. Two tries round the half-hour mark restored Barrow's lead and Hornets went to the half time break trailing 16–12. The second half was a complete Barrow blow-out, the visitors scoring 38 unanswered points to win 54–12. The attendance of 501 felt like an encouraging starting point.

Hornets faced Oldham at Boundary Park on the following Wednesday night. Hornets only try scorer was John Walker in a 54–4 defeat to the team that would get to the Championship

1 Grand Final. On the following weekend, the fledgling Hornets celebrated their first ever win, beating Blackpool Panthers 28–26. Despite going 10 points behind in the second half, Hornets dragged themselves back into contention with a try from John Gillam. On the hooter, prop Paul Raftery crashed in to level the scores. Wayne Corcoran, the coolest head in the ground, added the extras to spark the celebrations on and off the field.

The Manchester Evening News was impressed: "A word for the Hornets' steering committee, as the organisation of the match, before, during and after ran like clockwork. They may have been disappointed with the crowd, their hard work deserves better. It's time those armchair fans went along to support their efforts."

With the real business of the league and Challenge Cup fast approaching, the RFL confirmed that the Hornets would start the season with a nine-point deduction for going into administration.

The Challenge Cup would provide the highlights of this inaugural season. It started brightly with a 38–24 victory over Leeds Metropolitan University at Headingley Stadium on 8 March 2009, a little over a month since the club had gone into administration. Round four saw Hornets grab an impressive 28–22 win at Swinton, before eventually being knocked out by Super League side Huddersfield Giants. It was a gutsy performance at the Galpharm Stadium; Hornets went down 38–12 after being 26–0 behind at half-time.

The first home fixture of the league campaign was against the Championship 1 favourites Dewsbury Rams, who would go through the entire league campaign undefeated. Hornets put in a superb performance, losing narrowly 33–31, the closest Dewsbury came to a league loss all season. The rest of the season was hit-and-miss. With six league wins out of 18 games, Hornets finished eighth in a 10-team league. This wouldn't have changed even without the nine-point deduction. A three-game winning run that saw Hornets go undefeated in July made little difference to their league position.

The season did finish on a high, though. A solid 42–20 victory over Workington Town brought the curtain down on a frantic year for the supporter-owned Hornets. On the plus side, an average attendance of 637 was up 51 on the last season of the 'old' Hornets and was the sixth best in the division.

Off the field it was, at times, a season of acrimony and recrimination among some but, thankfully one of hope and endeavour amongst the majority. Having been told pre-season by an RFL representative that the Rochdale Hornets brand was 'toxic', one of the big tasks of the co-operative was to repair the tarnished image of the club. As part of the brand's rehabilitation, a new, modern and exciting logo was commissioned from award-winning Manchester graphic designer Ben Gerrard. The new logo wasn't without its critics, but it was important that a club looking forward to a bright future should be branded to engage with a new, younger audience. Since its first appearance on a Hornets shirt, the 'Battling Hornet' has become the longest-used badge in the club's history.

The other important tool in the modern world is an organisation's website. In 2009 Rochdale Hornets was the only club in professional rugby league, and possibly professional sport, without its own website. Thankfully, supporter Mark Webster allowed the club to use his Hornets fan-website while the club began the process of creating and launching an official club website. The club had no social media presence either, so the co-operative launched both Facebook and Twitter accounts.

Indeed, the inaugural season had thrown-up a whole range of challenges. Mid-season the fledgling co-operative club was shaken when chair of the Steering Group, Jim Stringer, was compelled to stand-down due to work commitments. The Steering Group elected Mark Wynn as chair in his place.

During the early weeks of the inaugural season, SponsorBank took an active role in the running of the club, appointing Joe Pitts as CEO. A former player with Bradford and Batley, Pitts had previously been a senior sales executive at BT. At Hornets, he had the difficult task of not only trying to bring together all the competing factions at the club, but also of following the instructions of SponsorBank.

As the season progressed, the tensions between the Steering Group and SponsorBank grew more intense, with Joe Pitts caught in the middle as SponsorBank were his employers. Also, the Steering Group had no legal authority until elections had been held, so the relationship with SponsorBank continued to be difficult. By mid-August, Pitts had revealed that he would be stepping down as CEO at the end of the season to work full-time at SponsorBank.

When payments to players and suppliers began to bounce, the Steering Group was given increasingly unbelievable explanations about was happening and why the club's liabilities weren't being met. Eventually, a face-to-face meeting between some members of the Steering Group and SponsorBank was arranged. The meeting was a simmering affair that boiled over when Steve Ferres attempted to defend SponsorBank's performance by saying that the Steering Group was focusing too much on where the club's money had gone!

Thankfully, preparations for the elections for the first Hornets co-operative board were now well advanced. Supervised by Supporters Direct, the election of a board that would have legal authority to take on the management of the club couldn't come quickly enough.

On 4 September, Supporters Direct announced the results of the first elections to the board of Rochdale Hornets Rugby Football League Club Society Limited. The members elected to make up the historic first board of a co-operative club were: Brian Belfield, Andrew Birch, Alan Brett, Julie Clarke, Geoff Hurst, Paul Ormerod, Walter Tann and Mark Wynn

Immediately after the announcement, the board met to elect officers. Paul Ormerod became club President, with the board electing Mark Wynn as chair and Brain Belfield as vice-chair. Julie Clarke took on the role of secretary and work began to sever any connection with SponsorBank and to find a new CEO.

References
Email from Jim Stringer to working group 6 January 2009
Email from Mark Wynn to Debbie Troops 8 January 2009
Email from Jim Stringer to working group 9 January 2009
The Guardian: "Rochdale Hornets face financial crisis ahead of new season" 13 January 2009
Letter from Clarion Solicitors to Rochdale Hornets Shareholders 24 February 2009
Email from Jim Stringer to the Steering Group 15 May 2009
Email from Joe Pitts to the Steering Group 21 August 2009
Minutes of Rochdale Hornets Board Meeting 7 September 2009

16. A new start - with a less than clean slate

Delving into the issues the club faced was frustrating, especially with the difficulty in obtaining useful information that would help the board get a clear picture of the financial position of the club.

Local accountancy firm Wyatt, Morris, Golland & Co. (WMG) had the unenviable task of trying to unpick the mess, a process which would take several months. When WMG finally completed the accounts for the period under SponsorBank's management, the figure outstanding to creditors was an eye-watering £180,454.

In addition, a figure of £27,186 was reported in the accounts as being owed to Rochdale Hornets by SponsorBank. After months of chasing, including instigating legal action, this money had to be written off as SponsorBank were wound up in the High Court in June 2010 by other creditors trying to unsuccessfully recover their outstanding debts.

Given that the 'old' Hornets had gone into administration owing around £700,000, and had also spent the £1,000,000 from the sale of the Athletic Grounds, one season with SponsorBank had left the new club with a debt of over £180,000. As such, it was understandable that questions were asked whether Hornets could operate at any level of competitiveness while working within a prudent financial framework.

On top of the financial headache, the new board also faced an upsetting campaign of personal attacks, anonymous abuse and threats sent through the post to members of the Hornets Steering Group and Board, targeting Julie Clarke, Andrew Birch and, in particular, chair Mark Wynn. The abuse ranged from name calling on the internet and criticism of people associated with the co-operative club to threats against board members' businesses. Thankfully, the abuse tapered off, but not before matters were brought to the attention of the police.

With SponsorBank gone, the new board had to start running the club: bringing in its own employees, developing business and community plans to develop the club and the sport of Rugby League across the Borough. It also had to plan for the 2010 season and put a competitive team out on the field.

Working with the RFL, former Leeds CEO Alf Davies was brought in to advise the board. Davies was an expert on lotteries, and he worked hard to turn the Hornets Lottery into an income stream – some achievement, given that the old lottery was actually losing money when the new board took over. There were changes in the backroom staff too. The board acted swiftly to appoint Mike Banks as CEO. Banks had an impressive CV, having previously worked at Widnes RLC, Everton, Sale Sharks, and Brands Hatch. Off-field issues saw Darren Shaw and his coaching staff move on from the club, so the board set about recruiting his replacement.

Among the applications for the post, there was one standout candidate: former St Helens and Widnes forward John Stankevitch. Having cut his rugby league coaching teeth at Widnes and Doncaster, he came with excellent recommendations from several well-respected judges of what makes a great coach. In his autobiography, Stankevitch recalls his meeting with Mark Wynn and Mike Banks, saying: "I was confident that I could get a squad of players together in a short amount of time and, in actual fact, unbeknown to them, I had already spoken to a handful ... the opportunity to put my mark on a team and on a club was one that I'd be a fool to turn down."

What was obvious was that Stankevitch had a pool of players that he could call on who were loyal to him and who would sign at Hornets. One of these was influential goalkicking half-back and captain-in-waiting Paul Crook. Along with Wayne English, these signings would prove inspirational, providing the cornerstone of the club for several seasons. Arguably, Stankevitch's most impactful signing was Dave 'Rammy' Ramsbottom as assistant coach/team manager. Stankevitch approached Mark Wynn with a job description of a person he needed to join his coaching staff. The description said that the person should be well known and, most importantly, well-respected within the local amateur game in Rochdale.

Ramsbottom fitted that description perfectly. Certainly, a major part of Stankevitch's legacy at Hornets, 'Rammy' became a mainstay of the successful development of the co-operative club's culture.

With the 2010 season fast approaching, an early pre-season open trial game was highlighted as a way to put more local players and unidentified, unsigned talent on the club's radar. Constantly looking to bring in the best local players, the last pre-season game saw Hornets take on a Rochdale Town team coached by Dave Ramsbottom. With players drawn from several local sides a good selection signed for the co-operative club.

Hornets kicked-off the 2010 campaign in confident style. The first game saw John Stankevitch's Hornets beat his previous club Doncaster 56–24 at Spotland. Next up, Hornets faced French Champions Lézignan in the Challenge Cup. Having gone 12–0 down in the early exchanges, Hornets forced their way back into contention to trail 18–12 at the break. A scrappy second half suited the visitors and they took advantage to edge away from a hard-working Hornets. An Andy Saywell hat-trick gave the Hornets fans something to cheer, but Hornets went down 32–22.

Back in the league, Hornets had a stuttering spell and it wasn't until May that they hit form, going undefeated in the month. Hornets began June with a great 28–22 victory over that season's runaway league leaders Hunslet, inflicting the second of just two defeats in their entire league campaign. However, as so often happens, the Herculean effort against Hunslet came at a cost. Hornets slumped to three back-to-back losses, before a home win against South Wales steadied the ship.

Despite three defeats in the run-in, a home win over Swinton gave Hornets 10 wins from 20 games. The addition of seven bonus points saw Hornets finish in a creditable fifth place, which saw the new club qualify for its first end of season play-offs. A convincing 60–26 home win against South Wales Scorpions saw Hornets head for big-spending Blackpool Panthers in the semi-finals. With the game in the balance until the final quarter, Hornets pushed Blackpool all the way before eventually succumbing 34–26.

Salt was further rubbed into the wounds when Blackpool kept the monies from the shared gate. Then, within days of losing to York in the Elimination Final, the club folded, taking Hornets' share of the gate money with them.

On the field, the season had ended in disappointment, but off it the stringent financial management structures that the board and CEO had put in place saw the losses accrued under SponsorBank all but wiped out.

From net liabilities of over £180,000 and an operational loss of £122,874, the board reported a near break-even position with a small operational loss of £1,902 – a £120,000 improvement in the performance of the business, although the £180,000 debt would remain an albatross around the co-operative club's neck. This strong financial performance was presented to members at the AGM, along with a proposal for the club to incorporate the word 'Rochdale' back into the playing name now that enough time had elapsed after the block by the shareholders of the old company. The news on finance was well received and the vote to incorporate Rochdale back into the badge was passed with great enthusiasm.

At the end of December 2010, Rochdale Hornets made the news on a global level when they announced they would be bidding to host the fixture between Ireland and Fiji in the 2013 Rugby League World Cup. The brainchild of Hornets chairman Mark Wynn, the audacious bid saw Hornets hit the headlines worldwide, with the story carried by news outlets including the *Mumbai Times* and *Florida Today*. It gained attention nearer home too, on *Sky Sports* and *Look Northwest*.

Despite making headlines, the announcement was met by a huge degree of scepticism. Thankfully, a small group who believed in the project, including future Hornets CEO Ryan Bradley, started work on turning the dream of hosting a Fiji fixture into a reality.

The 2011 season was one of so near and yet so far. A narrow 22–20 home victory over Workington Town in the Challenge Cup set the scene for a slow start to the season, with Hornets falling as low as seventh in the division. However, with results starting to gain momentum in late April, the team really hit its straps by mid-July. Leading the charge for Hornets were wingers Dale Bloomfield and Andy Saywell who ended the season with 37 tries between them. Half-back Paul Crook contributed 10 tries, 100 goals and five drop-goals for the 245 points that made him the league's second highest points scorer.

With 12 wins from 20 games, four bonus points and a superior points difference, Hornets climbed into 4th place above Doncaster and entered the play-offs in a confident mood. First up for Hornets in the play-offs were local rivals Oldham. A dominant display from Hornets saw them finish comfortable 39–18 winners. Hornets then faced Doncaster in another do-or-die game, putting in another solid performance to win a tense encounter 26–18.

This win set-up a semi-final away to high-flying Keighley Cougars, who hadn't been outside the top three all season, but who Hornets had beaten 31–30 at Cougar Park earlier in the season. On the morning of the semi-final, coach John Stankevitch rang Mark Wynn to say that an off-field matter involving Craig Ashall had left him with no option but to drop one of the team's star players. The decision caused a huge reaction from the players, but they unanimously backed the coach's decision, despite it weakening the team.

Shorn of one of the team's leaders, but with rock solid team spirit, Hornets took the game to Keighley, holding a 16–0 lead after 34 minutes. Leading until the 58th minute, Hornets eventually succumbed to the Cougars' relentless pressure, conceding three tries in the last eight minutes down the infamous Lawkholme Lane slope. Keighley went on to defeat Workington Town in the final to secure promotion. After the game, a supporter approached

175

Wynn and said: "That's Hornets, they always let you down." It felt almost embedded in the Hornets psyche that they would fail in the games that really mattered.

A disappointing end to a season was tempered by another good performance off the field, with the club returning a profit of £4,376 and an increase in turnover of £18,000.

The 2012 campaign started brightly with a home victory over London Skolars and wins in three of the next four games, including a 48–20 Challenge Cup win over East Hull. The season then went off the rails after a heavy 68–18 defeat at Leigh in the next round. Hornets went on to lose the next three league fixtures too, conceding nearly 200 points in the process.

The board sought an unusual fix which, if it all went to plan, could get the team back on track and secure Hornets some much needed publicity. The club was approached by the television company Tiger Aspect and Channel 4, about making a documentary on how dance can have a positive effect on performance. The programme was a vehicle for Peter Lovatt, a flamboyant dance professor and psychologist who was studying how the brain responds to music and how dance can help people make positive changes in their lives.

After much debate on the potential pros-and-cons of the documentary on perceptions of the club and its playing and coaching staff, and possible ramifications with the RFL, it was agreed to go ahead. However, the positive influence of dance didn't really materialise in the team's performances. Despite a good run-in with five wins from the last eight games, Hornets crashed out of the play-offs at the first hurdle, going down 40–12 at Whitehaven.

The season had not gone as well as expected. John Stankevitch had told the board in June that he would be standing down as coach at the end of the season to focus on a role helping Hornets develop the commercial side of the club, although he also stepped away from that shortly after the end of the season.

Hornets began the search for a new head coach to help drive the club forward for the 2013 season. Thanks to the club's improved standing in the game, the traditional route of advertising the post drew plenty of interest. Unlike three years previously when Hornets received few credible applications, the number and quality of candidates now took everyone by surprise. This appointment had to be part of a bigger, more strategic plan to progress the club and recruit the right calibre of personnel.

Stankevitch had been contacted by St Helens to see if Hornets would be interested in a dual registration agreement. Known as 'dual reg.', the system had grown in popularity with clubs as a way of sharing players and resources and minimising costs. Hornets chairman, Mark Wynn, met with St Helens CEO Mike Rush, to discuss what a potential partnership would look like. The meeting proved fruitful with both sides seeing huge potential benefits to partnering.

What struck Wynn most in his discussions with Rush was the culture at St Helens, where everything was based around winning. Wynn recounted the story of the fan at the Keighley game who believed that Hornets would always let the supporters down. Discussions with St Helens continued over several months, as both sides wanted to create a best practice model for dual reg. During the many conversations it became clear that, for Hornets to be successful, they needed to adopt the winning mentality that was ingrained in Saints' DNA.

At St Helens it was deemed a disaster if they went much more than a season without a piece of silverware. The contrast with Hornets who, by 2013, hadn't lifted a major trophy in

91 years was stark. The offer of young up-and-coming players to supplement the core Hornets squad was certainly an attractive one. For the project to work, though, the players would have to operate under a similar system and methodology. The ideal solution was to take a coach from within the Saints set-up who knew the systems, but most importantly, was able to embed St Helens' winning culture into Rochdale Hornets.

The person who best fitted the bill was Ian Talbot, a former Super League hooker with Wigan and Wakefield who had progressed up the coaching hierarchy at St Helens. As a supporter-owned co-operative, Hornets had to ensure the members were happy with any dual registration agreement. Members were updated regularly during September, October and November and they gave the green light to the partnership ahead of the new season.

In an interview with *Sky Sports*, Saints CEO Mike Rush gave more details of the dual reg. agreement, announcing that, to supplement Talbot, Saints legend Steve Prescott would join Hornets' coaching team alongside David Ramsbottom. In addition, former Hornets player Matt Calland would also join the set up as head of youth.

One signing that was made which would have a massive positive benefit to the club was the appointment of new CEO, Ryan Bradley. Previously the rugby league Development Manager for Rochdale with local health charity Link4Life, he was the stand-out candidate for the post and immediately began to make his mark at Hornets. 2013 was already destined to be a ground-breaking season for Rochdale Hornets after the Rugby League World Cup organisers confirmed that Hornets would host the Ireland versus Fiji fixture.

As a supporter-owned club, recognising Hornets' history and tradition was always a major priority. One of Ryan Bradley's early successes was to secure funding for a Hornets Heritage Room, a museum dedicated to the club's rich history. The envy of most rugby league clubs, it charts the triumphs and disasters of Hornets since its inception in 1871. In line with the club's respect for its history, the home kit for the 2013 season was a contemporary take on the jerseys worn in 1922, the last time Hornets won any major silverware. More unusually, the away jersey was Fiji-themed and trimmed with the Irish colours to help promote the forthcoming World Cup fixture.

With the Saints partnership in place, major heritage projects underway, and a World Cup fixture confirmed, the icing on the cake was the announcement that Fiji would play Rochdale Hornets in a World Cup warm-up game. Everything was in place for a stellar year.

References

Letter from Wyatt, Morris, Golland & Co. to SponsorBank 26 February 2010

Rochdale Hornets Accounts 29 January 2009 to 30 November 2009

High Court of Justice Chancery Division Manchester: "Company Winding Up Order, Insolvency 0715 SponsorBank Limited" 21 June 2010

Companies House: "Company Report - SponsorBank Limited 05070669" - accessed 26 September 2021

Rochdale Hornets Accounts December 2009 to November 2010

Rochdale Hornets Accounts December 2010 to November 2011

manchestereveningnews.co.uk: "Rochdale Hornets 28 Blackpool Panthers 26" - 24 February 2009

manchestereveningnews.co.uk: "Hornets 22 FC Lézignan 32" - 10 March 2010

manchestereveningnews.co.uk: "Keighley 38 Rochdale Hornets 23" - 27 September 2011

League Publications Limited: Being John Stankevitch - John Stankevitch, 2011

skysports.com: "St Helens have formed partnerships with Rochdale Hornets and Whitehaven RLFC" - 11 October 2012

17. Writing new history

The 2013 season got off to the perfect start with a 28–18 win at Oldham, who, as they had so many times in the past, would become the defining opponent in a season that ebbed and flowed towards a date with destiny at the end of September.

The victory over Oldham was followed by a 40–4 Challenge Cup win over Hunslet Old Boys, in a match which, at times, threatened to boil over. Two weeks later Hornets faced a rampant Bradford Bulls in the next round, going down 70–10. The following two fixtures saw consecutive defeats to both South and North Wales, but Hornets rallied with a mid-season run of five consecutive wins to go second in the league. The run was ended by three away defeats at the end of a near two-month stint playing on the road. The last of them, a dismal 38–18 defeat away to Hemel Stags, had the vultures circling, with some calling for the sacking of Ian Talbot, despite Hornets still being fourth in the table.

Talbot wasn't the type of coach to shout and scream. After the Hemel defeat, he spoke to the players in calm tones about loyalty, playing for each other, respect and being on the right side of history. This measured response had a far greater effect on the team than an old school 'spraying'. Hornets went on to win four out of their last five league fixtures, the only stumble a narrow defeat in a bad-tempered televised game against potential nemesis Oldham.

This late run of form saw Hornets finish third in the regular season. Confidence was high for the play-offs. First up in the play-offs was a resurgent London Skolars. The Skolars had finished just one place behind Hornets in the regular season and they came to Spotland buoyant after defeating Hornets 32–16 when the teams met in June.

In a real blood and thunder encounter, the result remained in doubt until the last seconds. Hornets started the brighter of the two sides, opening up a 12–0 lead through tries from Jordan Case and Dave Sutton. But the Skolars wouldn't lie down, with Thomas and former Great Britain International Raynor crossing. Skee missed a conversion to give Hornets a 12–10 advantage at half-time. As the team walked to the dressing rooms, Jim Stringer, now operating the tannoy, played *Don't Stop Believin'* by Journey, a prophetic choice.

After the break, Raynor scored his second try to give Skolars the lead for the first time. They then pulled further away through an Anthony try. Crucially, the conversion was missed. Chris Baines scored to put Hornets back in contention and a Paul Crook penalty from inside his own half edged Hornets ahead 20–18. But this game was far from over. With 10 minutes remaining, the Skolars scored again through Skee. This time the conversion was good and, with the clock ticking down, Hornets trailed 24–20.

All seemed lost when John Cookson was adjudged to have knocked on in the act of scoring. Skolars were awarded the scrum with just two minutes on the clock. As the Skolars drove the ball out from their own line, the Hornets defenders threw everything into the tackle and the ball spurted loose, Dave Llewellyn was on hand to make the most of the mistake and score to level the scores at 24–24. With time almost up, the trusty boot of Paul Crook sealed the win 26–24. The game had everything including controversy, as the Skolars were incensed that Gaz Langley hadn't been sent off for a high challenge late in the second half.

Victory sent Hornets back to Oldham in the qualifying semi-final; the winners would go directly to the play-off final at Leigh, the loser would have to battle for another week in an attempt to reach the final.

If the Skolars game was a last-minute affair, then the Oldham game went down to the last seconds. The conditions at Whitebank were atrocious. With rain lashing down, the game was never going to be pretty. Oldham took an early lead through a converted Ford try, but Hornets hit back with a try from Joe Greenwood and a Paul Crook conversion. A Paul Crook penalty nudged Hornets further in front before some sloppy Oldham handling close to their own line gifted Jordan Case a simple try. Crook added the extras to give Hornets a deserved 14–6 half-time lead.

Oldham began the second half brightly; Hughes snaffling a bouncing ball to score, Palfrey the conversion. But a Paul Crook grubber kick, pounced upon by Wayne English produced a try that stretched Hornets' lead. Crook added the extras. Two late converted Mo Agoro tries levelled the score at 22–22. However, this game had a sting in the tail. With Hornets in possession in the dying seconds, Paul Crook slammed home a 40-metre drop-goal to break Oldham hearts and send Hornets to their first final in 22 years; the longest gap between finals by any club in professional rugby league. Hornets' celebrations with their jubilant, sodden fans showed just how much it meant.

Speaking to the *Manchester Evening News*, proud Hornets coach Ian Talbot gave a hint to his motivation: "The goal at the beginning of the season was promotion," he said. "We've played two very tough games to get to the final, but the fans deserve some success."

Preparations for the Final began at the final whistle of the semi-final win over Oldham. The game had been played in wretched conditions and the players were ingrained with mud. Hornets former CEO Ryan Bradley recalls events: "The final whistle went and, while the celebrations went on, Ian Talbot pulled me to one side with a serious question: 'How the f*ck do I get the kits clean for the final?'"

At the time, Hornets were paying £30 a week for the kit to be washed which, over at least 20 games, was setting the club back £600 a season. As a benefit of the dual reg. deal, it had been agreed with St Helens' CEO Mike Rush that, in order to free up some budget for post-match protein shakes, Talbot would take the kit to Saints' training base and launder it himself.

Bradley continues: "The Monday after the semi-final I rang Ian, as I probably did every other day to see what he was up to. He was already on with power washing the kit."

Hornets had the luxury of two weeks to prepare for the final, but there was much to do. Bradley remembers: "We decided that we had to do the little things right for the final. We were already at the extent of our credit limit with our kit partner, which meant we had to get the players' matchday polos embroidered locally and unbranded. We also got the playing shirts embroidered for the occasion."

As part of the build-up, Ian Talbot had the idea holding a shirt presentation the Friday before the game. The club had been working with local restaurant Peritos, so after the captain's run at Spotland, the team was brought together for a meal and the presentation of their cup final shirts.

"We got a couple of guests in to give a motivational talk," says Bradley. "Leeds Rhinos and England captain Kevin Sinfield was a mate of Chris Hough. He talked the lads through what it's like to play in finals. He talked about the need for leaders, calmness, sticking to systems. And the irony of an Oldham lad helping us out wasn't lost."

"Ian Talbot had also asked for a supporter or former player to speak about what Hornets meant to them. There was only one guy we could ever pick: Ray Myers. Ray was known to everyone at the club through his long-standing role as timekeeper but, due to ill health, he had stepped back a little. The lads knew who Ray was, but he hadn't been at every game with the team as he had been before."

"I sat with Ray and his wife Ena throughout the meal, listening to his jokes and stories. Ena had him on a strict warning to behave and to keep it brief. We needn't have worried. What Ray did next would win us the final. Ray told some stories and we had a few laughs, but then his tone changed and you could hear a pin drop. The lads were on the edge of their seats and they'd have run through a brick wall for Rochdale Hornets after hearing him speak."

29 September 2013: a sunny afternoon at Leigh Sports Village (LSV) as Hornets lined up to take on the Oldham Roughyeds in no ordinary game of rugby league. The team on the day was: Wayne English, Gareth Langley, Danny Davies, Dave Hull, Martin Waring, Paul Crook, Steve Roper, Carl Forster, Chris Hough, Warren Thompson, Dave Llewellyn, Alex Trumper, Joe Greenwood. Subs: John Cookson, Alex McClurg, Chris Baines, Jordan Case

At stake, not only the chance of promotion to Rugby League's Championship, but, almost more importantly, the chance for a Hornets team to end a 91-year drought and bring silverware back to Rochdale, a feat not achieved since 1922.

After the tensions that the Hornets faithful had to endure in the two previous play-off games, was it perhaps too much to ask that the final would be a straightforward affair. No such luck. In an absolute classic, Hornets took a fifth minute lead with a try from Dave Llewellyn. Oldham replied through Ford to draw level. Danny Davis restored Hornets' lead at 12–6, but a converted Hughes try near half-time saw the scores tied 12–12 at the interval.

During the break, Ryan Bradley walked round to chat with the Hornets fans: "I was worried, but the fans weren't. There was an air of confidence that we were going to do it. It'd been a tough season. Defeat at Hemel was the lowest point and fresh in the memory. But for some reason, they all knew we were going to do it."

Oldham started the second half the stronger taking an 18–12 lead with a Cookson try on 44 minutes. Hornets levelled the score at 18–18 with a converted Dave Hull try on the hour. In a game played at a furious pace it wasn't until the 65th minute that a penalty was conceded by either team. Oldham the culprits, Paul Crook stroking the ball between the sticks to give Hornets a slender 20–18 lead. On 70 minutes, John Cookson forced his way in from close range, the video referee deciding in his favour after denying him in the first half. Paul Crook added the two points and Hornets had a little breathing space at 26–18.

In the closing minutes, Hornets faced wave after wave of Oldham attacks as the Roughyeds tried to get back into the game. But with the clock ticking down, an Oldham knock-on gave Hornets possession at a scrum in their own half.

Most people in the ground expected Hornets to play it safe and run out the set with five drives and a kick. However, Carl Forster, packing down at loose-forward, broke from the scrum. He dummied his way across the field to feed a rampaging Gaz Langley who skipped out of a tackle, turning defenders inside out before slipping a perfect pass to Rochdale's own

Wayne English. Nicknamed 'The Bolt from Kirkholt', English slammed the ball down to put the result beyond doubt. Paul Crook converted from wide out to land his sixth goal from six attempts. A perfect day.

With the noise of the Hornets supporters ringing around the ground, the Hornets players waited with anticipation to climb the steps for the presentation. No medals were issued that day, but for the first time since 1922, a Rochdale Hornets captain had a trophy to collect.

One by one, the players and Ian Talbot climbed the steps to shake hands with the assembled dignitaries. After the longest of waits, team captain Paul Crook and club captain Wayne English were handed the gleaming piece of silverware. Turning to face the Hornets faithful in the far stand, the pair hoisted the trophy aloft.

Paul English, reporting for *League Publications* wrote: "Rochdale lifted their first trophy since 1922 with a hard-fought victory over local rivals Oldham as a fairy tale try from local boy Wayne English cemented promotion just two minutes from time."

Amid the confetti and cheers, there were grown men in tears as the Hornets players each in turn lifted the trophy. The 91 year wait was over.

In the years since Jack Bennett lifted the Challenge Cup, Hornets had gained promotions and avoided relegations; won pre-season 7-a-sides, local Charity Cups and reserve team competitions, but the symbolism of lifting a trophy won in open competition wasn't lost on Hornets' long-suffering supporters, in the ground and further afield. The post-match lap of honour saw the Hornets in front of their euphoric supporters to receive a heroes' welcome!

One of the things Ian Talbot had brought to the club was a victory song, which had been plagiarised from the Australian side Penrith Panthers. *Hornets Are You Ready, Ready?* had become a fans' favourite during the season, with the club producing t-shirts with the lyrics on as a special cup final memento. David Hull led the song to the wild cheers from the fans, with the entire Hornets contingent, players, staff and supporters nearly bringing the roof down when Hull asked, "Hornets are you ready, ready?" The answer was most certainly: "Yes, we are ready, ready." Ryan Bradley recalls: "After the game, Gaz Langley made a beeline for Ray Myers with the cup, plonking it on the table for him like a cat bringing its owner a mouse. Ray stood proud with that trophy, taking pictures with everyone at the LSV. He epitomised the long-suffering Hornets supporter and had earned the right to carry that cup around as much as Ian Talbot and the lads."

Ian Talbot summed up the day: "I am very proud of the players. We have done things right and it has worked out right. We did go through some dark times when we went on the road in the middle of the season. It was tough and we had to bounce back. The doubters doubted and I took some stick, but I knew we had it in us to be up there challenging."

Heading back to Rochdale after the game, Hornets had one last laugh. "The journey from the LSV was a little rowdy as you'd imagine," says Bradley. "Especially when we passed the Oldham bus, with our trophy in the window."

In 1922, the Hornets team returned with the Challenge Cup and pulled into the Rochdale Town Hall Square on a coach. Ninety-one years later this trophy-winning Hornets team also pulled up in the town hall square with silverware. There may not have been as many fans to meet them in 2103, but those that did had as much pride and passion as their forebears.

The post-game reception at *The Flying Horse* went on long into the night, with players, staff and supporters celebrating together, passing round the trophy, taking photographs. Ian Talbot in particular was happy to show-off the trophy. Bradley says: "He'd had his critics that season and now those people wanted a picture with 'his' trophy. He made sure he got photos with a few of the supporters who had knocked him publicly. They had been his motivation."

After 91 years between drinks, everyone connected with Hornets would wake up the day after, some worse for wear than others, knowing that the club would be playing Championship rugby league in 2014.

The last fixture Hornets would play in 2013 was against the Fijian national team in a World Cup warm-up fixture. Missing several of their cup-winning side, Hornets were no match for a rampaging Fiji team full of NRL superstars. The Fijians ran out 78–0 winners, but the score mattered little for the majority of Hornets supporters.

The lasting image from the day was of the last survivor of the original Fijian pioneers, Voate Drui embracing Fijian superstar and rugby league legend Petero Civoniceva. The link between a small Lancashire mill town and the South Sea Islands was captured in that moment. If that embrace was the image of the day, the sound was definitely the Fijians singing their team hymn, *Qo na noqu masu* (This is my Prayer) in the Spotland lounge after the game. The room fell silent, their harmonies stirring the emotions of everyone present.

While the singing and the warm-up game were a fantastic celebration of Rochdale's links to Fiji, they were just a sideshow to the main event of Fiji versus Ireland in the 2013 Rugby League World Cup, the first time Rochdale had hosted a World Cup fixture in any sport.

The game itself had a real carnival atmosphere, with a capacity crowd of 8,872 enjoying the excitement of international rugby league. The Irish team had a large and noisy following, but the majority of the supporters present were cheering on the adopted Rochdalians from Fiji, who ran out 32–14 winners in a tough, physical contest. The successful event proved the World Cup organisers right in backing Rochdale to host the game, especially given that, in the early conversations, some people said that the game would not attract 1,000 people. Certainly, those that had started the project and had faith in it could feel justifiably satisfied.

The connections made around the Fijian game allowed Hornets to dip back into their history and look to add a new name to Hornets' Fijian legacy. After conversations with coach Ian Talbot, CEO Ryan Bradley targeted Ryan Millard, who played stand-off against England in the group stages of the World Cup. Hornets chairman, Mark Wynn, met with Millard in the dressing rooms at Wembley Stadium after Fiji had been beaten in the World Cup semi-final against Australia, in a bid to assure Millard that the club was serious about getting his signature on paper. Bradley continued the conversation and, eventually, Millard signed, joining that distinguished group of Fijians who had crossed the world to play for Hornets.

The signing of Millard for the 2014 season brought the curtain down on what was possibly Hornets' greatest post-war season. Promotion, the first trophy in 91 years, playing the Fijian national team, hosting a sell-out World Cup fixture, forming the first ladies team in the club's history and posting a healthy financial surplus all made for a great end of season celebration.

However, reality would bite in 2014 as the scale of the task required to remain in the second tier hit home. The euphoria of promotion quickly changed to the challenge of building a side capable of competing in the Championship. The task of fielding a side that could perform to the level required in the Championship moved beyond difficult to near impossible when it was announced that, in 2014, five clubs would be relegated to the third tier. To avoid relegation Hornets would have to make the play-offs, a daunting task to say the least.

Hornets started the 2014 league campaign badly with three heavy defeats and conceding an average of 46 points a game. There was some respite in the Challenge Cup. Hornets gained some confidence with a 76–4 win over Gloucestershire All Golds. Hornets won four of the next five league games with only back-to-back defeats to Leigh in the league and cup.

This run of form pushed Hornets to the edge of what was required to escape the drop, but eight back-to-back defeats, the majority when Hornets had to play away from home for several weeks in the summer, pretty much sealed their fate.

Hornets reserved their best performance of the season for their return to Spotland after the enforced summer break. The opponents were Featherstone Rovers who arrived having lost only once in their previous seven games, sitting second in the league table and odds-on favourites to win. However, Fijian star Ryan Millard had other ideas, delivering a virtuoso performance that almost single-handedly steered Hornets to a 38–34 victory. Millard's contribution was so influential that Featherstone chased Millard for the rest of the season to secure his signature for 2015.

A clear 54–22 win over Barrow the following week offered the faintest hope of salvation, but with just one win in the next eight games, Hornets were relegated having finished third from bottom. In any other year, this would have been enough to escape the drop.

One bright spot for the club in 2014 was the progress of the new Rochdale Hornets Ladies team. They had an excellent first season, reaching the WARLA Women's Rugby League Challenge Cup Final at Post Office Road, Featherstone against local rivals Whitworth Warriors. Despite two tries from Terri Davey, Whitworth proved too strong, beating Hornets by 50–8.

2015 was a year of transition. Any hopes of an immediate return to the Championship were dashed after Hornets failed to take points off the teams above them in games that mattered. Oddly, the win ratio for league games was marginally higher than in the promotion year of 2013, but defeats to those teams who finished in the top five cost Hornets dearly.

Things had looked promising at the end of May when four straight wins had lifted the Hornets into second place in the table, but a stuttering second half of the season saw them slip down the ladder. With 14 wins from 22 games, Hornets finished sixth and outside the play-offs. It was clear that changes had to be made to enable the club to grow and succeed. With chairman Mark Wynn and CEO Ryan Bradley undertaking a strategic review of all aspects of the club's operations, one major change was forced upon them.

Having become increasingly frustrated, Ian Talbot had the chance to coach St Helens reserves and help with the first team. With the job security in a full-time role offered, he took Saints' offer and left the club. The search began for a new coach to take the club forward.

References
rochdaleonline.co.uk: "Oldham Roughyeds 22 - 23 Rochdale Hornets" - 15 September 2013
manchestereveningnews.co.uk: "Hornets home and dry for final after defeating rivals Oldham" 17 September 2013
www.totalrl.com: "Hornets end trophy drought in style" – 29 September 2013
League Publications Limited: *League Express Rugby League Yearbook 2013–2014*
Conversation with Ryan Bradley, September 2021

18. Miracles happen

Before the 2016 season even began, everyone in League 1 knew that the challenge of aiming to be champions would be made more daunting with the addition of French champions Toulouse Olympique.

Toulouse was a million-Euro operation that included a full-time squad peppered with internationals of all nationalities. Lining-up up against them was a division of semi-professional clubs whose players had regular jobs while playing rugby league part-time.

Prior to the season, the RFL had reviewed the competition and shared a sliding scale of the clubs in League 1 that showed where each respective club's player budget stood in comparison to its rivals. Toulouse were obvious leaders. Hornets were seventh on the list. This was reflected by the bookmakers' odds. At the start of the 2016 season, they had Hornets as ninth favourite to be crowned champions at the end of the campaign, with odds in the hundreds to one.

Not even the most ardent Hornets fan would have thought the team could have upset those odds; but every now and then an outsider comes good. All Hornets needed was a coach that could make up the difference.

The task of recruiting a new head coach in 2015 was a very different experience than it was in 2009. The number and quality of candidates applying eclipsed what the club had to choose from previously as the perception of the club had significantly improved. From the huge number of candidates, a really strong four-person shortlist was created and there was one stand-out candidate: Alan 'Killer' Kilshaw.

'Killer' came with the perfect pedigree of what Hornets needed from a head coach. A protégé of former England and Warrington Wolves head coach Tony Smith, he had cut his coaching teeth in an impressive range of appointments including England and Warrington's development squads before moving up to assist with the first team at Warrington.

His ambitions then took him to Australia where he took a head coaching role with Sarina Crocodiles in the Mackay District of North Queensland. With a population of 5,500, the town of Sarina is a dot on the map, but its rugby league team has produced top-class players including Wendell Sailor, Martin Bella, Dale Shearer and Kevin Campion. Manly Sea Eagles and Australia star Daly Cherry-Evans also had a spell with Sarina as a junior when his father Troy was the captain-coach of the side.

During his spell at Sarina, Kilshaw took the Crocodiles to their first Minor Premiership and Grand Final in 13 years. He also gained coaching experience at the Mackay Cutters in the Queensland Cup, as well as establishing coaching connections with the North Queensland Cowboys. Coming with a good coaching pedigree and excellent recommendations from Tony Smith, Kilshaw was the front-runner throughout the process. While he passed under the radar of the average fan, he had a good reputation within the game. St Helens CEO Mike Rush flagged him as one of the best up-and-coming coaches – and the chair of one successful Championship side said Kilshaw had been their target, but at the time was settled in Australia.

Fortunately for Hornets, a change in circumstances led to Kilshaw returning to England just as the job at Hornets became available. It felt like destiny. From the get go, Kilshaw began to assemble a competitive squad. He had taken a handful of young British players to play for him in Sarina and they too were returning at the same time. Key signings from this group were hooker Ben Moores and centre Lewis Galbraith.

He also assembled a strong Rochdale core including Wayne English, Michael Ratu, Dave Cookson and Jack Francis. Added to these were Fijian Jo Taira and Northern Irishman Matty Hadden, neither of whom were born in Rochdale, but both were drawn from local sides Rochdale Cobras and Rochdale Mayfield.

The retention of Paul Crook and the signing of Oldham-born Danny Yates gave Kilshaw a strong half-back pairing. He also brought in the talismanic Jono Smith and the six feet seven inch Samir Tahraoui alongside no-nonsense prop Warren Thompson.

The last major signing before the start of the season was former Warrington and England Knights winger Chris Riley. Three times Challenge Cup winner and two times Grand Finalist, Riley would bring experience to this new squad.

A solid pre-season saw the Alan Kilshaw-coached Rochdale Hornets take the field in the iPRO Sport Cup at Barrow on a wet February afternoon. Tries from Corey Lee, James Dandy and Chris Riley saw Hornets grab a respectable 14–4 victory to put them into the next round against York. Hornets' York hoodoo struck again in a 40–16 defeat in April.

One week later came the Challenge Cup, where a quirk of fate had seen Hornets drawn away to local amateur side Rochdale Mayfield. The tie caught the imagination of rugby league fans in the town and even made it onto the local television news in what was billed as 'The Battle of the Borough'. In an exciting encounter, Mayfield put up a strong display, pushing Hornets hard at times and arguably scoring the try of the game through Dec Sheridan. But in the end Hornets had too much size, power and pace, running in seven tries to win 40–14.

One of the key tenets of the supporter-owned Hornets was to commemorate, acknowledge and celebrate the history of the club. For cup fixtures in 2016, Hornets had produced a commemorative 'Heroes of Hornets' jersey to mark the selection by supporters of their greatest ever Hornets XIII and coach.

The 'Heroes of Hornets' project was created to celebrate former players, teams and supporters who had made an outstanding contribution to the club. Early recipients included Ray and Ena Myers, hooker Kevin Lowe and the Rochdale Hornets squad that had undertaken the pioneering tour to France in the 1960s

This time, supporters were invited to vote for their favourite Hornets players across all eras. The result produced the All Time Heroes of Hornets XIII:
1: Alan Hodkinson. 2: Norman Short. 3: Paul Crook. 4: Malcom Price. 5: Teddy Cahill. 6: John Cookson. 7: Apisai Toga. 8: Wayne English. 9: Graham Starkey. 10: Chris Churm. 11: Karl Marriott. 12: Walter Gowers. 13: David Taylor. Coach: Frank Myler

As part of the on-going Hornets Heritage Project, supporter Neil Bruckshaw began the monumental task of listing every player who has ever played for Rochdale Hornets since the great split of 1895. The sequential heritage numbers awarded to each player became a badge of honour for players past and present. Neil continues to keep a meticulous record of every player to have made a first team debut.

Certainly, if Hornets were to achieve anything in 2016, it would need a heroic effort. The 2016 Kingstone Press League 1 campaign got off to a solid start. A 28–18 home win against

Hunslet, followed by convincing victories over Coventry, North Wales and the Gloucestershire All Golds pushed Hornets to the top of the table. An expected defeat to Super League side Widnes Vikings brought Hornets' Challenge Cup run to an abrupt halt; but, in the league, next in line was full-time glamour side Toulouse Olympique. The French outfit headed to Spotland with both Hornets and Toulouse undefeated in the League, sitting first and second respectively.

However, rather than talking about the excitement of a top of the table clash, the weeks leading up to the Toulouse game at Spotland had seen the ownership of the stadium in the headlines. The 'Old Hornets' had secured an emergency loan of £120,000 from the Rugby Football League (RFL) to pay pressing debts, and had used its shares in the stadium company as security. That meant that, when the club went into administration in 2009, the RFL became part-owners of a stadium, with accounts showing the stadium company as having outstanding debts of £505,967.

Fast forward to 2016 and Rochdale AFC wanted to take full ownership of the stadium to provide investment and to stop the stadium company going bankrupt and then being snapped up in a fire sale by a hostile investor.

When the co-operative Hornets formed, the negotiations around rent to play at Spotland Stadium were fractious as the stadium company were aggrieved that the debt owed by the 'Old' Hornets would have to be written off. The accounts for the stadium company in May 2008 show that debt as £69,422. With the 2009 season looming, the new Hornets were faced with having nowhere to play unless they agreed to pay a stadium rent of £45,000 a year plus VAT and stewarding costs of around £600 per game.

Given little choice, Paul Ormerod paid the rent for the first year in advance as part of seed fund for the new Hornets. It would later transpire that the rent set for the new Hornets was more than double that of any League 1 or Championship rugby league club.

Six years on and, somehow, Hornets had managed to pay the rent and put out a competitive side. But it was obvious for all concerned that changes had to be made. From the RFL perspective, they were still owed £120,000 from the loan. The level of rent that Hornets were paying was an albatross around the club's neck and holding them back. Plus, behind the facade, the stadium was in a poor state of repair with major infrastructure problems with the electrics, plumbing and drainage.

The RFL, through its CEO Nigel Wood, began negotiations to sell its share in the stadium company back to Rochdale AFC. Wood was clear, though, there would be no deal unless Hornets were 100 percent happy with it.

As a supporter-owned club, substantial decisions such the RFL's sale of the shares and the subsequent deal offered to Hornets required discussion by the members and a vote of approval. Nigel Wood was an experienced negotiator, and the deal approved by Hornets members was for a 60 percent reduction in rental and steward costs as part of a guaranteed 25-year lease. As a result of the vote, the RFL would get its £120,000 back and the football club could start renovations on the stadium.

Back on the field, the club pulled out the stops to publicise the visit of Toulouse. To promote the game Hornets acquired huge billboard sites across town, with posters featuring Jo Taira, Matty Hadden and Samir Tahraoui ready to welcome the big spending French outfit.

Even though the two clubs were first and second and both undefeated, it was something of an uneven contest. Toulouse's full-time players faced a semi-professional Rochdale Hornets side, made up of bricklayers, teachers, welders and community workers.

The early stages of the game followed most Hornets fans' worst expectations. With Curran crossing after two minutes for the French outfit, followed by Minga and Bentley, Hornets were 16–0 down with only 10 minutes on the clock.

It took 18 minutes before Hornets hit back through James Tilley before Tom Lineham, playing on dual reg, crossed twice around the half hour mark. Hornets were back in the game; 16–16 at half time. In the second half the game ebbed-and-flowed. At first Hornets had the upper hand with tries from Jono Smith and Danny Yates. Then Toulouse regained the lead with tries from White and Curran. A late Paul Crook penalty goal snatched the draw for Hornets and raised the roof.

What became clear during the game was that this was the first time that Toulouse had been put under pressure in a league fixture and they reacted badly. Their discipline slipped and the game threatened to boil over, especially after Toulouse player Ader was put on report for biting. Even after the final whistle tempers threatened to explode in the tunnel, where players and officials became embroiled in heated exchanges. Certainly, the rivalry had gone up several notches. Grudges had developed and Hornets now knew they could get under Toulouse's skin and match them when the pressure was on.

Hornets maintained the top spot until early June when a 40–12 loss at York blemished their undefeated league record, but four straight wins in the run-in guaranteed them a second place finish in the regular season.

Next up was a new concept, the Super 8s – effectively an extended play-off series. Hornets got off to a bad start losing 34–12 at Barrow, before two wins away to London Skolars (38–28) and Keighley (18–4) steadied the ship. However, it was York, again, that brought Hornets back to earth, handing them a 36–16 beating at Spotland.

The following week, Hornets faced a re-match against Toulouse in France. Travelling without a few key injured players, there was little to play for in this game, but Toulouse saw it as revenge for the torrid time they'd had at Spotland earlier in the year. As expected, Toulouse ran out easy 46–6 winners, which they took as a return to normal service. That assumption would be their downfall.

Post-game, the coaching staff used the time in Toulouse as a bonding exercise for the team. The 2016 Hornets were probably one of the strongest groups during the co-operative era and that night out in Toulouse cemented that bond. And as the team grew closer, it developed the 'siege mentality' needed to achieve great things. After the trip to Toulouse the team had a different mindset; complete as a unit, single-minded about their objectives and focused on achieving its absolute goal.

Next up for Hornets were Doncaster and Hunslet, both dispatched ruthlessly, to secure second spot in the table. More importantly, it ensured that Hornets would return to Toulouse and face their rivals in the promotion play-off final.

It was only confirmed on the evening of Sunday 11 September that Hornets would fly to Toulouse and play them in the final on the following Saturday, 17 September. The bad news was that the direct summer flight schedule to Toulouse had ended, forcing Hornets to travel by coach to Gatwick on the Thursday 15 for a Friday morning flight to Toulouse. A less than perfect preparation. With the lateness of arrangements, centre Dave Cookson couldn't get time off work and had to fly in separately for the game.

On arrival in Toulouse, the Hornets team was transported to a hotel on the edge of town which had been closed since the summer season had finished, leaving Hornets as the only guests. From there the team was taken to Toulouse's crumbling old ground in the city centre for the captain's run.

As this was potentially the last game of a long season, several Hornets players were carrying injuries. Forward Jono Smith's knee was causing a huge amount of concern, centre Michael Ratu had a major abdominal problem. The strapping area before training was like a MASH unit where the busiest member of the squad was the physio.

The coaching team decided to keep the captain's run as brief as possible to minimise the risk of exacerbating the players' injuries. But even in an abridged session Jono Smith's knee gave way and he was looking increasingly doubtful for the following day's final.

The team went back to the hotel and an evening meal was laid on for the players and staff. After eating together, Alan Kilshaw took his team through the game plan for one last time. Then, for inspiration, he showed the team the film *The Class of 92*, which focuses on the friendships built up by Manchester United's Golden Generation charting their seven-year rise from FA Youth Cup winners to Premier League dominance.

After the film, Kilshaw asked each player to say what it would mean to them to win the following day. One-by-one the players spoke. Chris Riley who had been in major finals spoke about his family and making them proud. Jono Smith spoke of how this was a very personal battle and he had come to win. Others spoke of achievement; a desire to win against the odds; of proving people wrong.

Kilshaw finished by asking chairman Mark Wynn to say what winning would mean to him. An emotional Wynn spoke of his late father; how, as a boy, he had gone to watch Hornets with his dad. His father, like so many Hornets fans, hadn't witnessed Hornets winning any competitions. This was a piece of history that this group could put right.

Alan Kilshaw asked the players to go back to their rooms, have a good night and prepare for the morning. Hornets media director, Luke Harrison, who was in the team meeting, has since said that, when the team left that room, no-one was in any doubt that Hornets would win the day, such was the atmosphere.

The morning of the match was sunny. After breakfast and a dynamic stretching session in the swimming pool, Alan Kilshaw went through how the day would pan out. The trip to Toulouse a couple of weeks previously had been a scouting mission; understanding the stadium, the dressing rooms and pitch-side facilities. Hornets had to use every piece of information to enhance their performance and distract, disturb and disrupt Toulouse's. On the last visit, the heating in the dressing room was turned up uncomfortably high.

So, this time, Hornets would get changed and prepare at their hotel – playing kit, strapping, massages, everything. The plan was to arrive just 30 minutes before kick-off instead of the expected one and a half hours.

While Hornets were preparing in the comfort and calmness of the hotel rather than the tiny over-heated dressing rooms of the Stade Ernest Argelès, Luke Harrison would go ahead and make sure the dressing rooms were set up for the team when they did arrive. Once there, an increasingly irate match commissioner and several Toulouse officials lambasted Harrison, as they feared Hornets wouldn't even turn up. The trap was set.

The mood back at the hotel was beginning to change. The relaxed atmosphere was changing into one of tension as volume levels began to drop. Chris Riley completed his pre-game rituals and began to write a message on the strapping on his wrist, he became visibly emotional and quietly left the room. Other players looked anxious; others drained of colour. Some, like Jono Smith, were ready to take on whoever Toulouse put in front of them. Jo Taira, simply quiet, but looking around for a release for his energy. The time had come to finally board the bus for the final and destiny.

After weaving through the busy city traffic, the Hornets team bus arrived at the stadium, much to the relief of the match commissioner. Hornets disembarked and ran straight out onto the pitch for their warm-up. Up in the main stand, RFL CEO Ralph Rimmer was glad-handing the Toulouse directors: warm handshakes, wide smiles, champagne flutes and big cigars all-round. Across town Toulouse had booked a sports centre for their after-match celebrations. A coronation was clearly expected. Toulouse's jour de gloire est arrivé.

Time for a last-minute team talk and then it was game on! The Hornets team that day was: Chris Riley, Jack Holmes, Dave Cookson, Lewis Galbraith, Dale Bloomfield, Paul Crook (c), Danny Yates, Samir Tahraoui, Ben Moore, Warren Thompson, Jono Smith, Josh Crowley, James Tilley. Subs: Ryan Maneely, Jo Taira, Matty Hadden, Michael Ratu.

There was little between the teams in the opening exchanges, with both sides running and tackling hard, but in the 11th minute the Hornets dam broke as prop Canet opened the scoring for Toulouse. That score was followed just four minutes later by a try from Curran.

Hornets' woes were further increased when centre Dave Cookson took a knock to the head and failed the subsequent head injury test. He could not take any further part in the game. Hornets had to rush a substitution to replace the injured Cookson, with Michael Ratu coming on to cover the right centre position. Toulouse took advantage of this upset in the defensive structure; centre White ghosting through the right channel to extend the lead to 16–0 with just 16 minutes gone. It looked ominous, but Hornets had been here before and turned the result around.

Ratu's first contribution after coming on was to give away a penalty for a high shot. The penalty initially felt like another nail in the Hornets coffin, but the incident did seem to have an impact on the Toulouse players. In their next two tackles, Toulouse knocked players distracted by looking at who was approaching to put the hit in.

Hornets regathered, pushing up the field through Tahraoui and Smith. Then a set move, ending with Ratu slipping the ball back for Jack Holmes to score in the corner. Crook converted from the touchline to take the score to 16–6. Suddenly, Toulouse didn't seem to run as hard, handling began to falter and their key men seemed less eager to get their hands on the ball. Slowly, the game began to change. Hornets were now able to weather the Toulouse attacks. And when Hornets were in possession, yards were easier to gain.

Also, Hornets seemed to have more energy. As the high tempo of the game took its toll on Toulouse, Hornets finished the half stronger. On the stroke of half-time, a desperate late high tackle gifted Hornets a penalty. Paul Crook stroked it home and Hornets were very much back in the game at 16–8.

Hornets dominated the start of the second half and were unlucky to have a Lewis Galbraith try chalked off for a forward pass. Jono Smith disagreed with the decision and was sinned binned for dissent.

Even with Hornets down to 12 men, it was Toulouse's discipline that slipped. Penalties for foul play were now happening with increasing frequency, much to the displeasure of a now edgy home crowd. Hornets' next passage of play involved a moment of genius from Danny Yates. His amazing footwork dazzled the Toulouse defenders before he slipped out a peach of a pass for the on-rushing Galbraith to score out wide. Paul Crook hit the target from the touchline. 16–14 after 50 minutes.

The game was still in the balance on the hour when Joe Taira became the victim of a lifting tackle by Kriouache that saw the Toulouse player sin binned. There then followed a bizarre argument as the Toulouse players tried to get Taira removed from the field for a head test, while the Hornets medical staff and Taira himself were saying it was a shoulder injury.

Hornets weren't fazed by such gamesmanship and continued to take the game to Toulouse. With just nine minutes remaining on the clock, a teasing cross-field kick from Danny Yates was plucked out of the air by Michael Ratu. As he fell to the ground, he fed Jack Holmes who plunged in at the corner. Paul Crook's conversion went just wide, but Hornets were in front for the first time. Eight minutes to go and Hornets led by two points.

In the next set, Toulouse's lack of discipline was their downfall again: This time Jono Smith the victim of an elbow to the face by Hepi. Seven minutes to go. Off the back of the penalty Hornets had all the momentum. A forceful drive by Josh Crowley from the play-the-ball, quick hands via Maneely, Crook and Yates and the ball found Chris Riley with, seemingly, nothing on. But a dummy, a spin, and last second jink saw Riley crash over to extend the Hornets lead.

Paul Crook converted to equal Walter Gowers' 80-year all-time Rochdale Hornets points scoring record of 1,497. Three minutes to go: Toulouse 16 Rochdale Hornets 24. In desperation, Toulouse threw everything they had at Hornets and, with one minute 45 seconds on the clock, Ader scored in the corner. Kheirallah's kick was good. 24–22 to Hornets with 40 seconds on the clock and Hornets to kick off

Paul Crook slammed the ball deep and Toulouse spun the ball wide to create a half break. With Hornets defenders scrambling for their lives Toulouse winger Minga was bundled to the floor. Luke Harrison, on radio commentary duty, screamed down the microphone: "It's over! It's over! It's over" But it wasn't quite over. In the final play Minga had conceded a penalty for obstruction. Paul Crook kicked the ball dead and then it was over.

Rochdale Hornets were League 1 Champions. The first time in 97 years that any Rochdale Hornets team could claim a league title.

Celebrating the victory in Toulouse. The authors of this book are in the photo.

Hornets produced a Rugby League miracle to beat full-time French side Toulouse Olympique 24-22 in the League 1 promotion final. Not only was this co-operative's second trophy in three years, it was the first time Rochdale Hornets had been crowned champions of any competition since 1919.
(Jackie Meredith/JM Sportpix)

A mix of euphoria, relief and disbelief ran through the group. Just 29 people were able to make the trip to Toulouse for the final. We were few, but we were a happy few and that day we were most certainly a band of brothers (and sisters). The 29 were: The 17-man squad plus Jack Francis as travelling reserve; Alison Roby masseuse and Brian Carroll, physio; Alan Kilshaw, head coach, Paul Berry and Jason Viller, assistant coaches, David Ramsbottom, team manager, Steve Wordsworth, statistics, Luke Harrison, media, Jackie Meredith, club photographer and Mark Wynn, chairman.

Given the limited amount of time to arrange a trip, the lack of direct flights to Toulouse and the prohibitive cost of over £1,000 to get to the game, only one supporter was able to make the journey. Jim Stringer was there too.

The group cheered and sang, embraced each other and a few tears were shed. Ben Moores came up to Mark Wynn and said: "That's for your dad" a reference to the speech Wynn had given the night before. There were phone calls home, text messages sent and the winning song was sung! Hornets were champions!

Unlike the 2013 Final, the Hornets players would receive medals, albeit from a hastily assembled table, from a somewhat surprised Ralph Rimmer. Ever the diplomats, the players gave Rimmer some grief about how a Hornets win had put a spanner in the works by denying Toulouse their expected promotion.

Then came the cup presentation; a beautiful silver rose bowl that had been re-purposed by the RFL over the years to fit changing competition structures. The only problem was that the traditional winners' ribbons that adorned the trophy were blue and white, the colours of Toulouse.

When asked about why they weren't in amber and black, the Hornets colours for the day - or even red, white, and blue, Rimmer could only say: "They've only sent one set." The assumption has to be that an upset wasn't even considered. Still, those blue ribbons found a nice home in the Hornets Heritage Room back at Spotland Stadium.

Going back to the dressing rooms, tensions rose as players were selected for substance testing. The Toulouse players were dealt with quickly, but the Hornets players made to wait. When the samples were eventually taken, the stadium was empty. Toulouse and their supporters had left for their civic reception in the city, pre-booked to celebrate their 'victory'. Like the person ordering the ribbons for the cup, they were a little presumptuous.

Interestingly, there was no post-match hospitality for visitors at Toulouse. Just a bit of pizza in a deserted bar area under the main stand as the Hornets group waited for the coach to take them to the airport.

The journey home was eventful. Getting a team of championship winning rugby league players home while enduring a 12-hour journey interspersed with a visit to duty free wasn't without its issues. However, after a coach to Toulouse airport, a flight to Gatwick and a six-hour trip back to Rochdale the weary band of Hornets arrived home at 5am on Sunday morning. Indeed, the gulf between the two finalists was starkly evident on the return home. Chris Riley tried to get as much sleep as possible on the journey as he was back on shift at work at 6am.

The traditional town centre reception was arranged for noon at the *Flying Horse* pub on the day after the game. The fans were waiting in good number as the trophy was carried into 'The Flyer'. The players arrived in pockets coming from different locations, but they gathered for a celebratory team photo with the statue of Gracie Fields which had been a recent addition to the Town Hall Square.

On a glorious afternoon Jono Smith took a dip in the town centre's Packer Spout fountain to cool off as players and supporters celebrated for the rest of the day.

19. Optimism and change

Having learned from the harsh lessons of the 2014 season, Alan Kilshaw set about building a much stronger squad for life in the Championship. While retaining the core of the 2016 team, some real quality was added, including Rob Massam, Gaz Middlehurst, Miles Greenwood, Gavin Bennion and Lewis Palfrey. To the disappointment of some supporters, Paul Crook, Dale Bloomfield and Warren Thompson moved on.

A strong pre-season included a comprehensive 24–12 Law Cup victory over Oldham at Stalybridge. Celebrations were marred when Oldham's George Tyson attacked Hornets' new signing Jake Eccleston as the players were shaking hands after the final hooter and about to leave the field. Incredibly Tyson was only given a four-match ban.

The season-opener was at home against perpetual Championship survivors Dewsbury Rams. Dewsbury came in confident mood, but Hornets announced their return to the Championship with a near perfect display, running out 46–0 winners.

Next came a visit to Odsal to take on the Bradford Bulls. Hornets had not had a victory there in over 50 years. In a game threatened by persistent snowfall, Hornets showed that they could grind out a win as well as play flamboyant rugby. A 22–14 victory kept Hornets top of the Championship and the noisy Hornets contingent in the crowd took great delight in pointing that out to the Bradford fans who hadn't left early.

The following week brought Hull KR to the Crown Oil Arena. The Robins had been relegated from Super League the previous season and, like Hornets, had made a 100 percent positive start to the 2017 season. The game had the feel of an old-fashioned cup tie. A grey overcast afternoon in February, a big vocal crowd of over 2,000 and two sides prepared to give it their all. Hornets matched Hull KR all the way. Late in the game, and with less than a score between the sides, they had Rovers pinned on their own goal-line with a full set of six tackles to come. But Hornets panicked, and the chance to take another major scalp was lost. A late converted try for Rovers made the final score 28–18 to the visitors.

In the dressing rooms after the game, Alan Kilshaw laid down the law: to compete in Championship we had to do what had been practised; don't move away from the plan; don't panic. A harsh reminder of what was needed at this level.

A flat Hornets performance then saw a 20–6 defeat at Halifax, but Kilshaw's men displayed some of their early season steel with a 10–9 victory at Featherstone seven days later. It was Hornets' first win at Post Office Road since Deryck Fox's side won there in May 1998. The following week, Hornets snatched a point in a 26–26 home draw with Oldham. This was the last league point Hornets achieved for 10 games, until they again faced Oldham at the Summer Bash at Blackpool, the Championship's equivalent of Super League's Magic Weekend, where the whole of one weekend's fixtures were played at a single venue and televised worldwide via *Sky Sports*.

The chances of Hornets getting anything from the game looked slim after half an hour, with the score 26–8 to Oldham. However, just before half-time there was a hint of a comeback as Jake Eccleston dived over to make the score 26–12 at the break. Despite an early Oldham penalty, the momentum of the game shifted 10 minutes into the second half when Lewis Galbraith laid on the pass for Welsh international Rob Massam to score in the corner. He was followed swiftly by a Ben Moores try to put Hornets six points behind the Roughyeds. A 57th minute Jordan Case try brought the Hornets fans to their feet. Palfrey added the conversion to tie up the scores at 28–28. The final quarter looked set to be a thriller.

Hornets' comeback was completed when centre Lewis Galbraith snaffled a stray Oldham pass to sprint 75 metres and score. As this was a televised game, the try was sent to be confirmed by the video referee. Not only was the try awarded, the video referee awarded a penalty after an Oldham defender's use of the knees in the act of scoring. This rare 8-point try put Hornets in front 36–28. Incredible stuff.

With 15 minutes remaining, a late tackle on Danny Yates was penalised. The half-back got off the floor to kick the goal and increase Hornets' lead to 10 points. Oldham were put on a team warning. What had looked like an unlikely victory was complete, but not before the game erupted in the dying seconds. leading to a red card for Oldham's Gee and a yellow for Danny Yates. The miraculous 38–28 victory over Oldham helped get the season back on track, with four wins and five losses from the remaining nine league games giving Hornets a creditable 9th place finish. This not only retained their Championship status, but also secured additional funding for the 2018 campaign.

The aim of the co-operative Rochdale Hornets was to build a sustainable Championship club; to gain promotion to the Championship and remain there, while maintaining prudent control of the club's finances. Chairman Mark Wynn had set this as his personal goal and had discussed privately that, once he felt this had been achieved, he would step down from the board. An action that would hopefully encourage new blood and new ideas to come forward. At the end of the 2017 season, Hornets had consolidated their position in Championship, the club finances were in reasonable shape and the off-field structures such as the Hornets Foundation and the media department were the envy of many of Hornets' peers.

Off the field, the continuous cycle of preparing for the new season continued; recruitment and retention of players, the setting of budgets and the endless search for new sponsors and new income streams continued. To bolster the squad Alan Kilshaw signed brothers Luke and Toby Adamson and former Wigan and Widnes back-row forward Dave Allen; all experienced Championship campaigners. They were joined by Warrington Wolves academy forward Lewis Hatton, Salford Red Devils academy hooker Dec Gregory and experienced Italian international, and former Oldham full-back, Richard Lepori. With some exciting new talent on board, it was hoped the club would kick on from its 9th place finish the previous season.

However, a simmering problem behind the scenes came to the boil before a ball had been kicked. Hornets were caught in a perfect financial storm as two of their major sponsors went to the wall. Local firm TBA, the club's main sponsor, went into administration and Tap2 – their online ticketing partner – into liquidation. The accounts for that season show that the £43,415 owing to Hornets left a major hole in the club's finances.

This meant that cuts to the already agreed budget would have to be put in place. Wynn postponed his decision to step down until new budgets had been agreed and reductions in player contracts had been signed off. Supported by Paul Ormerod, new CEO Steve Kerr had the unenviable task of working through individual contracts to reduce the player spend in order to balance the budget and bring finances back onto an even keel.

Inevitably, the club lost some players and the atmosphere within the group changed. There certainly wasn't the feeling of positivity that had become a cornerstone of the co-operative club's culture. In discussions with members, it was decided to review the club's model to see how it could be improved to better weather such damaging financial storms.

One business model that members agreed to look at was similar to the one in place in the German Bundesliga, which allows additional private investors to own part of the club. Also up for consideration were models that allowed philanthropic investors to get involved and, potentially, the prospect of full private ownership.

The 2018 season started as it had the year before, with a visit from Dewsbury Rams. This time, though, there would be no repeat of the 2017 heroics as Hornets crashed 38–6. This game was followed by two more defeats before a 24–12 comeback win against Barrow, having trailed 12–0 at half-time.

This was followed by an unconvincing 20–8 Challenge Cup victory against National Conference side Normanton Knights at Featherstone's Post Office Road, played in freezing Siberian conditions. Next up for Hornets at the Crown Oil Arena was big spending glamour club Toronto Wolfpack. Owned by a multi-millionaire mining magnate, and with an annual budget of $3,000,000, the full-time Canadian side was packed with former Super League and NRL players on a mission to bulldoze their way to Super League. The game was televised worldwide and for 80 minutes Rochdale Hornets showed the world what they could do.

Right from the kick-off, Hornets shook their rich rivals. Billy Brickhill outmuscled his opposite number to a short kick-off to give Hornets possession. Five tackles and 60 seconds later, Earl Hurst showed greater appetite than Kay to challenge for a high ball to score out wide. Lewis Palfrey was on target from wide out to give Hornets a blistering 6–0 start.

The visitors shuttled the ball wide for a converted Kay try, but Hornets weren't fazed. After a long period of soaking up the best Toronto had to offer, Hornets drove the visitors back under their own posts where debutant Morgan Smith unleashed a neat flat pass for Gary Middlehurst to squeeze between the defenders and score. Palfrey added the two and Hornets were good value for their 12–6 half time lead.

Hornets continued in the same vein after the break, defending heroically and matching Toronto blow for blow. Then, a moment of magic. Hornets kept the ball alive across a scrambling Toronto defence, sucking the visitors' pack into centre field. Lewis Palfrey hoisted a high kick to the corner where Rob Massam out-jumped Laulu-Togaga'e, producing a miracle one-handed catch to score. Hornets 16–6 up. Total bedlam in the stands.

A converted Toronto try from former Canberra Raiders half-back McCrone closed the gap to 16–12. Just past the hour, Hornets centre Earl Hurst landed a big shot and Toronto players started jumping in from all directions, Kay threw a punch and, for all the world, it looked like the outcome was only going one way. Referee Mr Rossleigh showed Toronto's' Kay and O'Brien yellow cards. Having dispatched Lewis Palfrey similarly he then gave the penalty to Toronto. In the resulting reshuffle, Maitua squeezed through a shifting Hornets defence to tie the scores at 16–16.

One more time Hornets drove the Toronto defence back to their goal-line, and, when the ball was snapped to Morgan Smith, he slotted the drop-goal to re-establish Hornets' lead. Leading 17–16 with just minutes to go it looked like Hornets would pull off the shock of the season, until the intervention of a touch judge to award a penalty for an infringement way back in play that no one else in the ground saw, including the television commentators. Toronto were in front, at the death, 18–17.

Hornets had one last roll of the dice, though. In the dying seconds they were awarded a penalty five metres inside the Toronto half. Hornets pointed to the posts, fans' hearts in mouths. The impossible just one kick away. As it was, Lewis Palfrey pulled his kick short and Toronto were able to hold out for a one-point win that broke Hornets' hearts.

The physical and emotional toll of this defeat knocked the stuffing out of Hornets' mini-revival. It was another six games before Hornets tasted victory. This time it was Hornets with a last-minute score of their own. Morgan Smith set up Dec Kay to score under the posts at Dewsbury. The conversion took the game 32–27.

Although not perfect, the financial position of the club was now sufficiently stable for Mark Wynn to feel confident enough to announce that he would step down at the AGM, so the process could begin to choose a successor.

The win at Dewsbury didn't produce the hoped-for spark to re-ignite the season. Hornets managed just two more wins, both against Swinton who, at the time were led by Andy Mazey, a former Leigh director who had formed a consortium to take ownership of the Lions.

Wynn's last official game as chair of the club was against Swinton on 8 July; another game that ended in a dramatic last-minute win for the Hornets as Morgan Smith charged down a kick to regather and score by the posts. His conversion gave Hornets a 28–26 victory.

Hornets didn't win again until late in the Championship Shield, now locked in a relegation battle rather than having any chance of silverware. After the despair of 2014 when Hornets lost their place in Championship due to five teams being relegated, rugby league karma offered Hornets a chink of hope as the RFL decided that only one club would be relegated after a play-off with the League 1 winners. A 26–22 home win against Dewsbury set up the final game against Sheffield Eagles. At the same time Swinton would play Batley. The maths was simple: Hornets had to win and Swinton lose to secure Hornets' Championship status.

The Hornets fans travelled to South Yorkshire in good numbers hoping that Alan Kilshaw could again work his magic and pull-off a 'Great Escape'. It was a tense evening on and off the field. All eyes and ears equally on Swinton's performance at Mount Pleasant. Once again, Alan Kilshaw defied the odds. The Hornets boys rose to the occasion, running out 32–22 winners. Swinton crashed 40–6. As the hooter sounded, players and coaching staff embraced. The 'Great Escape' was done. Hornets would be in the Championship in 2019.

Ultimately, 2018 was a year of change. Longstanding chairman Mark Wynn and directors Wendy Hamer and Luke Harrison left the board room. On the coaching staff Alan Kilshaw stood down, as did assistant coach Jason Viller and team manager Dave Ramsbottom.

Without doubt, Rochdale Hornets in 2019 would be a different place. Stepping into Alan Kilshaw's shoes was new head coach Carl Forster, a 2013 promotion final hero. He had the difficult task of keeping Hornets' Championship status on a limited budget. His signing of winger Shaun Ainscough was a good choice, as was keeping Lee Mitchell and Ben Moores.

20. 2019 to 2021: The end of the beginning

Off the field early in 2019, there were early rumblings of impending change. Interim vice-chair Brian Belfield was replaced by Peter Rush after a just few weeks. When the fixtures for the 2019 season were released, Carl Forster looked set for a baptism of fire, with opening fixtures against the favourites Toronto Wolfpack, followed by a trip to Toulouse Olympique. Any off-season optimism soon evaporated. The Toronto fixture went as many expected, ending in a heavy 56–6 loss. The 42–12 defeat in Toulouse was hardly better.

By the end of April 2019, Hornets – and their player coach Carl Forster – appeared to be in deep trouble. Having delivered just one victory in nine games, Forster was conspicuous by his absence from Hornets' 54–16 defeat at Bradford Bulls, a game in which Hornets led 12–0 after 10 minutes.

Amid press speculation that he was heading for the exit, there seemed to be some confusion within the club as to what was actually going on. Reports suggested that at least some of the players were aware of Forster's absence from the club as early as the previous Thursday. Rumours were rife that he'd been sacked - and then, somehow, un-sacked. The mystery deepened when Hornets issued a "vague statement" on the matter, which was "hastily withdrawn" shortly afterwards.

By Thursday 2 May, Forster's departure was confirmed. Whatever the truth of the matter, a statement claimed that there was a "mutual agreement to part ways". 24 hours later, Hornets unveiled Matt Calland as the club's new head coach. In three spells with Hornets, Calland had made 120 appearances and scored 60 tries. Having cut his teeth coaching Halifax to their 2010 Grand Final win, he'd gone on to coach Rochdale Mayfield in the National Conference League and lead player development as the head coach of Hopwood Hall College's academy side.

For a couple of years there had been a growing groundswell of support to have Calland installed as Hornets' coach and he was delighted to seize the opportunity, saying: "There is a lot of hard work to be done and I can't wait to get stuck into it. Rochdale Hornets was my first professional club and it is a job I have always wanted."

Hornets CEO Steve Kerr saw it as an exciting appointment: "[Calland] brings with him a wealth of experience, a winning attitude and a no-nonsense approach. He is a missing piece of the puzzle that we have been trying to put together for a number of years. He is a local coach, whose experience of the game in Rochdale is second to none."

The scale of the challenge became apparent in that weekend's 56–10 defeat by Featherstone Rovers. Things didn't improve. The following week at the Blackpool Bash – in the archetypal game of two halves – Hornets tossed away a 24–10 half time lead over Swinton to crash 40–30. Having dominated the first half with a display brimming with confidence and ideas, Hornets melted in the seaside heat. Leading 30–14 after 45 minutes, they then shipped 26 unanswered points in the last 27 minutes in a capitulation that left the Hornets fans in stunned silence.

The shockwave shattered Hornets' confidence, as they slid to 13 straight defeats. In five of those games, they were nilled, conceding 314 points in the process. By the time Hornets lost 46–0 in Toronto (the game was abandoned in the 74th minute due to a lightning storm) they had used 50 players over the season. Relegation felt like a mercy. While Hornets were falling apart on the field, cracks had started to appear off it too.

As a Provident and Industrial Society, the club was legally bound by a set of rules and was regulated by the Financial Conduct Authority (FCA). The rules regarding directors was straightforward: the board had to comprise between eight and 12 members, covering a variety of skills. Directors could be co-opted, but such members could not outnumber elected members. Officers were then elected by the board members.

However, by April the board had dropped to just two directors, Councillors Peter Rush, acting as Chair, and Ray Dutton, both of whom had been co-opted rather than elected. This meant that the club was operating outside the terms of its rules and, as such, was not legally able to take business decisions.

As the member with responsibility for governance, Society secretary Julie Clarke saw that action needed to be taken to put the board back into compliance, but the AGM was still almost three months away. Under the Society's rules 20 members could call for a meeting to be held within 28 days of the request. The signatures were easily obtained and the request delivered to Peter Rush. When no meeting was called, Clarke took advice from Supporters Direct Europe's Advisory Board member Andy Walsh and an emergency meeting of the members was called for 29 April. The sole agenda item was to find sufficient volunteers to join the board on an interim basis pending the AGM on 8 July.

At the emergency meeting, 19 members volunteered to step up to the board, 10 of whom were elected. This interim board would then steer the club as far as its AGM in July, when a new board of six would be formally elected, with the intention of co-opting the others. It was a bad tempered meeting, described by *TotalRL.com* as a night "... when the different factions first became apparent through the way people spoke to others in front of the room."

In the wake of the emergency meeting and in the weeks leading up to the AGM, something strange happened. Hornets' membership saw a 61 percent increase, something never before achieved in the 10 year history of the co-operative. *TotalRL.com* reported the anomaly: "... the club's membership surged dramatically shortly before it closed for the election, and it emerged this was through the Hornets Past Players' Association – who had seen little connection with the club in recent years – joining en masse, apparently all intending to vote in a certain way."

In a five-day period, the club received 70 applications, 50 of which were delivered in person by Peter Rush accompanied by Ray Dutton. Given this sudden spike in interest, it was agreed by the temporary directors that nine board places would be made available rather than six, but voting forms had already gone out by that stage.

Come the AGM, all hell broke loose. The meeting began with an unscheduled proposal from the floor to block the move to nine directors. As this move ran contrary to the club's legally-binding constitution – because it was not on the original agenda sent 28 days previously, so absent members had no knowledge of it and could not vote remotely on it or by proxy – there were arguments in the room as to the validity of the unscheduled proposal.

Despite secretary Julie Clarke's efforts to challenge proceedings and explain the rules of conduct for an AGM, not only was the proposal allowed to stand by the chair Peter Rush, it was passed by a show of hands and a significant number of proxy votes held by the chair. *TotalRL.com* wrote that: "Issues became personal, some left the room in disgust and one message-board poster described the meeting as "outrageous"." Having descended into a shouting match, the meeting went on to elect Councillors Rush and Dutton, Denise Dawson, Martin Hall, Mark Harris and Gavin Reynolds as directors.

Incensed by what they considered to be an open breaching of the club's democratic, co-operative principles, a group of supporters tabled a vote of no-confidence in Councillors Rush and Dutton for their failure to adhere to the terms of the club's legally-binding rules.

In a tense meeting with the new board at the Flying Horse Hotel on 19 September, the signatories of the vote of no-confidence put their concerns about the AGM directly to Councillors Rush and Dutton, and invited them to resign. The board withdrew to consider their position.

On 2 October, *Rochdale Online* reported that both Rush and Dutton had stood down form the board, with Dutton stating: "Unfortunately, a situation arose with a small band of supporters, who didn't feel we were fit to continue, stemming from in-house reasons following our AGM, which I will not divulge." In a statement, the remaining four members of the board of directors said: "They have stepped aside to allow the board to find a new focus and attract new investment to take the club forward in the future. The board will meet this week to discuss options to strengthen its skills set moving forward."

However, just a week later, 9 October, the remaining four members of the board announced that they too had also decided to stand down. Their statement said: "After outlining the exact details of a number of pressing issues to members we felt that we had no other alternative. We are all committed to ensuring a smooth handover and will remain in a supporting role until the election of a new board. We are willing to assist the new board with sharing information and knowledge regarding the club's current situation, and to help complete any current ongoing projects that have been worked (sic). At the same time we wish the club the very best success in these testing times."

In a case of déjà vu, yet another election was called for 7 November, the earliest date possible under the club's 28-day notice rule. Six directors were elected: Martin Hall was re-elected as director of rugby to sit alongside Emma Conway, Carl Halstead, David Heaton, Alex Orange and Jim Stringer. Conway said: "We are committed to keeping the members informed and will make some decisions in the coming weeks. Our priority as a board is to support Martin and Matt [Calland] with the recruitment of a squad ahead of the 2020 season."

However, at the first board meeting, CEO Steve Kerr handed the new board a dossier that would change the direction of the club once again. Inside was a proposal from a consortium led by former Swinton chairman Andy Mazey to take over the running of Rochdale Hornets. The proposal included a five-year plan for development designed to make the club sustainable over the long-term; a plan to not only invest in the first two years, but also to restructure the club and make it fit for life beyond the Sky Television deal that was due to expire in 2021.

As such, the new board's first act was to agree unanimously to meet the consortium. In a statement that was stark in its realistic appraisal of the club's situation, the board said: "At present, the club is losing money and struggling to raise sufficient revenue to meet its obligations. The club needs investment, resource and a strategic vision to build value in the product, the team and the sport in the town."

"The co-operative model has served us well, but it's unsustainable. Given the size of our membership we have reached the extreme of our limitations, and we are currently over-reliant on RFL distribution and the generosity of benefactor loans to make us viable."

In their meeting with the Rochdale Hornets board, the consortium committed to providing coach Matt Calland with a budget to make the team competitive in League 1 and displayed a longer-term intention of turning Hornets into a viable, sustainable Championship club. To do that, the consortium's investment would run across all areas of the club – including non-playing activities and infrastructure. As *TotalRL.com* put it: "All investment from the consortium will be used for strengthening the club – not servicing its debts."

After extensive talks between the board, Steve Kerr and the consortium, the formal takeover proposal was tabled. The board prepared to recommend to the membership that they back the move from being a supporter-owned co-operative to become a privately-owned club, saying: "The board has a responsibility to do what it feels best secures the club's long-term viability and delivers future success. It feels that the proposal received from the consortium is exciting and has lots of potential to grow Rochdale Hornets into a club that all members and fans can be proud of in a way that can't be achieved under the current ownership model."

In order to proceed with changing the status of the club from an Industrial and Provident society to a private Limited Company, members had to deliver a two-thirds majority in favour of the proposal. At a members meeting on 9 December, 136 members – 69% of the total membership – voted to back the move, with no opposition. Under the rules of the Society, the decision had to be ratified by a second vote, scheduled for 23 December. The vote was a formality and the deal brought the curtain down on Hornets' 10-year co-operative adventure.

As an experiment born of necessity, the co-operative achieved a great deal, modernising the club, bringing a sustained period of stability and delivering success on the pitch. From the basics of establishing the Hornets' first website, developing its social media presence and reinventing the club shop both at the stadium and online, to more fundamental issues like repairing a tarnished brand, building bridges with the local media and developing relationships with the wider business community, even the harshest critics would concede that things changed for the better.

There was also success in reconnecting the club with its rich history through initiatives like the Heritage Room, Heroes of Hornets and the Heritage Numbers project. Also important was the revitalising of the historic link between Rochdale Hornets and Fiji, which produced one of the greatest sporting occasions the town has ever seen, when Fiji met Ireland on that amazing night in 2013.

The development of the wider game wasn't ignored either. The creation of the Rochdale Hornets Sporting Foundation introduced rugby league to thousands of local children and launched both women's and wheelchair sides to put Hornets at the forefront of inclusion and sporting diversity.

Despite its difficult start, the co-operative also managed a level of economic stability. When the club picked up the reins from SponsorBank, debts stood at £180,454. When the club was handed over, the debt stood at £185,012 – an increase of £4,558 over a decade: an average loss of £458 a year. The major change was to whom the debt was owed, with Paul Ormerod shouldering the majority of the financial burden.

In reality, though, any sporting club is judged by its performance on the field. Raising the club's first trophy in 91 years and being the first Hornets side to be crowned champions in 97 years are unarguable successes. Of the last seven years as a co-operative club, six of them were either in the Championship or winning trophies to get there. Not a bad time to be a Hornets fan.

Ultimately the major downfall of the co-operative club was that, while success on the field and relative stability silenced the factions that have beset rugby league in Rochdale, they didn't go away. Whether through naivety or misplaced optimism, when a number of board members stood down a lack of succession planning left a void, and once there was a chink in the club's armour the in-fighting started again. Although attempts were made to bring all parties into the fold, these attempts ultimately failed and the early ideal of a mass membership club never materialised.

All these things played a part, but the major flaw was that the initial investment by Paul Ormerod was squandered by SponsorBank. This meant that money that should have been a seed fund to develop the club was wasted, leaving Hornets severely undercapitalised. As such, instead of spending time growing and developing the business, all the effort and energies were devoted to firefighting in order to put a competitive team on the field.

That said, if it hadn't been for that hardy group of supporters, there would be no Rochdale Hornets to hand over to the new consortium and no 150th anniversary to celebrate.

With the consortium given the green light, the new directors were to be chairman Andy Mazey plus Tony Sheridan, Richard Heyes, Peter Smith and club president Paul Ormerod, who wrote off £170,000 of loans to clear the way for the takeover.

While the legal cogs turned slowly in the background to process the transfer, incoming chairman Andy Mazey began to articulate his vision for Rochdale Hornets: "We'd taken a bit of a leap of faith and have been helping out behind the scenes with building a quad for several weeks now... it was important that we got to Christmas and we weren't in a bad place, with the pre-season games due to start in the New Year. It is exciting times (sic). Now that everything has gone through we can start investing more into the club and start executing our plans and vision."

"I can see huge potential in the club and I feel that I can do here, what I couldn't do at Swinton. There is a first-class stadium in the town, first-class training facilities at Hopwood Hall, a player pathway and a great amateur game in the town. So there is a lot of the building blocks here that you would need for a successful club already in place. It just needs some investment, strong leadership and people who can put all those blocks together to build a strong club."

Mazey was also keen to recognise the role played by the supporters who'd battled to keep their club alive for a decade. "Let's not forget the fans owned the club for ten years and they did some fantastic work in not just keeping the lights on, but they had a degree of success and I think it was time to come together with some private ownership, but keeping strong supporter input, and if everyone works together, we can really grow it and maximise its potential."

2020 began in positive mood. In a pre-season 34–24 defeat by Championship side Widnes Vikings, a Hornets side featuring several new signings showed promise and a desire to play good football. A week later, Hornets' confidence was boosted further when they took the Law Cup 18–12 over newly promoted Oldham.

Competitive games began with two rounds of the Challenge Cup. Hornets' Round 3 game against York Acorn was initially postponed due to the effects of 'Storm Ciara'. With more bad weather in the forecast, the game was moved to Salford Red Devils' AJ Bell Stadium the following week. In front of a crowd of just 200, Hornets ran out comfortable winners 54–10. Round 4 saw Hornets drawn at home against the British Army.

On 23 February, the same day that a ruthless Hornets dispatched the Army side 54–10, news broke that 13 people in the United Kingdom had been confirmed as having the dangerous new Coronavirus Covid–19. Concern within rugby league at this point was pretty low. By the time Hornets beat Keighley 29–14 in the first league game of the season on 8 March, there were 23 cases, with three people having died.

By 15 March, there were already rumours that some restrictions may soon be put in place. The virus had surged to over 1,000 cases and the death-toll had doubled in just 24 hours from 11 to 21. On the same day, Hornets fans travelled to Featherstone to play York City Knights in Round 5 of the Challenge Cup. The game had been moved at just 24 hours notice due to the unavailability of Bootham Crescent. On paper, it looked set to be an interesting contest: York firmly anchored to the bottom of the Championship with no wins, Hornets on a roll of four consecutive victories. But the York hoodoo remained firmly in place, as Hornets crashed out of the cup 70–12.

As a result of the spread of Covid–19, on the following day, 16 March, the RFL suspended the 2020 season in-line with government advice warning against mass gatherings. The suspension was to last, initially, until 3 April. At that point, three weeks off seemed like a minor inconvenience. However, as Covid surged in the UK to 38,168 cases and 3,605 deaths, the 3 April deadline came and went, with no clear idea of when it might be lifted.

As the national lockdown tightened, uncertainty on the future of the 2020 season – and the wider game – grew. RFL chief executive, Ralph Rimmer declared that the future of many clubs could be under threat. In May, the Government gave the RFL a £16 million emergency loan to help clubs deal with the extreme financial impact of the coronavirus outbreak while the season remained suspended.

Rimmer admitted that, with finances tighter in rugby league than other mainstream sports, the suspension of games left clubs facing a precarious future. He said: "All of them have different business models, but they are based on having a certain amount of home games. There's a threat, we recognise it."

For Hornets, that suspension soon became a cancellation. On 20 July, after a consultation with Championship and League 1 found that the majority of teams would not support the cost implications of playing behind closed doors, the RFL announced that the 2020 Championship and League 1 seasons would not resume and declared all results null and void.

Thankfully, Hornets CEO Steve Kerr and the new board acted swiftly to put an action plan in place that would reduce Hornets' financial exposure and stabilise the club through the coming months of inactivity. The Government's Coronavirus Job Retention Scheme, which paid up to 80 percent of a person's wage, was used to cover furloughed players' salaries, while Kerr and Matt Calland both took significant pay cuts.

Kerr and his team also worked behind the scenes to access Covid-related business grants, including a business recovery grant from the local Council and a technology grant for a computerised ticketing system that would enable the club to be compliant with regulations in place on the game's eventual return. Another major factor that helped Hornets through was the number of fans and sponsors who generously donated the cost of their season tickets and sponsorships back to the club, despite the loss of the 2020 season.

In combination, these actions allowed Hornets to operate without the revenues they had forecast for the season. More importantly, such decisive action ensured that Hornets didn't have to take on any debt from the RFL's emergency loan scheme.

Despite the sport's complete shutdown, Andy Mazey remained upbeat, reassuring supporters that Hornets were well-set to recover from the impacts of the coronavirus lockdown, saying: "Covid-19 might have put a bit of a speed bump in the road for us all, but rest assured the Rochdale Hornets New Era remains firmly on track and the future is filled with optimism."

And his upbeat mood was justified. After months of painfully slow progress, Companies House eventually ratified the conversion of the club from a co-operative into private ownership. Mazey said: "We are absolutely delighted to finally announce that the company conversion and take-over of Rochdale Hornets has been completed. On behalf of the board, I would like to place on record a huge thank you to the members who voted unanimously for this exciting new direction of travel for the club. Our thanks must also go to outgoing chairman and the former board, all who have been extremely supportive and involved in the transitional period."

"There is much work ahead of us and, of course, with the current situation surrounding Covid-19, we have had to work around this, however we remain excited and incredibly focused on forward planning to ensure progression on and off the field."

With the 2020 season abandoned, the board showed its faith in coach Matt Calland, extending his contract for another season. Speaking of his new deal, Calland said: "I had no hesitation in agreeing to remain as coach through to the end of the 2021 season and hopefully beyond."

He went on: "Covid-19 related issues mean that we are in unprecedented times for both Rochdale Hornets as a club and the sport of rugby league in general. The game will not be the same on the resumption, how we operate, what the financial impact has been, what restrictions we will have to adhere to, all these matters will have to be thoroughly assessed as we slowly start to understand what the 'new normal' will look like for the sport of rugby league."

The most obvious manifestation of the 'new normal' came when Super League restarted in August 2020. In order to try and control the Covid transmission risks, games were played at a restricted number of venues and behind closed doors. The return of rugby league at the top level also saw a significant change to the shape and flow of the to the game, as the RFL suspended scrums as a precautionary measure, replacing them with a tap restart to the non-offending team.

Hornets' own 'new normal' became apparent with the lifting of restrictions that allowed Hornets to commence pre-season training in late November 2020, with sessions run in line with strict Covid protocols. Strength and conditioning coach Miles Greenwood said: "We had a good period in November and December. We had some really good sessions. All the lads [were] in their bubbles, [so we] tapped into the competitiveness element of the bubbles and doing some competitions with bubbles against each other. All the lads bought into it and it was really good, it was flying. The lads came back in really good shape."

However, in early January, the RFL advised clubs in the Championship and League 1 to pause their pre-season training programmes in response to the worsening national Covid crisis. Following a virtual meeting between the RFL and Championship and League 1 clubs a couple of weeks later, Hornets were cleared to return to training in February, but only for 'Stage 1 plus' which permitted socially distanced (non-contact) training outdoors. 'Stage 2', contact training, would be confirmed at "a later date", with all clubs required to satisfy the RFL that they were able to meet "strict conditions regarding testing and biosecurity".

CEO Steve Kerr pointed out the challenges of making the 'new normal' a reality in a semi-professional sporting environment: "The RFL protocols will be placing the club under significant administration, logistical and financial strain. Matt, his team and all our essential staff will now need to be tested weekly at considerable expense. If that wasn't difficult enough to manage, we are balancing our finances on a 20 percent reduction in central funding and we are faced with the prospect of playing behind closed doors."

However, the prospect of playing at all felt even more remote when Hornets were also told that the start of the League 1 season would be moved back by two months, due to public health concerns and the potential risks involved in welcoming fans back into stadia. The much delayed release of the 2021 fixtures brought a mix of good news and bad news for supporters.

The good news was that, after 406 days of no rugby league, Hornets fans could see their team in action. The bad news was that the first three games – a pre-season friendly against North Wales Crusaders on 25 April and the first two league games against West Wales Raiders and Doncaster – would be played behind closed doors and only available to watch online. But after a 13 month drought, it felt, in the words of Andy Mazey, 'like Christmas Eve'.

Behind the scenes, significant adjustments were made to enable the safe return of rugby league to the Crown Oil Arena. There were Covid protocols to follow, processes to be learned and practices to be adopted as game-day became a series of strict medical checkpoints.

To create a Covid-safe environment, the stadium was divided into Zones. The Green Zone comprised the stadium's exterior areas, the car park and open spectator areas. The Amber Zone was restricted to match day staff and media. Anyone entering this area was subject to a temperature check and required to sign a health declaration.

The Red Zone was the most severely restricted area and included the pitch, the tunnel, technical areas, medical room, socially distanced dugouts and dressing rooms. Access was strictly limited to players, coaching staff, match officials and essential staff who had tested negative for Covid-19 in the previous five days. All Hornets players arriving for games were required take a lateral-flow test, overseen by the club's new 'Covid Officer' Dave Ramsbottom, before being handed their credentials to enter the Red Zone. Inside the stadium there were hand sanitiser points at almost every turn and the removal of masks was only permitted in the Green Zone.

To make matters even stranger, given the risk of postponements due to Covid, the RFL announced that league positions would be decided on a win percentage basis, with clubs having to playing at least 70 percent of their scheduled fixtures to be eligible for the play-offs.

With those play-offs in mind, the board had invested heavily, bringing in former NRL star Fuifui MoiMoi to run off Sean Penkywicz. They'd added half-back Rob Fairclough and Prop Gavin Bennion from Championship Swinton and brought Danny Yates and Lewis Galbraith 'home' from Batley. Proven talent to augment a squad containing a solid core of local players.

On 25 April, only five days after their 150th Anniversary, Rochdale Hornets kicked off their 2021 season. And expectations were high.

The opening exchanges of Hornets' pre-season game with North Wales were steady if unspectacular, but with Lewis Galbraith given a yellow card for an outrageous off the ball tackle in the 13th minute, the visitors capitalised with two quick tries to take a 10–0 lead. On the half-hour, the game took a decisive turn when Crusaders' full-back Johnson was sent off for a high tackle on Josh Jordan-Roberts.

This time it was Hornets' turn to work the numbers and send Ben Calland in for a converted try that left Hornets trailing 10–6 at the break. Hornets started the second half in decisive mood; Jordan-Roberts with the break, Danny Yates the finish, Jordan-Roberts with the extras and Hornets 12–10 in front. A Crusaders penalty gave the visitors parity, but, as both sides rotated their squads, the game became a scrappy arm-wrestle. Hornets did finish stronger. Two tries in the closing stages for Callum Marriott and Lee Registe gave Hornets a 22–12 winning return after more than a year away.

The visit of West Wales Raiders in the opening league game on 9 March came with its own interesting sideshow. Having been League 1's whipping boys before the Covid break with only one win in two seasons, the Raiders had signed former Super League Man of Steel, England international and rugby league enfant- terrible Rangi Chase. That alone would have been enough to give the game a frisson of anticipation. But West Wales had produced a headline-grabbing double coup, signing 38-year-old former Welsh rugby union megastar Gavin Henson.

Henson had made a passable debut in West Wales's heavy Challenge Cup defeat to Widnes a couple of weeks previously, but there was a palpable exhalation of disappointment in a busy press box when his name wasn't listed on the team-sheet. In the event, even the presence of Rangi Chase couldn't prevent Hornets sweeping the Raiders aside 40–16.

The following week at Doncaster, Hornets started miserably slowly, shipping three unanswered tries in the first 28 minutes to trail 18–0. Hornets did find a rare moment of lucidity when, with the hooter imminent, Ben Calland slipped a pass wide for winger Shaun Ainscough to score and make it 18–4 at the break. Hornets continued in the same lackadaisical vein, conceding another sloppy try within 10 minutes of the restart to go 24–4 down. In a desperate attempt to chase down the game, Hornets played their best rugby of the day, producing tries from Zak Baker and Luke Fowden to give the Hornets fans watching at home a glimmer of hope. But a lapse of concentration under a Doncaster kick to the corner led to a simple Doncaster try that all but extinguished Hornets' chances. A 71st minute try by Jack Higginson put Hornets within nine minutes of an unlikely upset, but Doncaster stood firm to win 30–22.

For supporters, the next game at Keighley came as blessed relief. Having spent three weekends shouting at their laptops, the Government's easing of restrictions meant that fans could attend the game at Cougar Park. The excitement was tempered somewhat by the imposition of Covid protocols. The 'new normal' meant that cash could no longer be taken at the turnstiles, and clubs were initially requesting that fans arrive early at a pre-defined time slot to avoid the gathering of large numbers at the last minute. By 2.15pm, a 60 metre queue snaked back up the street, fans waiting patiently as tickets were scanned at the gate. Then there were the awkward questions: Mask on or mask off? Am I standing two metres away from the next fan? Once the game began, neither seemed to matter.

In their first 80 minutes back in over a year, the Hornets faithful were treated to a rollercoaster game that encapsulated life as a Hornets fan in microcosm. The first half was, initially, a nip and tuck affair: both sides trading scores, with Keighley just in front at 12–10 on the half-hour. Then Hornets exploded into life, with Sean Penkywicz as the catalyst. First his pinpoint short ball hit Gavin Bennion who crashed in to restore Hornets' lead. Then his jump out of dummy half caught the Cougars napping, Rob Fairclough hoisted a lethal kick and Shaun Ainscough finished neatly. Right on the hooter, Fairclough sneaked in a cheeky drop-goal and Hornets looked good value for their 21–12 lead. After such a long time, it felt good to have the fans cheer Hornets from the field.

Hornets began the second half as they had ended the first, this time Fairclough scored a try to take Hornets' further ahead. Then came two forward power-plays, with Josh Jordan-Roberts and Fuifui Moimoi scoring to give Hornets a convincing 37–18 lead. With just 10 minutes to play Hornets collapsed spectacularly, conceding three tries in five minutes to find themselves desperately clinging to a 37–36 lead. Salvation came in the 75th minute when Dec Sheridan sent Shaun Ainscough racing in to score. Jordan-Roberts, with the conversion, secured a 43–36 victory.

Highs as a Hornets fan don't last long. Hornets careered directly into a month of four consecutive defeats and a run of cruel bad luck that saw injuries mount week on week. At one point Hornets were missing 13 first-team players due to injury or suspension.

Influential half-back Rob Fairclough received a serious knee injury in the frankly awful 38–30 defeat at Coventry. Then came a lacklustre 36–22 defeat at Hunslet, at which the travelling Hornets fans were corralled into the worst seats in the house at the very back corner of the top tier of the stand, reserved usually, judging by the state of the seats, for pigeons. By the time Hornets went to Barrow, they were down to their last 17 willing bodies. Never really in the game, Hornets succumbed 40–4. Then came a heart-breaking defeat at Workington. A Hornets side shored up by fringe players and loanees played out of their skins, only to throw away victory with a loose pass as the final hooter sounded to go down 34–28. The travelling fans were left stunned in disbelief. It was a long, silent drive back to Rochdale.

In a quest to add quality to the squad, Hornets' board produced another major coup, signing Rangi Chase from West Wales Raiders. After just a couple of training sessions he went straight into the side for the visit of North Wales Crusaders. For 15 minutes he ran the show, working his way through a high quality repertoire of teasing runs, perfectly timed passes and line-busting breaks. But when he was slow to get up after an innocuous tackle, the doctor was called onto the field. Word came back to confirm everyone's greatest fear, he had broken his arm. Andy Mazey spoke for all Hornets when he said: "But for bad luck we would have none at all, but we will keep going, head down and keeping fighting."

Hornets recovered their composure to grab three vital wins, against North Wales Crusaders (38–28), London Skolars (22–4) and in Llanelli against West Wales Raiders (30–18), where a hardy band of Hornets supporters came close to outnumbering the locals.

Having gained some momentum, Hornets' next home game with Workington Town was then postponed when 11 players and three staff tested positive for Covid-19. Due to the compulsory 10-day isolation period and the RFL's seven-day return to play protocols, an already threadbare Hornets were unable to field a team. The game was never rearranged.

Still beset with injuries, and in the wake of the Covid outbreak, it's hardly surprising that Hornets then struggled against Keighley, losing 42–20. A narrow 38–34 away win against London Skolars, another game at which the Hornets fans equalled the home fans in number, and a 44–8 thumping of a poor Doncaster perfectly teed-up Hornets' final push to get into the play-offs.

However, a 34–34 draw with Hunslet, in which Hornets took the lead in the 76th minute, only to concede a penalty in the last tackle of the game, followed by defeats away to North Wales (36-10) and by champions elect Barrow (32–30), put paid to any chance of Hornets making the cut. In both defeats, Hornets had players dismissed for what the referees saw as high tackles, but which the RFL disciplinary panel declared as 'no case to answer'. This added to the frustration felt by everyone at the club. Hornets ended the first full season of the 'new era' with a 50–22 blow-out against Coventry Bears.

Despite the disappointment that Hornets never quite fulfilled their potential in 2021, there was a greater concern in rugby league that some clubs were facing an economic and existential crisis. This threat came from an impending cut in RFL central funding, the result of a much reduced television deal. For clubs like Hornets, the maths made for uncomfortable reading.

Until 2021, the RFL had received a quarter of Super League's £40million per year Sky Television deal, of which Championship and League 1 clubs received a share of £4million in central distribution. But everything was about to change.

Announced just eight days after Hornets' 150th Anniversary, the new deal for 2022 and 2023 was revealed to be £24million per year. With the RFL now scheduled to receive just £5million, it was expected that the clubs outside Super League would only receive a share of £2million.

In 2021, League 1 clubs received around £75,000 per year in central funding from the RFL. But under the terms of the new deal, third tier clubs, including Rochdale Hornets, were bracing themselves for cuts of around 75 percent. Andy Mazey spoke of the harsh reality of such a severe reduction: "... we at Rochdale are set for a 78 percent cut in central funding for 2022... it just means the town will need to rally for its professional club and we will all have to work much harder now!" How many chairmen have made that plea since 1871?

As 2021 draws to a close, we find rugby league mired in uncertainty, with the game threatened by a potential split caused by the way clubs are funded. Some things, it seems, never change. While the game wrestles, as it always has, with financial, structural and operational issues, the challenge for Rochdale Hornets is how it finds a place in rugby league's new landscape.

At many points throughout its 150 year history, the club has faced extinction, but there have been two constants that have remained a source of pride and hope. The first is the players. Their willingness to strain, scrap, sweat and bleed for our club is a tale of gladiatorial proportions. There have been heroic acts, displays of freakish athleticism, unwavering loyalties and, certainly, commitment beyond the cause.

The other constant is the club's loyal and long-suffering supporters. Down the years they have been served a diet of brief joy, harsh criticism and crushing disappointment. Yet they remain the one source of unshakable faith that glory is just around the corner. They also come out of this story as the one group of people that the club has always turned to for assistance in its darkest hours. To date, the supporters have always answered that call.

Looking ahead, it is into a new era, a new normal and a new rugby league landscape that we must step. As always, onward into the future, where triumph and disaster undoubtedly await.

References

loverugbyleague.com: "Carl Forster set for Rochdale exit" - 29 April 2019
loverugbyleague.com: "Rochdale Hornets confirm Carl Forster departure" - 2 May 2019
thetelegraphandargus.co.uk: "Carl Forster parts company with Rochdale Hornets" - 2 May 2019
rugby-league.com: "Rochdale Hornets part ways with Carl Forster" - 3 May 2019
Supporters Direct: "Model Rules for a Community Owned Sports Club: Rules for Rochdale Hornets Rugby Football League Club Society Limited" - 8 July 1019
rochdaleonline.co.uk: "Peter Rush and Ray Dutton step down from Rochdale Hornets board" - 2 October 2019
rochdaleonline.co.uk: "Remaining members of Rochdale Hornets board resign" - 9 October 2019
loverugbyleague.com: "Rochdale have no directors after remaining board members resign" - 10 October 2019
totalrl.com: "The curious case of Rochdale Hornets... from the journalist who found himself involved" - 19 October 2019
rochdaleonline.co.uk: "Rugby League: New board of directors for Rochdale Hornets" - 7 November 2019
loverugbyleague.com: "Former Swinton chairman Andy Mazey leading consortium to take over Rochdale" - 19 November 2019
www.totalrl.com: "Andy Mazey holds talks over potential takeover of Rochdale" - 19 November 2019
rochdaleonline.co.uk: "Rugby League: Rochdale Hornets could become a privately-owned club" - 19 November 2019
rochdaleonline.co.uk: "Rugby league: Hornets' supporters unanimously back ownership change" - 10 December 2019
loverugbyleague.com: "Rochdale supporters back ownership change" - 10 December 2019
hornetsrugbyleague.co.uk: "A Christmas message from the Chairman" - 23 December 2019

totalrl.com: "Andy Mazey's Rochdale Hornets vision" - 27 December 2019

totalrl.com: "Rochdale Hornets takeover completed" - 17 June 2020

theguardian.com: "Coronavirus: 15 March at a glance" - 15 March 2020

bbc.co.uk: "Coronavirus: Rugby Football League suspends season until 3 April" - 16 March 2020

theguardian.com: "RFL admits clubs are under threat after suspending season over coronavirus" - 16 March

bbc.co.uk: "Coronavirus: Latest updates for England" - 3 April 2020

gov.uk: "Government pledges £16 million to rescue Rugby League" - 1 May 2020

bbc.co.uk: "Super League: No relegation in 2020 as Toronto Wolfpack withdraw" - 20 July 2020

seriousaboutrl.com: "Championship and League One null and void" - 20 July 2020

skysports.com: "Super League's strategies to ensure a safe season restart" - 30th July 2020

walesonline.co.uk: "Gavin Henson explains shock cross-code switch to rugby league as ex-Wales and Lions star to be watched for World Cup" - 19 September 2020

hornetsrugbyleague.co.uk: "An insight into club's pre-season so far" - 10 January 2021

rochdaleonline.co.uk: "Start of 2021 season delayed for Hornets" 21 January 2021

loverugbyleague.com: "Championship and League 1 seasons delayed: - 14 January 2021

walesonline.co.uk: "Gavin Henson takes to a rugby field for the first time in 765 days as ex-Wales star makes 13-a-side debut for West Wales Raiders" - 21 March 2021

hornetsrugbyleague.co.uk: "Pre-season friendly announced" - 27 March 2021

thesportsman.com: "Rochdale Hornets Have Their Buzz Back For 2021 League One Season" - 9 May 2021

examinerlive.co.uk: "The worrying numbers behind rugby league's drop in central distribution funding" - 7 September 2021

@andy_mazey via Twitter: "Harsh reality! I wrote my programme notes last night for this Sunday's game as we at Rochdale are set for a 78% cut..." - 7 September 2021

@andy_mazey via Twitter: "Thanks Ian. It won't stop us @RochdaleHornets it just means the town will need to rally for its professional club..." - 7 September 2021

Conversation with Steve Kerr, Friday 1 October 2021

Appendix 1: Statistics and Records

League results: Rugby Union

Season	Comp	Place	Played	Won	Drawn	Lost	Points
1892–93	LCC	9/10					7
1893–94	LCC	8/10	18	5	3	10	13
1894–95	LCC*	7/7	12	3	1	8	7

*Leigh, Salford and Wigan suspended due to allegations of professionalism
LCC: Lancashire Club Competition

League results: Rugby League

Season	Comp	Place	Played	Won	Drawn	Lost	For	Against	Points
1895–96	NRL	22/22	42	4	8	30	78	388	16
1896–97	LSC	12/14	26	8	1	17	121	167	17
1897–98	LSC	13/14	26	7	0	19	146	247	14
1898–99	LSC	10/14	26	9	3	14	112	216	21
1899–00	LSC	11/14	26	9	1	16	90	181	17*
1900–01	LSC	10/14	26	8	2	16	103	257	18
1901–02	LSC	8/13	24	11	2	11	163	98	24
1902–03	D2	4/18	34	20	6	8	323	88	46
1903–04	D2	4/17	32	22	2	8	319	104	46
1904–05	D2	6/14	26	11	4	11	154	145	26
1905–06	NRL	29/31	32	3	6	23	105	327	12 (18.75%)
1906–07	NRL	20/26	26	9	1	16	292	312	19 (36.53%)
1907–08	NRL	17/27	30	13	0	17	232	290	26 (43.33%)
1908–09	NRL	25/31	30	8	2	20	195	384	18 (30.00%)
1909–10	NRL	19/28	32	13	0	19	272	371	26 (40.62%)
1910–11	NRL	13/28	34	17	1	16	355	320	35 (51.47%)
1911–12	NRL	16/27	34	16	0	18	335	397	32 (47.05%)
1912–13	NRL	12/26	34	17	2	15	327	277	36 (52.94%)
1913–14	NRL	7/25	34	18	4	12	356	270	40 (58.83%)
1914–15	NRL	4/25	34	24	2	8	306	194	50 (73.53%)
1915–16	War EL	19/24	33	9	3	21	146	261	21 (31.81%)
1916–17	War EL	24/26	26	5	1	20	73	283	11 (21.15%)
1917–18	War EL	22/22	7	0	0	7	7	156	0 (0.00%)
1918–19	Lanc L	1/12	12	9	0	3	92	52	18 (75.00%)
1919–20	NRL	7/25	34	22	1	11	363	203	45 (66.18%)
1920–21	NRL	10/25	34	18	2	14	311	301	38 (55.88%)
1921–22	NRL	7/26	34	20	2	12	352	225	42 (61.76%)
1922–23	NRL	9/27	36	22	0	14	389	355	44 (61.11%)
1923–24	NRL	8/27	36	19	4	13	318	330	42 (58.33%)
1924–25	NRL	12/27	36	18	2	16	348	329	38 (52.72%)
1925–26	NRL	22/27	36	13	1	22	320	410	27 (37.50%)
1926–27	NRL	8/29	36	23	0	13	378	285	46 (63.88%)
1927–28	NRL	24/28	34	11	1	22	192	448	23 (33.82%)
1928–29	NRL	26/28	34	10	0	24	235	434	20 (29.41%)
1929–30	NRL	22/28	34	13	2	19	258	442	28 (41.17%)
1930–31	NRL	24/28	38	10	2	26	330	557	22
1931–32	NRL	12/28	38	19	2	17	458	458	40
1932–33	NRL	15/28	38	19	1	18	497	533	39
1933–34	NRL	17/28	38	17	0	21	442	524	34

1934–35	NRL	19/28	38	16	1	21	395	521		33
1935–36	NRL	20/30	38	17	0	21	380	439		34
1936–37	NRL	21/30	38	15	1	22	311	468		31
1937–38	NRL	25/29	36	9	1	26	338	567		19
1938–39	NRL	28/28	40	4	0	36	261	817		8
1939–40	War EL	9/12	21	8	0	13	197	306		16
1945–46	NRL	24/27	36	9	1	26	221	513		19
1946–47	NRL	27/28	36	9	0	27	223	430		18
1947–48	NRL	22/28	36	11	2	23	231	311		24
1948–49	NRL	22/29	36	12	3	21	230	335		27
1949–50	NRL	27/29	36	5	2	29	200	547		12
1950–51	NRL	22/29	36	14	1	21	321	534		29
1951–52	NRL	26/31	36	10	1	25	328	585		21
1952–53	NRL	22/30	36	13	3	20	443	536		29
1953–54	NRL	19/30	36	14	3	19	404	457		31
1954–55	NRL	12/31	36	20	3	13	396	346		43
1955–56	NRL	20/30	34	15	0	19	475	514		30 (44.11%)
1956–57	NRL	16/30	38	19	0	19	510	611		38
1957–58	NRL	19/30	38	17	1	20	466	642		35
1958–59	NRL	26/30	38	11	1	26	398	649		23
1959–60	NRL	23/30	38	15	0	23	435	519		30
1960–61	NRL	28/30	36	9	0	27	296	733		18
1961–62	NRL	24/30	36	9	4	23	317	595		22
1962–63	D2	5/14	26	14	1	11	282	243	29	26
1963–64	D2	8/13	24	8	1	15	209	271	17	24
1964–65	NRL	29/30	34	7	1	26	293	493		15
1965–66	NRL	25/30	34	10	0	24	284	387		20
1966–67	NRL	18/30	34	15	4	15	408	395		34
1967–68	NRL	23/30	34	13	0	21	335	489		26
1968–69	NRL	21/30	34	13	0	21	342	485		26
1969–70	NRL	20/30	34	13	3	18	334	524		29
1970–71	NRL	25/30	34	9	3	22	318	533		21
1971–72	NRL	8/30	34	21	1	12	429	306		43
1972–73	NRL	11/30	34	20	1	13	438	426		41
1973–74	D1	10/16	30	13	2	15	379	415		28
1974–75	D1	15/16	30	8	0	22	219	400		16
1975–76	D2	2/14	26	19	3	4	347	200		41
1976–77	D1	13/16	30	11	0	19	367	449		22
1977–78	D2	3/14	26	21	0	5	437	200		42
1978–79	D1	15/16	30	8	0	22	297	565		16
1979–80	D2	7/14	26	9	5	12	315	373		23
1980–81	D2	10/15	28	13	0	15	406	418		26
1981–82	D2	13/17	32	10	1	21	361	484		21
1982–83	D2	13/17	32	10	5	17	361	469		25
1983–84	D2	12/18	34	13	3	18	551	667		29
1984–85	D2	12/20	28	12	2	14	436	466		26
1985–86	D2	5/18	34	21	0	13	763	485		42
1986–87	D2	5/18	28	19	1	8	519	369		39
1987–88	D2	18/20	28	10	0	18	322	514		20
1988–89	D2	9/20	28	15	0	13	655	677		30
1989–90	D2	2/21	28	24	0	4	977	422		48
1990–91	D1	14/14	26	1	0	25	317	912		2
1991–92	D2	5/8	28	12	2	14	619	489		26
1992–93	D2	4/8	28	14	0	14	622	607		28
1993–94	D2	8/16	30	18	0	12	704	532		36
1994–95	D2	6/16	30	18	0	12	805	544		36

213

1995–96	Cen D1	8/11	20	8	1	11	365	483	17
1996	D1	10/11	20	2	2	16	348	602	6
1997	D2	2/11	20	15	0	5	680	347	30
1998	D1	10/11	30	6	1	23	571	912	13
1999	NFP	15/18	28	9	0	19	539	724	18
2000	NFP	13/18	28	10	0	18	563	696	20
2001	NFP	3/19	28	21	0	7	863	433	42
2002	NFP	3/18	27	19	1	7	809	582	39
2003	NL1	3/10	18	13	0	5	647	477	26
2004	NL1	8/10	18	7	1	10	472	587	15
2005	NL1	6/10	18	9	1	8	468	506	19
2006	NL1	5/10	18	8	0	10	462	435	16
2007	NL1	9/10	18	3	0	15	302	700	10
2008	NL2	7/12	22	10	1	11	715	610	36
2009	Ch1	8/10	18	6	0	12	500	557	15**
2010	Ch1	5/11	20	10	0	10	630	498	37
2011	Ch1	4/10	20	12	0	8	652	498	40
2012	Ch1	5/10	18	9	0	9	496	460	28
2013	Ch1	3/9	16	10	0	6	536	375	32 (p)
2014	Ch	12/14	26	7	0	19	509	919	25
2015	L1	5/14	22	14	0	8	731	459	28
2016	L1 (S8)	2/8	21	16	1	4	709	440	33 (p)
2017	Ch (S)	5/8	30	8	1	21	569	956	17
2018	Ch (S)	7/8	30	6	0	24	465	1093	12
2019	Ch	14/14	27	1	0	26	342	1268	2
2021	L1	7/10	17	8	1	8	505	488	50%

* Two points deducted for breach of rules
** Nine points deducted
(p) Promoted through play-offs in 2013 and 2016

NRL: Northern Rugby League
LSC: Lancashire Senior Competition
War EL: War Emergency League
Lanc L: Lancashire League
D1: Division One
D2: Division Two
Cen D1: Centenary Division One

NFP: Northern Ford Premiership
NL1: National League 1
NL2: national League 2
Ch1: Championship One
L1: League 1 L1(S8): League 1 Super 8
Ch (S): Championship Shield
Ch: Championship

League play-offs

Season	Opponents	Venue	Score	Round
2010	South Wales S	Home	60–26	Elimination play-off
2010	Blackpool P	Away	26–34	Elimination semi-final
2011	Oldham	Home	39–18	Elimination play-off
2011	Doncaster	Home	26–18	Elimination semi-final
2011	Keighley C	Away	23–38	Final elimination
2012	Whitehaven	Away	12–40	Elimination play-off
2013	London S	Home	26–24	Qualifying play-off
2013	Oldham	Away	23–22	Qualifying semi-final
2013	Oldham	Leigh	32–18	Grand Final
2016	Toulouse O	Away	24–22	Promotion Final

Challenge Cup results

Season	Round	H/A	Opponents	For	Agst	Notes
1896–97	1	H	Waterhead Hornets	63	3	
	2	H	St Helens Recs	8	0	
	3	H	Swinton	3	3	
	3R	A	Swinton	0	10	
1897–98	1	H	Holbeck	10	6	
	2	H	Bramley	3	4	
1898–99	1	H	Dalton	28	0	
	2	A	Bradford	5	19	
1899–00	1	A	Windhill	11	0	
	2	H	Hull KR	13	5	
	3	H	Warrington	3	0	
	4	A	Salford	3	11	
1900–01	1	H	Bramley	3	7	
1901–02	1	A	Aspatria	4	2	
	2	H	Huddersfield	9	19	
1902–03	1	H	Alvethorpe	33	0	
	2	A	St Helens	8	2	
	3	H	Salford	0	15	
1903–04	Int	H	Rochdale A	28	6	
	1	H	Leigh	3	10	
1904–05	Int	H	Chadderton	2	0	
	1	A	Swinton	3	8	
1905–06	1	H	Salford	0	6	
1906–07	1	A	Leeds	11	18	
1907–08	1	A	Wigan	3	20	
1908–09	1	H	Swinton	3	3	
	1R	A	Swinton	0	3	
1909–10	1	A	Bramley	3	3	
	1R	H	Bramley	11	5	
	2	A	Leeds	3	13	
1910–11	1	H	Hunslet	11	5	
	2	H	Widnes	8	0	
	3	A	Oldham	8	8	
	3R	H	Oldham	4	3	
	SF	N	Broughton R	9	12	Salford
1911–12	1	A	Bradford N	13	0	
	2	A	Hull	5	27	
1912–13	1	H	Featherstone R	15	3	
	2	H	Wigan	0	16	
1913–14	1	H	Hunslet	9	3	
1914–15	1	A	York	0	0	
	1R	H	York	19	2	
	2	H	Broughton Moor	75	13	
	3	H	Hull	11	0	
	SF	N	St Helens	5	5	Warrington
	SFR	N	St Helens	2	9	Wigan
1919–20	1	H	Dewsbury	10	7	

	2	H	Leeds	0	5	
1920–21	1	A	Keighley	10	5	
	2	A	Broughton R	5	3	
	3	A	Dewsbury	0	0	
	3R	H	Dewsbury	5	2	
	SF	N	Leigh	0	10	Wigan
1921–22	1	H	Broughton Moor	54	2	
	2	H	Leeds	15	7	
	3	H	Oldham	5	2	
	SF	N	Widnes	23	3	Salford
	F	N	Hull	10	9	Leeds
1922–23	1	H	Huddersfield	3	5	
1923–24	1	A	Oldham	0	5	
1924–25	1	H	Barrow	7	0	
	2	H	Huddersfield	5	0	
	3	H	St Helens Recs	9	5	
	SF	N	Oldham	0	9	Wigan
1925–26	1	A	Bramley	11	0	
	2	A	Oldham	3	12	
1926–27	1	H	Leigh	8	2	
	2	H	Hull KR	0	14	
1927–28	1	H	Leigh	5	2	
	2	H	Hull	3	3	
	2R	A	Hull	0	16	
1928–29	1	H	Barrow	2	6	
1929–30	1	A	Dewsbury	10	24	
1930–31	1	A	Lindley	13	2	
	2	H	Broughton R	7	15	
1931–32	1	A	Oldham	18	8	
	2	A	Leigh	7	14	
1932–33	1	A	Oldham	8	13	
1933–34	1	A	Hull	5	6	
1934–35	1	H	Barrow Marsh H	28	18	
	2	A	Widnes	4	13	
1935–36	1	A	Castleford	3	16	
1936–37	1	H	Hull	0	10	
1937–38	1	H	Glass Houghton	50	2	
	2	A	St Helens Recs	10	18	
1938–39	1	H	Warrington	3	29	
1945–46	1–1L	H	Barrow	9	11	
	1–2L	A	Barrow	5	21	Agg: 14–36
1946–47	1–1L	A	Widnes	2	13	
	1–2L	H	Widnes	0	11	Agg: 2–24
1947–48	1–1L	H	Pemberton Rovers	13	0	
	1–2L	A	Pemberton Rovers	11	0	Agg: 24–0
	2	H	Belle Vue Rangers	3	2	
	3	A	Keighley	6	4	
	SF	N	Wigan	0	11	Swinton
1948–49	1–1L	A	Huddersfield	5	4	
	1–2L	H	Huddersfield	0	11	Agg: 5–15

216

1949–50	1–1L	A	Widnes	2	15	
	1–2L	H	Widnes	0	27	Agg: 2–42
1950–51	1–1L	H	Wigan	0	32	
	1–2L	A	Wigan	5	18	Agg: 5–50
1951–52	1–1L	H	Featherstone R	7	8	
	1–2L	A	Featherstone R	2	17	Agg: 9–25
1952–53	1–1L	A	Wigan	7	27	
	1–2L	H	Wigan	15	24	Agg: 22–51
1953–54	1–1L	H	Bradford Northern	9	9	
	1–2L	A	Bradford Northern	2	11	Agg: 11–20
1954–55	1	H	Wakefield Trinity	11	9	
	2	H	Liverpool City	15	5	
	3	H	Barrow	2	15	
1955–56	1	H	Stanningley	55	0	
	2	H	Bradford Northern	2	5	
1956–57	1	H	Blackpool Borough	10	18	
1957–58	1	A	Hull	16	13	
	2	H	Bradford Northern	11	8	
	3	H	York	8	5	
	SF	N	Wigan	3	5	Swinton
1958–59	1	H	Halifax	9	10	
1959–60	1	A	Doncaster	15	0	
	2	H	Bramley	0	4	
1960–61	1	A	Bramley	6	5	
	2	H	Whitehaven	9	2	
	3	A	Halifax	5	18	
1961–62	1	A	Workington Town	2	14	
1962–63	1	H	Hunslet	3	16	
1963–64	1	A	Hull KR	12	12	
	1R	H	Hull KR	7	22	
1964–65	1	A	Halifax	12	17	
1965–66	1	A	Featherstone R	6	22	
1966–67	1	A	Hull KR	2	18	
1967–68	1	A	York	2	24	
1968–69	1	A	Leigh	13	4	
	2	H	Bramley	7	7	
	2R	A	Bramley	7	4	
	3	A	Wakefield Trinity	10	10	
	3R	H	Wakefield Trinity	2	15	
1969–70	1	H	York	2	0	
	2	A	Doncaster	5	5	
	2R	H	Doncaster	3	4	
1970–71	1	A	Warrington	7	13	
1971–72	1	A	York	5	13	
1972–73	1	A	Keighley	44	8	
	2	A	Featherstone R	19	30	
1973–74	1	H	Halifax	13	6	
	2	H	Wigan	8	15	
1974–75	1	A	Huddersfield	21	18	
	2	H	Oldham	10	10	

	2R	A	Oldham	3	15	
1975–76	1	H	Bradford Northern	2	15	
1976–77	1	H	Leigh	23	8	
	2	H	Castleford	2	10	
1977–78	1	A	Widnes	8	15	
1978–79	1	H	Batley	15	0	
	2	H	St Helens	10	11	
1979–80	1	H	Doncaster	11	3	
1980–81	1	A	Workington Town	8	17	
1981–82	1	A	Doncaster	7	6	
1982–83	1	H	Fulham	4	24	
1983–84	1	H	York	8	17	
1984–85	1	H	York	11	5	
	2	H	Hull KR	4	18	
1985–86	1	A	Huddersfield	10	4	
	2	A	Widnes	20	36	
1986–87	1	H	Carlisle	4	4	
	1R	A	Carlisle	22	30	
1987–88	1	H	Barrow	6	4	
	2	A	Halifax	6	30	
1988–89	1	H	Hull KR	24	28	
1989–90	1	H	Carlisle	38	6	
	2	A	Widnes	16	22	
1990–91	1	H	Chorley	14	10	
	2	H	Wigan	4	72	
1991–92	1	H	Hull	28	32	
1992–93	1	H	Doncaster	34	13	
	2	A	Leeds	6	68	
1993–94	3	H	Millom	32	0	
	4	H	Leeds	18	40	
1994–95	3	H	Lock Lane	48	16	
	4	A	Ryedale-York	12	18	
1995–96	4	H	Thatto Heath	54	8	
	5	H	St Helens	20	58	
1997	3	H	Walney C	30	6	
	4	A	Oldham	6	48	
1998	3	H	Leigh Miners R	44	4	
	4	H	Bradford Bulls	10	48	
1999	3	H	Wigan St Judes	52	12	
	4	H	York	19	22	
2000	3	H	The Army	66	6	
	4	H	Oldham	30	14	
	5	A	Hull	10	82	
2001	3	H	Wigan Rose Bridge	52	0	
	4	H	Hunslet	38	4	
	5	H	Villeneuve	19	26	
2002	3	H	Farnworth	44	28	
	4	H	Leigh	20	24	
2003	3	A	Oldham St Anne's	62	18	Played at home
	4	H	Hull KR	20	27	

2004	3	H	Dinamo Moscow	60	24	
	4	H	Warrington	0	80	Played away
2005	3	H	Illingworth	120	4	
	4	H	Salford	24	30	
2006	3	A	Leigh Miners R	34	6	Played at Leigh
	4	H	Celtic Crusaders	32	8	
	5	A	Leeds	66	0	
2007	3	H	Saddleworth	48	6	
	4	H	Celtic Crusaders	20	16	
	5	A	St Helens	10	70	
2008	3	H	York Acorn	50	8	
	4	H	Hull	5	42	
2009	3	A	Leeds Met Carnegie	38	24	Played at Headingley
	4	A	Swinton	28	22	
	5	A	Huddersfield	12	38	
2010	3	H	Lézignan	22	32	
2011	3	H	Workington Town	22	20	
	4	H	Castleford	10	72	
2012	3	A	East Hull	48	20	Played at home
	4	A	Leigh	18	68	
2013	3	H	Hunslet Old Boys	40	4	
	4	H	Bradford Bulls	10	70	
2014	3	H	Gloucestershire AG	76	4	
	4	H	Leigh	22	28	
2015	3	A	Kells	29	12	Played at Whitehaven
	4	A	Swinton	12	30	
2016	3	A	Rochdale Mayfield	40	14	
	4	H	Siddal	48	20	
	5	H	Widnes	6	62	
2017	4	A	York	20	26	
2018	4	A	Normanton	20	8	Played at Featherstone
	5	A	Whitehaven	0	38	
2019	4	A	Whitehaven	22	21	
	5	A	Salford	6	76	
2020	4	H	British Army	54	10	
	5	A	York City Knights	12	70	
2021			Did not play			

Lancashire Cup Finals

Season	Opponents	Score	Venue
1911–12	Oldham	12–5	Broughton
1912–13	Wigan	5–21	Salford
1914–15	Wigan	3–2	Broughton
1918–19	Oldham	22–0	Salford
1919–20	Oldham	0–7	Salford
1965–66	Warrington	5–16	St Helens
1991–92	St Helens	14–24	Warrington

John Player No.6 Trophy Final

1973–74	Warrington	16–27	Wigan

BBC2 Floodlit Trophy

1971–72	St Helens	2–8	St Helens

Great Britain internationals
Johnny Baxter (1907)
Tommy Woods (1911)
Jack Robinson (1914)
Joe Bowers (1920)
Ernest Jones (1920)
Jack Bennett (1924)
Malcolm Price (1967)
Terry Fogerty (1974)
John Butler (1974)
Alan Hodkinson (1977)

NB Butler and Hodkinson were in British Lions squads but did not play in test matches or World Cup fixtures.

England internationals
Johnny Baxter 1904
Tommy Woods 1911 to 1913
Ernest Jones 1913 to 1914
Walter Roman 1914
Tommy Harris 1924
Jack Bennett 1924 to 1926
Stanley Langshaw 1925
Derrick Schofield 1952 to 1953
Ted Cahill 1953

Wales internationals
E Jenkins 1910 to 1912
Bernard McNally 1953
Byron Smith 2007

Ireland internationals
Stuart Littler 2014
Bradley Hargreaves 2015
Danny Bridge 2015

Appendix 2: Player Heritage Numbers

Compiled by Neil Bruckshaw

No.	Name	Debut
1890s		
1	Buckley E	07/09/1895
2	Dearden A	07/09/1895
3	Dex GT	07/09/1895
4	Hill A	07/09/1895
5	Hill J	07/09/1895
6	Kershaw F	07/09/1895
7	Leach A	07/09/1895
8	Leach J	07/09/1895
9	Leach P	07/09/1895
10	Mason A	07/09/1895
11	Midgeley C	07/09/1895
12	Sucksmith S	07/09/1895
13	Trevor C	07/09/1895
14	Uttley F	07/09/1895
15	Wood J	07/09/1895
16	Fletcher H	14/09/1895
17	Higgin J	14/09/1895
18	Melledew E	14/09/1895
19	Rigg W	14/09/1895
20	Atkinson	21/09/1895
21	Ogden J.	21/09/1895
22	Rothwell	21/09/1895
23	Turner J	21/09/1895
24	Ogden W	28/09/1895
25	Sutcliffe	28/09/1895
26	Whitworth J	28/09/1895
27	Fletcher J	05/10/1895
28	Horsefield E	05/10/1895
29	Kelly JJ	05/10/1895
30	Higgin F	08/10/1895
31	Knowles A	08/10/1895
32	Rangeley J	19/10/1895
33	Hanson W	09/11/1895
34	Hewitt	09/11/1895
35	Wightman C	23/11/1895
36	Tetlow E	14/12/1895
37	Egerton E	25/12/1895
38	Gorman J	01/01/1896
39	Melledew T	01/01/1896
40	Isherwood A	22/02/1896
41	Nuttall H	07/03/1896
42	Coop T	03/04/1896
43	Kershaw A	07/04/1896
44	Smith W	07/04/1896
45	Simpson J	18/04/1896
46	Bates W E	12/09/1896
47	Davies W	05/09/1896
48	Evans D	05/09/1896
49	Hickey G	05/09/1896
50	House P	05/09/1896
51	Jones T	05/09/1896
52	Lancaster W	05/09/1896
53	Ashworth GE	12/09/1896
54	Gibbon T	26/09/1896
55	Broughton CH	31/10/1896
56	Howarth T	26/12/1896
57	Every L	02/01/1897
58	Bonynge CH	23/01/1897
59	Tarr S	30/01/1897
60	Childs W	06/02/1896
61	Leach W	20/02/1897
62	Taylor	20/02/1897
63	Harrison J	04/09/1897
64	Harrison K	04/09/1897
65	Johnstone T	04/09/1897
66	Whatmough j	04/09/1897
67	Rigg L	11/09/1897
68	Vaughan S	11/09/1897
69	Garnett G	18/09/1897
70	Davies D	09/10/1897
71	Griffiths	09/10/1897
72	Coupe	30/10/1897
73	Halkyard	30/10/1897
74	Wilson J	30/10/1897
75	Jardine	06/11/1897
76	Stevenson	06/11/1897
77	Tweedale JS	19/12/1897
78	Hardiker J	26/01/1899
79	McKie	26/01/1898
80	McLean W	26/01/1898
81	Edwards S	05/02/1897
82	Wilson A	02/04/1898
83	Chadwick R	15/03/1897
84	Hawkins	17/09/1898
85	Henderson	17/09/1898
86	Butterworth T	24/09/1898
87	Farmer F	15/10/1898
88	Ellis J	29/10/1898
89	Hunter	29/10/1898
90	Field A	10/12/1898
91	Kruger	10/12/1898
92	Metcalfe P	10/12/1898
93	Schofield	17/12/1898
94	Thompson E	31/12/1898
95	Berry J	11/02/1899
96	Cooper	18/02/1899
97	Allen A	16/09/1899
98	Boothroyd	16/09/1899
99	Hutchinson H	16/09/1899
100	Wood W	16/09/1899
101	Smethurst	28/10/1899
102	Trembath	04/11/1899
103	Corrie	11/11/1899
104	Jackson	11/11/1899
105	Langhorn	09/12/1899
106	Handley	26/12/1899
1900s		
107	Beckwith W	01/01/1900
108	Platt J	06/01/1900
109	Gillielands	13/01/1900
110	Martin T	27/01/1900
111	Blincow F	08/09/1900
112	Greenhalgh	08/09/1900
113	Smith O	08/09/1900
114	Cross	15/09/1900
115	Hurst C	15/09/1900
116	Berrill	27/10/1900
117	Triggs	01/12/1900
118	Richardson AJ	15/12/1900
119	Charnock	22/12/1900
120	Harris	22/12/1900
121	Roebuck	25/12/1900

122	Grindrod W	29/12/1900		189	Dawson	20/10/1906
123	Owens R J	05/01/1901		190	Ward G	20/10/1906
124	Thomas A B	05/01/1901		191	Stubbs	27/10/1906
125	Williams E	26/01/1901		192	Williams	07/09/1907
126	Williams J	26/01/1901		193	Hartley	07/09/1907
127	Gibson A	16/02/1901		194	Wormald	28/09/1907
128	Tetlock E	16/02/1901		195	Farrar	05/10/1907
129	Leeson	06/04/1901		196	Storey	12/10/1907
130	Saunders	18/03/1901		197	Ward E	12/10/1907
131	Heap A	02/09/1901		198	Earnshaw	26/10/2007
132	Crabtree F	07/09/1901		199	Cockle	09/11/1907
133	Oldershaw A	14/09/1901		200	Kirk	07/12/1907
134	Baron S	28/09/1901		201	Walker	18/01/1908
135	Leach S	28/09/1901		202	Ledgard	28/01/1908
136	Smallwood L	28/09/1901		203	Sutcliffe	21/03/1908
137	Forshaw R	26/10/1901		204	Hammond	05/09/1908
138	Leach G	26/10/1901		205	Thomas G.	05/09/1908
139	Wilkinson S	26/10/1901		206	Pearson A.	26/09/1908
140	Prescott	23/11/1901		207	Thomas F.	10/10/1908
141	Baxter J	14/12/1901		208	Hale	24/10/1908
142	Dearden J	01/01/1902		209	White	24/10/1908
143	Fitton E	08/03/1902		210	Mullin E.	31/10/1908
144	Harling W	29/03/1902		211	West T.	07/11/1908
145	Hurst H	29/03/1902		212	Marshall	14/11/1908
146	Quinn	29/03/1902		213	English M	21/11/1908
147	Upton E	29/03/1902		214	Fitzsimmons	28/11/1908
148	Eckersley	10/04/1902		215	Collins	09/01/1909
149	Croson	20/09/1902		216	Bamber J	23/01/1909
150	Turner A	29/11/1902		217	Hobson	23/01/1909
151	Phennah	05/09/1903		218	Brumsley J	03/03/1909
152	Richardson W	05/09/1903		219	Wallwork	03/04/1909
153	Brooks A	19/09/1903		220	Hayes	04/09/1909
154	Liley M	26/09/1903		221	Whitaker	04/09/1909
155	Lord F	31/10/1903		222	Kaye	18/09/1909
156	Mort	31/10/1903		223	Measor	18/09/1909
157	Walker J	07/11/1903		224	Emerson	25/09/1909
158	Fielding J	21/11/1903		225	Loftus	16/10/1909
159	Mellor	23/01/1904		226	Bowers J	23/10/1909
160	Hallsworth	30/01/1904		227	Woods T	27/11/1909
161	Lewis	06/02/1904		*1910s*		
162	Mallinson	06/02/1904		228	Paddon HL	22/01/1910
163	Morton	24/09/1904		229	Roman W	22/01/1910
164	Dodd	08/10/1904		230	Jenkins	17/09/1910
165	Booth	15/10/1904		231	Rowe H	27/12/1910
166	Potter	05/11/1904		232	Dowd	04/02/1911
167	Devitt	07/01/1905		233	Barber JE	25/02/1911
168	Hyde J	07/01/1905		234	Burton CJ	01/04/1911
169	Smith F	11/02/1905		235	Jones EW	02/09/1911
170	Eastwood	22/04/1905		236	Stott H	16/09/1911
171	Evans D	22/04/1905		237	Jones T	23/09/1911
172	Hollinrake D	02/09/1905		238	Ward W	23/09/1911
173	Thorpe	02/09/1905		239	Hodgson E	07/10/1911
174	Swindell	16/09/1905		240	Belshaw	11/11/1911
175	Kiley	23/09/1905		241	Burton B	21/10/1911
176	Charles	30/09/1905		242	Taylor C.	25/11/1911
177	Chorley	21/10/1905		243	Taylor T	25/11/1911
178	Shaw	21/10/1905		244	Prudence GA	13/01/1912
179	Robinson	28/10/1905		245	Holmes	27/01/1912
180	Shore	04/11/1905		246	Slade VB	10/02/1912
181	Lee T	25/11/1905		247	Reed CF	07/09/1912
182	Christison	02/12/1905		248	Williamson W	21/09/1912
183	Ashton	23/12/1905		249	Carter S	04/10/1912
184	Ashworth W	21/04/1906		250	Hopwood	18/10/1912
185	Crudden	21/04/1906		251	Morrisey	09/11/1912
186	Threlfall	01/09/1906		252	Collins E	15/02/1913
187	Hardman	15/09/1906		252	Collins T	15/02/1913
188	Proctor	15/09/1906		254	Green F	22/03/1913

255	Corsi Jack	06/09/1913		321	Butterworth	30/10/1924
256	Bibby	13/09/1913		322	Brooks	22/11/1924
257	Newman	26/12/1913		323	Butler	22/11/1924
258	Fairhurst	03/01/1914		324	Foy	29/11/1924
259	Goulden J	23/03/2014		325	Langshaw	13/12/1924
260	Twigg	23/03/1914		326	Cooper	20/12/1924
261	Smith	13/04/1914		327	Willis	07/09/1925
262	Webb	05/09/1914		328	Ainsworth	19/09/1925
263	Mole	26/09/1914		329	Evans W	24/10/1925
264	Goulden M	07/04/1915		330	Evans H	25/12/1925
265	Roman G	07/04/1915		331	Whatmough	09/01/1926
266	Bennett J	18/01/1919		332	May	06/02/1926
267	Bowmer	18/01/1919		333	Millard	02/04/1926
268	Brannan J	18/01/1919		334	Hinam	11/09/1926
269	Goulding	18/01/1919		335	Valentine	11/09/1926
270	Groves A	18/01/1919		336	Ireson	02/10/1926
271	Heaton J	18/01/1919		337	Carr	30/10/1926
272	Lowe	18/01/1919		338	Grimes	30/10/1926
273	Dewhurst	25/01/1919		339	Dixon	12/02/1927
274	Spencer	25/01/1919		340	Welsby James	27/08/1927
275	Richardson	25/01/1919		341	Milne	10/09/1927
276	Jones EW	15/02/1919		342	Murray	10/09/1927
277	Hesketh	01/03/1919		343	Martin	15/10/1927
278	Blan	23/08/1919		344	Felton	17/12/1927
279	Corsi Lou	20/09/1919		345	Welsby Joseph	14/01/2028
280	Winstanley	27/09/1919		346	Cronshaw	04/02/1928
281	Corsi Joe	29/11/1919		347	Parkes	03/03/1928
281	Hodgkins	13/12/1919		348	Green	10/04/1928
283	Prince	13/12/1919		349	Wade	14/04/1928
284	Bradbury J	16/12/1919		350	Todd	25/08/1928
1920s				351	Campbell	01/09/1928
285	Rhoda	14/02/1920		352	Whitney	15/09/1928
286	Hamblin	24/03/1920		353	Fenwick	06/10/1928
287	Powell WJ	04/09/1920		354	Halton F	20/10/1928
288	McLean	18/09/1920		355	Sutcliffe B	03/11/1928
289	Dacres	02/10/1920		356	Schofield	10/11/1928
290	Kynan WR	09/10/1920		357	Ellis	22/12/1928
291	Catterall	10/11/1920		358	Mahan	26/12/1928
292	Harris TH	11/12/1920		359	Bradley	09/03/1929
293	Prescott F	29/01/1921		360	Rossi	06/04/1929
294	Edwards D	27/08/1921		361	Baldwin	31/08/1929
295	Fitton T	27/08/1921		362	Beattie JE	31/08/1929
296	Wild H	17/09/1921		363	Condren	21/09/1929
297	Copestick	19/11/1921		364	Donohoe	21/09/1929
298	Gore	03/12/1921		365	Anderton	23/10/1929
299	Shore	03/12/1921		366	Hall	25/12/1929
300	McLoughlin E	28/01/2022		*1930s*		
301	Forrest	09/09/1922		367	Simpson	11/01/1930
302	Gowers W.	30/09/1922		368	Whittle	18/01/1930
303	Hennessy	21/10/1922		369	Davies L.	15/02/1930
304	Wills	21/10/1922		370	Hill E	22/03/1930
305	Bamford	18/11/1922		371	Slater	05/04/1930
306	Tetlow	25/11/1922		372	Lindley	13/09/1930
307	Turner	13/01/1923		373	Whitehead	27/09/1930
308	Chadwick	30/03/1923		374	White	04/10/1930
309	Clayton	14/04/1923		375	Aynsley CJ	25/10/1930
310	Jones W.	25/08/1923		376	Gaunt R	06/12/1930
311	Pascoe	25/08/1923		377	Edmonds	07/02/1931
312	Reed	01/09/1923		378	Dean J	19/03/1931
313	Thomas	22/09/1923		379	Allen	11/04/1931
314	Rudman	14/11/1923		380	Close	25/04/1931
315	Tucker	17/11/1923		381	Dewhirst	29/08/1931
316	Owen	19/04/1924		382	Bennett	05/09/1931
317	Wood	30/08/1924		383	Parkinson W	05/09/1931
318	Walker	06/09/1924		384	Williams J	05/09/1931
319	Bertram	20/09/1924		385	Ambruster V	19/09/1931
320	Hesketh	20/09/1924		386	Burkhill R	19/09/1931

387	Ogden F	03/10/1931
388	Knapman JH	17/10/1931
389	Falwasser AG	12/12/1931
390	Lister R	01/01/1932
391	Ring J	23/01/1931
392	Beattie RK	30/01/1932
393	Stephens Frank	06/02/1932
394	Clarke R	27/08/1932
395	Halhead W	27/08/1932
396	Thompson R	27/08/1932
397	Helme J	10/09/1932
398	Walker	10/09/1932
399	Fox H	22/10/1932
400	Tolan T	22/10/1932
401	Flathers	19/11/1932
402	Baines J	07/01/1933
403	Skillen	07/01/1933
404	Mills GE	02/09/1933
405	Neuman	04/11/1933
406	Selway F	02/12/1933
407	Abbot	09/12/1933
408	Moore W J	20/01/1934
409	Birkinshaw	03/02/1934
410	Moaby	25/08/1934
411	Downey	15/09/1934
412	Bethel	17/11/1934
413	Sayer	17/11/1934
414	Gaunt S	29/12/1934
415	Johnson	29/12/1934
416	Cadd	19/04/1935
417	Lees	31/08/1935
418	Lister GE	17/09/1935
419	Frodsham	28/09/1935
420	Logan	26/10/1935
421	Hesketh	28/12/1935
422	Matthews	11/01/1936
243	Ellison	11/04/1936
242	Wardle	13/04/1936
425	Blacklaws	29/08/1936
426	Barlow	12/09/1936
427	Haigh	19/09/1936
428	Mason	03/10/1936
429	Lewis	03/10/1936
430	Wolstencroft	17/10/1936
431	Read	31/10/1936
432	Lamb Freddie	01/01/1937
433	Cooper	02/01/1937
434	Stephens Mortimer	23/01/1937
435	Cutbush	06/02/1937
436	French	20/02/1937
437	Wood A.	20/02/1937
438	Steeden	20/03/1937
439	Wood H.	28/08/1937
440	Aspinall	11/09/1937
441	Rankin	09/10/1937
442	Shaw	23/10/1937
443	Fleming	30/10/1937
444	Stuart	08/01/1938
445	Miller	19/03/1938
446	Ward	18/04/1938
447	McDonald	26/04/1938
448	Stephens W	26/04/1938
449	Grounds	24/09/1938
450	Brook	11/03/1939
451	Cattlin R	11/03/1939
452	Harker	25/03/1939
453	Parker	25/03/1939

454	Schofield J.	25/03/1939
455	Cattlin S.	08/04/1939
456	Jones	10/04/1939
457	Binns	26/08/1939
458	Fairhurst	26/08/1939
459	Forber	26/08/1939
460	Howard	26/08/1939
461	Pickford	26/08/1939
462	Brown	02/09/1939
463	Holding	30/09/1939
464	Leach	14/10/1939
465	Hampson	28/10/1939
466	Yates	18/11/1939
467	Spencer	09/12/1939
1940s		
468	Prescott	23/03/1940
469	Dacre	24/02/1940
470	Bell	04/05/1940
471	Pendlebury	11/05/1940
472	Ayres	25/08/1945
473	Brown A	25/08/1945
474	Callison	25/08/1945
475	Joel	25/08/1945
476	Mark	25/08/1945
477	McKendry	25/08/1945
478	Nicholson Walter	25/08/1945
479	Stockbridge	25/08/1945
480	Milne	08/09/1945
481	Tweddle	06/10/1945
482	Brogden	20/10/1945
483	Suart	20/10/1945
484	Harrison	17/11/1945
485	Devlin	24/11/1945
486	Hennigan	24/11/1945
487	Holmes	24/11/1945
488	Thompson	24/11/1945
489	Brierley	12/01/1946
490	Winstanley Arthur	26/01/1946
491	Booth Douggie	02/02/1946
492	Lynch	23/02/1946
493	Jennings	02/03/1946
494	Gabriel	09/03/1946
485	Park	09/03/1946
496	Fearnley Albert	16/03/1946
497	Denton	23/03/1946
498	Houghton	30/03/1946
499	Eastwood	02/04/1946
500	Kearns	02/04/1946
501	Edwards	06/04/1946
502	Combes	09/04/1946
503	France	09/04/1946
504	Barton	13/04/1946
505	Oxley Bill	19/04/1946
506	Colley	31/08/1946
507	Dickinson	31/08/1946
508	Halliwell	31/08/1946
509	Lamb Fred	31/08/1946
510	Martindale	31/08/1946
511	Singleton	31/08/1946
512	McGurrin	07/09/1946
513	Nicholson Harold	07/09/1946
514	Fairclough	14/09/1946
515	Lowrey	14/09/1946
516	Molyneux J	28/09/1946
517	Molyneux R	05/10/1946
518	Disley	26/10/1946
519	Whitworth	09/11/1946

520	Fletcher	16/11/1946
521	North	16/11/1946
522	McCreary	23/11/1946
523	Wagstaffe Frank	30/11/1946
524	Lord	28/12/1946
525	Bitters	11/01/1947
526	Davies G.H.	11/01/1947
527	Fenton	11/01/1947
528	Turton	11/01/1947
529	Rothwell Jack	08/02/1947
530	Lloyd	29/04/1947
531	Ellison	06/05/1947
532	Gummer	23/08/1947
533	Robinson	02/09/1947
534	Butler	10/09/1947
535	Farmer A	10/09/1947
536	Hertzmann	20/09/1947
537	Rees D	25/12/1947
538	Griffiths Billy	17/01/1948
539	Kerr	24/01/1948
540	Jackson	29/03/1948
541	Williams Glyn	21/08/1948
542	Davies E	06/09/1948
543	Jones R	06/09/1948
544	Musgrave	06/09/1948
545	Gronow	09/10/1948
546	Davies T	16/10/1948
547	Jones G	01/01/1949
548	McGilvray	15/01/1949
549	Schofield D	15/01/1949
550	Schofield K	05/02/1949
551	Thorning	16/04/1949
552	Ellis	18/04/1949
553	Foster	18/04/1949
554	Caine	20/08/1949
555	Hayes	20/08/1949
556	Wilde	20/08/1949
557	Tucker	31/08/1949
558	Taylor Alan	24/09/1949
559	Lomas	01/10/1949
560	Croft Arnold	08/10/1949
561	Fallon	08/10/1949
562	Hirons	12/11/1949
563	Rostron	19/11/1949
564	Spooner	19/11/1949
565	Pickles	03/12/1949
566	Cahill Ted	10/12/1949
567	Mitchell Frank	17/12/1949
568	Rigby	24/12/1949
569	Stockley	31/12/1949
1950s		
570	Grice	04/02/1950
571	Powell	18/03/1950
572	Genders	22/04/1950
573	Ellean Wally	16/09/1950
574	Kelly C.	16/09/1950
575	Stanford Ron	16/09/1950
576	Duffy Tom	07/10/1950
577	Ferguson	07/10/1950
578	Redford Billy	07/10/1950
579	Heaton Jeff	14/10/1950
580	Stanford Reg	21/10/1950
581	Kelly Geoff	04/11/1950
582	Dagnall Bob	21/12/1950
583	Jimmeson	21/12/1950
584	Fletcher Dave	03/02/1951
585	Ward Alec	23/03/1951
586	McKeown Mick	07/04/1951
587	Holland	14/04/1951
588	Watt	24/04/1951
589	Gibson H	18/08/1951
590	Cotton	06/10/1951
591	Hardman James	17/11/1951
592	Slater Ralph	08/12/1951
593	Healey	15/12/1951
594	Oldroyd Peter	15/12/1951
595	Fisher Ron	02/02/1952
596	Stevenson Norman	08/03/1952
597	Helme Ronnie	24/04/1952
598	Harris Norman	23/08/1952
599	Hawkins Eynon	30/08/1952
600	McNally Bernard	27/09/1952
601	Vallet Austin	27/09/1952
602	Cunliffe	04/10/1952
603	Jones Walter	18/10/1952
604	Rowley B.	13/12/1952
605	Short Norman	13/12/1952
606	Gill Jack	31/01/1953
607	Jones H.	31/01/1953
608	Livesey Ken	07/02/1953
609	Baines Joe	21/02/1953
610	Chisnall John	31/03/1953
611	Reilly Peter	03/04/1953
612	Bradley Dennis	26/09/1953
613	Sivill Jack	24/10/1953
614	Appleton Bill	07/11/1953
615	Bell	14/11/1953
616	Dooney Jim	12/12/1953
617	McArthur Wally	12/12/1953
618	Roach Wilf	23/01/1954
619	Wilcox Charlie	13/02/1954
620	Unsworth Norman	13/03/1954
621	Jones Les	20/03/1954
622	Gallagher Maurice	14/08/1954
623	Trumble Eddie	24/08/1954
624	Evans Ray	04/09/1954
625	Scholes Alan	01/01/1955
626	Kay John	28/04/1955
627	Wareham	28/04/1955
628	Tierney Mel	20/08/1955
629	Horrocks Tom	17/09/1955
630	Smith Danny	08/10/1955
631	Unsworth Gerry	19/11/1955
632	Blan Billy	24/12/1955
633	Featherstone Jim	24/12/1955
634	Hanson Bill	07/01/1956
635	Mullane Joe	28/01/1956
636	Buxton Ray	24/03/1956
637	Fishwick John	07/04/1956
638	Howarth Rudy	22/09/1956
639	Bowden Eddie	29/09/1956
640	Ralph Bert	29/09/1956
641	Baxter Mick	26/01/1957
642	Platt Frank	06/04/1957
643	Lill Harold	19/04/1957
644	Bailey Reg	24/08/1957
645	Parsons George	27/08/1957
646	Jennings Bill	21/09/1957
647	Richardson Peter	05/10/1957
648	Hollis Bob	07/12/1957
649	Corsi Ferdi	01/02/1958
650	Parr Jim	01/02/1958
651	Lawrenson John	15/02/1958
652	Sheridan	22/03/1958

653	Wareing Albert	19/08/1958		717	Hope Frank	11/04/1964
654	Hilton Ralph	08/11/1958		718	Noon Johnny	22/08/1964
655	Emmott John	22/11/1958		719	Pratt Tony	22/08/1964
656	Thomas Grosvenor	22/11/1958		720	Starkey Graham	22/08/1964
657	Grundy Tom	20/12/1958		720a	Williams George	24/08/1964
658	Sedgwick	27/12/1958		721	Crocker Mick	05/09/1964
659	Tobin John	28/02/1959		722	Owen Stan	10/10/1964
660	Ashworth Irwin	27/03/1959		723	Ashcroft Kevin	28/11/1964
661	Kettleton Brian	28/03/1959		724	Harvey John	23/01/1965
662	Turner Kevin	28/03/1959		725	Gregory J	20/02/1965
663	Melling Joe	02/05/1959		726	Chamberlain Joe	21/08/1965
664	Parry Geoff	02/05/1959		727	Ratu Mike	16/10/1965
665	McFarlane J.	15/08/1959		728	Measures Jim	04/12/1965
666	McFarlane W.	15/08/1959		729	Gaskell Jimmy	27/12/1965
667	Williams	01/09/1959		730	Mitten Harry	04/03/1966
668	Ledger Eric	03/10/1959		731	Hindley Tom	08/03/1966
668a	Atherton Bill	14/11/1959		732	Taylor David	12/03/1966
669	Cox	19/12/1959		733	Lewis Jim	21/03/1966
1960s				734	McGuigan Mick	26/03/1966
670	Allander Danny	23/01/1960		735	Price Malcolm	06/08/1966
671	McGurrin Bernard	23/01/1960		736	Payne Ken	06/08/1966
672	Simms Trevor	06/02/1960		737	Cribaillet Henri	28/09/1966
673	Berry T	16/08/1960		738	Parkinson George	29/10/1966
674	Berry C	20/08/1960		739	Brown Eddie	02/12/1966
675	Rowbotham	20/08/1960		740	Goddard Peter	13/01/1967
676	Lingard	22/08/1960		741	Robinson Geoff	13/01/1967
677	Tunney Brian	22/08/1960		742	Reilly Peter	27/03/1967
677a	Smith Dick	15/10/1960		743	Earl Glynn	08/04/1967
678	Walsh Alan	29/10/1960		744	Smith Dick	12/08/1967
679	Pritchard Roy	12/11/1960		745	Pimblett Tom	18/08/1967
680	Dickinson T	10/12/1960		746	Tighe Ken	22/08/1967
681	Birchall Peter	18/03/1961		747	Entwistle Tony	30/08/1967
682	Wolstencroft	25/03/1961		748	Fletcher Ray	30/08/1967
683	Woodcock	03/04/1961		749	Gill Kevin	01/09/1967
684	Heap	19/04/1961		750	Delooze Henry	20/09/1967
685	Brophy Tom	19/04/1961		751	Worswick Steve	20/09/1967
686	Jones Wally	22/04/1961		752	Argent Joe	23/09/1967
687	Ince Norman	29/05/1961		752	Brelsford Norman	23/09/1967
688	Pugsley Yendal	19/08/1961		754	Dawson Trevor	14/10/1967
689	Kilduff Phil	02/09/1961		755	Cook Colin	25/11/1967
690	Ashworth	09/09/1961		756	Greenall Les	25/11/9167
691	Evans David	23/09/1961		757	Crowther Geoff	22/12/1967
692	Lea	23/09/1961		758	Murray Denis	23/02/1968
693	Keegan	21/10/1961		759	Holt Alan	09/03/1968
694	Brown Derek	11/11/1961		760	Ackersley Terry	17/08/1968
695	Dawai Orisi	11/11/1961		761	Roberts Ken	17/08/1968
696	Levula Joe	11/11/1961		762	Tees Eddie	06/09/1968
697	Parr Ken	11/11/1961		763	Mooney Mick	14/09/1968
698	Ravouvou Laitai	24/03/1961		764	Dolly Terry	15/10/1968
699	Morgan	31/03/1962		765	Corcoran Terry	07/03/1969
700	Sanderson Bill	18/08/1962		766	Clarke Peter	07/04/1969
701	Lowe	08/09/1962		767	Worrall Norman	12/04/1969
702	Edwards	15/09/1962		768	Machen Paul	17/08/1969
703	Drui Voate	22/09/1962		769	Rogers Tony	16/08/1969
704	Warren Bernard	29/09/1962		770	Owen Ray	20/08/1969
705	Taylor	01/12/1962		771	O'Neill	16/09/1969
706	Scott Mick	24/08/1963		772	Snape George	16/09/1969
707	Slevin Ted	24/08/1963		773	Flanagan Kevin	20/09/1969
708	Aspinall Alf	26/08/1963		774	Hodkinson Alan	16/11/1969
709	Brown Jeff	21/09/1963		775	Rabbitt Trevor	22/11/1969
710	Fairclough	09/11/1963		*1970s*		
711	Mulligan Terry	25/12/1963		776	Crellin Jim	15/03/1970
712	Garforth Malcolm	28/12/1963		777	Earl Kelvin	20/03/1970
713	Stansfield G.	15/02/1964		778	Plant Tony	08/04/1970
714	Toga Apisai	15/02/1964		779	Reynolds Colin	22/08/1970
715	Miller Sid	21/03/1964		780	Watson Mike	22/08/1970
716	Bradley Frank	27/03/1964		781	Hammond John	05/09/1970

782	Delooze Walter	06/10/1970		849	Brierley Jeff	02/04/1978
783	Robinson Alan	08/01/1971		850	Prime Steve	23/04/1978
784	Kvouve John	13/02/1971		851	Lowe Kevin	20/08/1978
785	Sheffield Bill	28/02/1971		852	Bailey Alan	20/08/1978
786	Gourley Tony	20/03/1971		853	Rathbone Allan	20/08/1978
787	Hillman Albert	07/08/1971		854	Holland Ian	10/09/1978
788	Myler Frank	07/08/1971		855	Langan Terry	10/09/1978
789	Welding Bob	07/08/1971		856	Bucys Roy	17/09/1978
790	Gartland Peter	15/08/1971		857	Manning	08/10/1978
791	Cooke Tony	25/08/1971		858	Woods John	22/10/1978
792	Aspinall Willie	04/09/1971		859	Grimes John	26/11/1978
793	Willacey Alan	09/10/1971		860	Horton Wayne	24/12/1978
794	Glover Brian	19/10/1971		861	Doherty Joe	23/01/1979
795	Brophy Tom	20/08/1972		862	Gorvin Graham	25/04/1979
796	Harris Ray	20/08/1972		863	Fletcher Tex	25/04/1979
797	Wood Harry	27/08/1972		864a	Bailey Gary	19/08/1979
798	Whitehead Stuart	05/11/1972		864	Smith Steve	16/09/1979
799	Holliday Bill	26/11/1972		865	Ashton Alan	30/09/1979
800	Butler John	16/03/1973		866	Wilson Andy	30/09/1979
801	Halmshaw Tony	25/03/1973		867	Banks Glen	05/10/1979
802	Tickle Rod	19/08/1973		868	Coates Mick	09/10/1979
803	Simpkins Colin	05/09/1973		869	Nolan Mick	04/11/1979
804	Fogerty Terry	23/09/1973		870	Campbell Ian	18/11/1979
805	McGiffen Steve	05/01/1974		*1980s*		
806	Farrow Michael	26/03/1974		871	Turley Norman	10/02/1980
807	Green Alan	26/03/1974		872	Wharton Dale	10/02/1980
808	Leadbetter Mike	22/09/1974		873	Cheetham	23/03/1980
809	Marsh Derek	22/09/1974		874	Price Billy	17/08/1980
810	Rouski John	22/09/1974		875	Gill Henderson	31/08/1980
811	Woodyer Eric	25/10/1974		876	Glover John	31/08/1980
812	Harris Les	30/10/1974		877	Hoare Shaun	14/09/1980
813	Hughes John	26/12/1974		878	Frodsham Peter	21/12/1980
814	Maloney John	05/01/1975		879	Breheney Steve	15/03/1981
815	McLoughlin Mick	19/01/1975		880	Deakin Chris	19/04/1981
816	Allen Tony	14/03/1975		881	Stondin Uri	16/08/1981
817	Nellist Paul	28/03/1975		882	Bates Alan	06/09/1981
818	Warlow John	17/08/1975		883	Lockwood Dave	23/09/1981
819	Burke David	25/08/1975		884	Armitage Paul	27/09/1981
820	Jones Wally	25/08/1975		885	Corcoran John	27/09/1981
821	Ayres Warren	28/09/1975		886	Canning John	04/10/1981
822	Kurtianyk Steve	23/11/1975		887	Pickavance Kieron	04/10/1981
823	Storey Chris	26/12/1975		888	Schofield Alan	18/10/1981
824	Longstaff Paul	08/02/1976		889	Molyneux Jim	25/10/1981
825	Middlehurst Peter	22/02/1976		890	MacCorquodale Ian	22/11/1981
826	Hawley Dave	07/03/1976		891	Fitzpatrick Paul	29/11/1981
827	Hartley Dave	22/08/1976		892	O'Donovan John	03/01/1982
828	Henighan Mick	22/08/1976		893	Wiltshire Roy	07/03/1982
829	Johnson Jim	22/08/1976		894	Whitehead Craig	12/04/1982
830	Rawlinson John	22/08/1976		895	Henshaw Mark	18/04/1982
831	Baker Gordon	05/09/1976		896	Kirkbride Bill	22/08/1982
832	Handforth	12/09/1976		897	Standidge George	22/08/1982
833	Smethills Colin	19/09/1976		898	Hughes Brian	19/09/1982
834	Barham	26/09/1976		899	Jones Wally	24/09/1982
835	Duffy Andy	26/09/1976		900	Murphy Martin	24/10/1982
836	Crabtree Nigel	08/10/1976		901	Brown Graham	07/11/1982
837	Coslett Kel	28/11/1976		902	Haslam Rodney	02/01/1983
838	Hoyle Granville	28/11/1976		903	Buckley Denis	16/01/1983
839	Kelly Ken	28/11/1976		904	Ellis Ian	23/01/1983
840	Wainwright Tony	09/01/1977		905	Bruen Bob	14/04/1983
841	Heaton Jeff	23/01/1977		906	Davies Gary	14/04/1983
842	Sanderson Mark	04/04/1977		907	Gratton Martin	14/04/1983
843	Gilmore John	30/08/1977		908	Stapleton John	21/04/1983
844	Ashcroft Kevin	10/09/1977		909	Claughton George	21/08/1983
845	Jenkins David	20/11/1977		910	Morris Geoff	21/08/1983
846	Garside Brett	08/01/1978		911	Simpkin Kevin	24/08/1983
847	Burns Martin	15/01/1978		912	Keaveny Alan	28/08/1983
848	Birdsall Charlie	05/02/1978		913	Turner Steve	03/09/1983

914	Ubermanowicz Tony	23/10/1983		981	Sawyer Aaron	20/09/1987
915	Hartley Neil	30/10/1983		982	Barrow Scott	27/09/1987
916	Munro Geoff	27/11/1983		983	McGinty Rob	27/09/1987
917	Barker Andy	02/09/1984		984	Connell Pomare	02/10/1987
918	Cartwright Phil	02/09/1984		985	Vaafusu Olson	25/10/1987
919	Chisnall Dave	02/09/1984		986	Broxton David	01/11/1987
920	Fairhurst Alan	02/09/1984		987	Ruane David	22/11/9187
921	Feeney Steve	02/09/1984		988	Diamond Jason	27/03/1988
922	Massa Mark	02/09/1984		989	Nanyn Mick	27/03/1988
923	Platt Billy	02/09/1984		990	O'Neill Sean	27/03/1988
294	Burgess Mark	23/09/1984		991	Marriott Karl	01/04/1988
295	Brown Dave	14/10/1984		992	Stokes Bob	01/04/1988
926	Leathley Trevor	21/10/1984		993	Brown Jeff	28/08/1988
927	Dean Tony	28/10/1984		994	Derbyshire Alan	28/08/1988
928	Bilsbury Terry	12/12/1984		995	Garrett Colin	28/08/1988
929	Saville David	26/12/1984		996	Myler Chris	28/08/1988
930	Howarth Michael	20/03/1985		997	Edwards Jeff	04/09/1988
931	Mellor Ian	21/04/1985		998	Edwards Anthony	11/09/1988
932	Duane Ian	01/09/1985		999	Tupaea Shane	25/09/1988
933	Dunn Brian	01/09/1985		1000	Higgins Brian	28/09/1988
934	Edge Phil	01/09/1985		1001	Charnock Lee	02/10/1988
935	Fitzsimmons Eric	01/09/1985		1002	Simcott Stuart	02/10/1988
936	Harcombe Kevin	01/09/1985		1003	Sealey Camrel	09/10/1988
937	Hardy Alan	01/09/1985		1004	Wilson Walter	09/10/1988
938	Timpson Andy	01/09/1985		1005	Gamble Paul	16/10/1988
939	Wood David	01/09/1985		1006	Edwards Logan	23/10/1988
940	Nash Steve	15/09/1985		1007	Bamber Simon	11/12/1988
941	Austin Greg	22/09/1985		1008	Scott Alan	11/12/1988
942	Evans David	22/09/1985		1009	Higgins John	15/01/1989
943	McKenzie Phil	22/09/1985		1010	Chadwick Les	05/02/1989
944	Shaefer Derek	06/10/1985		1011	Hall Martin	03/09/1989
945	Austin Tony	13/10/1985		1012	Humphries Tony	03/09/1989
946	Bancroft Phil	27/10/1985		1013	Lord Mark	03/09/1989
947	Kuiti Mike	27/10/1985		1041	Marsden Bob	03/09/1989
948	Idle Graham	22/12/1985		1051	McDermott Paul	03/09/1989
949	Fellows Paul	01/01/1986		1016	Nixon Mark	03/09/1989
950	Willis Chris	19/01/1986		1017	Sullivan Andy	03/09/1989
951	Shaw Glyn	16/03/1986		1018	Woods John	03/09/1989
952	Meachin Colin	28/03/1986		1019	Lonergan Dean	06/09/1989
953	Dobson Mark	20/04/1986		1020	McCormack Kevin	17/09/1989
954	Causey Mark	23/04/1986		1021	Molloy Dale	17/09/1989
955	Hitchin Gary	27/04/1986		1022	Webb Vinny	05/11/1989
956	Byron Gerry	07/09/1986		*1990s*		
957	Harrigan Mark	07/09/1986		1023	Viller Mark	17/01/1990
958	Jones Glen	07/09/1986		1024	Myler John	21/01/1990
959	Round Mike	07/09/1986		1025	Barrett David	11/02/1990
960	Aspey Steve	21/09/1986		1026	Fox Phil	11/03/1990
961	Purcell Craig	21/09/1986		1027	Blackburn John	25/03/1990
962	Thomson Darren	21/09/2986		1028	Gormley Ian	19/08/1990
963	Caffey Brian	28/09/1986		1029	O'Neill Mike	19/08/1990
964	Roe Peter	05/10/1986		1030	Whitfield Colin	19/08/1990
965	Cowie Neil	19/10/1986		1031	Gallagher David	09/09/1990
966	Hughes Eric	02/11/1986		1032	Belle Aidan	16/09/1990
967	Williams Dean	09/11/1986		1033	Grogan Bob	16/09/1990
968	Kelly	16/11/1986		1034	Holding Neil	16/09/1990
969	Sanby Tony	14/12/1986		1035	Lever David	04/11/1990
970	Dwyer Mark	24/12/1986		1036	Abram Darren	11/11/1990
971	Johnson Willie	25/01/1987		1037	Galbraith Stuart	18/11/1990
972	Rule Steve	05/04/1987		1038	Pitt Darren	18/11/1990
973	Geldard Steve	12/04/1987		1039	Halsall Ian	25/11/1990
974	Carter Phil	17/04/1987		1040	Kay Martin	25/11/1990
975	Clucas Geoff	20/04/1987		1041	Hall Rob	30/11/1990
976	Connell Chris	20/04/1987		1042	Dean Mike	20/01/1991
977	Davies Warren	20/04/1987		1043	Williams Mike	27/02/1990
978	Garrity Brian	30/08/1987		1044	Cheval Robert	10/03/1991
979	Ruane Andy	30/08/1987		1045	Gartland Steve	10/03/1991
980	Mellor Terry	30/08/1987		1046	Calland Matt	24/03/1991

1047	Viller Paul	24/03/1991
1048	Hulme Mike	14/04/1991
1049	Clark Brett	02/09/1991
1050	Eccles Cliff	22/09/1991
1051	Eccles Bob	29/09/1991
1052	Webster Dave	06/10/1991
1053	Okesene Paul	13/10/1991
1054	Bimson Jeff	29/10/1991
1055	Platt Alan	12/01/1992
1056	Reddican Mal	23/02/1992
1057	Heugh Cavill	30/08/1992
1058	Reynolds Paul	30/08/1992
1059	Stewart Mike	30/08/1992
1060	Jones Ken	20/09/1992
1061	O'Keefe Paul	27/09/1992
1062	Brown Colin	25/10/1992
1063	Phillips Rowland	25/10/1992
1064	Green Jason	29/11/1992
1065	O'Brien Darren	13/12/1992
1066	Pachniuk Richard	21/02/1993
1067	Warburton Steve	21/02/1993
1068	Chrimes David	14/03/1993
1069	Worrall Mick	28/03/1993
1070	Hourigan Paul	04/04/1993
1071	Bates Ian	29/08/2993
1072	Partington Carl	29/08/2993
1073	Ratu Emon	29/08/1993
1074	Cullen Brett	05/09/1993
1075	Harmer Dave	12/09/1993
1076	Gibson Steve	10/10/1993
1077	Cannon Glen	24/10/1993
1078	Gotts Richard	07/11/1993
1079	Cassidy Frank	14/11/1993
1080	Waddell Hugh	28/11/1993
1081	Pugsley Stuart	19/12/1993
1082	Strett Martin	19/12/1993
1083	Miller Vinnie	16/01/1994
1084	Fell David	13/03/1994
1085	Churm Chris	04/04/1994
1086	Bunce Martin	21/08/1994
1087	England Keith	21/08/1994
1088	Hilton Tony.	21/08/1994
1089	Maudsley Steve	21/08/1994
1090	Reid Wayne	21/08/1994
1091	Whitehead Sean	21/08/1994
1092	Laugier Serge	28/08/1994
1093	Ryan Matt	04/09/1994
1094	Gilfillan John	11/09/1994
1095	McCarthy Brain	18/09/1994
1096	Atherton Lee	25/09/1994
1097	Grayshon Paul	25/09/1994
1098	Anderson David	09/10/1994
1099	Griffiths Mark	06/11/1994
1110	Higginson Paul	27/11/1994
1101	Mort Craig	27/11/1994
1102	Pratt Gareth	11/12/1994
1103	Sharp Henry	11/12/1994
1104	Mannion Kevin	22/01/1995
1105	Robey Nick	22/01/1995
1106	Coop Chris	29/01/1995
1107	McAllister Charlie	29/01/1995
1108	Diggle Craig	22/03/1995
1109	Bailey David	02/04/1995
1110	Meadows Mark	02/04/1995
1111	Poynton Phil	20/08/1995
1112	Hilton Chris	20/08/1995
1113	Alvarez Sean	20/09/1995
1114	Flanagan Neil	01/11/1995
1115	Booth Craig	12/11/1995
1116	Agar Richard	29/11/1995
1117	Greenwood Adam	29/11/1995
1118	Lowe Rob	11/02/1996
1119	Mackie Damien	31/03/1996
1120	Crowther Steve	05/05/1996
1121	Edwards Logan	12/05/1996
1122	Morrison Tony	31/05/1996
1123	Fa'aoso James	09/06/1996
1124	Nuttall Nick	16/06/1996
1125	Durrant Lee	30/06/1996
1126	Pucill Andy	07/07/1996
1127	Jewitt Roy	14/07/1996
1128	Ventola Roy	14/07/1996
1129	Farrell Mick	19/07/1996
1130	Hayes Ian	30/01/1997
1131	Parr Chris	30/01/1997
1132	Scarisbrick Chris	30/01/1997
1133	Stevens Paul	30/01/1997
1134	Viller Jason	30/01/1997
1135	Picchi Nathan	18/05/1997
1136	Appleby Darren	06/07/1997
1137	Holland Chris	27/07/1997
1138	Cameron Steve	30/07/1997
1139	Quinlan Brian	30/07/1997
1140	Winroe James	17/08/1997
1141	Bradbury Gary	25/08/1997
1142	Milligan Paul	25/08/1997
1143	Salisbury Lee	25/08/1997
1144	Casey Leo	01/02/1998
1145	Dixon Keith	01/02/1998
1146	Eyres Andy	01/02/1998
1147	Fitzgerald Peter	01/02/1998
1148	Hall Steve	01/02/1998
1149	Jones David	01/02/1998
1150	Maher Adam	01/02/1998
1151	McKinney Chris	01/02/1998
1152	Opetaia Scott	01/02/1998
1153	Eyres Ritchie	22/02/1998
1154	Swann Willie	22/02/1998
1155	Topping Paul	03/03/1998
1156	Aston Jon	05/04/1998
1157	Gray Kevin	05/04/1998
1158	Jukes Neil	05/04/1998
1159	Kerr Ken	19/04/1998
1160	Webster John	19/04/1998
1161	Fox Deryck	17/05/1998
1162	Shaw Mick	21/06/1998
1163	Sculthorpe Danny	24/06/1998
1164	Coult Mick	15/07/1998
1165	Waters Ryan	02/08/1998
1166	Burgess Andy	31/01/1999
1167	Coussons Phil	31/01/1999
1168	Hough Chris	31/01/1999
1169	Hudson Lee	31/01/1999
1170	Knowles Matt	31/01/1999
1171	Stephenson Dave	31/01/1999
1172	Wilde Steve	31/01/1999
1173	Best Jason	28/02/1999
1174	Best Dave	14/03/1999
1175	Cooper Sean	02/04/1999
1176	Hepi Brad	02/04/1999
1177	Marsh Steve	02/04/1999
1178	Kelly Chris	28/04/1999
1179	Sherratt Ian	03/05/1999
1180	Rose Robert	17/05/1999

1181	Newall Chris	30/05/1999
1182	Powell Mark	06/06/1999
1183	Robinson Darren	13/06/1999
1184	Francis Michael	18/07/1999
1185	Miller Marlon	29/08/1999
1186	Dorahy Dane	27/12/1999
1187	Durose Darrell	27/12/1999
1188	Martin Scott	27/12/1999
1189	McMenemy Shayne	27/12/1999
1190	Moore Adrian	27/12/1999
1191	Price-Jones Gavin	27/12/1999
1192	Waring Phil	27/12/1999
1193	Wood Danny	27/12/1999

2000s

1194	Ashton Paul	02/01/2000
1195	Prest Lee	09/01/2000
1196	Swinson Gavin	09/01/2000
1197	Maher Lee	30/01/2000
1198	Forber Paul	20/02/2000
1199	Harrison Phil	27/02/2000
1200	Edwards Mike	01/03/2000
1201	Martindale Mick	05/03/2000
1201	Demetriou Jason	12/03/2000
1203	Ireland Andy	26/03/2000
1204	Sculthorpe Lee	02/04/2000
1205	Simeonovich James	09/04/2000
1206	Hooson Gareth	16/04/2000
1207	Murray Anthony	07/05/2000
1208	Green Peter	14/05/2000
1209	Simpson Ben	11/06/2000
1210	Alexander Neil	03/12/2000
1211	Billy Marlon	03/12/2000
1212	Coates Mick	03/12/2000
1213	Fearon Danny	03/12/2000
1214	Larder Dave	03/12/2000
1215	O'Meara Brendan	03/12/2000
1216	Owen Paul	03/12/2000
1217	Campbell Steve	10/12/2000
1218	Mayberry Casey	10/12/2000
1219	Watson Dave	10/12/2000
1220	Rogers Wes	07/01/2001
1221	McHugh Wayne	18/02/2001
1222	Radley Dave	18/02/2001
1223	Blake Ryan	07/03/2001
1224	Bunyan James	07/03/2001
1225	Ramsden Neil	13/03/2001
1226	Tawhai Latham	18/03/2001
1227	Berry Joe	06/05/2001
1228	Ball Damian	02/12/2001
1229	Long Matt	02/12/2001
1230	Smith Paul	02/12/2001
1231	Sinfield Ian	30/12/2001
1232	Davidson Paul	13/01/2002
1233	Higgins Ian	05/05/2002
1234	Wilson Lee	21/07/2002
1235	Wallace Andy	04/08/2002
1236	Grundy Andy	19/01/2003
1237	Nanyn Mick	19/01/2003
1238	Price Gareth	19/01/2003
1239	Southern Paul	19/01/2003
1240	Watson Ian	19/01/2003
1241	Leigh Matt	26/01/2003
1242	Roper Jon	02/02/2003
1243	Doherty Stepen	09/03/2003
1244	Bowker Radney	17/04/2003
1245	Hamilton John	15/06/2003
1246	Irwin Chris	22/06/2003

1247	Anderson Paul	01/02/2004
1248	Ball Rob	01/02/2004
1249	Billings Janan	01/02/2004
1250	Birdseye Lee	01/02/2004
1251	Braddish John	01/02/2004
1252	Butterworth Sam	01/02/2004
1253	Campbell Chris	01/02/2004
1254	Costello Mark	01/02/2004
1255	Gorski Andy	01/02/2004
1256	Hansen Lee	01/02/2004
1257	Leatham Andy	01/02/2004
1258	Platt Michael	01/02/2004
1259	Ratcliffe Kris	01/02/2004
1260	Shaw Darren	01/02/2004
1261	Westmore Ashley	01/02/2004
1262	Williams Liam	01/02/2004
1263	Kirwin Tony	08/02/2004
1264	Varkulis Richard	15/02/2004
1265	Hodgkinson Tommy	22/02/2004
1266	Yates Danny	02/03/2004
1267	Sturm Matt	07/03/2004
1268	Newton Dave	04/04/2004
1269	Butler Danny	09/04/2004
1270	Cunliffe Dave	09/04/2004
1271	McGovern Liam	09/04/2004
1272	Taylor Alex	09/04/2004
1273	Soro Lepani	18/04/2004
1274	Naulumatua Komai	09/05/2004
1275	McCully Mark	23/05/2004
1276	Saywell Andy	30/05/2004
1277	Goulding Bobbie	20/06/2004
1278	Picton Kevin	20/06/2004
1279	Alstead David	04/07/2004
1280	Cantillon Phil	13/02/2005
1281	Doran Lee	13/02/2005
1282	Farrell Phil	13/02/2005
1283	Giles Chris	13/02/2005
1284	McConnell Dave	13/02/2005
1285	Hill John	24/04/2005
1286	Durbin Jamie	24/07/2005
1287	Goulden Tommy	14/08/2005
1288	Royle Nicky	21/08/2005
1289	Benjafield Ryan	15/02/2006
1290	Firth Matt	15/02/2006
1291	Norman Paul	15/02/2006
1292	Robinson Craig	15/02/2006
1293	Patterson Lee	19/02/2006
1294	Sanderson Lee	22/03/2006
1295	Gordon Ian	23/04/2006
1296	King Kevin	14/05/2006
1297	Dean Craig	04/06/2006
1298	Pickersgill John	04/06/2006
1299	Hasty Phil	11/06/2006
1300	Bailey Andy	09/07/2006
1301	Ross Jordan	03/09/2006
1302	Andrews Eric	11/02/2007
1303	Baldwin Simon	11/02/2007
1304	Blanchard Mark	11/02/2007
1305	Corcoran Wayne	11/02/2007
1306	Fagborun Bolu	11/02/2007
1307	Hulse Gary	11/02/2007
1308	Smith Byrom	11/02/2007
1309	Svabic Simon	11/02/2007
1310	Gledhill John	18/02/2007
1311	Marsh Iain	18/02/2007
1312	Whitaker Matt	18/02/2007
1313	Johnson Nick	04/03/2007

1314	O'Brien Todd	08/07/2007	
1315	Johnson Eric	19/07/2007	
1316	Attwood Brad	29/07/2007	
1317	Law Scott	29/07/2007	
1318	Sheriffe Jode	29/07/2007	
1319	Barber Gareth	05/08/2007	
1320	Ainscough Martin	03/02/2008	
1321	Alcock Paul	03/02/2008	
1322	Brocklehurst Mark	03/02/2008	
1323	Brown Alex	03/02/2008	
1324	Elston Jimmy	03/02/2008	
1325	Marsh Adam	03/02/2008	
1326	Spurr Chris	03/02/2008	
1327	Stout Mike	03/02/2008	
1328	Wild Tom	03/02/2008	
1329	Bower Craig	10/02/2008	
1330	Callan Mike	10/02/2008	
1331	Forster Chris	24/02/2008	
1332	Lloyd Benji	24/02/2008	
1333	Farrimond Crig	24/02/2008	
1334	Sneyd Carl	05/03/2008	
1335	Gorey Andy	09/03/2008	
1336	Roughneen Mark	09/03/2008	
1337	Cookson John	14/03/2008	
1338	Highton Craig	30/03/2008	
1339	Hughes Carl	27/04/2008	
1340	Sozi Yusuf	05/05/2008	
1341	Muir Jonathan	11/05/2008	
1432	Ashe Matt	29/06/2008	
1343	Neal Kyle	29/06/2008	
1344	Rolls Paul	13/07/2008	
1345	Rivett Leroy	20/07/2008	
1346	Samuel Danny	15/02/2009	
1347	Fogerty Mike	15/02/2009	
1348	Gambles Martin	15/02/2009	
1349	Gillam John	15/02/2009	
1350	Grundy Liam	15/02/2009	
1351	Isherwood Andrew	15/02/2009	
1352	Johnson Craig	15/02/2009	
1353	McLoughlin Martin	15/02/2009	
1354	Rafferty Paul	15/02/2009	
1355	Smith Andy	15/02/2009	
1356	Bretherton Liam	18/02/2009	
1357	Cunliffe Dale	18/02/2009	
1358	Donoghue Dayne	18/02/2009	
1359	Walker John	18/02/2009	
1360	Gallagher Tommy	10/05/2009	
1361	Houghton David	10/05/2009	
1362	Robinson Brett	10/05/2009	
1363	Strong Matthew	10/05/2009	
1364	Thomas Adam	10/05/2009	
1365	Brindell Tommy	17/05/2009	
1366	Hobson Mark	31/05/2009	
1366a	Roper Steve	31/05/2009	
1367	Kay Darrell	02/08/2009	
1368	Hatton Dean	16/08/2009	
1369	Powell Ryan	16/08/2009	

2010s & 2020s

1370	Ashall Craig	08/02/2010	
1371	English Wayne	08/02/2010	
1372	Hayes Gareth	08/02/2010	
1373	McPaul Ryan	08/02/2010	
1374	Ostick Michael	08/02/2010	
1375	Smith Danny	08/02/2010	
1376	Tunstead Craig	08/02/2010	
1377	Wood Phil	08/02/2010	
1378	Bloomfield Dale	14/02/2010	

1379	Bostock Liam	14/02/2010	
1380	Duffy Jay	14/02/2010	
1381	Cocker Semisi	17/02/2010	
1382	Gorton Dean	17/02/2010	
1383	Hore Andy	17/02/2010	
1384	Taylor Andy	17/02/2010	
1385	Crook Paul	23/02/2010	
1386	Reid Damien	23/02/2010	
1387	Wayne Adam	23/02/2010	
1388	Bowman Adam	07/03/2010	
1389	Fleming Danny	02/04/2010	
1390	Blackmore Dale	04/07/2010	
1391	Fairhurst Peter	04/07/2010	
1392	Clough Chris	06/02/2011	
1393	Yates Scott	06/02/2011	
1394	Mansfield Scott	13/02/2011	
1395	Meakin Danny	13/02/2011	
1396	Peasnall Jamie	13/02/2011	
1397	McDermott Steve	27/02/2011	
1398	Pyke Danny	27/02/2011	
1399	Biggins Mark	27/03/2011	
1400	Ekis Danny	27/03/2011	
1401	Kearney Martin	27/03/2011	
1402	Mervill Richard	10/04/2011	
1403	Stewart Mike	17/04/2011	
1404	Middlehurst Gary	10/07/2011	
1405	Baines Chris	19/02/2012	
1406	Lucas Steve	19/02/2012	
1407	O'Connor Paul	19/02/2012	
1408	Stewart Anthony	19/02/2012	
1409	Bannister Steve	26/02/2012	
1410	Brearly Paul	04/03/2012	
1411	Kellett Mark	04/03/2012	
1412	Leather Johnny	04/03/2012	
1413	Turner Damien	04/03/2012	
1414	Davies Danny	11/03/2012	
1415	Braddish Phil	01/04/2012	
1416	Chadwick Will	15/04/2012	
1417	Brown Ryan	09/05/2012	
1418	Clarke Barry	09/05/2012	
1419	Fitzpatrick Joe	09/05/2012	
1420	Jones-Lake Fraser	09/05/2012	
1421	Marsden Ben	09/05/2012	
1422	Moore Charles	09/05/2012	
1423	Unsworth Andy	09/05/2012	
1424	West Alex	09/05/2012	
1425	Pryce Danny	03/06/2012	
1426	Hickney Stephen	03/06/2012	
1427	Mitchell Henry	03/06/2012	
1428	Case Jordan	03/03/2013	
1429	Forster Carl	03/03/2013	
1430	Hand Jordan	03/03/2013	
1431	Hull Dave	03/03/2013	
1432	Langley Gareth	03/03/2013	
1433	Makinson Tommy	03/03/2013	
1434	McClurg Alex	03/03/2013	
1435	Sutton Dave	03/03/2013	
1436	Thompson Warren	03/03/2013	
1437	Trumper Alex	03/03/2013	
1438	Frodsham Gareth	10/03/2013	
1439	Lee Gaskell	10/03/2013	
1440	Waring Martin	10/03/2013	
1441	Ashe Nathan	17/03/2013	
1442	Greenwood Joe	17/03/2013	
1443	Ratu Mike	17/03/2013	
1444	Bate Joe	29/03/2013	
1445	Goodman Mark	29/03/2013	

1446	Ainscough Andy	01/04/2013	1513	Crowley Josh	26/06/2016
1447	Llewellyn Dave	01/04/2013	1514	Holmes Jack	24/07/2016
1448	Sheridan Lewis	01/04/2013	1515	Penny Kevin	24/07/2016
1449	Whalley Liam	01/04/2013	1516	Cartwright Harry	30/07/2016
1450	Speakman Dom	01/04/2013	1517	Bennion Gavin	05/02/2017
1451	Yates Danny	26/05/2013	1518	Eccleston Jake	05/02/2017
1452	Swift Adam	02/06/2013	1519	Greenwood Miles	05/02/2017
1453	Crow Matty	09/06/2013	1520	Massam Robert	05/02/2017
1454	Tyrer Chris	07/07/2013	1521	Palfrey Lewis	05/02/2017
1455	Wheeler Gary	07/07/2013	1522	Blythe Matty	26/02/2017
1456	McGoff Ruairi	04/08/2013	1523	Lobwein Jay	05/03/2017
1457	Casey Sean	23/02/2014	1524	Fowden Luke	26/03/2017
1458	Dandy James	23/02/2014	1525	Livett Harvey	09/04/2017
1459	Dawson Matt	23/02/2014	1526	Savelio Andre	02/04/2017
1460	Flanagan Mark	23/02/2014	1527	Mitchell Lee	14/04/2017
1461	Richards Greg	23/02/2014	1528	Prell Taylor	14/04/2017
1462	Suffolk Tony	23/02/2014	1529	Moran Patrick	21/05/2017
1463	Walker Anthony	23/02/2014	1530	Foster Lewis	10/06/2017
1464	Dwyer Connor	02/03/2014	1531	Hatton Lewis	10/06/2017
1465	Marsh Steve	02/03/2014	1532	Kay Declan	10/06/2017
1466	Millard Ryan	02/03/2014	1533	Rasool Danyal	10/06/2017
1467	T'eo Sam	02/03/2014	1534	Whittaker Tyler	10/06/2017
1468	Tilley James	09/03/2014	1535	Adamson Luke	19/02/2018
1469	Clare Alex	30/03/2014	1536	Deon Cross	19/02/2018
1470	Gilchrist Liam	06/04/2014	1537	Earl Hurst	19/02/2018
1471	Robinson Shaun	18/04/2014	1538	Johnson Luis	19/02/2018
1472	Galbraith Lewis	18/05/2014	1539	Adamson Toby	25/02/2018
1473	Jones Josh	01/06/2014	1540	Allen Dave	25/02/2018
1474	Littler Stuart	01/06/2014	1541	Lepori Richard	25/02/2018
1475	Percival Mark	01/06/2014	1542	Brickhill Billy	03/03/2018
1476	King Ryan	22/06/2014	1543	Gregory Declan	03/03/2018
1477	Beaumont Richard	29/06/2014	1544	Turner Blake	03/03/2018
1478	McDonell Shannon	13/07/2014	1545	Hema Aidan	17/03/2018
1479	Bridge Danny	01/03/2015	1546	Smith Morgan	23/03/2018
1480	Hadden Matty	01/03/2015	1547	Talatoka Setareki	23/03/2018
1481	Hargreaves Brad	01/03/2015	1548	Mulkeen Callum	02/04/2018
1482	Mignacca Dean	01/03/2015	1549	Gaskell Alex	08/04/2018
1483	Brooks Sam	07/03/2015	1550	Welch Taylor	15/04/2018
1484	Smith Ryan	07/03/2015	1551	Cunningham Jonah	06/05/2018
1485	Ashworth Jack	15/03/2015	1552	Syme Jordan	12/05/2018
1486	Charnock Lewis	03/04/2015	1553	Fox Jack	03/06/2018
1487	Thompson Luke	16/05/2015	1554	King George	10/06/2018
1488	Fozzard Matty	27/06/2015	1555	Pomeroy Ben	17/06/2018
1489	Jones Danny	05/07/2015	1556	Calcott Will	24/06/2018
1490	Haggerty Matthew	12/07/2015	1557	Ryan Joe	24/06/2018
1491	Cookson Dave	21/02/2016	1558	Millington Ryan	12/08/2018
1492	Files Harry	21/02/2016	1559	Abram Dan	10/02/2019
1493	Francis Jack	21/02/2016	1560	Ainscough Shaun	10/02/2019
1494	Lee Corey	21/02/2016	1561	Carberry Liam	10/02/2019
1495	Moores Ben	21/02/2016	1562	Davies Matthew	10/02/2019
1496	Riley Chris	21/02/2016	1563	Gillam Ellis	10/02/2019
1497	Tahouroui Samir	21/02/2016	1564	Howarth Stuart	10/02/2019
1498	Biscomb Stuart	27/02/2016	1565	Jenkins Elliott	10/02/2019
1499	Walpole Kieran	27/02/2016	1566	Lawton Adam	10/02/2019
1500	Evans Ben	06/03/2016	1567	Moore Scott	10/02/2019
1501	Johnson Jack	06/03/2016	1568	Morris Ben	10/02/2019
1502	Philbin Joe	06/03/2016	1569	Wheldon Mike	10/02/2019
1503	Taira Jovili	06/03/2016	1570	Wood Brandon	10/02/2019
1504	Murray	25/03/2016	1571	Akauloa Sitaleki	16/02/2019
1505	Smith Jono	25/03/2016	1572	Cottingham Jack	16/02/2019
1506	Julien Ben	03/04/2016	1573	Flynn Paddy	24/02/2019
1507	Wilde Sam	03/04/2016	1574	Reidy Nathan	17/03/2019
1508	Patton Dec	10/04/2016	1575	Wood Callum	17/03/2019
1509	Lineham Tom	24/04/2016	1576	Robson Ellis	24/03/2019
1510	Shoel Jake	15/05/2016	1577	Higginson Jack	31/03/2019
1511	King Toby	19/06/2016	1578	Walker Danny	28/04/2019
1512	Maneely Ryan	19/06/2016	1579	Coleman Michael	12/05/2019

1580	Hamlett Reece	12/05/2019	1606	Whitehead Matt	15/03/2020
1581	Worthington James	12/05/2019	1607	Fairclough Rob	09/05/2021
1582	Gleeson Aidan	18/05/2019	1608	Jordan-Roberts Josh	09/05/2021
1583	Marriott Callum	18/05/2019	1609	Moimoi Fuifui	09/05/2021
1584	Baker Zac	26/05/2019	1610	Forshaw Ryan	16/05/2021
1585	Farrell Issac	09/06/2019	1611	Ogden Callum	16/05/2021
1586	Thomas Oscar	09/06/2019	1612	Registe Lee	30/05/2021
1587	Williams Daley	09/06/2019	1613	Connaughton Jimmy	06/06/2021
1588	Shelford Kyle	21/06/2019	1614	Forster Ben	06/06/2021
1589	Bourrell Pierre	30/06/2019	1615	Nixon Ben	06/06/2021
1590	Brown Kevin	07/07/2019	1616	Brearley Paul	12/06/2021
1591	Kilner Ben	07/07/2019	1617	Watson Tyler	12/06/2021
1592	Barran James	04/08/2019	1618	Freeman Ben	20/06/2021
1593	Grant Sam	01/09/2019	1619	Oakley Cole	20/06/2021
1594	Calland Ben	16/02/2020	1620	Chase Rangi	27/06/2021
1595	Carr Adam	16/02/2020	1621	Tate William	04/07/2021
1596	Freeman Sam	16/02/2020	1622	Whur Tom	04/07/2021
1597	Hesketh Adam	16/02/2020	1623	Hughes Kenny	10/07/2021
1598	Hopkins Sam	16/02/2020	1624	Dean Reece	01/08/2021
1599	Lea Andy	16/02/2020	1625	Ashton Tom	07/08/2021
1600	Sheridan Dec	16/02/2020	1626	Harrison Myles	07/08/2021
1601	Tracey Jamie	16/02/2020	1627	Littlewood Luke	07/08/2021
1602	Holroyd Brad	08/03/2020	1628	Towse Alwyn	07/08/2021
1603	Penkywicz Sean	08/03/2020	1629	Tyrer Cian	07/08/2021
1604	Ridyard Martin	08/03/2020	1630	Warren Todd	07/08/2021
1605	Ngawati Quinn	15/03/2020			

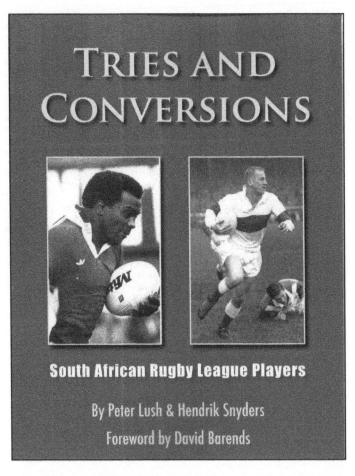

TRIES AND CONVERSIONS

South African Rugby League Players

By Peter Lush & Hendrik Snyders

Foreword by David Barends

In 1910, James Megson and William Mart became the first native-born South Africans to sign for British rugby league clubs. Since then, South African players have made a significant contribution to rugby league. This book is the first comprehensive study of their contribution to rugby league. It covers players who played in Great Britain and Australia. Some were very successful, such as Attie van Heerden and George van Rooyen in the 1920s, Tom van Vollenhoven, Alan Skene, Jan Prinsloo and Len Killeen in the 1950s and 1960s, and Mark Johnson and Jamie Bloem in the Super League era. But there were also players who never made it after switching codes to play rugby league, and their stories are also told here.

Available for just £13.95 post free in the UK direct from London League Publications Ltd or from Amazon.co.uk . Credit card orders via www.llpshop.co.uk; payment by cheque to PO Box 65784, London NW2 9NS. Available in bookshops at £14.95.

Also available as an E-Book for Kindle from Amazon.

The King of Brilliance: Great book about one of the sport's genuine legends. James Lomas played for Bramley, Salford, Oldham and York, and won representative honours for Lancashire, Cumberland, England and Great Britain. He captained the first Lions team to tour Australia and New Zealand in 1910. This is the first biography of him.

Published in October 2011 at £16.95 (hardback). Special offer: £9.95 post free in the UK available direct from London League Publications Ltd. Also available on Amazon and Abe Books.

Also available as an E-Book for Kindle from Amazon.

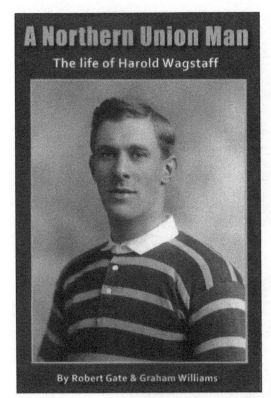

A Northern Union Man

The life of Harold Wagstaff

By Robert Gate & Graham Williams

Harold Wagstaff, known as the 'Prince of Centres', was one of the key players in the development of rugby league in the early twentieth century.

He made his debut for the Huddersfield first team in November 1906, at the age of 15, having previously played for Underbank. He joined the professional game at an important time for the sport. The number of players had been reduced to 13, and other rule changes made, including the introduction of play-the-ball after a tackle. This made Northern Union rugby a more open game, and Wagstaff and the Huddersfield team took full advantage of the changes.

He played for Yorkshire in 1908, and in January 1909 made his Great Britain debut against Australia, the first player aged under 18 to play for his country. He was made captain of Huddersfield in 1911, and under his direction the club won the Challenge Cup three times, the Northern Rugby League Championship three times, the Yorkshire League six times and the Yorkshire Cup five times. They won 'All Four Cups' in 1914–15, and were known as the 'Team of all the Talents'. For Great Britain, Wagstaff captained the 1914 and 1920 Lions tours to Australia and New Zealand. This included the 1914 'Rorke's Drift' test, when a Great Britain team reduced to 10 men through injuries hung on to beat the Australians and win the Ashes.

However, it was not just his success that made him one of the sport's greatest players. It was the way he played the game, seeing the sport as a passing and handling game, rarely kicking the ball. He was made a founder member of the Rugby League Hall of Fame in 1988.

This book, as well as contributions from the two authors, includes an autobiographical newspaper series that Wagstaff wrote in the 1930s, excerpts from an autobiographical series published in 1921 and contributions from other rugby league writers, including Tony Collins and Harry Edgar. It is book that every rugby league fan will enjoy.

Published in July 2019 at £12.95. Special offer: £12.50 post free in the UK available direct from London League Publications Ltd. Also available on Amazon and Abe Books.

Also available as an E-Book for Kindle from Amazon.